STUDIES IN EVANGELICAL HISTORY AND THOUGHT

When the Lord Walked the Land

The 1858-62 Revival
in the North East of Scotland

STUDIES IN EVANGELICAL HISTORY AND THOUGHT

A full listing of all titles in this series will be found at the close of this book

STUDIES IN EVANGELICAL HISTORY AND THOUGHT

When the Lord Walked the Land

The 1858-62 Revival
in the North East of Scotland

Kenneth S. Jeffrey

Foreword by David Bebbington

Wipf & Stock
PUBLISHERS
Eugene, Oregon

Wipf and Stock Publishers
199 W 8th Ave, Suite 3
Eugene, OR 97401

When the Lord Walked the Land
The 1858–62 Revival in the North East of Scotland
By Jeffrey, Kenneth S.
Copyright©2002 Paternoster
ISBN: 1-59752-746-7
Publication date 6/6/2006
Previously published by Paternoster, 2002

This Edition Published by Wipf and Stock Publishers
by arrangement with Paternoster

Paternoster
9 Holdom Avenue
Bletchley
Milton Keyes, MK1 1QR
Great Britain

STUDIES IN EVANGELICAL HISTORY AND THOUGHT

Series Preface

The Evangelical movement has been marked by its union of four emphases: on the Bible, on the cross of Christ, on conversion as the entry to the Christian life and on the responsibility of the believer to be active. The present series is designed to publish scholarly studies of any aspect of this movement in Britain or overseas. Its volumes include social analysis as well as exploration of Evangelical ideas. The books in the series consider aspects of the movement shaped by the Evangelical Revival of the eighteenth century, when the impetus to mission began to turn the popular Protestantism of the British Isles and North America into a global phenomenon. The series aims to reap some of the rich harvest of academic research about those who, over the centuries, have believed that they had a gospel to tell to the nations.

Series Editors

David Bebbington, Professor of History, University of Stirling, Stirling, Scotland, UK

John H.Y. Briggs, Senior Research Fellow in Ecclesiastical History and Director of the Centre for Baptist History and Heritage, Regent's Park College, Oxford, UK

Timothy Larsen, Associate Professor of Theology, Wheaton College, Illinois, USA

Mark A. Noll, McManis Professor of Christian Thought, Wheaton College, Wheaton, Illinois, USA

Ian M. Randall, Deputy Principal and Lecturer in Church History and Spirituality, Spurgeon's College, London, UK, and a Senior Research Fellow, International Baptist Theological Seminary, Prague, Czech Republic

To Linda

Contents

	Page
List of Tables	xi
List of Maps	xv
Foreword	xvii
Acknowledgements	xxi
List of Abbreviations	xxiii
Chapter 1 : The Revivalist Tradition	1
Chapter 2 : Theories of Revivalism	27
Chapter 3 : The Revival in Aberdeen Timing and Manner	49
Chapter 4 : The Revival in Aberdeen Analysis and Results	75
Chapter 5 : The Revival in the Rural Hinterland Timing and Manner	113
Chapter 6 : The Revival in the Rural Hinterland Analysis and Results	141
Chapter 7 : The Revival in the Fishing Villages Timing and Manner	181
Chapter 8 : The Revival in the Fishing Villages Analysis and Results	203
Chapter 9 : The Relative Failure of the Revival to affect Peterhead	233
Chapter 10 : Conclusion	253
Bibliography	265
Appendix 1: The method by which those who were affected by the revival were identified	287
Appendix 2: Social Classification System Used	289
Index	291

List of Tables

Table	Title	Page
4.1.	Greyfriars Parish Church: Communion rolls 1855-64	80
4.2.	Holburn Parish Church : Young communicants 1859-61	80
4.3.	Woodside Parish Church: Young communicants 1859-64	81
4.4.	Free South Church: Young communicants 1857-63	82
4.5.	Newhills Free Church: Young communicants 1858-62	83
4.6.	St Nicholas Lane United Presbyterian Church: Young communicants 1857-64	83
4.7.	George Street Congregational Church: New members 1857-62	84
4.8.	St Paul Street Evangelical Union Church: New members 1855-62	84
4.9.	Union Terrace Baptist Church: New members 1857-63	85
4.10.	Holburn Parish Church: The religious background of young communicants in 1861	87
4.11.	Woodside Parish Church: The religious background of young communicants between 1859 and 1861	87
4.12	The class composition of 188 people who joined Aberdeen churches at the height of the revival	92
4.13.	The distribution of new church members in each congregation according to class	92
4.14.	An analysis of the class composition of new church members during the Aberdeen revival	93
4.15.	The marital status of 256 people who joined Aberdeen churches at the height of the revival	96

4.16.	The distribution of new church members in each congregation according to their marital status	96
4.17.	An analysis of the marital status of new church members during the Aberdeen revival	97
4.18.	The ages of 142 people who joined Aberdeen churches at the height of the revival	100
4.19.	The distribution of new church members in each congregation according to their age	101
4.20.	An analysis of the ages of new church members during the Aberdeen revival	101
4.21.	The gender status of those who joined Aberdeen churches before, during and after the revival	104
4.22.	An analysis of the gender status of those who joined Aberdeen churches before, during and after the revival	105
6.1.	Millbrex Parish Church: Young communicants 1862-66	143
6.2.	Cluny Parish Church: Communion rolls 1857-63	143
6.3.	Daviot Parish Church: Young communicants 1857-63	144
6.4.	Rhynie Parish Church: Communion rolls 1858-64	144
6.5.	Insch Free Church: Young communicants 1856-65	146
6.6.	Banchory Ternan Free Church: Communion rolls 1856-61	146
6.7.	Pluscarden Free Church: Young communicants 1858-66	147
6.8.	Elgin High Free Church: Young communicants 1858-66	147
6.9.	Huntly United Presbyterian Church: Young communicants 1856-63	148
6.10.	New Deer United Presbyterian Church: Young communicants 1856-63	148
6.11.	Craigdam United Presbyterian Church: Young communicants 1857-63	149

6.12.	Shiels United Presbyterian Church: Total membership 1857-97	149
6.13.	Shiels United Presbyterian Church: Young communicants 1859-63	150
6.14.	St James Episcopal Chapel, Cruden: Confirmations 1853-65	150
6.15.	St James Episcopal Chapel, Cruden: Communicants 1857-63	151
6.16.	St Ternan's Episcopal Chapel, Banchory Ternan: Communicants 1857-62	151
6.17.	The comparative size of farms in Aberdeenshire and East Lothian, c1885	153
6.18.	The demographic pattern of parishes unaffected by the revival	157
6.19	The demographic pattern of parishes affected by the revival	157
6.20.	The religious background of those who joined Millbrex and Rhynie Parish Churches during the revival	168
6.21.	The class composition of those who joined a number of rural churches during the revival	171
6.22.	The marital status of those who joined a number of rural churches during the revival	172
6.23.	The ages of those who joined a number of rural churches during the revival	173
6.24.	The gender status of those who joined a number of rural churches before, during and after the revival	175
6.25.	An analysis of the gender status of those who joined a number of rural churches before, during and after the revival	175
7.1.	The relative success of the herring fishing industry along the Moray Firth between 1850 and 1861	186
7.2.	The population of several Moray Firth fishing villages in 1860	197
8.1.	Drainy Parish Church: Young communicants 1860-64	211
8.2.	Macduff Free Church: Young communicants 1857-61	213

8.3.	Bellie Free Church: Young communicants 1857-63	213
8.4.	Nairn Free Church: Young communicants 1858-61	214
8.5.	Portsoy Free Church: Communion rolls 1857-62	214
8.6.	Banff Free Church: Young communicants 1859-63	215
8.7.	Banff United Presbyterian Church: Young communicants 1858-63	216
8.8.	Banff Free Church: The religious background of young communicants in 1860	217
8.9.	The previous lives of a number of fishing village revival converts	218
8.10.	The class composition of Banff new church members during the revival	219
8.11.	The occupations of fifteen fishing village revival converts	220
8.12.	The marital status of Banff new church members during the revival	220
8.13.	The relationships that existed among fifty one of the fishing village revival converts	221
8.14.	The ages of Banff new church members during the revival	222
8.15.	The 'age' at which fishing village people were converted during the revival	222
8.16.	The gender status of Banff new church members before, during and after the revival	224
9.1.	The 1851 Religious Census, Peterhead	237
9.2.	Employment patterns in Peterhead, c1840	241
9.3.	Employment patterns in Gardenstown, c1840	242
9.4.	The class composition of a random selection of people living in Peterhead in 1861	242
9.5.	The class composition of the inhabitants of Portessie in 1861	243

List of Maps

Map	Title	Page
4.1.	The Aberdeen churches that embraced the revival and the homes of some of those who joined these congregations at the height of the religious movement	88
5.1.	The spread of some Free Church revival prayer groups that met before the religious movement began in the north east of Scotland, compared with the distribution of the rural revival	121
5.2.	The main centres from which the rural revival was diffused across the north east of Scotland	123
6.1.	The settlement pattern in the north east of Scotland, from the atlas by James Thomson, 1828, compared with the distribution of the rural revival	154
6.2.	The planned villages in the north east of Scotland, 1730-1830, compared with the distribution of the rural revival	156
6.3.	The demographic growth and decline of a number of selected parishes in the north east of Scotland between 1851 and 1861, compared with the distribution of the rural revival	158
6.4.	The remote and underpopulated parishes in the north east of Scotland in 1860, compared with the distribution of the rural revival	160
6.5.	The relative strength of the Roman Catholic Church in the north east of Scotland in 1860, compared with the distribution of the rural revival	161
6.6.	The pattern of parishes in the north east of Scotland where there was no Free Church congregation in 1860, compared with the distribution of the rural revival	163
6.7.	The Free Church presbyteries in the north east of Scotland which appear to have been relatively unaffected by the rural revival	164

6.8.	The relative strength of the Moderates and Evangelicals in the Established Church in the north east of Scotland in 1842, compared with the distribution of the rural revival	166
6.9.	The line of the Great North of Scotland Railway, compared with the distribution of the rural revival	167
6.10.	The parishes of the eleven rural congregations that were examined	169
7.1.	The itinerary of James Turner's evangelistic preaching tour along the Moray Firth in 1859 and 1860	188
7.2.	The fishing villages that were affected by the revival as it spread along the Moray Firth	194
8.1.	The distribution of new churches and religious groups that emerged along the Moray Firth in the wake of the 1859 revival	225

Foreword

The phenomenon of revival has been a striking feature of the history of the Evangelical movement over the centuries. It has normally been a time when whole communities, and not merely individuals, have become intensely concerned about the welfare of their souls. Members of the communities have looked inside themselves to discover their capacity for wickedness; and they have turned outside themselves to find a profoundly reassuring sense of divine forgiveness. The subjects of these experiences were sure that they had a supernatural dimension, but that does not prevent revivals from having had, as it were, a natural history. There has been an evolution in the style of revival over the years: a development in the way these events have been conducted and in the pattern of conversions that have taken place during their course. Revivals have changed over time.

The oldest tradition of revival is associated with religious practice in seventeenth-century Scotland. In that Presbyterian land, holy communion was an infrequent happening. When a communion service was held, it was a profoundly solemn occasion, standardly entailing several services of preparation immediately beforehand and also including an occasion of thanksgiving afterwards. People would gather from far around to join in the event in a particular parish. During this communion season, and especially at the last act of worship, a sense of the awesome issues raised by the remembrance of Christ crucified might stir the crowds to deep contrition. There would be weeping, anguished prayer and a hunger for authentic Christian experience. The community could be stirred for days, weeks or months, as dozens took up a new found faith. During this period ministers would continue preaching, nurture the converts and draw them into the life of the church. Revival along these lines was closely connected with the life of the existing ecclesiastical structures.

In the second tradition of revival, rooted in the practice of eighteenth-century Methodism, preachers would gather crowds to hear gospel messages in the open air or some convenient building. Like John Wesley, his followers travelled around the countryside to proclaim a message that demanded a response. Conversions were often immediate. Revival events were frequently noisy affairs, commonly marked by clapping, screaming and jumping and sometimes attended by involuntary physical phenomena such as falling or shaking. Propriety, especially ecclesiastical propriety, was thrown to the winds. These revivals seemed specially suited to humble folk living in out-of-the-way places remote from traditional centres of population. The Methodists would subsequently gather in their own societies rather than in existing churches, would sing their own hymns by Charles Wesley and would adopt their own Arminian theology that marked them off from Calvinists such as the Presbyterians.

The third tradition, developed in the growing cities of the nineteenth century, was far more businesslike. Charles Finney, its original mastermind, believed that revivals could be analysed scientifically and so, like experiments, replicated. Planning was essential, methods were calculated to maximise results and modern advertising techniques were not spurned. Emotional display was discouraged, private counselling was undertaken and sensible arrangements were made for follow-up work. The approach was evident in the 'businessmen's revival' in New York in 1857-58, in the missions of Moody and Sankey from the 1870s and in many a campaign organised by lesser figures into the twentieth century. This style, in fact, looked forward to the city-wide crusades of Billy Graham in the latter half of that century.

Ken Jeffrey's study of revivalism in the north-east of Scotland brings these three contrasting traditions into much sharper focus than hitherto, isolating some of the distinctive features of each of them for the first time. He shows that in the years around 1860 the three types of revival were operating simultaneously. It was not so much that they were intertwined, although there certainly was interaction between the different styles, as that all three were going on in adjacent areas at he same time. The areas were distinct in their patterns of life, and the form of revival that struck the community was the one that most suited its socio-economic structure. Thus traditional Presbyterian ways dominated the farming regions on the edges of the Grampian Mountains; characteristic Methodist enthusiasm broke out in the fishing villages along the coast; and the revival in the city of Aberdeen was organised in a highly businesslike manner. Drawing extensively on census returns as well as church records and the local press, the author demonstrates that the type of convert was also affected by the form the revival took in each of the areas. So the movement in this region, which was often seen at the time as a unity, turns out to have been a strikingly heterogeneous affair. This book shows a refreshing sensitivity to place, revealing that the phenomenon was an immensely powerful force in the life of the various communities it struck. Future historians will want to ask whether the internal diversity of revival in the north-east of Scotland was reproduced in other parts of the Evangelical world. Ken Jeffrey has provided an invaluable yardstick for the analysis of global revivalism.

David Bebbington
University of Stirling
July 2002

Acknowledgements

I have received help from a large number of people during the preparation of this book, all of whom it would be impossible to cite individually. Nevertheless there are those whose knowledge of congregations and the work of various denominations in the north east of Scotland has been particularly beneficial. J. S. Fisher suggested sources that revealed the work of Baptists in Aberdeenshire, while Harold Bowes shared his knowledge of the history of the Methodists along the Moray Firth. Dr C. Johnson, archivist of the Scottish Catholic Church, provided information on Roman Catholicism, and Ian MacDonald recommended several important sources that proved most illuminating. Also Harry Sprange highlighted the effect which the revival had upon children.

Three of my fellow post-graduate students at Stirling University shared some useful insights that proved invaluable. Brian Talbot revealed the witness of the Baptists in the north east of Scotland, and Pat Meldrum brought to the fore the effect the revival had upon the Episcopal Church. Meanwhile Neil Dickson uncovered the significant influence which the 1859 religious movement exercised upon the emergence of Open and Close Brethren assemblies in Aberdeenshire.

Moreover I enjoyed spending time in conversation with Professors D. E. Meek and S. J. Brown, whose insights into revivalism were most profitable. In particular I would like to record my thanks to Dr John Smith, of the Geography Department at Aberdeen University. He gave of his time generously and aided me greatly in the preparation of the maps that appear in the book.

I have appreciated the assistance of the staff of several libraries and archives. Among them are those who work at Aberdeen City Archives, the north east's regional archives at Oldmeldrum, the local studies section of Aberdeen City Library, and the public libraries of Elgin and Peterhead. I wish to thank those who work in the libraries and special collections at the Universities of Aberdeen, Edinburgh, Glasgow, and Stirling for their help in finding obscure nineteenth- century pamphlets and books. In addition, I am grateful to the staff of the National Archives of Scotland, the National Library of Scotland, the British Library and its Press Library at Colindale for their cooperation in locating church records, religious journals and newspapers.

Undoubtedly this work would not have been possible without the financial assistance that was provided by the Hope Trust during the period of my research. Hence I am obliged to the trustees for their support. Also I wish to thank the Drummond Trust, 3 Pitt Terrace, Stirling for their award of a grant that met the publication costs of this book.

It is noteworthy that the origins of my interest in religious movements lie in a Christian Union meeting held at Stirling University in 1990 on the subject of Revival. This was led by the Reverend James Taylor, who was the minister of Stirling Baptist Church. Accordingly I acknowledge the importance of this first influence upon my affection of awakenings.

I am greatly indebted to Professor D. W. Bebbington for his outstanding supervision of the research that lies behind this work. Besides his enormous expertise, he guided me, by his encouragements and constructive criticisms, in a consistent and gracious manner. I am indeed privileged to have been afforded the benefits of his knowledge and friendship.

Finally, I reserve my most profound thanks for Linda, my wife. She has listened patiently to my outbursts of deep frustration and overwhelming excitement, while her constant encouragement helped me to persevere when my enthusiasm faltered. She has supported me faithfully throughout the course of all my studies. Without the strength and the hope which her love has provided, this work would not have been written. I owe a special debt to Linda, to whom I dedicate this book.

K.S.J.
Cupar, Fife, 2002

List of Abbreviations

A.C.	Aberdeen Citizen
A.F.P.	Aberdeen Free Press
A.H.	Aberdeen Herald
A.J.	Aberdeen Journal
A.S.P.	Aberdeen Saturday Post
B.J.	Banffshire Journal
B.My.	Banffshire Mercury
B.Me.	The Baptist Magazine
B.E.	British Evangelist
B.F.E.R.	British and Foreign Evangelical Review
B.Mr.	The British Messenger
D.S.	The Day Star
E.Ct.	Elgin Courant
E.Cr.	Elgin Courier
F.E.N.G.	Forres, Elgin and Nairn Gazette
F.A.	Fraserburgh Advertiser
F.C.M.R.	The Free Church Monthly Record
F.C.W.R.	The Free Church Weekly Record
H.F.R.C.S.	The Home and Foreign Record of the Church of Scotland
H.F.R.F.C.S.	The Home and Foreign Record of the Free Church of Scotland
M.R.UP.C	Missionary Record of the United Presbyterian Church
M.A.	Morayshire Advertiser
N.T.	Nairnshire Telegraph
N.C.J.M.	The News of the Churches and Journal of Missions
N.A.	Northern Advertiser
N.T.N	Northern Telegraphic News
P.S.	Peterhead Sentinel
T.R.	The Revival
T.S.	The Scotsman
S.C.M.	The Scottish Congregational Magazine
S.J.	Stonehaven Journal
T.T.	The Times
U.P.M.	The United Presbyterian Magazine
W.T.	Wesleyan Times
W.J.	The Wynd Journal

Chapter 1

The Revivalist Tradition

'The Lord', wrote Henry Williamson, 'is walking through the land.'[1] Williamson, an Ulster-born Free Church minister at Huntly, was describing the revival of 1859 as it spread across the north east of Scotland. It was 'a day', he said, 'the like to which may not appear for many generations'.[2] Scotland was by no means the only country affected by this awakening. Its origins lay in America where it began in 1857, but beyond Britain it also affected other parts of Europe, Africa and Asia.[3] Nor was it unique. Such times of renewal have appeared at different periods throughout the church's history. However it was not until around the middle of the eighteenth century that they came to be called 'revivals'. In 1745, for example, John Gillies entitled them 'historical narrations of the success of the Gospel' and 'extraordinary dispensations of grace'.[4] Jonathan Edwards in his account of the movement that affected the parish of Northampton, New England, was probably one of the first people to describe these remarkable events as a 'revival'.[5] Today the word is considered to have a number of different meanings. Donald Meek has outlined at least three that include: 'the revitalisation of a body which once possessed spiritual life'; 'a movement which "awakens" the unregenerate to a sense of sin and spiritual lostness'; and 'the reassertion or rediscovery of aspects of doctrine or practice which have been neglected in the life of a congregation or Church'.[6] According to T. T. Matthews, the editor of *Reminiscences of the Revival of Fifty-nine and the Sixties*, published in Aberdeen in 1910, 'the one deep dominant note [of the 1859 movement] was an overpowering sense of sin'.[7] Similarly, David Henry, Free Church minister at New Marnoch in rural Aberdeenshire during the revival, described how many were brought to 'deep conviction of sin, great concern about their souls, and lively anxiety for their salvation'.[8] Accordingly the spiritual movement of 1859 fits Meek's second definition of revival. It began with the reawakening of Christians to a renewed spirit of prayer, and led not only to remarkable church growth through numerous conversions, but also to the revitalisation of congregations in Scotland, and indeed across the world.

Although it was perhaps one of the most important revivals to affect Scotland, the 1859 awakening was preceded and has been succeeded by a number of other similar movements. The first 'modern' Scottish revival, which became associated with Stewarton, began in Irvine in 1625. It lasted for upwards of five years, and was followed in 1630 by another movement that affected the parish of Shotts in Lanarkshire.[9] Then it appears that 'vital religion' suffered decay in Scotland for over a hundred years. By 1740, Arthur Fawcett suggests 'the situation was indeed critical for the Church of Scotland. Within it was a new and growing generation of ministers who were more concerned about culture than conversion – a group of "Senecan" clergy who spoke of their Covenanting forbears with contempt and amusement.'[10] However following his success in leading several religious movements in America, George Whitefield arrived in Scotland and led a revival at Cambuslang in 1742. Subsequently the movement spread to nearby Baldernock, Kirkintilloch and Kilsyth, and Muthill in Perthshire the following year.[11] Once more there was a lull in fervent spiritual activity and a revival did not occur in Scotland again until 1798, when a movement appeared in the parish of Moulin, near Pitlochry. This signalled the beginning of a series of revivals that affected the Highlands and Western Isles. Awakenings emerged in Arran in 1804, in Skye in 1812, and in Lewis between 1824 and 1835.[12] Perhaps the first broad-based revival in Scotland began in Kilsyth in 1839. Its greatest impression was felt around Perth and Dundee, but it affected other churches at Kelso and Jedburgh in the south, and Aberdeen in the north east of the land.[13] However, it was not until 1859 that the first truly national revival in Scotland occurred. It was followed in 1873 when the American evangelist Dwight Moody and his singing companion Ira Sankey led a successful evangelistic crusade that spread over the greater part of the country.[14] In the twentieth century Scottish revivals appear to have become more localised again. For instance, a remarkable movement influenced the Rose Street Baptist Church in Edinburgh in 1905 after the pastor Joseph Kemp visited scenes of the great awakening in Wales in 1904. Within twelve years of his ministry 1,148 members were added to this church.[15] Sixteen years later, in 1921, a revival that began among the fisherfolk at Lowestoft appeared in a dramatic manner along the Moray Firth.[16] The last 'traditional' revival that has affected Scotland occurred in the Island of Lewis between 1949 and 1953 and was led by the evangelist Duncan Campbell.[17] However, the Billy Graham crusade that took place in Glasgow for six weeks during March and April 1955 was the most recent and successful evangelistic campaign in Scotland. It affected 26,457 inquirers.[18] Accordingly a number of different revivals have appeared in various parts of Scotland during the course of the last four hundred years.

Yet revival studies have been largely ignored by Scottish church historians. Untidy and often seemingly inexplicable affairs, religious awakenings have been regularly passed over with only a brief passing remark. J. H. S. Burleigh does not make a single reference to a revival in his history of the church in Scotland.[19] Meanwhile Andrew Drummond and James Bulloch refer fleetingly to the 1859 revival in order to suggest simply that it stimulated a rise in hymn singing in the church.[20] The 1859 revival has not received any published scholarly attention for more than fifty years. Indeed J. E. Orr's account, that appeared in 1949, gave the impression that it was a uniform event and thus grossly misrepresented the movement.[21] Yet this inaccuracy has been left uncorrected for more than half a century. There has been a regrettable dearth of serious academic study of both this and other religious movements. Hence this book will seek to offer a new interpretation of this movement, building upon the most recent work that has been undertaken within this field of study. This chapter will begin by charting the development of the revival tradition as it has evolved over the last four hundred years, particularly in Scotland and with some references to other parts of Britain and in America.

I

When revivals began to occur in early seventeenth-century Presbyterian Scotland they were considered to be spontaneous outbursts of divine favour. It appears that communities simply prayed, waited and hoped for a religious movement. Christians generally embraced a providential belief that periodic 'showers of blessing' would fall according to God's sovereign purposes. Such an understanding is revealed by contemporary descriptions of these awakenings before the word 'revival' began to be used to describe them. For instance, the Stewarton movement of 1625 was reported by Robert Fleming as an 'extraordinary out letting of the Spirit'.[22] He portrayed the events at Shotts five years later as 'a convincing appearance of God and down pouring of the Spirit'. Elsewhere he commented upon how 'God sometimes works without his people'.[23] Even a century later, in 1744 after the Cambuslang revival, a concert of prayer was established by English and Scottish Evangelicals which described how 'before the late revivals prayer for such blessings was so much neglected that in some respects it may be said, the Lord was found of people when they sought Him not and did wonderful things which we looked not for'.[24] These descriptions demonstrate that during this period Christians understood revival as a sovereign work of God's Spirit which occurred according to his will and purpose. Men and women, they believed, could not manufacture that which God alone could cause to occur.

In the seventeenth century revivals appeared most frequently in small, close-knit communities and although they spread across local regions of Scotland they did not become national religious movements.[25] The first 'modern' Scottish revival began in Stewarton, a hamlet that 'was little more than a cluster of houses that surrounded the parish church'.[26] Although it attracted many pilgrims and affected a large area of south west Scotland, it was not diffused over the entire country. Likewise the revival at Kirk of Shotts in 1630, notwithstanding its effect upon the surrounding countryside, did not extend its influence across the whole of the land.[27] Similarly, each of the eighteenth-century Scottish religious movements was confined to a small village or town. Many that appeared in the Highlands, such as at Obsdale in 1675, Tongue in 1773, Kiltearn in 1782 and Moulin in 1800, were parochial affairs.[28] They affected the communities within which they appeared and their immediate vicinities, but their influence did not stretch throughout the whole of Scotland. Also religious movements, at this time, appeared as a process over an extended period of time, rather than as a single event of short duration.[29] For upwards of five years a heightened state of spiritual awareness was maintained over Stewarton after the revival began in 1625. Meanwhile the movement that affected Moulin more than a hundred years later, in 1799, did not exhaust itself until 1802.[30] Hence seventeenth- and eighteenth-century Scottish revivals were, on the whole, local community-based movements that tended to last for quite a considerable length of time.

Indeed the pattern of these rural-based revivals regularly followed the seasons of the year, and frequently became associated with communion seasons which were interwoven around the agricultural events of planting and harvest. In this way they were confined usually to the late spring and early autumn, with the result that the period from May to October was often called the 'holy season', a time which people expected to be one of conversion and renewal.[31] When Presbyterianism emerged in Scotland, these community-based, religious festivals, which usually lasted from Thursday to Monday, replaced the high days of mediaeval Catholicism and became important local events within the annual cycle of society. Held infrequently, they attracted large crowds of men and women and created a sense of religious expectancy. Infused with spiritual influence, they became the occasion of a large number of Scottish revivals in the seventeenth and eighteenth centuries. Therefore the coincidence of communion and revival became established.[32] These events affected deeply the rhythm of people's piety and were anticipated as moments of spiritual renewal.[33] Thus according to M. J. Crawford, 'throughout the British American evangelical community, the celebration of the Lord's supper, however it varied in form, was a revivalistic ritual that served as a conduit for the outpouring of grace'.[34] The sacrament of communion, a significant rite within the religious culture of Scotland, became the occasion of many seventeenth- and eighteenth-century revivals.

Yet there is no record of the preparatory services or the actual celebration of the sacrament being the moment when these movements began. Rather it appears that the stimulus was the Monday thanksgiving day service. For instance, the Kirk of Shotts revival in 1630 began after a sermon was preached by John Livingston on Monday 21 June.[35] Similarly at Cambuslang in 1742 the Monday following the celebration of the sacrament was said to have been the greatest day of the revival.[36] Almost one hundred years later, as an awakening engulfed the parish of Kilsyth in 1839, it was acknowledged that the most notable day of that movement was Monday 22 July, the day following the celebration of the Lord's supper.[37] Likewise, the minister of the parish of Tain reported how the 1840 revival began 'in the parish of Tarbat . . . on the Communion Monday, being the 6th of July last . . . it commenced in this parish . . . on the following Monday, being also the communion here'.[38] The fact that five separate revivals all started during the Monday thanksgiving service that followed the celebration of the Lord's Supper suggests there was something peculiar about these particular gatherings that was especially conducive towards religious movements. Communion seasons had a specific order of events. The Thursday preceding the celebration was the fast day, Friday was set aside for the 'Question Meeting', a preparatory service was held on the Saturday, and after the sacrament was served on the sabbath, a thanksgiving service was held on the Monday.[39] Each day's meeting had a special theme and the Monday services, as thanksgiving implies, focused upon praise to God for his grace. Hence it would appear that the celebration of God's favour provided the specific context within which these revivals flourished.

The nature of these exclusively Presbyterian revivals is revealed further by examining the key people who were involved. Repeatedly, in many of the contemporary reports, the local minister was presented as the most important figure. According to W. J. Couper the name most popularly associated with the Stewarton revival was David Dickson, the parish minister at Irvine.[40] Similarly John Livingston was the chief instrument in the Kirk of Shotts revival. Despite having been called by several churches, Livingston was, at the time, unlicensed to preach because the church authorities had obstructed his ordination. Nevertheless, although he was untitled, Livingston was essentially a minister of the gospel.[41] Furthermore, despite the celebrated role that was exercised by the evangelist George Whitefield, the parish ministers of Cambuslang and Kilsyth, William M'Culloch and James Robe, were widely credited as having been the principal agents in the revivals that affected their churches in 1742.[42] Local parish ministers were also at the centre of the movements that appeared after the 'Cambuslang Wark'. John Sutherland of Golspie, William Halley at Muthill and John Balfour of Nigg were acknowledged as the main protagonists of the movement in these places.[43] Accordingly the position of the local minister at times of revival during the seventeenth and eighteenth centuries was significant. There is little doubt he played a prominent role during these days of religious excitement and that he exercised considerable control over the course of events.[44]

Certainly ministers had a profound influence upon the nature of revival sermons. At this time the accustomed means of grace, the preaching of the word of God and the dispensation of the Lord's Supper, were considered to be the principal tools in the work of revival. Salvation came through hearing the gospel preached, which was represented by the elements of the sacrament. Ministers did not threaten their congregations with the prospect of the angry judgment of God. The 'terror of the Lord' was not generally employed in an attempt to awaken the conscience of men and women. On the contrary, it has been observed that during this period ministers sought to excite a sense of guilt among their congregations by arousing the moral conscience of those who listened to them preach.[45] Moreover the grace of God was the dominant theme within revival preaching. The sermon which John Livingston preached at Kirk of Shotts, which acted as the catalyst of that revival, was based upon Ezekiel chapter 36 verses 25 and 26, which describe God's desire to forgive and recreate his people.[46] He also recalled the preaching of another minister, James Durham, who was instrumental in revival work during communion seasons near Glasgow. He described how Durham made

> a glorious display of the banner of free grace, holding forth the riches of it very clearly and convincingly, and bringing the offers of it very low, wonderfully low ... some of his hearers were made to think, that the cord of the offer of salvation was let down and hung so low to sinners, that those of the lowest stature among them all, might have caught hold of it, who, through grace, had any mind to do so.[47]

Later William McKenzie, the minister at Tongue during a season of revival in 1773 told a fellow minister 'that the truth which seemed above all others to impress and awaken his people was the dying love of Christ'.[48] In this manner ministers held before their congregations the mercy of God and his offer of forgiveness. The saving grace of God, not fear of his judgment, lay at the heart of their revival sermons.

The influence of ministers also extended to how men and women understood and experienced religious conversion. Traditionally it was understood to be 'an unanticipated exercise of divine sovereignty . . . [that was] waited for rather than contrived'.[49] According to Stewart, parish minister during the Moulin revival in 1799, 'all our converts have been brought to serious concern and inquiry in a quiet, gradual manner'.[50] Consequently it was not uncommon for men and women to suffer from conviction of sin for a period of time before they were converted and found peace in believing. Ned Landsman discovered that almost all the Cambuslang converts claimed that their awakening arose from a sense of sin and dishonour which they experienced as shame, rather than a fear of damnation. Spiritual anxiety, it seems, did not arise from a sense of inherent depravity, but rather from a concern for social position within their own community.[51] Accordingly it appears that early eighteenth-century conversions were often protracted, subjective, personal affairs that proceeded from an inherent sense of embarrassed shame.

In addition a proportion of those who became Christians at Presbyterian communion season revivals were affected in a physical manner and often suffered from prostrations. During this period Evangelical piety was often intensely visual. Consequently lapsing into trances, fainting or falling down as if dead, hearing voices, dreaming and seeing visions were all commonplace within this tradition.[52] Lady Robertland, whose estate lay close to Stewarton, described how during the revival in 1625 'many were so choked and taken by the heart through terror, the Spirit in such measure convincing them of sin in hearing of the Word, that they have been made to fall over and thus carried out of the church'.[53] As a result the revival became popularly known and was discredited as the 'Stewarton sickness'. At Kirk of Shotts, five years later, it was recalled by an elderly man that 'several upon that remarkable Monday after sermon lay so long as if they had been dead, that their friends and others scarce thought they would recover'.[54] During the July communion season, which marked the high point of the 1742 Cambuslang revival, George Whitefield described how 'there was such weeping, so many falling into deep distress and manifesting it in various ways, that description is impossible. The people seemed to be smitten by scores. They were carried off and brought into the house like wounded soldiers taken from the field of battle'.[55] Even mid-nineteenth-century rural, sacrament-based revivals that affected the Highlands and Islands of Scotland continued to be accompanied by dramatic displays of physical manifestation. James McQueen, pastor of the Baptist church in Broadford, described one revival scene at a communion weekend on Skye, in a letter he addressed to the Baptist Home Missionary Society in September 1841. He wrote, 'they had a sacrament last week, and I hear that between 12000 and 15000 attended, and that hundreds fell down as if they were dead'.[56] People weeping and falling over unconscious were common features of these sacrament-based revivals. It is noticeable, nonetheless, that these manifestations appear to have been comparatively quiet and orderly rather than rowdy and boisterous. Nevertheless they created suspicion and disgust amongst the sceptical, while those who led these religious movements accepted them, albeit in an unwilling manner.

The Cambuslang movement also provides a valuable insight into the type of person who was affected by this traditional form of revival. In an attempt to make a record of the movement, William M'Culloch, the parish minister, interviewed 110 converts. These accounts formed the basis of a study undertaken by T. C. Smout, who analysed the material and classified the converts according to their previous religious experience, gender, occupation, marital status and age. He discovered that each of them attended church with some regularity. Seventy had been taught to pray when they were children and a large number had recently joined a local praying society and were actively seeking spiritual counsel. Sixty eight per cent were women and thirty two per cent were men. Also two thirds of those whose work was specified came from the background of small tenants or low status craftsmen, thirteen were from more humble backgrounds, and approximately one ninth were from what may be regarded as the 'middle class'. A fifth of those influenced were teenagers and seventy two per cent were less than thirty years of age. The average age of the female and male converts was 24.9 and 27.9 respectively. It is regrettable that the marital status of a large proportion of the male converts is unknown. Nevertheless of those whose conjugal position was noted, almost three quarters were unmarried, and the greater number of them were women.[57] Supposing the 110 people M'Culloch interviewed were a fair representation of those affected during the Cambuslang revival, it emerges that the typical convert of this eighteenth-century Scottish movement was the church-attending, unmarried, daughter of a skilled craftsman who was in her early twenties.

Despite bearing the general characteristics of the rural community-based revivals of this period, the 'Cambuslang Wark' does not fit neatly into the pattern of these seventeenth- and eighteenth-century movements. Like similar seasons of grace, it was inextricably linked to the local communion season. The preaching of the gospel did not differ from that delivered at previous revivals, and people experienced conversion in a protracted and often colourful manner. Crucially however, this was not a wholly spontaneous revival. Rather its origins lay in the religious movement that had appeared in New England in 1734, led by Jonathan Edwards. Accounts of these awakenings, which M'Culloch read to his congregation, created the desire and expectancy for a similar movement to appear amongst them.[58] Also, without ignoring the central role played by the parish minister M'Culloch, the revival became popularly associated with two large communion seasons at which George Whitefield preached. For the first time an awakening became identified with the work of an ordained deacon.[59] Furthermore this was the first Scottish revival in which laymen were reported to have played a leading role. Robert Bowman, a local weaver, and Ingram More, a shoemaker, were credited as having been important protagonists of the movement.[60] Fourthly, the Cambuslang movement was comparatively short. It did not continue for upwards of five years like previous revivals, but lasted for only six months, from 18 February to 15 August 1742.[61] Perhaps most significant was the manner in which revival impulses were not contained within this parish or local area as they had been before, but were diffused widely across Scotland. From Irvine in the south-west through Stirling in the central belt to Golspie in the north and Aberdeen in the east, the excitement of this movement spread through the land.[62] Hence even though it resembled the traditional Presbyterian, local, rural, sacrament-based revival in many respects, the events at Cambuslang demonstrated, as early as 1742, that religious movements were beginning to change.

II

Although the long-established, seventeenth-century Presbyterian model of revival continued to appear in the nineteenth and twentieth centuries, a second tradition of religious movements began to emerge around the 1790s. The origins of this were found in the accelerated growth of Methodism and other independent churches such as the Baptists and Congregationalists. It appeared almost simultaneously and yet separately in America, England, Scotland and Ulster. Across the Atlantic the Methodists experienced almost thirty years of continuous revival towards the end of the eighteenth century with the result that they became the largest of America's denominations by 1830.[63] In England the Wesleyans made gains through the same period during the course of a series of local revivals.[64] Meanwhile in Scotland success accompanied the evangelistic work of the Baptist and Congregational churches in the Highlands and Islands of Scotland.[65] Despite being, in several respects, autonomous religious movements, the revivals in each of these situations shared common characteristics, which set them apart from those that had occurred previously.

In the first instance they arose in communities that lay along the isolated, 'neglected' fringes of society. They appeared in America through the western and southern frontier areas, especially in the Cumberland region of Kentucky, where, in this far-off area among recent settlements, there were few churches.[66] Similarly the English Primitive Methodist revivals at the start of the nineteenth century prospered in remote places like Cornwall and the West Riding, but only rarely penetrated within a seventy-five mile radius of London.[67] Indeed it has been suggested that Cornwall's geographical isolation was a key factor that helps to explain why the Methodists in that area were so susceptible to religious movements in the first half of the nineteenth century.[67] In Scotland the revivals that arose between 1790 and 1820 emerged in the Highlands and Islands which had been neglected by the church for several generations. At the heart of Perthshire, in the district of Breadalbane, for example, the biographer of the Haldanes recorded that before there was a revival in this district 'there were actually no Bibles, scarcely any Testaments, and the people lived without prayer'.[69] Likewise it was found that late eighteenth-century Methodist revivals in the south of Ulster thrived where the long-established denominations were weak, but did not flourish where the older churches retained their influence and authority. According to David Hempton 'the most conducive environments were those interstitial and marginal areas where traditional hierarchical structures were either absent or perceived to be antithetical to new interests'.[70] It is significant that religious movements, as they appeared in America, England, Scotland and Ulster at the end of the eighteenth century, arose within these isolated communities.

Also the places that became hotbeds of religious enthusiasm, where people had a limited education and where new ideas were slow to penetrate, were highly superstitious.[71] It appears they embraced the evangelical faith of Methodist revivalists in particular because it was considerably more supernatural than the rationalist religion offered by the institutional church, and hence it appealed to their paranormal view of the world. It has been argued that superstitious beliefs exercised considerable influence over the fishing communities of Yorkshire, and that the religious void created by the absence of the Anglican Church was filled comfortably by the Methodists.[72] Likewise Methodism flourished among the Cornish fishermen and became absorbed into their superstitious culture after Established clergymen became averse to their popular beliefs.[73] Also in South Lindsey, where the Church of England failed to proselytise the local community, Methodism imbibed the spirituality of the local people and prospered in this area.[74] It was suggested that the religion of 'the Men', the itinerant evangelists who led the Highland revivals towards the end of the eighteenth century, was more readily accepted amongst these people than the Enlightenment-influenced preaching of the Moderate ministers because it was considerably more supernaturalist.[75] According to Major-General Stewart of Garth, the people of the Highlands, although having lost, as a result of their conversion, 'a great portion of their belief in fairies, ghosts, and second-sight', nevertheless retained 'their appetite for strong impressions [and] have readily supplied the void with the visions and inspirations of the "new light", and in this mystic lore have shown themselves such adepts as even to astonish their new instructors'.[76] Late eighteenth-century religious movements were regularly charged with a heightened sense of eternal and supernatural matters. Communities that were already inclined to consider such issues, albeit in a superstitious manner, often embraced these revivals more readily than other places where belief in the paranormal was not as common.

Another difference, that separated this late eighteenth-century revival tradition from that which belonged previously to the Scottish Presbyterians, was the length and the internal dynamic of these movements. They were regularly short and intense affairs. At Breadalbane in 1802, for instance, it was recorded how 'they all flocked together, and continued to go from house to house, praying and praising God, for eight or ten days, with only two hours' sleep each morning; and many of them were several nights without any sleep'.[76] Then the awakening finished abruptly. Similarly in Cornwall when revival broke out at Redruth in 1814 a meeting was held continuously for nine successive days and nights, at the end of which two thousand people were converted. However, the movement soon came to an end.[77] A chief characteristic of these revivals was the protracted all-night meeting held in homes which began during the day and seldom finished until the following morning.[78] These short, excited, spontaneous outbursts of religious enthusiasm, which appeared most regularly among Methodist, Baptist and

Congregational churches in remote and isolated places, established quite clearly a second, distinctive tradition of revival.

Another distinguishing feature of these revivals was the central role played by local, lay, itinerant evangelists.[80] Along the American frontier, revivals at the end of the eighteenth century followed the work of 'poorly educated but physically robust itinerant preachers' who travelled from town to town conducting large, open-air religious meetings.[81] It was observed how a close relationship between the evangelists and a community was an important feature of these movements.[82] Similarly the presence of William Bramwell and Ann Cutler, two popular local evangelists, was a critical determinant of the pattern of revival that affected the West Riding in 1795.[83] Meanwhile in Ireland, Gideon Ouseley, born in Galway in 1762, spent forty years travelling as a missionary preacher throughout Ireland and was instrumental in a number of local Methodist revivals.[84] In Scotland too, bands of itinerant preachers from the Relief, Baptist and Congregational churches had a great effect upon the religious climate of the West Coast and Highlands of Scotland in the second half of the eighteenth century.[85] The crucial factor in the success of this work was the social position of the evangelist, who was considered trustworthy because he was counted as one of the people.[86] It was significant that he shared the same social and intellectual background as his audience. There is no doubt his success lay within his ability to contextualise the gospel message to fit the particular conventions of the community within which he lived and worked.[87] Accordingly local men and women frequently emerged as the leaders of these late eighteenth-century revivals. In this way, they replaced ministers, and began to exercise considerable influence upon the nature of these movements.

The work of women evangelists was another distinctive feature of revivals during this period.[88] Although their role within religious movements was often ignored by their male contempories who recorded these events, and consequently has been frequently understated by historians, women exercised a crucial role during Methodist revivals in the 1790s as previous constraints of gender disappeared. Ann Cutler became the most popular female evangelist of this period in England.[89] She was widely credited as being 'the principal instrument in the beginning of the late revival of the work of God in Yorkshire and Lancashire' between 1792 and 1796.[90] Mary Barritt was another famous evangelist who played a leading role in the Yorkshire revivals of the 1790s.[91] Like the character Dinah Morris who appeared preaching the gospel at Hayslope in George Eliot's novel *Adam Bede*, published in 1859, similarly many young women travelled around the north of England engaged in revival

The Revivalist Tradition

work.[92] Female preachers became very popular in Methodist circuits towards the end of the eighteenth century. Indeed in 1818 a fifth of all Primitive Methodist preachers were women.[93] Consequently they played a very prominent role in the work of revival during this period.

It is noteworthy that the lay, itinerant evangelists presented the gospel as a 'free, full and present salvation through and by faith', because herein lies another deviation from the previous tradition of revival.[94] As Methodism became more popular towards the end of the eighteenth century, conversion was offered, increasingly, as an immediate experience of spiritual regeneration which everyone could decide to receive. Although regularly it continued to be presented as a gradual process over time, the exact moment of the 'new birth' became more climactic. The conversion of William Clowes, co-founder of the Primitive Methodist Connexion, was quite typical. He described how he had been burdened by a sense of sinfulness for a considerable time before he was 'born again', but the moment of his conversion was sudden. He recounted how 'the power of Heaven came down upon me, and I cried for help to Him who is mighty to save. It was towards the close of the meeting . . . in an agony of prayer, I believed God would save me, – then I believed he was saving me, – then I believed he had saved me, and it was so.'[95] Around the same time Hugh Bourne, the other co-founder of the Primitive Methodist Connexion, commented that conversions 'do not depend on length of time, but on [a person's] faith'.[96] David Bebbington, in his study of evangelical conversions from 1740 to 1850, has observed that around the start of the nineteenth century 'it was increasingly believed that the sinner did not have to wait until the moment of divine appointment for conversion'.[97] In this way conversion, during this second tradition of religious movements, became a less protracted, more immediate experience which lay within the ability of people to choose.

Nevertheless late eighteenth-century revival conversions continued to be accompanied by physical manifestations, and these were becoming more dramatic and emotional. Joseph Entwisle, a Methodist evangelist, provided a graphic account of revival scenes when he complained about the enthusiasm that characterised some Yorkshire meetings he attended in the 1790s. He deplored the manner in which 'they had gone beyond all bounds of decency, such screaming and bawling I never heard. Divided into small companies in different parts of the chapel, some singing, others praying, others praising, clapping of hands, etc, all was confusion and uproar . . . they continued thus until five o'clock in the morning.'[98] Physical manifestations continued, among the Methodists at least, to be an integral feature of revivals. However, compared with the relatively quiet prostrations that accompanied the Scottish Presbyterian movements in the seventeenth century when people wept softly and fell unconscious, these demonstrations of spiritual anxiety appear to have become more boisterous and noisy.

This particular style of excited revivalism served to alienate many Christians from religious movements, and as a result it did not endure. The Methodists, among whom it began, were unable to remain united at the beginning of the nineteenth century as the excesses of these awakenings created a gulf between the provincial revivalists and the respectable urban elite who sought to bring greater order and decency to their chapels.[99] There is no doubt, given the manner in which revivals were becoming increasingly rowdy, that churches were embarrassed by the unrestraint of those who led religious movements. As people moved from isolated rural villages, and the scenes of excited revivals, into larger towns and cities where such behaviour was not considered acceptable, they quickly discarded their enthusiasm and became more inhibited in their religious conduct. Therefore, anxious to be purged of revival excesses in an attempt to become more respectable, Methodists began to legislate against these uncontrolled outbursts of excitement in 1800.[100] In 1807 the Wesleyan Conference banned revival camp meetings in England and as a result the Primitive Methodist Connexion, which embraced this technique, was formed.[101] Nevertheless this revival tradition appears to have come to an end by around the 1830s, when a new organised style of religious movement began to emerge.[102] The tides of social and religious change were flowing against this revival tradition which persisted in the more remote fringes of Britain, such as Cornwall. Elsewhere however a new approach towards religious movements was about to appear.

III

An important agent of change that began to transform religious ideas during the eighteenth century was the Enlightenment. This liberalising movement, which effectively reconstructed the world view of western society, encouraged people to put their trust in reason and the discoveries of modern science. Accordingly American and British societies grew to invest more confidence in what they considered to be the reliable, rational laws which governed the world in which they lived. The sense of mystery that occupied people's minds in relation to what had been the great unknowns of life was being replaced by a bold faith in the findings of scientists. Subsequently, by the 1830s, a third tradition of revival arose. It is revealed clearly in the textbook of religious movements of this period, Charles Finney's *Lectures on Revival of Religion*, that was published in 1835. In it he wrote 'a revival is as naturally a result of the use of the appropriate means as a crop is of the use of its appropriate means . . . it consists entirely in the right exercise of the powers of nature'.[103] Revivals were unable to stand apart from the winds of change that were sweeping through the western world. Increasing political enfranchisement, the rise of an industrial economy and an urban society, not to mention the accompanying evolution of culture and science, influenced religious movements in a fundamental manner. A new period in the history of revivals was about to begin.

This third tradition of religious movements was conceived by several men who had experienced extraordinary success as evangelists in small-town America during the 1820s before creating an impression in British cities in the 1840s and 1850s.[104] They published the theories and methods of their work, and these books heralded the beginning of this new era of revivals. The first was Calvin Colton, a New England minister, whose influential work, *The History and Character of American Revivals of Religion*, was published in 1832. He described traditional, spontaneous revivals, such as the seventeenth-century Presbyterian and late eighteenth-century Methodist movements, as those which 'Christians waited for as men are wont to wait for showers of rain' which he considered to be 'an expression of sloth'.[105] Instead he believed that revivals had become 'matters of human calculation by the arithmetic of faith in God's arrangements'.[106] The second and more influential exponent of the new approach towards revivals was Charles Finney, a converted trainee-lawyer. He popularised further the belief that religious movements could be expected and achieved regularly provided that certain preconditions were met. 'A revival,' he wrote, 'is not a miracle . . . it is a purely philosophical result of the right use of the constituted means'.[107] His *Lectures on the Revivals of Religion* was a practical handbook that marked a turning point in the history of religious movements. It prescribed means, in accordance with divine laws, by which, he believed, a revival could be planned and arranged. The methods it recommended included preaching tours undertaken by itinerant evangelists, camp meetings, a four-day evangelistic campaign that was broadly based upon the Presbyterian communion season, and the use of an 'anxious seat' or penitent form, a special pew placed at the front of a church where those who were spiritually concerned could be counselled and where public professions of faith might be expected.[108] Shortly these new measures had become the customary practice in many of the major evangelical denominations in America, and by the late 1830s churches in Britain had also begun to embrace these techniques.[109]

In many respects these methods grew out of the church's response to the challenge of reaching the new heterogeneous communities that were emerging in towns and cities at this time. Although 'traditional' religious movements had appeared previously in large settlements, the church needed a new evangelistic approach and thus urban revivalism became increasingly important from the 1830s.[110] As a result cities, during the nineteenth century, grew to become the centres of religious movements from which spiritual impulses were diffused into the surrounding areas. The series of revivals that affected Scotland in 1840 was dispersed principally from Dundee and Perth into the surrounding countryside.[111] The 1857 American revival, which spread across large parts of the nation, began in a church in lower Manhattan at the very heart of New York's business district.[112] Later the Moody and Sankey revival, that affected parts of Scotland in 1873-4, began in Edinburgh before it travelled across the land.[113] Therefore during the second half of the nineteenth century, revivals became increasingly an important strategy of urban evangelism.[114] Indeed during this period, they became almost a synonym for special mission crusade, religious events that were staged in halls, theatres and specially constructed tents and buildings.[115] Significantly, cities became the birthplace of this particular type of religious movement.

The urban context, within which this new type of revival was born, affected the length of its appearance. The work and leisure patterns of the city did not allow men and women to attend to religious matters continuously over a four-day period as their forefathers had previously done during their rural communion seasons or small-town protracted gatherings. Businessmen could not afford to suspend their commercial activities for an extended period of time. Also the increased variety of available recreational activities meant that the church was no longer the central social focus of the lives of city dwellers as it had been in the smaller townships. Revival preachers had to compete against the latest show at the theatre and other cultural attractions. The famous noontime prayer meeting, which was restricted to an hour and which came to epitomise the 1857 American revival, demonstrated how city inhabitants could not devote whole days to spiritual exercises. Religious movements were becoming increasingly tailored to fit this busy context. Therefore the chief instrument used in city crusades was a series of special evening services that were held over the period of a week or a fortnight.[116] As a result city revivals ebbed and flowed over the course of up to eighteen months depending upon the particular success of these courses of meetings. Accordingly it appears that the third tradition of revivals included shorter, organised periods of intensive evangelism that focused on specially arranged events.

Perhaps the most distinguishing feature of these modern religious movements was their organised nature. The psychological technique of conducting specially arranged assemblies for people who belonged to the same occupational or social group was adopted. Specific gatherings were organised for businessmen, firemen, policemen, sailors and even waiters.[117] Also during the principal meeting Christians were afforded the opportunity of making a public profession of their faith, while the unconverted were invited to indicate whether they were spiritually anxious and wanted to be prayed for. A special pew, set aside at the front of the meeting hall where those in a state of spiritual concern were prayed for and exhorted to be converted, was regularly used. Later this was replaced by the inquiry room where, after the main service, a second meeting was conducted when those who had been affected by what they had heard could be interviewed individually by a Christian counsellor. In addition, every effort was made to prevent any outburst of religious excitement. According to Richard Carwardine 'the emotional, cruder excrescences of revivals were being pruned by ministers anxious not to alienate the more respectable, sophisticated members of their congregations . . . [who] wanted a more decorous and polished revivalism'.[118] Finney, the chief architect of these gatherings, said that 'the only thing insisted upon under the gospel dispensation, in regard to measures, is that there should be decency and order'.[119] It is noteworthy that the *Glasgow Herald* praised Moody for the 'promptitude, tact and practical wisdom with which he presides over meetings, so as to prevent mere physical excitement, and so let the word of the Lord have free course without the obstructions and perversions of nervous feeling or prostration'.[120] The dignified and respectable manner of the new revival meeting reflects, above all, the methodical planned nature of this particular tradition of religious movements.

The most visible new aspect of this school of revival was the role played by the professional itinerant evangelist, who was employed to initiate a movement. Unconcerned with the long-term interests of a church, their primary responsibility was simply to produce an immediate effect. Frequently these entertaining preachers, several of whom became quite famous for their glamorous antics, delivered remarkable results.[121] By the late 1860s almost every religious movement had become popularly associated with a particular preacher. For instance the revival which affected the Congregationalists of Brantford, Ontario, in 1869 was perceived to have been principally the result of the labours of Douglas Russell, a young Scottish evangelist en route to Chicago. Henry Varley, an English independent Baptist preacher, was the leader of another movement in the same town in 1875, while E. P. Hammond, an American Congregationalist, instigated another series of revivals there in 1879.[122] Meanwhile the evangelist Moody and his singing companion Sankey were the principal directors of the 1873 revival in Scotland. In this manner later nineteenth-century revivals increasingly became personality-centred gospel campaigns.

Certainly in Scotland at least, Moody and Sankey became the best known revival team during this period. They, more than anyone else, represented most clearly the style of religious movement which Finney had cultivated. By 1873 Moody had perfected the techniques and organisation of modern urban revivalism which had appeared in Britain thirty years previously.[123] Dismissed by some as a dignified form of religious entertainment, it was suggested that their meetings resembled a travelling circus, with their varied and fast moving programme. Advertised widely in the press and by posters, sandwich boards and handbills, distributed from house to house, these crusades were intricately planned. Portable buildings and tents were specially constructed, inside which large canvas sheets were hung from the ceiling with huge religious texts. Long rows of regimented chairs led to an enormous platform that accommodated up to 100 ministers and a 200-strong choir. At the front was a raised rostrum from which Moody preached gospel addresses that were preceded with solos and communal singing. Inquiry rooms had replaced the 'anxious seat' as the more respectable means by which those who were interested in the Christian faith could be interviewed after services.[124] Traditional Calvinists felt uncomfortable with these professional techniques and their reliance upon human methods. Yet undoubtedly these men succeeded in reaching the urban masses.[125] Moody and Sankey's campaigns in Britain between 1873 and 1875 represented the 'high point of evangelical self confidence and influence' in Britain.[126] This was indeed the golden age of the modern, organised religious movement.

The content and style of Moody's addresses reflected revival preaching as it appeared in the modern religious movements during the second half of the nineteenth century. In many respects he reflected the changing social and theological attitudes of this period. Essentially Moody focused on the love of God in his preaching. The American literary critic, H. L. Mencken, writing about him in the late 1940's, commented, 'it was by putting the soft pedal on Hell that Moody beat all his competitors'.[127] Henry Moorhouse, an English Brethren assembly member, visited Moody in Chicago in 1868 and persuaded him to preach more about love and less about the anger of God towards sinful people. Certainly Moody made only rare references to the cruder aspects of eternal damnation, and spoke more about the pain of the act of God which condemned one to go to hell, rather than the actual pain of hell itself. Moody preached about heaven at length, and of the absolute necessity of conversion, in the dramatic, instantaneous, sense. He did not say much about repentance or sin, but simply repeated that the new birth was mandatory.[128] Also he had a unique conversational preaching style which attracted many critics who judged his manner to be too bold and brash.[129] However the success of his campaigns could only assuage such people who had to admit that his preaching produced a remarkable effect upon those who heard him. The emphasis of Moody's sermons lay firmly upon the love of God, an approach that appealed to many people in his audiences.

Also the experience of conversion had continued to evolve over the course of the nineteenth century and this reflected further the changes that were taking place within the revival tradition during this period. Charles Finney, the influential architect of modern revivals, rejected the idea that the human will was incapable of choosing God apart from his preparatory grace. He believed that, 'neither God, nor any other being, can regenerate him, if he will not turn'.[130] Gradually people turned away from the traditional 'protracted conviction of sin and repentance' model of religious experience. The perceived balance between human and divine agency was shifting as men and women began to believe that they could be converted without the help of the Holy Spirit.[130] 'Self conversionism' became increasingly fashionable, with the result that nine students were expelled from at the Glasgow Congregational Theological Academy for adopting this doctrinal position. Eagerness to see people saved had led to this modifying of conversion theology among Evangelicals.[132] Bebbington concludes his study of 'Evangelical Conversions between 1740 and 1850' by commenting that 'the trend in the nineteenth century was for the human component to become exclusive so that divine participation in conversion tended to diminish'.[133] Similarly K. D. Brown, in his study of the conversion experiences of Nonconformist ministers between 1800 and 1930, has observed that towards the end of the nineteenth century spiritual regeneration had become more formal and mechanistic and bore little resemblance to the passionate, protracted struggles that were more common during the earlier part of the period under examination.[134] This is illustrated by a comment made by Gordon Reith, a Free Church minister, who recalled how 'we were in 1859 all Simon Peters falling at Jesus' knees and crying: "Depart from me, for I am a sinful man, O Lord!" In 1874 we were all Lydias, "the Lord opening our hearts" with the golden Key of His great love to sinners.'[135] Accordingly it appears that revival conversions in Scotland, in the second half of the nineteenth century, were not charged with the same spiritual anxiety that had existed previously. Instead they had become less emotionally complicated.

Another important feature of religious movements that belonged to this third tradition of revivals was the concerted effort made to target specific groups of people. As early as 1835 Charles Finney was encouraging the separation of those who attended meetings into specific groups such as 'the children of believing parents' and 'unbelieving husbands of believing wives'. Then specific addresses and hymns were employed that were designed to have a certain appeal for particular groups of people. In this way, he advocated 'all legitimate means, psychological and moral, that could be thought of were employed to arrest the attention and awaken the conscience'.[136] Consequently, concerned that in an increasingly materialistic world the church was losing a large number of men, mid-nineteenth-century American revivalists sought to readjust congregational gender imbalance with a concerted evangelistic campaign among men.[137] The Young Men's Christian Association, whose founder George Williams was heavily influenced by Finney and his new revival methods, spearheaded with considerable success these aggressive crusades.[138] The American revival of 1857, which began at a businessmen's prayer meeting and was diffused principally through the networks of the YMCA, was a distinctly masculine affair. According to one journal the revival 'prevails chiefly among a class of men who are usually the least affected by revivals – the practical business men of the cities'.[139] Also Couper, commenting upon the Moody and Sankey Scottish campaign in Scotland during 1873 remarked that 'perhaps the most striking feature of the whole mission was the way it seized upon young men'.[140] He described how in various reports from across the country special attention was paid to the large number of men who attended the meetings, and how on occasions they outnumbered women. Again the YMCA played a pivotal role in the work of this movement.[141] There was a noticeable deviation in the gender proportion of those affected in urban revivals in the second half of the nineteenth century. Previously the general ratio of converts had been roughly two thirds female and one third male, but, largely as a result of the work of the YMCA, men became more represented among those affected by religious movements during this period.

It is apparent that revivals evolved considerably between the seventeenth and nineteenth centuries, and that there have been at least three main traditions that are separated by a number of broad differences. Firstly each began to appear during a particular period in history. Secondly they emerged within distinctive theological persuasions. Thirdly, and perhaps most significantly, they were conceived in dissimilar social contexts. Yet it is quite remarkable that manifestations of each of these traditions of revival appeared at different times in various places in Scotland during the twentieth century. In 1921 a revival affected the fishing communities along the Moray Firth. Jock Troup, a lay evangelist, was the main personality of this excited movement which resembled those that affected the Methodists and other smaller denominations in neglected places towards the end of the eighteenth century.[142] Then between 1949 and 1953 a revival appeared among the crofting community of the parish of Barvas in Lewis, in the Western Isles. Duncan Campbell, a leader of this revival, was anxious to distinguish this movement from a successful, modern evangelistic campaign, and in several respects it was similar to the seventeenth-century Presbyterian revivals.[143] Within two years of the Lewis revival, Scotland was overtaken by another religious movement. The 'Tell Scotland' campaign and the Billy Graham crusades in the Kelvin Hall were highly organised.[144] Heralded rather presumptuously as 'the greatest evangelistic campaign in the history of Scotland' it bore a likeness to the nineteenth-century Evangelical urban campaigns.[145] Religious movements have clearly not appeared in a uniform manner in the last four centuries. Rather, conditioned fundamentally by the social and theological contexts in which they have been conceived, their manner and expression have varied enormously.

Notes

1. *A Report of a Conference on the State of Religion and Public Meeting, held in the Free Church, Huntly, January 5, 1860* (Huntly, 1860), p. 6.
2. Ibid.
3. J. E. Orr, *Evangelical Awakenings in Africa* (Minnesota, 1975), pp. 53-55, J. E. Orr, *Evangelical Awakenings in India* (New Delhi, 1970), pp. 29-33.
4. J. Gillies, *Historical Collections relating to Remarkable Periods of the Success of the Gospel* [H. Bonar ed.,Kelso, 1845] (Pennsylvania, 1981), pp. i-iv.
5. J. Edwards, *An Account of the Revival of Religion in Northampton* [1743] (Edinburgh, 1995), p. 149.
6. N. M. de S. Cameron (ed.), *Dictionary of Scottish Church History and Theology* (Edinburgh, 1993), pp. 711-12.
7. T. T. Matthews, *Reminiscences of the Revival of Fifty-Nine and the Sixties* (Aberdeen, 1910), p. xii.
8. *Conference on the State of Religion*, p. 31.

9. J. D. MacMillan (ed.), *Restoration in the Church: Reports of Revival 1625-1839* (Tain, Ross-shire, 1989), pp. 47-58.
10. A. Fawcett, *The Cambuslang Revival: The Scottish Evangelical Revival of the Eighteenth Century* (London, 1971), p. 27.
11. MacMillan, *Restoration in the Church*, pp. 11-46.
12. Ibid., pp. 59-66, 91-102, 115-30.
13. *Evidence on the Subject of Revivals taken before a Committee of the Presbytery of Aberdeen* (Aberdeen, 1841), pp. 57-76.
14. W. J. Couper, *Scottish Revivals* (Dundee, 1918), pp. 141-52.
15. W. Whyte, *Revival in Rose Street: A History of Charlotte Baptist Chapel, Edinburgh* (Edinburgh, nd), pp. 35-42.
16. D. E. Meek, '"Fishers of Men": The 1921 Religious Revival – Its Cause, Context and Transmission', *Scottish Bulletin of Evangelical Theology*, 17, (1999), p. 44.
17. Cameron, *Dictionary of Church History and Theology*, p. 127.
18. T. Allan (ed.), *Crusade in Scotland: Billy Graham* (London, 1955), p. 8.
19. J. H. S. Burleigh, *A Church History of Scotland* (London, 1960), pp. 427-56.
20. A. L. Drummond, J. Bulloch, *The Church in Victorian Scotland 1843- 74* (Edinburgh, 1975), p. 185.
21. J. E. Orr, *The Second Evangelical Awakening* (London, 1949), pp. 58-77.
22. Couper, *Scottish Revivals*, p. 3.
23. MacMillan, *Restoration in the Church*, p. 58.
24. Couper, *Scottish Revivals*, p. 69.
25. Cameron, *Dictionary of Church History and Theology*, p. 715.
26. Couper, *Scottish Revivals*, p. 26.
27. Ibid., p. 38.
28. MacMillan, *Restoration in the Church*, p. 5.
29. M. J. Crawford, *Seasons of Grace: Colonial New England's Revival Tradition in its British Context* (Oxford, 1991), p. 219.
30. Couper, *Scottish Revivals*, pp. 31, 85.
31. L. E. Schmidt, *Holy Fairs: Scottish Communions and American Revivals in the Early Modern Period* (New Jersey, 1989), p. 156.
32. Ibid., p. 22.
33. L. E. Schmidt, 'Time, Celebration and the Christian Year in Eighteenth Century Evangelicalism' in M. A. Noll, G. A. Rawlyk, D. W. Bebbington (ed.), *Evangelicalism: Comparative Studies of Popular Protestantism in North America, the British Isles and Beyond 1700-1990* (New York, 1994), pp. 95-103.
34. Crawford, *Seasons of Grace*, p. 219.
35. Gillies, *Historical Collections*, p. 198.
36. Fawcett, *Cambuslang Revival*, pp. 113-23.
37. MacMillan, *Restoration in the Church*, p. 133.
38. Couper, *Scottish Revivals*, pp. 126-7.
39. Cameron, *Dictionary of Church History and Theology*, p. 200.
40. Couper, *Scottish Revivals*, p. 27.
41. Gillies, *Historical Collections*, pp. 198-9.
42. Fawcett, *Cambuslang Revival*, pp. 94-143.
43. Couper, *Scottish Revivals*, pp. 60, 65-6.
44. N. Landsman, 'Evangelicals and their Hearers: Popular Interpretations of

Revivalist Preaching in Eighteenth-Century Scotland', *Journal of British Studies*, 28, 1989, pp. 127-8.
45. Couper, *Scottish Revivals*, p. 157.
46. Ibid., p. 36.
47. Gillies, *Historical Collections*, p. 185.47.
48. Couper, Scottish Revivals, p. 13.
49. D. W. Bebbington, 'Evangelical Conversion c1740-1850' *North Atlantic Missiology Project*, Position Paper No 21, University of Cambridge, 1996, p. 15.
50. *A Letter from Rev Alexander Stewart, Minister of Parish of Moulin to Rev David Black, Minister of Lady Yesta's Church, Edinburgh* (Glasgow, nd), p. 5.
51. Landsman, 'Evangelicals and their Hearers', p. 137.
52. Schmidt, *Holy Fairs*, p. 145.
53. Couper, *Scottish Revivals*, p. 30.
54. Ibid., p. 37.
55. Ibid., p. 46.
56. D. E. Meek, 'Gaelic Bible, Revival and Mission: The Spiritual Rebirth of the Nineteenth-Century Highlands' in J. Kirk (ed.), *The Church in the Highlands* (Edinburgh, 1999), pp. 114-45.
57. T. C. Smout, 'Born Again at Cambuslang: New Evidence on Popular Religion and Literacy in Eighteenth-Century Scotland', *Past and Present*, 97, (1982), p. 116.
58. Couper, *Scottish Revivals*, p. 43.
59. Fawcett, *Cambuslang Revival*, p. 115
60. Landsman, 'Evangelicals and their Hearers', p. 125.
61. Couper, *Scottish Revivals*, p. 49.
62. Fawcett, *Cambuslang Revival*, pp. 124-42.
63. R. Carwardine, *Transatlantic Revivalism: Popular Evangelicalism in Britain and America, 1790-1865* (Westport, Connecticut, 1978), p. 10.
64. R. B. Walker, 'The Growth of Wesleyan Methodism in Victorian England and Wales', *Journal of Ecclesiastical History*, 14, (1973), p. 267.
65. J. MacInnes, *The Evangelical Movement in the Highlands of Scotland 1688-1800*(Aberdeen, 1951), pp. 154-67.
66. Carwardine, *Transatlantic Revivalism*, p. 4.
67. J. S. Werner, *The Primitive Methodist Connexion: Its Background and Early History* (Wisconsin, 1984), p. 33.
68. D. Luker, 'Revivalism in Theory and Practice: The Case of Cornish Methodism', *Journal of Ecclesiastical History*, 37, (1986), p. 609.
69. A. Haldane, *The Lives of Robert Haldane of Airthrey, and of His Brother, James Alexander Haldane* (London, 1852) quoted by Couper, *Scottish Revivals*, p. 100.
70. D. Hempton, *The Religion of the People: Methodism and Popular Religion c1750-1900* (London, 1996), pp. 2, 27.
71. R. Carwardine, 'The Welsh Evangelical Community and 'Finney's' Revival', *Journal of Ecclesiastical History*, 29, (1978), p. 469.
72. D. Clark, *Between Pulpit and Pew: Folk Religion in a North Yorkshire Fishing Village* (Cambridge, 1982), pp. 140-51.
73. J. Rule, 'Methodism, Popular Beliefs and Village Culture in Cornwall, 1800-50' in R. D. Storch (ed.), *Popular Culture and Custom in Nineteenth-Century*

England (London, 1982), p. 63.
74. J. Obelkevich, *Religion and Rural Society: South Lindsey 1825-75* (Oxford, 1976), p. 259.
75. S. Bruce, 'Social Change and Collective Behaviour: The Revival in Eighteenth-Century Ross-shire', *British Journal of Sociology*, 34, (1983), p. 567.
76. Couper, *Scottish Revivals*, p. 109.
77. Ibid., p. 101.
78. W. R. Ward, *Religion and Society in England, 1790-1850* (London, 1972), p. 83.
79. M. Smith, *Religion in Industrial Society: Oldham and Saddleworth 1740-1865* (Oxford, 1994), p. 183.
80. W. McLoughlin, *Revivals, Awakenings and Reform* (Chicago, 1978), p. 86.
81. Carwardine, *Transatlantic Revivalism*, p. 4.
82. Carwardine, 'Welsh Evangelical Community', p. 472.
83. J. Baxter, 'The Great Yorkshire Revival 1792-6: A Study of Mass Revival among the Methodists' in *A Sociological Yearbook of Religion in Britain 7* (London, 1974), p. 47.
84. Hempton, *Religion of the People*, pp. 130-8.
85. D. E. Meek, 'Evangelicalism and Emigration': Aspects of the Role of Dissenting Evangelicalism in Highland Emigration to Canada' in G. MacLennan (ed.), *Proceedings of the First North American Congress of Celtic Studies* (Ottawa, 1988), p. 17.
86. Bruce, 'Social Change and Collective Behaviour', pp. 558, 566-69.
87. Carwardine, 'Welsh Evangelical Community', p. 469.
88. Werner, *Primitive Methodist Connexion*, p. 35.
89. D. M. Valenze, *Prophetic Sons and Daughters: Female Preaching and Popular Religion in Industrial England* (New Jersey, 1985), pp. 52-5.
90. Baxter, 'Yorkshire Revival', p. 54.
91. Valenze, *Prophetic Sons and Daughters*, pp. 52-5.
92. G. Eliot, *Adam Bede* [1859] (London, 1980), pp. 58-77.
93. Werner, *Primitive Methodist Connexion*, p. 142.
94. Ibid., p. 150.
95. Ibid.
96. Ibid., p. 151.
97. Bebbington, 'Evangelical Conversion', p. 17.
98. Baxter, 'Great Yorkshire Revival', p. 54.
99. Hempton, *Religion of the People*, p. 17.
100. Werner, *Primitive Methodist Connexion*, p. 49.
101. Ward, *Religion and Society*, pp. 75-85.
102. Smith, *Religion in Industrial Society*, p. 194.
103. C. G. Finney, *Revival Lectures* [1832] (np, nd), p. 5.
104. Carwardine, *Transatlantic Revivalism*, pp. 198-9.
105. C. Colton, *The History and Character of American Revivals of Religion* (London, 1832), p. 6 quoted by J. Kent, *Holding the Fort: Studies in Victorian Revivalism* (London, 1978), p. 18.
106. Kent, *Holding the Fort*, p. 18.
107. Finney, *Revival Lectures*, pp. 4-5.
108. Carwardine, *Transatlantic Revivalism*, p. 4.
109. Ibid., pp. 4-18.

110. Ibid., p. 18.
111. Couper, *Scottish Revivals*, pp. 123-24.
112. K. T. Long, *The Revival of 1857-58: Interpreting an American Religious Awakening* (New York, 1998), p. 13.
113. Couper, *Scottish Revivals*, pp. 141-52.
114. Cameron, *Dictionary of Scottish Church History and Theology*, p. 714.
115. D. W. Bebbington, 'Mission in Scotland, 1846-1946', in D. Searle (ed.) *Death or Glory: The Church's Mission in Scotland's Changing Society*, (Edinburgh, 2001), p. 44.
116. Carwardine, *Transatlantic Revivalism*, pp. 20-21.
117. Ibid., p. 20, 27.
118. Ibid., p. 23.
119. Finney, *Revival Lectures*, p. 276.
120. J. Holmes, 'Religious Revivalism and Popular Evangelicalism in Britain and Ireland 1859-1905', unpublished D.Phil thesis, Queen's University, Belfast, 1995, p. 253.
121. Carwardine, *Transatlantic Revivalism*, pp. 21-3.
122. M. Van Die, 'The Marks of a Genuine Revival: Religion, Social Change, Gender and Community in mid Victorian Brantford, Ontario', *The Canadian Historical Review*, 79, (1988), p. 548.
123. Carwardine, *Transatlantic Revivalism*, p. 200.
124. Kent, *Holding the Fort*, p. 178.
125. J. Coffey, 'Democracy and Popular Religion; Moody and Sankey's Mission to Britain, 1873-75' in E. F. Biagini (ed.), *Citizenship and Community: Liberals, Radicals and Collective Identities in the British Isles, 1865-1931* (Cambridge, 1996), p. 99, 116.
126. Ibid.
127. Kent, *Holding the Fort*, p. 170.
128. Ibid., p. 176.
129. Ibid., p. 178.
130. Finney, *Revival Lectures*, pp. 409-31.
131. Bebbington, 'Evangelical Conversion', p. 15.
132. D. W. Bebbington, *Evangelicalism in Modern Britain: A History from the 1730s to the 1980s* (London, 1989), pp. 8-9.
133. Bebbington, 'Evangelical Conversion', p. 15.
134. K. D. Brown, *A Social History of the Nonconformist Ministry in England and Wales 1800-1930* (Oxford, 1988), p. 53.
135. Matthews, *Reminiscences*, p. 34.
136. E. Davies, *Revivals in Wales: Facts and Correspondence supplied by Pastors of the Welsh Churches* (London, 1859), p. 21 quoted by Carwardine, 'Welsh Evangelical Community', p. 479.
137. Van Die, 'Genuine Revival', p. 534.
138. C. Binfield, *George Williams and the YMCA: A Study in Victorian Social Attitudes* (London, 1973), p. 18.
139. *Christian Advocate and Journal*, 29 March 1858, quoted by Long, *Revival of 1857-58*, p. 68.
140. Couper, *Scottish Revivals*, p. 148.
141. Binfield, *George Williams and the YMCA*, pp. 212-14.

142. Meek, 'Fishers of Men', p. 47.
143. C. N. Peckham, *Heritage of Revival* (Edinburgh, 1986), p. 165.
144. C. G. Brown, 'Religion and Secularisation', in A. Dickson, J. H. Treble (ed.), *People and Society in Scotland* Volume 3, 1914-1990 (Edinburgh, 1992), pp. 52-3.
145. Allan, *Crusade in Scotland*, p. 15

CHAPTER 2

Theories of Revivalism

Beyond the unfolding history of the revival tradition, a number of scholars have suggested that differing factors have determined the appearance of these religious movements, with the result that a variety of circumstances have been proposed as definitive influences upon the timing of these events. Indeed the historiography of revivals has developed considerably, especially during the last fifty years. Each of the main distinct schools of analysis will be examined. In this way it is hoped the strengths and weaknesses of these theories of revival will be highlighted, and that it will become clear how they have evolved during the last half century. In addition an outline will be made of the subject and method of this particular study.

I

The first group of revival historians may be called the 'religious school'. They include John Gillies whose *Historical Collections of Accounts of Revival* was first published in 1745, W. J. Couper who authored *Scottish Revivals* in 1918, James Edwin Orr, the famous itinerant evangelist who wrote *The Second Evangelical Awakening* that appeared in 1949, and latterly Iain H. Murray, whose *Pentecost-Today? The Biblical Basis for Understanding Revival* appeared in 1998. All of these men were or are committed Evangelicals and they have maintained that religious movements are strictly the work of God. Accordingly Gillies described revivals as 'extraordinary dispensations of grace, with which the Lord has favoured so many different corners'.[1] Subsequently Couper, commenting upon revivals as 'the story of the abundant supply of grace', said that 'the Spirit of God is without limits and bonds, and over and over again He caused revival to come which cannot be traced to any particular source'.[2] Latterly Orr affirmed that 'any explanation of the [1859] Revival other than that of an outpouring of the Spirit is considered inadequate'.[3] Most recently Murray has said that 'a revival is an outpouring of the Holy Spirit . . . an extraordinary communication of the Spirit of God, a superabundance of the Spirit's operations, an enlargement of his manifest power'.[4] It is now generally accepted that this purely spiritual interpretation of revivals is inadequate. In the first place these men have described religious movements in a straightforward narrative manner as they appeared. They have recounted the stories of revival, but have done so uncritically. Hence their presentation of religious movements as homogeneous, uniform movements is misinformed.[5] Also they have failed to deal with people who were affected by revivals in their totality. Treated rather simply as religious agents, little attention has been given to their background, marital status, occupation, age or gender. Presently even Evangelical scholars, who include Donald Meek and David Bebbington, acknowledge that a number of other factors have exercised considerable influence upon the appearance of these movements.[6] Hence the 'religious school' offers an insufficient understanding of revivals.

II

A political interpretation of revivals started to appear at the beginning of the 1960s. It arose when E. J. Hobsbawm found that Methodism and radicalism flourished together in the same places at the same time for what he considered the same reasons. He believed awakenings were religious and political manifestations of the same social processes of change.[7] Edward Thompson in his epoch-book, *The Making of the English Working Class*, published in 1963, offered a similar, and highly influential, but alternative analysis to Hobsbawm. Thompson, building upon Halévy's work, believed that towards the end of the eighteenth century many working people turned to religion as a 'consolation' for the failure of their political ambitions. Methodist revivalism, he said, acted as the 'chiliasm of the defeated and the hopeless . . . [which] took over just at the point where political or temporal aspirations met with defeat'.[8] Political disappointment, he contended, acted as the spur of religious movements. Later Hobsbawm agreed with Thompson when he considered the religious movements which followed the Swing riots in 1830 as 'an escape from, rather than a mobilisation for social agitation'.[9] John Baxter, in his study of the great Yorkshire revivals between 1792 and 1796, published in 1974, further endorsed Thompson's position. 'At the moment that the hopes of popular radicalism were finally extinguished' he says, 'religious revival burst into flame'.[10] Accordingly a group of historians emerged which argued that revivals occurred because of political influences and in particular, when the public affair ambitions of people met with defeat.

This interpretation quickly met with considerable opposition. R. Currie and R. M. Hartwell, in a review of Thompson's study, criticised both his use of evidence, which in their opinion provided a 'minimum of analysis', and his prejudicial commitment to Marxist social theories.[11] In particular they considered that his interpretation of Methodist revivalism was inaccurate. According to their research they could find 'no sign of a significant association between repression or failure of political activity and the expansion of Methodism'.[12] Similarly David Hempton has, more recently, said that the weakness of Thompson's analysis lay within the partiality of his ideological convictions and the consequent biased nature of his assumptions which, he suggests, were based on selected evidence drawn from particular regions of a specific country.[13] Also Julia Werner, amid the evidence which she reveals surrounding the rise of the Primitive Methodists in the early nineteenth century, has concluded that 'no very clear picture emerges when political agitation and reform activities are set alongside Ranter revivals and missioning efforts'.[14] Consequently the political theories of revival of Hobsbawm and Thompson have become largely discredited.

Notwithstanding the judgment which has been passed upon Thompson's interpretation of the relationship between political movements and revival, it does appear that a particular bond has existed between them. Meek has commented upon the Cambuslang revival and its appearance immediately before the Jacobite Rising of 1745 during a period of considerable political uncertainty in Scotland.[15] Also Carwardine has demonstrated the varied association between religious movements and periods of political activity in mid-nineteenth-century America. Although some church leaders complained how 'politics diverted time and energy from religious activity', Carwardine shows how the two were not mutually exclusive. Instead he reveals that political campaigns could, on occasions, stimulate revival.[16] Hence, although Thompson's oscillation theory is now refuted, it remains true that revivals and political movements have 'enjoyed a rich and textured relationship'.[17] They have not belonged to separate spheres. On the contrary, they have often been simultaneous and complementary movements within the same context.

Thereafter a 'social school' of revival theorists appeared who argued that religious movements were reactions to periods of intense community change. For instance, Steve Bruce examined late eighteenth-century revivals in the Highlands of Scotland and found that contemporary observers of the movements considered them to be a response to the social changes of that period.[18] Although Bruce employed a different analytical method from Hobsbawm, he still 'sees the economic and social transformation of the Highlands as the cause of the religious transformation' during this period.[19] Similarly Callum Brown believes that the collapse of the traditional social order through the clearances was a significant contributory factor towards the early nineteenth-century Highland revivals.[20] Also Peter Gibbon, an Irish social historian, considers the Ulster revival of 1859 among rural labourers and new factory workers to have been a reaction to the social dislocations created by industrialisation and urbanisation in the 1850s.[21] Accordingly it became popular to claim that revivals were a response to significant social changes that affected a community of people.

Other commentators found that revivals coincided with periods of economic depression. Whitney Cross discovered in his investigations into religious movements in Western New York during the 1830s how 'the revival cycle had long been inclined to an inverse conformity with the business cycle, rising with hard times and falling with good.'[22] Likewise David Luker suggested that the threat of economic depression and mass unemployment was a significant factor during the 1799 revival in the tin mining villages of Cornwall.[23] Similarly Werner has said that the economic distress suffered in Nottingham and West Riding was 'an especially powerful goad to revivalism'. She associates directly the Bramwell-Pipe revival, which came to its climax in 1800, with the extreme privation which people suffered at that time.[24] Also J. L. Duthie believes the 1921 Moray Firth fishing revival was a direct consequence of the economic slump experienced by the herring industry that year. '1921', he contends, 'was an annus terribilis for the fishing communities of north east Scotland, and the despair of the fisher folk led them to religious fervour for consolation.'[25] This interpretation of the Moray Firth revival is supported by Callum Brown and Nancy Dorian.[26] Thus, a number of historians have associated incidents of awakening with periods of economic recession.

By contrast other revival historians have found occasions when religious movements flourished during periods of financial prosperity. Ned Landsman has observed how the Cambuslang revival appeared at a time of prosperity, when Glaswegian merchants had just begun to make substantial investments into the nearby, rural infrastructure with the result that new textile industries were beginning to flourish.[27] Notwithstanding his previous observations, Luker found that the Cornish revival of 1799 followed the good harvest of 1798, and the 1814 movement succeeded a fall in the price of wheat. Meanwhile, according to a local minister, the 1847 revival did not extend beyond the town of Truro into the adjacent countryside because of the considerable economic distress in rural areas that was caused by a poor harvest and high prices.[28] Hence other scholars have argued that revivals have prospered when the local economy has been buoyant.

Perhaps more significantly, the political, social and economic evidence demonstrates the irregular relationship that has existed between these trends and revivals. R. B. Walker, who examined a large number of nineteenth-century Methodist revivals, concluded 'no clear pattern of relationship between religious revivals and economic changes emerges'.[29] Similarly Marguerite Van Die, who studied two periods of revival that affected the people of Brantford, Ontario, found that a first wave of religious enthusiasm in 1853 arose during a period of material boom which created optimism within the churches and their community, while a second movement began in 1857 immediately after the economic crash of that year which had a devastating effect upon the people.[30] This appears to confirm that there is not a consistent correlation between social and economic cycles and religious movements.

There is no doubt that scholars who have argued that political, social and economic factors influenced the appearance of revivals have usefully highlighted the important role which these circumstances have, on occasions, played. However, they are mistaken when they suggest these external circumstances were determinative agents of religious movements. More recently, scholars have recognised that while periods of political agitation and socio-economic change may have acted as the stimulus of religious movements or served to modify or intensify a revival cycle, they have not been definitive causes.[31] Even Thompson was forced to concede in reply to criticism of his 'oscillation' theory in the 1968 revised edition of *The Making of the English Working Class* that 'revivalism is not a phenomenon which admits of a single hold-all explanation ... different contexts may require different explanatory methods'.[32] Luker has warned historians that 'there are very real pitfalls in approaching revivals essentially from the outside and attempting to explain their occurrence merely by reference to secular trends or preoccupations'.[33] External factors have often served to create an environment in which revivals have flourished, but they have not been absolute causes of religious movements.

III

A third, heterogeneous school of revival historians appeared in 1978. This year witnessed the publication of three separate, influential studies which contributed further to the discussion surrounding these moments. The first of these, *Revivals, Awakenings, and Reform:*

An Essay on Religion and Social Change in America, 1607-1977, was written by William G. McLoughlin, an American scholar. He distinguished great awakenings from religious revivalism. The former, he contended, are periods of cultural revitalisation which change the world-view of a whole people, while the latter alter the lives of individuals.[34] He argued that the five periods of American awakenings, which he identified, reshaped fundamentally the culture of the nation.[35] Essentially McLoughlin sought to reassert the significance which religious movements had played in the history of modern America, but he also suggested that their influence had declined over time. Nonetheless his principal concern was the wider cultural implications of revivals.

The second book exploring religious movements published in 1978 was *Holding the Fort: Studies in Victorian Revivalism*, whose author was the British Methodist minister, John Kent. He focused his attention upon the significance of revivals in late nineteenth-century Britain, during the period when, he believed, 'popular Protestantism began to lose its grip on English society'.[36] In a sardonic manner he criticised revivalism as having been 'an aspect of that anti-modernist, anti-materialist, anti-democratic and often anti-intellectual movement'. He said that Victorian revivals failed to affect the working classes, that their greater influence lay within the Christian sub-culture, and that they failed to hold back the tides of secularisation which were sweeping over Britain.[37] Essentially Kent displayed an unsympathetic attitude towards late nineteenth-century religious movements. However, John Coffey, in an article published in 1996, disproved many of Kent's bold assertions. He showed how Evangelicals were socially active during this period and that the appeal of Moody and Sankey, the popular revivalists of the 1870s, 'transcended barriers of gender, age and class'.[38] Indeed he went on to demonstrate, contrary to what Kent suggested, that Evangelicalism commanded its greatest influence upon British social and political life during the second half of the nineteenth century.[39] Hence Kent's contribution to the history of revivals has, more recently, become rather discredited.

The third study of revivals published in 1978 was Richard Carwardine's *Transatlantic Revivalism: Popular Evangelicalism in Britain and America, 1790-1865*. As the title suggests, Carwardine highlighted the significance of the relationship that spanned the Atlantic between Evangelicals during the nineteenth century. In particular he discussed the influence of Finney and the development of the new measures of American revivalism, and how they were imported into Britain.[40] Among a number of noteworthy observations, Carwardine revealed the importance of 'the cultural and ethnic homogeneity of a relatively tightly knit community' in producing a traditional small-town revival.[41] Perhaps the most vital contribution he made to the discussion of religious movements was the discovery that 'the only stable factor amongst the whole complex of influences that operated at times of revival was the existence of a desire for and expectancy of revivals in the churches involved'.[42] Unfortunately Carwardine failed to examine in any substantive detail the history of nineteenth century religious movements in Scotland. Instead he concentrated his attention upon awakenings in England, Wales and Northern Ireland. Nevertheless there is no doubt that he has made a valuable contribution to the understanding of the changes that overcame revivals in the nineteenth century.

IV

Another school of revival historians emerged in the 1980s which began to pay greater attention to the local factors that had influenced the appearance of long established community-based revivals. A broad consensus has arisen which suggests there have been at least three experiences that have served to create the environment in which these movements have flourished. In the first instance it appears that epidemic illnesses have heightened people's sensitivities to religious matters. Meek has described the profound effect which the cholera epidemic of 1832 had upon the Baptist church at Grantown on Spey.[43] Similarly R. B. Walker found that at Bilston in the Black Country, which suffered one of the worst outbreaks of the illness, the membership of the Wednesbury and Dudley Methodist circuits rose from 3,315 to 5,382. Likewise the Methodist circuits grew by 11.9 per cent, compared with 5.7 per cent for the connection as a whole, in seven places which suffered acutely from another epidemic. At the same time the Wesleyan president of the Sunderland circuit warned his hearers, in light of the rampant disease, to prepare for eternity. He said, 'the utter inability of human skill, either to explain the cause or provide a remedy for this plague, shows it to be a special visitation of Almighty God'.[44] Werner discovered also, that at the height of the widespread illness, 250 new members were added during a single quarter to the Primitive Methodist Connection in Hull and North Shields, and that even 'hard' Liverpool experienced revival.[45] Hence there have been instances of revival where disease appears to have been a significant contributory factor.

Yet there have been other occasions when epidemic illnesses have not precipitated revival. At Kilsyth in 1732, for instance, the parish minister, James Robe, had hoped that a malignant fever that claimed the lives of sixty people in the course of three weeks might awaken spiritual concern, but instead he found that the religious state of his parish grew worse.[46] Similarly one hundred years later, around 1830, the minister of the same parish, William H. Burns, believed the 'scourges' which fell upon Kilsyth would awaken the people, but he discovered, like his predecessor, that they made no impression.[47] Furthermore, notwithstanding the connection between revival and the cholera epidemic in 1832, subsequent outbreaks of the disease in 1854 and 1866 were not accompanied by religious movements. The threat of illness, together with the fear which this can engender within a community, has sometimes aroused an intense interest in spiritual matters amongst men and women which has led to revival. In this way the risk of disease has influenced the timing of certain religious movements. Nevertheless a regular relationship has not been established between illness and revival, and therefore the former cannot be judged as a primary cause of increased spiritual activity.

Another noteworthy influence at work in small local communities at times of revival has been an inherent sense of fear. Ian Muirhead was, in 1980, one of the first to identify, among a number of revival causes, the fundamental importance of 'insecurity, theological, social, personal'.[48] It is significant that many revivals have been advanced by various movements of religious or cultural change which have threatened the perceived identity of a local community. The first Scottish movements, for instance, at Stewarton and Irvine in 1625, began after conflict arose among those who would not accept the forms of church government and practice which were being imposed by the Crown.[49] The great Yorkshire revival of 1792-6 began during the local organisational crisis that followed the death of Wesley in March 1791. This movement provided unity and consolidation at a critical time when Methodism was threatened with fracture.[50] Other commentators have argued that the Scottish revivals of the 1830s and 1840s were associated with the Ten Years' Conflict and were a reaction against the intrusion of ministers into congregations of the Established Church.[51] More recently W. R. Ward has argued that the origins of the great eighteenth-century revivals, in Europe and America, lay within the defiance of groups of people against the threat of assimilation they felt from powerful states and established churches.[52] In this manner he accounts for the advance of Methodism in England around the period of the French Revolution. Similarly David Hempton has connected the dramatic expansion of the Methodists in southern Ulster to the rebellion of the United Irishmen in 1798.[53] In his view 'there seems little doubt that religious revivalism thrived on the perceived vulnerability of individuals and social groups when confronted by . . . threats to health and personal security'.[54] Also S. J. Brown believes that the renewed interest in revivalism in Ulster that preceded the 1859 movement 'was in large part a response by Ulster Presbyterians to the new strength and confidence of the Roman Catholic Church'.[55] This particular interpretation of revival has remained largely unchallenged. Accordingly the timing of revivals appears to have been affected by the fear of a community created by a perceived threat to its religious identity.

Perhaps of greatest significance, the community crisis created by an unexpected death has provided the context within which a number of local revivals have appeared. Jonathan Edwards, in his account of the revival at the village of Pascommuck, near Northampton, Massachusetts, in 1743 described how 'the very sudden and awful death of a young man in the bloom of his youth' which 'was followed with another death of a young married woman . . . seemed to contribute to render solemn the spirits of many young persons; and there began evidently to appear more of a religious concern on people's minds'.[56] Orr has recorded how the deaths of local men in a fishing tragedy at Cellardyke, Fife, was the stimulus of the 1859 revival in that village.[57] Likewise John McGibbon, a local historian, described how the death of a fisherman, Tammas Reid in the early 1880s at a village near Peterhead, acted as the spur to a religious movement that swept through that community.[58] Julia Werner has noticed how fear induced by the threat of an imminent death was often a factor in the conversion of Primitive Methodists during times of revival.[59] Similarly Carwardine describes how the precarious nature of life in industrial Wales created a favourable context for the spread of religious movements. According to James Kendall, writing in 1853, 'terrible accidents and fearful deaths [are] not uncommon in these iron and coal districts . . . [H]ence funeral sermons are frequent and often attended with good moral and religious effect'.[60] Likewise Christopher Turner has described how an ever-present fear of death or serious injury which accompanied 'the harsh realities of work underground in Welsh industrial society' regularly served to intensify revival cycles when they appeared.[61] Meanwhile James Obelkevich observed from the pattern of mortality in South Lindsey during the nineteenth century that death overcame a disproportionate number of young people in the prime of life, and these tragedies had a powerful effect on those who survived.[62] Bebbington has found, from his study of ninety one evangelical conversion accounts, collected from 1750 to 1850, that following sermons, the fear of death and illness was the second most common precipitating factor of spiritual regeneration.[63] Hence he judges that the crisis of death can 'provide a favourable context for the propagation of the faith'.[64] Accordingly the fear and experience of sudden death has been an important factor in a number of local religious movements, particularly within fishing and mining communities where people lived and worked daily with its constant threat. It is clear that the particular circumstances of a local situation have regularly influenced the timing of the appearance of revivals.

V

The most widely accepted current school of revival studies has moved beyond the concentration on the role of local factors in determining the appearance of religious movements. Instead scholars have begun to uncover the inner dynamic of religious movements and have been more anxious to discover who was affected by them. Myrtle Hill, for instance, in her study of the Ulster revival of 1859, published in 1990, dismantled many of the general myths that surrounded this movement and paid greater attention to the detail of its diffusion across the north of Ireland. In this way she revealed some of its local nuances, including the fact that it affected principally the Presbyterian community in Counties Down and Antrim. Moreover Hill went on to examine the gender, age, social status and church background of those who were converted. She did not ignore, as previous scholars had, the physical manifestations that accompanied the revival.[65]

Janice Holmes, in her doctoral thesis submitted in 1995, which examined revivalism in Britain and Ireland in the second half of the nineteenth century, offered another detailed study of the Ulster revival of 1859 and focused particular attention upon the groups of people who were affected by it.[66] Subsequently Marguerite Van Die wrote an article about a series of mid-nineteenth-century revivals that affected the town of Brantford, Ontario. She provided a comprehensive examination of the society, economy and religious character of this town before she discussed how revival began in this context. Then she went on to investigate, in considerable depth, the gender, age, occupation and church background of those who were affected during two separate religious movements. In this manner Van Die presented a comprehensive study of the inner dynamic of these revivals and how they were integrated in a particular location.[67]

Most recently Kathryn Long wrote a history of the American revival of 1857-58 that was published in 1998. Long provided a meticulous examination of this movement. She was concerned to

Theories of Revivalism

display the diversity of the revival as it appeared among the people who were affected by it. As a result she demonstrated how individuals experienced this religious movement in a variety of ways, depending upon a number of different features of the context in which they lived. Long drew attention to several factors that affected the various manifestations of this single religious movement.[68] Hence the latest school of revival studies has become, during the last ten years, concerned with the detail of revivals as they have appeared in particular contexts, and the identities of the people who have been affected by them.

The sands of revival historiography have shifted considerably since the 1960s. The explanations of religious movements that were based purely upon political and socio-economic factors have been found wanting. It is accepted that although such circumstances may have influenced the particular climate of a community within which revival was experienced, there has not been a direct or consistent correlation between them and incidents of a religious movement. It is generally accepted that revivals have not occurred in response to any one single aspect, but rather they have arisen as the result of the interplay of a variety of external and local factors. Scholars appreciate there are a number of different perspectives from which revivals ought to be examined. Hence an increased attention has been paid to the indigenous circumstances of the contexts within which they have occurred. Most recently there has appeared a greater sensitivity towards the appearance of a distinct revival in a given situation. It has been shown that far from being monolithic events, religious movements have appeared in a variety of different ways, and that their peculiar manifestations have been conditioned by the particular context in which they have arisen.

VI

This book proposes to examine in detail the 1859 revival as it affected the north east of Scotland in an attempt to uncover the various textures of this movement as it occurred in a range of separate situations. There are at least three reasons why it is important to examine this religious movement in particular. In the first place it is perhaps the most far-reaching awakening that has affected Scotland. Robert Buchanan, the Free Church moderator in 1860, remarked how

> from East Lothian to the Outer Hebrides – from the shore of the Moray Firth to those of the Solway – and all through the central mining and manufacturing districts of the Kingdom, we heard of scenes which carried us back to the days of the Lord, at Shotts and

Stewarton and Cambuslang. Unless we greatly deceive ourselves, no former revival of religion which our church and country have witnessed has ever spread over so wide a field.[69]

At the Free Church assembly the following year Dr Julius Wood reported that in two thirds of the church's presbyteries there had been 'decided awakening and revival', while in the greater proportion of the remaining third he described that 'whilst there is no decided awakening or revival there is in almost every instance without exception, increased attention to, and interest in, spiritual things'. Hence he concluded that 'the revival with which God has been pleased to bless us, extends over the length and breadth of the land'.[70] The 1859 revival was not preceded and has not been succeeded by a similar movement that stretched so far across the country. Unparalleled, it remains the largest, most widespread revival in Scotland's history, and thus it is worthy of examination.

Also this revival affords the opportunity to study a religious movement during an important period in its history when such movements were in a state of transition from spontaneous community based awakenings to organised urban crusades. Since the 1830s, Finney's *Lectures on Revivals* had received a mixed response in Britain. Some churches, including the Methodists, embraced his modern techniques wholeheartedly, while others remained more sceptical, suspicious of the 'human element' that had entered into revivalism.[71] Such people wanted an unplanned movement, but one that was also 'in strictest harmony with the profoundest devotion'.[72] Kent has remarked that 'the dividing line between the old and new revivalism may be drawn in the years 1857-62'.[73] According to Hempton and Hill, the 1859 revival, as it appeared in Ulster, was 'not an example of new-style technique revivalism imported from America, but was rather one of the last great folk revivals in the history of the British Isles'.[74] Accordingly it is necessary to examine the same movement as it appeared in Scotland in order to ascertain whether it was a traditional or a modern revival.

Perhaps the greatest reason for studying the 1859 revival in Scotland is that it has not been considered rigorously by any modern scholar. Couper, in his largely narrative account of Scottish revivals, committed only eleven pages to this movement. Despite being a useful description of the progress of the revival across the land, he recorded the events simply as a story and did not offer any criticism or analysis.[75] Similarly Orr, who devoted twenty pages to the revival in Scotland in *The Second Evangelical Awakening*, published in 1949, chronicled the movement in an anecdotal manner. There are two particular weaknesses in Orr's history of the revival. In the first instance he appears to suggest, by his descriptive technique, that it began in Glasgow and was diffused up the west coast and subsequently down the east coast of Scotland. In this way he does not describe accurately the spread of the revival. Secondly he presents the whole movement in a uniform manner without paying any attention to its various manifestations in different contexts.[76] Hence Orr's account of the revival in Scotland is inadequate. Muirhead, in his article on Scottish religious movements, manages only one paragraph on the 1859 revival.[77] The only recent academic work undertaken on the movement was by C. J. Marrs, who examined its appearance in Glasgow in his doctoral thesis, submitted in 1995. However, despite providing a detailed narrative of the revival, he does not move beyond describing its manifestation in Glasgow. Besides, occupied with demonstrating that the revival 'was not the major influential spiritual and social event of the Victorian era to which it has been popularly elevated', he does not manage to penetrate the revival and describe its effect upon the people involved.[78] It is clear that the historical analysis of the 1859 revival in Scotland has been poor and inadequate. It has been largely ignored and inadmissibly overlooked for a considerable time. Hence this study seeks to provide a thorough, modern understanding of this movement as it affected the north east of Scotland.

This region of Scotland has been chosen because it presents three separate, distinct social contexts for analysis. In the first instance the city of Aberdeen provides the opportunity to study this mid-nineteenth-century revival as it appeared in an urban setting. Like many other towns and cities during this period Aberdeen had experienced tremendous expansion. In the fifty years, from 1801 to 1851, the population of the city had grown almost threefold, from 26,992 to 71,973.[79] Aberdeen had experienced significant demographic change, with the result that the urban community had become increasingly heterogeneous. In addition to a considerable textile working class, the traditional artisan society continued to make up a large section of the labour force, with 4000 hand loom weavers, 800 shoemakers, 600 carpenters, 500 tailors, 500 blacksmiths and 200 cabinet makers and upholsterers.[80] Furthermore, there were shipwrights, mechanics, engineers and masons who were, on the whole, better off than those who belonged to the traditional skilled working class. There was also a substantial middle class. By 1861 there were eighty doctors, 170 male teachers and professors, 200 female teachers and 500 commercial clerks working in Aberdeen.[81] Also 3500 female domestic servants were employed in the city.[82] These people lived in various parts of Aberdeen. Beyond the city centre where 'grandeur and meanness [lived] side by side' it was surrounded by a number of smaller settlements.[83] Two miles north-west of the city lay the village of Woodside where rural immigrants settled and worked in textile factories. Meanwhile a large artisan community lived around Holburn in the south-west of Aberdeen, while Gilcomston 'was a thriving suburb of about 2000 inhabitants, mostly weavers'.[84] Accordingly Aberdeen was an expanding, Victorian city. Thus it affords a typical urban situation within which to examine the manifestation of a mid-nineteenth-century religious movement.

The rural hinterland of Aberdeenshire provides a different set of circumstances for a study of the appearance of this revival. The economic and social changes that prevailed upon the farming people during the early nineteenth century had a profound effect upon rural communities. The creation of larger farms, many of which were purchased by wealthy merchants, involved the consolidation of smallholdings; meanwhile subtenants were forced to accept new 'improving' leases on poorer land that had previously not been under cultivation. At the same time a new class of farm labourer emerged to work, within a rigid hierarchical structure, on larger farms. Many of these were managed by a grieve, because the owners of the farm were often absent, and thus the fabric of the rural community began to split apart.[85] Alexander Fraser lamented how 'old fashioned familiarity and friendly feeling, previously existing between masters and servants, began to die away . . . farm labourers came to be looked upon by many farmers and their families as little better than mere machines, not worthy of half the attention paid to their cattle or horses'.[86] By 1859 a generation of farming people had grown accustomed to the changes that had affected the agrarian economy and a new social order had been created. Nevertheless, advances of technology, which included the introduction of the horse-drawn reaper to replace the scythe in 1850, continued to bring further change to the lives of these communities.[87] Meanwhile a new market-driven culture was threatening to replace the traditional economy, while old networks of relationships were overtaken by commercial associations as the population decreased. Therefore, the rural situation offers an opportunity to examine how the 1859 revival arose within a mid-Victorian, agrarian community.

The homogeneous, tightly knit villages of the fisherfolk along the Moray Firth produced another distinct group of people who experienced this religious movement. Primarily these were one-occupation communities. Apart from a handful of shoemakers and grocers, everyone followed the same rhythm of work and earned their living from the sea. There was no hierarchy in the fishing crews. Each man contributed equally to the running costs and drew the same amount from the profits. In this way they formed a classless society, each man enjoying the same income and status, and sharing the risks of their profession.[88] Furthermore the whole family was involved with fishing. The men worked on the boats, while the women baited the lines, and prepared and sold the fish.[89] Also the fishing villages were visibly separate from the settlements of farmers and other people who lived near them. Even in the larger towns they lived in well defined districts that became known as the 'fishertown' or the 'seatown', and often they were regarded as an 'alien people'.[90] Even the seventy fishing villages along the one-hundred-and-fifty-mile stretch of the Moray coastline, whose average population was around 300 people, were separate one from another. There were six distinct communities within the ten miles from Cullen to Portgordon and six around the larger town of Fraserburgh. Each remained detached with clear boundaries and a different community identity.[91] Classless, isolated, distinct and close knit, these mid-nineteenth-century fishing communities along the Moray Firth present another distinct social context within which to study the manifestation of the 1859 revival.

It is noteworthy that this book will examine this religious movement as it appeared in a variety of different settings within a particular area of Scotland. Previous studies of revival have tended to approach these awakenings in two separate ways. Firstly some scholars have adopted a broad perspective and have considered them as large, national affairs. As a result they have discussed the appearance of a revival in a wide-ranging, general manner and consequently they have failed to consider local features. Meanwhile, other historians have focused sharply upon the peculiar exhibition of a movement in a single, specific location. In so doing they have concentrated on particular details, often at the risk of losing a more comprehensive understanding of the whole revival. Accordingly the approach of this study is novel because it will examine the 1859 revival in a thorough manner as it appeared in a socially varied region of Scotland.

The principal sources for this book were contemporary reports of the revival, biographies of people who were involved in the movement, religious newspapers, the local press and church records. There were three pamphlets produced in 1859 which followed the progress of the revival in Aberdeen during its first year. They were *Five Letters on the Religious Movement in Aberdeen*, *Times of Refreshing* and *The Appearance of God's Work in the Chief Towns of Scotland: with Special Reference to Aberdeen and Dundee*. These sources provided a rich source of eye-witness accounts of the movement when it began. There were also a number of other local reports, usually written by ministers of rural parishes, and proceedings of conferences published. The most insightful of these was *A Report of a Conference on the State of Religion, and Public Meeting, held in the Free Church, Huntly, January 5, 1860*. Twenty nine ministers who attended this gathering provided detailed descriptions of the movement as it affected their particular districts, and they represent an excellent source of information. In addition the life stories of the principal agents who led the revival, many of which were written before the end of the century, afford another record of the movement. James Turner, the Methodist fish curer and lay evangelist from Peterhead who led the revival along the Moray Firth, died in 1863. The story of his life and work was preserved by William Robbie in 1863 and again by Elizabeth M'Hardie in 1875. Jane, the daughter of the evangelist Reginald Radcliffe who was judged to have been the principal figure in the Aberdeen revival, wrote the history of her father's labours. Mrs M. M. Gordon published an account of the life story of Hay MacDowall Grant of Arndilly, another important leader in the revival in north east Scotland, in 1876. K. Moody-Stuart recorded the work of another key evangelist in the movement, Brownlow North, in 1878. These and other biographies of local ministers and evangelists provided an additional view of the revival as it unfolded in Aberdeenshire. All of these sources regarded the revival in a favourable manner, and as a result the inherent bias of their sympathetic treatment of the movement had to be considered.

At this time, on account of the fall in the printing taxes on papers and the press, there was a rise in the number of religious journals, several of which were devoted specifically to spreading the news of the revival. *The British Messenger*, published by Peter Drummond at Stirling, and *The News of the Churches and Journal of Mission*, produced in London and Edinburgh, appeared in 1853 and followed the progress of the revival closely. Also three further periodicals appeared in 1859 which were devoted specifically to reporting the course of the movement. They included *The Wynd Journal*, a Glasgow publication, and the *British Evangelist* and *The Revival* that were printed in London. *The Wynd Journal* and *The Revival* appeared weekly and consequently presented a detailed description of the movement as it unfolded. Notwithstanding the Evangelical bias of these publications, they have provided a comprehensive record of the events that followed this remarkable revival.

Besides the religious press, each of the sixteen local newspapers that were printed in the north east of Scotland in 1859 was examined. The extent and manner in which the movement was reported among these newspapers varied enormously. There were some which were clearly opposed to the revival. *The Aberdeen Herald*, for example, which was 'probably the most influential paper north of

Edinburgh' was 'decidedly liberal in tone' and vehemently opposed to the Free Church. It judged the events of the revival unfavourably.[92] Another important newspaper was the *Aberdeen Journal* which claimed to have 'no politics except the maintenance of the Constitution'. It also reported the movement in a disparaging fashion.[93] *The Aberdeen Saturday Post* was less than encouraging in its comments of the revival, which it reported under the headline of 'Religious Vagaries' before going on to describe it as an 'unhappy affair'.[94] In the same tone *The Aberdeen Citizen* condemned the work of the evangelists in the movement.[95] Meanwhile, the *Northern Telegraphic News*, which was published in Aberdeen, criticised the ministers who gave their support to the movement.[96] Beyond Aberdeen and along the Moray Firth the principal local newspaper was the *Banffshire Journal*. As *The Revival* put it, this was 'a paper by no means regarding the revival from a friendly point of view'.[97] Hence it appears that a significant proportion of the local newspapers which were read in Aberdeenshire were unsympathetic towards the 1859 revival. Nevertheless the *Aberdeen Free Press* was a staunch supporter of the movement. One of its owners, named Macallan, who died in 1858, 'was a leading member and chief supporter of the Baptist denomination in Aberdeen'.[98] Meanwhile the editor, during the movement, was a Mr M'Combie, who was described as 'a man of intense religious earnestness'.[99] Of all the newspapers, the *Aberdeen Free Press* covered the story of the revival in the most extensive manner. The partiality of these sources was observed, and the prejudice of their reporting was noted. Nevertheless each newspaper, in spite and often because of the considerable bias in their records of events, was an important source of information.

The last main source that was examined were the church records of the churches which existed at that time. Altogether documents that belonged to 113 congregations were investigated. These included fourteen communion rolls and twenty two sets of kirk session minutes that were owned by the Church of Scotland. They also contained all of the communion rolls, thirteen in total, and the kirk session minute books, which numbered sixty three, of the Free Church in the north east of Scotland that belonged to the period of the revival. In addition, the records of nine United Presbyterian churches, three Congregational chapels, four Episcopal chapels, an Evangelical Union and a Baptist Church were analysed. The kirk session minutes, particularly of the rural Free Church congregations, presented some interesting revelations of the movement, while the communion rolls revealed the actual growth which many of these churches experienced during the revival. Appendix 1 explains how these documents, together with the 1861 census, were used chiefly in an attempt to identify those who professed faith for the first time and became church members between 1858 and 1862 so that an examination could be made of those who were most likely affected by this religious movement.

This study will examine the 1859 revival as it appeared in the north east of Scotland. Firstly the movement as it emerged in Aberdeen will be considered. An attempt will be made to understand how and why the revival began in the city in 1858, and the manner in which it was accommodated within a busy, urban context will be investigated. In addition an analysis will be made of the particular manifestation of the movement, while those who joined the Aberdeen churches during this period will be scrutinised in an attempt to determine who was affected by the revival in the city. Furthermore an inquiry will be made into the movement as it affected the agricultural towns and villages of the rural hinterland. Indeed, the agrarian context and how this influenced the peculiar manifestation of the revival in this area, and the farmfolk who were affected are noteworthy. The revival among the fisherfolk along the Moray Firth will also be examined, and, in particular, consideration will be made of how and why this coastline, previously unknown for its spiritual fervour, was overwhelmed by this movement in 1860. The influence which the peculiar context of this area had upon the distinct expression of this revival, and the composition of those who were affected by this outbreak of the movement will also be studied. Finally, the relative failure of the 1859 revival to affect Peterhead will be explored.

This book will build upon the most recent research on revivals undertaken by Kathryn Long. She revealed that the American revival of 1857 'was a diffuse and multifaceted movement', and how its manifestation was conditioned by a number of factors including religious tradition, social context, class and gender.[100] It is hoped that this study will reveal the variety of different forms in which the 1859 revival appeared in the north east of Scotland. In this way it aims to reveal how the situation in which the movement emerged had a significant effect upon the separate ways in which it appeared. Most importantly, the analysis of those who were affected by the revival will demonstrate how the social context within which the movement arose affected the manner and expression of this particular awakening.

Footnotes

1. J. Gillies, *Historical Collections relating to Remarkable Periods of the Success of the Gospel* [H. Bonar ed., Kelso, 1845] (Pennsylvania, 1981), p. viii.
2. W. J. Couper, *Scottish Revivals* (Dundee, 1918), p. 155.
3. J. E. Orr, *The Second Evangelical Awakening* (London, 1949), p. 8.
4. I. H. Murray, *Pentecost Today? The Biblical Basis for Understanding Revival* (Edinburgh, 1998), pp. 23-4.
5. D. E. Meek, '"Fishers of Men": The 1921 Religious Revival – Its Cause, Context and Transmission', *Scottish Bulletin of Evangelical Theology*, 17, 1999, p. 40.
6. Ibid., D. W. Bebbington, *Evangelicalism in Modern Britain: A History from the 1730s to the 1980s* (London, 1989), pp. 116-17.
7. E. J. Hobsbawm, *Labouring Men* (London, 1964), pp. 23-33.
8. E. P. Thompson, *The Making of the English Working Class* (Harmondsworth, Middlesex, 1968), p. 419, 428.
9. E. J. Hobsbawn, G. Rude, *Captain Swing* (London, 1969), p. 291.
10. J. Baxter, 'The Great Yorkshire Revival 1792-6: A Study of Mass Revival among the Methodists' in *A Sociological Yearbook of Religion in Britain 7* (London, 1974), p. 65.
11. R. Currie, R. M. Hartwell, 'The Making of the English Working Class?', *Economic History Review*, 18, (1965), pp. 635-6.
12. Ibid., p. 640.
13. D. Hempton, *The Religion of the People: Methodism and Popular Religion c1750-1900* (London, 1996), p. 2.
14. J. S. Werner, *The Primitive Methodist Connexion: Its Background and Early History* (Wisconsin, 1984), p. 173.
15. N. M. de S. Cameron (ed.), *Dictionary of Scottish Church History and Theology* (Edinburgh, 1993), p. 716.
16. R. Carwardine, 'Religious Revival and Political Renewal in Antebellum America' in J. Garnett, C. Matthew (ed.), *Revival and Religion since 1700: Essays for John Walsh* (London, 1993), pp. 131, 134-5.
17. Ibid., p. 128.
18. S. Bruce, 'Social Change and Collective Behaviour: The Revival in Eighteenth-Century Ross-shire', *British Journal of Sociology*, 34, (1983), p. 559.
19. Ibid., p. 568.
20. C. G. Brown, *The Social History of Religion in Scotland since 1730* (London, 1987), pp. 119-20.
21. P. Gibbon, *The Origins of Ulster Unionism* (Manchester, 1975), pp. 44-66.
22. R. Carwardine, *Transatlantic Revivalism: Popular Evangelicalism in Britain and America, 1790-1865* (Westport, Connecticut, 1978), p. 54.
23. D. Luker, 'Revivalism in Theory and Practice: The Case of Cornish Methodism', *Journal of Ecclesiastical History*, 37, (1986), p. 617.
24. Werner, *Primitive Methodist Connexion*, p. 43.
25. J. L. Duthie, 'The Fisherman's Revival', *History Today*, (December 1983), p. 23.
26. C. G. Brown, 'Religion and Secularisation' in A. Dickson, J. H. Treble (ed.), *People and Society in Scotland Volume 3, 1914-1990* (Edinburgh, 1992), p. 59.
27. N. Landsman, 'Evangelicals and their Hearers: Popular Interpretations of

Revivalist Preaching in Eighteenth-Century Scotland', *Journal of British Studies*, 28, (1989), p. 124.
28. Luker, 'Revivalism in Theory and Practice', p. 616.
29. R. B. Walker, 'The Growth of Wesleyan Methodism in Victorian England and Wales', *Journal of Ecclesiastical History*, 14, (1973), p. 270.
30. M. Van Die, 'The Marks of a Genuine Revival: Religion, Social Change, Gender and Community in mid Victorian Brantford, Ontario', *The Canadian Historical Review*, 79, (1998), p. 532.
31. Bebbington, *Evangelicalism*, p. 114. Meek, 'Fishers of Men', p. 42.
32. Thompson, *English Working Class*, p. 919.
33. Luker, 'Revivalism in Theory and Practice', p. 604
34. W. McLoughlin, *Revivals, Awakenings and Reform* (Chicago, 1978), p. xiii.
35. Ibid., p. vii, ix.
36. J. Kent, *Holding the Fort: Studies in Victorian Revivalism* (London, 1978), p. 9.
37. Ibid., pp. 357-63.
38. J. Coffey, 'Democracy and Popular Religion: Moody and Sankey's Mission to Britain, 1873-5' in E. F. Biagini (ed.), *Citizenship and Community: Liberals, Radicals and Collective Identities in the British Isles, 1865-1931* (Cambridge, 1996), p. 97.
39. Ibid., p. 119.
40. Carwardine, *Transatlantic Revivalism*, pp. 198-200.
41. Ibid., p. 25.
42. Ibid., p. 56.
43. D. E. Meek, 'Gaelic Bible, Revival and Mission: The Spiritual Rebirth of the Nineteenth-Century Highlands' in J. Kirk (ed.), *The Church in the Highlands* (Edinburgh, 1999), pp. 122-3.
44. Walker, 'Growth of Wesleyan Methodism', p. 271.
45. Werner, *Primitive Methodist Connexion*, p. 154.
46. Couper, *Scottish Revivals*, p. 52.
47. Ibid., p. 118.
48. I. A. Muirhead, 'The Revival as a Dimension of Scottish Church History', *Records of the Scottish Church History Society*, 20, (1980), p. 194.
49. Cameron, *Dictionary of Church History and Theology*, p. 712.
50. Baxter, 'Great Yorkshire Revival', p. 58.
51. Brown, *Social History of Religion*, pp. 135-47.
52. W. R. Ward, *The Protestant Evangelical Awakening* (Cambridge, 1992), pp. 32-3.
53. Hempton, *Religion of the People*, p. 19.
54. Ibid., p. 25.
55. S. J. Brown, 'Presbyterian Communities, Transatlantic Visions and the Ulster Revival of 1859' in J. P. Mackay (ed.), *The Cultures of Europe: The Irish Contribution* (Belfast, 1994), p. 92.
56. J. Edwards, *A Narrative of Surprising Conversions* [1736] (Edinburgh, 1995), p. 17.
57. Orr, *Second Evangelical Awakening*, p. 73.
58. J. McGibbon, *The Fisherfolk of Buchan* (Edinburgh, nd), p. 97.
59. Werner, *Primitive Methodist Connexion*, p. 153.
60. J. Kendall, *Rambles of an Evangelist* (London, 1853), pp. 42-3 quoted by Car-

wardine, 'The Welsh Evangelical Community and 'Finney's' Revival', *Journal of Ecclesiastical History*, 29, (1978), p. 470.
61. C. B. Turner, 'Revivalism and Welsh Society in the Nineteenth Century' in J. Obelkevich, L. Roper, R. Samuel (ed.), *Disciplines of Faith: Studies in Religion, Politics and Partisantry* (London, 1987), p. 315.
62. J. Obelkevich, *Religion and Rural Society: South Lindsey 1825-75* (Oxford, 1976), p. 18.
63. D. W. Bebbington, 'Evangelical Conversion c1740-1850' *North Atlantic Missiology Project*, Position Paper No 21, University of Cambridge, 1996, p. 14.
64. Bebbington, *Evangelicalism*, p. 115.
65. M. Hill, 'Ulster Awakened: The '59 Revival Reconsidered', *Journal of Ecclesiastical History*, 41, (1990), pp. 443-462.
66. J. Holmes, 'Religious Revivalism and Popular Evangelicalism in Britain and Ireland 1859-1905', unpublished D.Phil thesis, Queen's University, Belfast, (1995), pp. 16-25.
67. Van Die, 'Marks of a Genuine Revival', pp. 524-63.
68. K. T. Long, *The Revival of 1857-8: Interpreting an American Religious Awakening* (New York, 1998), pp. 3-5.
69. Couper, *Scottish Revivals*, p. 130.
70. Ibid., p. 130
71. Kent, *Holding the Fort*, p. 73.
72. Ibid.
73. Ibid., p. 71.
74. D. N. Hempton, M. Hill, *Evangelical Protestantism in Ulster Society, 1740-1890* (London, 1992), p. 151.
75. Couper, *Scottish Revivals*, pp. 130-141.
76. Orr, *Evangelical Awakening*, pp. 58-77.
77. Muirhead, 'Revival as a Dimension', p. 183.
78. C. J. Marrs, 'The 1859 Revival in Scotland: A Review and Critique of the Movement with Particular Reference to the City of Glasgow', unpublished PhD thesis, University of Glasgow, Glasgow, 1995, p. 342.
79. J. S. Smith, D. Stevenson (ed.), *Aberdeen in the Nineteenth Century: The Making of the Modern City* (Aberdeen, 1988), p. 20.
80. R. Duncan, *Textiles and Toil: The Factory System and the Industrial Working Class in early Nineteenth-Century Aberdeen* (Aberdeen, 1984), p. 3.
81. J. Valentine, *Aberdeen as It Was and Is* (Aberdeen, 1871), p. 26.
82. Duncan, *Textiles and Toil*, p. 4.
83. F. H. Groome, *Ordnance Gazatteer of Scotland: A Survey of Scottish Topography, Statistical, Biographical and Historical* (Edinburgh, 1882), p. 7.
84. H. MacKenzie, *The Third Statistical Account of Scotland: The City of Aberdeen* (Edinburgh, 1953), p. 34.
85. M. Gray, 'Farm Workers' in T. M. Devine (ed.), *Farm Servants and Labour in Lowland Scotland* (Edinburgh, 1984), pp. 10-22.
86. A. Fraser, *Conditions of the Agricultural Population* (Edinburgh, 1859), p. 15.
87. Gray, 'Farm Workers', p. 21.
88. M. Gray, *The Fishing Industries of Scotland, 1790-1914: A Study in Regional Adaption* (Oxford, 1978), p. 14.
89. J. R. Coull, 'Fisherfolk and Fishing Settlements' in J. S. Smith, D. Stevenson

(ed.), *Fermfolk and Fisherfolk* (Aberdeen, 1989), p. 41.
90. Gray, *Fishing Industries of Scotland*, p. 12.
91. Ibid.
92. W. Robbie, *Aberdeen: Its Traditions and History* (Aberdeen, 1893), p. 386.
93. Ibid.
94. *A.S.P.*, (27 July 1861), p. 2.
95. *A.C.*, (5 March 1859), p. 3.
96. *N.T.N.*, (8 March 1859), p. 2.
97. *T.R.*, Vol 2, No 3, (10 March 1860), p. 77.
98. W. Alexander, *Twenty Five Years: A Personal Retrospect* (Aberdeen, 1878), p. 5.
99. Ibid., p. 7.
100. Long, *Revival of 1857-58*, pp. 5-7.

CHAPTER 3

The Revival in Aberdeen

Timing and Manner

Aberdeen was the birthplace of the 1859 revival in Britain. Indeed the movement began as early as November 1858, at least four months before it started at Ahoghill in Northern Ireland, to which has been usually attributed the first stirrings of the revival on this side of the Atlantic. An important question that needs to be addressed is why this religious movement appeared in Aberdeen in 1858. One way to approach an answer to this issue is to examine the industrial situation of the city at this time in order to consider whether economic circumstances exercised any influence upon its timing. However, the broader religious climate of Aberdeen was perhaps a more significant factor. The manner in which the revival was assimilated into a busy, urban context, and in particular how this movement was accommodated around the long working hours of the townsfolk, competing as it did with other various social attractions in the city, was a distinguishing feature of this awakening. In addition the nature of the movement in Aberdeen, and the reactions it provoked, reveal further the peculiar nature of this movement. Accordingly, the true character of this city revival will be revealed, enabling the location of this particular 'season of grace' within the broader tradition of religious movements.

I

The industrial and financial climate of Aberdeen in 1858 does not appear to have influenced the timing of the revival. Aberdeen developed economically at a remarkable rate during the first three decades of the nineteenth century. During this period improvements were made to the infrastructure of the city. New roads and bridges, not to mention the building of many fine public buildings, transformed Aberdeen from its appearance at the end of the eighteenth century when it 'was all an assemblage of narrow, ill built, badly arranged thoroughfares, without any good openings into the country' until it had 'noble streets in all directions'.[1] A number of relatively small but reasonably prosperous industries emerged in the first half of the nineteenth century which offered a variety of employment opportunities.[2] There were ten machine makers, four paper mills, eight rope making works and a comb making factory in Aberdeen in 1843.[3] Also, the ship building industry began to expand in the 1830s. In 1832, only two vessels which together weighed 198 tons were built in the city, but within six years twenty three ships, with a combined weight of 4058 tons, were made.[4] In addition, the introduction of a regular steamship service from Aberdeen to London in 1828 allowed the transport of cattle, which gave rise to developments in the beef industry.[5] Furthermore, the granite trade entered a new and lucrative stage at the beginning of the 1830s when Alexander MacDonald invented machinery for cutting, dressing and polishing blocks.[6] Accordingly, during the first half of the nineteenth century, the foundation of Aberdeen's economy was based upon a number of different industries, each of which enjoyed considerable prosperity at this time.

The city's economic progress was facilitated by several other developments. The 1846 Act for the Abolition of the Exclusive Privilege of Trading in Burghs in Scotland ended the law that forbade a person to open a shop or a trade unless he was a guild brother or a member of the craft. Subsequently, new shops and businesses began to appear in Aberdeen.[7] Perhaps of greater significance was the introduction of a railway line to the city which provided improved communications, both with the south of Britain from 1844, and across the north east of Scotland by the mid 1850s.[8] The railway wrought a complete revolution in travel, both commercial and personal, and served as 'a wonderful influence in promoting the wealth and prosperity both of town and country'.[9] However, it was the modernisation of the harbour, which began in 1770 but was accelerated after 1830, that made the most important contribution to the growth of Aberdeen's economy. The port was deepened in 1832 and converted into a wet dock in the 1850s. These developments were enormously beneficial to the industries of the city as they improved the harbour facilities for importing and exporting goods.[10] These improvements to the infrastructure of Aberdeen's economy between 1830 and 1850 contributed immensely to its development.

However, local commerce suffered a setback towards the end of the 1840s when the textile industry, which was the largest employer in the city, experienced a dramatic decline. The manufacture of linen, cotton and wool had received a boost at the end of the long French war when continental markets that were previously closed became open.[11] By 1840, there were three large firms which spun, weaved and bleached linen, employing 7,600 men and women.

Aberdeen also boasted three cotton factories that had 2,000 workers, and six woollen mills with a further 2,500 labourers.[12] Thus, forty-six per cent of the city's work force was employed in the textiles industry. According to Robert Duncan, 'the mill worker was the most conspicuous figure in the employment landscape'.[13] By the early 1850s, following the business crisis in 1848 that was caused by a fall in the value of railway shares, many of these factories were forced to close. The textile magnates had been the leading speculators in the new railway companies and they lost heavily. Only two factories were able to survive. Consequently, the number of bales of textiles exported from Aberdeen fell from 81,000 in 1845 to 9,000 by 1855. The demise of the Leys, Masson and Company mill at Woodside reduced the income of the people of this village from £50,000 to £8,000 per year. The collapse was described as 'little short of a major disaster' as thousands of people lost their jobs.[14] The clearest indication of the effect caused by the downfall of the textile industry upon Aberdeen was the dramatic slow down in the growth of the city. Its population, which had risen by an average of 28% in each decade from 1801 to 1831, increased by only 2.7% between 1851 and 1861.[15] In 1851, Aberdeen was the fourteenth largest provincial town in Britain, but by 1861 it was the twenty second.[16] Hence the growth of the city's economy suffered a considerable setback around the end of the 1840s.

Nevertheless, this situation was not prolonged and Aberdeen began to emerge from this depression in the mid 1850s. Alexander Keith, a local author, believes that 'the bad times lasted until the autumn of 1852', after which 'the north east moved steadily forward to a broad and sound prosperity during the next thirty five years'.[17] The remaining textile factories made a recovery. The import of flax rose from 346 tons in 1854 to 2024 tons in 1856. Similarly the ship building industry, which had been badly affected after the 1848 crisis, was restored to its former glory by 1860.[18] However, it was the herring and granite industries that laid the more secure foundations for what Mellor described as 'a time of considerable prosperity and wealth creation' in the second half of the nineteenth century that was evidenced in the erection of the large homes at the west end of the city from the 1870s.[19] Certainly the survey of the city's economic condition that was presented to the British Association, which met in Aberdeen in 1859, revealed a fairly affluent community.[20] At the time of the revival the city had recovered from its industrial depression and had entered another period of considerable prosperity. Accordingly there is no correlation between economic misfortune and this religious movement.

II

However, the religious climate in Aberdeen in 1858 had a more significant effect upon the timing of this revival. The origins of the movement can be traced back to the early 1850s when a new spirit of evangelism appears to have begun to affect the church. Around this time, Thomas Chalmers' urban community vision was revived in the Free Church, principally through the work of Robert Buchanan, the minister of Glasgow's Free Tron Church, in the Wynds district of Glasgow. Within a short period, other territorial missions emerged as the work of building churches in the city seized the imagination of young ministers. In 1854, the Home Mission and Church Extension Committee of the Free Church General Assembly made grants available to encourage those who had begun to engage in aggressive evangelism in towns and cities across Scotland. In this way, the Free Church initiated in the 1850s one of the most successful periods of urban mission in the nineteenth century.[21] Such work was encouraged by the appearance in 1853 of the *British Messenger*, 'a monthly journal [that was] devoted to the diffusion of scriptural knowledge, the promotion of vital religion, and the advancement of social reformation'.[22] As a result of the introduction of the railway and the penny post, which provided the new opportunity for mass circulation, this eight page journal had, within four years, a circulation of 110,000 copies. It played a fundamental role in the dissemination of the news of the American and Ulster revivals in Scotland.[23] According to *The Revival* of July 1859, it was 'a prominent instrument in deepening the tone of piety in the churches of Scotland and elsewhere'.[24] Around the same time, the Free Church began to send many of its most zealous ministers on summer open-air missions across Scotland.[25] At the General Assembly in 1858 it was reported that 'in regard to open-air preaching . . . during last summer ninety ministers of the Free Church, being nearly double the number employed in 1856, had engaged in this good work, and had visited a number of destitute districts'.[26] Indeed, in May 1858 *The British Messenger* said 'the gospel has been more widely, purely, earnestly and ably preached for some time than it has ever been in our land . . . now there is scarcely a parish in Scotland where the gospel is not preached'.[27] In this way, before the revival, the church had become engaged in evangelism across Scotland to a greater extent than it had been during previous years.

Meanwhile in Aberdeen the City Mission was established in 1854. This agency employed three workers who concentrated their labours in the poorer districts of the city. In their first annual report, they boasted that 'in recent years much has been done in comparison with the inactivity of previous periods'.[28] Homes that were largely ignored previously by the church were visited and personal spiritual matters were discussed. At the same time, churches in Aberdeen began to appoint their own missionaries to work in their parishes. For instance, George Greig, 'Preacher of the Gospel', was appointed 'to be Missionary' for the parish of St Clement's by the Established Church.[29] Later, in April 1859 the Aberdeen Evangelistic Association was formed. The object of this organisation was 'to provide such an arrangement and extension of missionary operations as that the entire spiritual destitution of our city should be overtaken'.[30] Within several months, the city was divided into forty districts and two women missionaries had been appointed. At their first annual meeting it was reported that 'within the past one or two years missionary operations have been prosecuted in our city on a more comprehensive scale than at any former period'.[31] Each of these developments demonstrates how through the 1850s a renewed zeal for outreach had started to appear amongst Evangelicals in Aberdeen.

The dramatic conversions of a number of so-called respectable gentlemen who subsequently became itinerant evangelists also served to create an atmosphere in Aberdeen that was conducive to revival. Firstly Brownlow North, the son of an Episcopalian minister, was dramatically converted in November 1854 during a game of cards. From 1856 he devoted himself tirelessly to travelling and preaching in the north east of Scotland.[32] Hay MacDowall Grant of Arndilly, a landed gentleman and another Episcopalian, was also 'born again' in a sudden manner in November 1854. He too committed himself to the work of an itinerant evangelist in Aberdeenshire from 1856.[33] In addition, Lord Kintore, Gordon Forlong and John Gordon of Parkhill dedicated themselves to presenting the gospel to the people of north east Scotland in the late 1850s.[34] Their impact was significant. The January 1857 edition of *The British Messenger*, for example, contained a letter from a farmer. He described how after Gordon Forlong's visit to the village where he lived, a group of around forty people had established a prayer meeting and that 'there are not a few serious inquirers and the work of the Lord is progressing in the midst of us'. Furthermore, it was reported from elsewhere that 'a considerable number of meetings for prayer and exhortation have been established where Mr Forlong has been labouring during the past summer, and the work of grace goes on hopefully'.[35] The *British Messenger* of January 1859 stated that 'these men have been instrumental appreciably in quickening the Christian life of Scotland'.[36] There can be no doubt, therefore, that by their endeavours the respectable gentlemen evangelists of Aberdeenshire prepared the people amongst whom the revival subsequently flourished.

As well as the prevalence of Evangelical preaching, the number of prayer meetings was growing at a tremendous rate in Aberdeen in the years before the revival. The minutes of the Bon Accord Free Church kirk session from 12 December 1856, for instance, record a discussion among the elders about resuming a prayer meeting in Gordon Street. The following March, William Rait, the master of Marywell Street School, reported that a schoolhouse had been obtained in Gordon Street and that a regular prayer meeting was held every Friday evening.[37] Similarly, in August 1857, the minutes of Peterculter Free Church chronicle how 'the session having taken into consideration the state of the congregation and the need of the revival of the Lord's work in the conversion and edification of souls by the outpouring of the Spirit of God and the preaching of the gospel resolve to establish more prayer meetings in different parts of the district'.[38] The members of the kirk session of Maryculter Free Church, also anxious to participate in revival, 'were of the opinion that what is mainly called for is not the adopting of any additional means ... [rather] it was thought that it might be of use to attempt a Sabbath morning congregational prayer meeting immediately before public worship'.[39] In May 1859, the elders at Woodside Free Church 'agreed to revive the prayer meeting among the office bearers'.[40] Meanwhile, in December 1859, the kirk session at the South Free Church 'proposed and approved ... that a weekly prayer meeting of members of Session should be held every Thursday at three o'clock'.[41] Revival prayer meetings were not confined to the Free Church. During a members' meeting of the Belmont Street Congregational Church 'Mr Riddle proposed that the members unite in prayer each evening ... for a revival of religion in the church'.[42] Undoubtedly the Aberdeen awakening was precipitated by a noteworthy rise in the number of prayer meetings across the city. It was within these gatherings that a desire and expectancy for a religious movement was fostered.

However, the immediate stimulus of the Aberdeen revival was the news of the American religious movement which started in New York in the autumn of 1857. Throughout 1858 a number of religious publications, including the *British Evangelist*, the *British Messenger* and the *British and Foreign Evangelical Review*, printed a number of articles that described the origins and progress of the American movement which stirred the interest of many readers.[43] The kirk session minutes of the Free West Church, for instance, of 17 May 1858 recorded that 'on the suggestion of Mr Sinclair the Session resolved that a tract on the present religious movement in the United States should be circulated in the congregation, by placing copies of it, in the pews'.[44] In addition to these channels of communication, there were a number of transatlantic ties between families and friends in Scotland and America which enabled a more direct and personal flow of revival news. J. MacLennan, a minister from Washington, upon his return to America from Britain sent a letter to some friends he had made in Aberdeen. He said, 'I have written to New York to have a copy of the last week's *New York Evangelist* forwarded to you by the steamer of next Saturday . . . I have also forwarded you from this place by this day's mail, the *National Intelligencer* of this city, in which there is reference made to the union prayer meeting here up to this time.'[45] In this way, people sent news to one another about the course of the revival as it spread across America with the result that the people of Aberdeen became well informed of its progress.

The accounts of the movement across the Atlantic rapidly served to excite the anticipation of the people of Aberdeen that they would experience a similar religious movement. They became, according to *The British Messenger*, 'arrested, aroused, solemnised and filled with prayerfulness, devotedness, living faith and hopeful anticipation'.[46] One eye-witness reported how, 'immediately after the news of the awakening in the United States came to Aberdeen, a spirit of earnest prayer . . . was poured out on many Christian people there for a similar blessing to descend on them'.[47] Professor David Brown told the Free Church General Assembly in 1859 that 'a solemn and prayerful spirit began to be diffused' across Aberdeen after it received news of the American revival.[48] The prayerfulness of the city's people was accompanied by an expectation of the imminence of a revival. According to the reminiscences of James Rae, a student in Aberdeen during 1859, the news of the American revival 'created in the Christian mind a spirit of great expectancy'.[49] Another student, Gordon Gray, recalled 'very distinctly the impression made . . . on the minds of very many, by the reports from America of the marvellous spiritual awakening . . . [how] a strange awe began to fall upon the minds of many in our own land, and an expectation of a like visitation took shape in their prayers'.[50] The thoughts of individuals became directed towards the notion that such an outpouring of the Spirit would occur in their city. Clearly, the news of the American revival caused a considerable stir in Aberdeen. A deep interest in religious movements was excited and a great longing for similar experiences was created.

This desire was released in a renewed and fervent spirit of prayerfulness. A period of concerted prayer began on Wednesday 1 September 1858 following a significant church service. The minister involved recalled how he 'felt assured, especially during the evening service, that God's Holy Spirit was working powerfully on the minds of the people'. Afterwards he spoke about the American revival and how prayer meetings had been recently formed in other towns in Scotland. He suggested that a similar gathering should be organised in Aberdeen.[51] The vision was captured by a group of young men, and within days the first union prayer meeting was held, from two to three o clock, in the upper room of the Mechanics' Institution. By the end of the week, attendance at the daily prayer meeting had risen to 600 and consequently a larger room in the County Buildings was found for the gathering. Shortly afterwards another evening prayer gathering was begun at eight o'clock for those who were unable, due to work commitments, to attend during the day.[52] During September, these meetings were addressed by three American ministers who described how the movement had started in their towns in the daily union prayer meetings they had established. According to the correspondent of the *British Evangelist*, their accounts 'produced a deep impression' among the people of Aberdeen.[53] Gordon Gray commented, 'too much stress cannot be laid on' the role which this prayer meeting played during the course of the revival.[54] Meanwhile J. C. Brown, minister of Belmont Street United Presbyterian Church, said that he attributed 'much of what I have seen to the preparation of heart produced by the daily meeting for prayer'.[55] The union prayer gathering exercised an important influence upon the timing of the appearance of the revival. It was within this meeting that the desire for and expectancy of this movement was encouraged and developed.

Besides praying, the Christians began to organise a series of week-long evangelistic campaigns. In September 1858, during the busy week of the Cattle Show which attracted up to 25,000 visitors to Aberdeen from the surrounding rural hinterland, a series of special religious services was conducted in the Albion Street Congregational Church by Peter Drummond, while open-air meetings were undertaken by Mr Gordon of Parkhill.[56] Following the success of these meetings the YMCA invited the evangelist Grattan Guinness to lead evangelistic services in Aberdeen. He started his campaign on 3 October. Each night he preached in various churches that were crowded to excess, while many hundreds were unable to gain admittance. These services made a strong impression upon those who attended, and according to one observer were 'chiefly useful in producing a general interest in divine things and preparing a people for the Lord'.[57] After Guinness, Brownlow North arrived in Aberdeen in November. Once again, he led a series of religious services which served to deepen and intensify the impact that had been made by Guinness. These meetings, which one observer described as being 'without precedent in the ecclesiastical history of the city of Aberdeen' were the means of creating a considerable sensation.[58] Everywhere these men appeared, the churches were crowded with anxious listeners. Later, in 1859, another eye-witness judged that these 'earnest labourers . . . were together instrumental in breaking up the fallow ground, in preparing the way for what was to follow'.[59] Without question, the religious climate in Aberdeen in 1858 was the chief factor in determining the timing of this revival. There was an unusual heightened state of spiritual anticipation in the city. The movement was awaited in the prayer meetings and expected at the evangelistic rallies.

Another significant event was the invitation by William Martin, the Professor of Moral Philosophy at Marischal College, to Reginald Radcliffe, a lawyer from Liverpool who had become an evangelist, to come and work in Aberdeen. He arrived on 27 November 1858 and, unable to find a church that would permit him the opportunity to preach, began leading services for children in a small Congregational mission-room in Albion Street. It was during one of these meetings that the revival began. One evening he invited those who wanted to speak with him to go to the vestry. A great number responded, 'all weeping and sobbing in the conviction of their sinfulness', and about thirty were converted that night.[60] As children's lives were changed, parents began to attend these gatherings and soon crowds of people began to attend Radcliffe's meetings. Radcliffe remained at Albion Street for a month until he was invited to preach at Greyfriars Parish Church by its minister James Smith on 22 December. Thereafter 'the blessing descended in large measure'.[61] Radcliffe conducted between three and six services for five days each week for the following three months and at every meeting between twenty and one hundred people fell under 'a deep conviction of sinfulness'.[62] According to James Stark, author of *The Lights of the North*, published in 1896, 'no man in such a short time ever so drew and stirred Aberdeen'.[63] Radcliffe had arrived in Aberdeen at an opportune moment. The Evangelical community of the city was ready and prepared for revival. Its members wanted to share the experience which their American relations had enjoyed and they had come to believe that they would. The timing of the 1858 revival in Aberdeen resulted from the desire and expectancy of the people that were created by the news of the American religious movement, and the visits of itinerant evangelists, chiefly Reginald Radcliffe, and manifested in the popular, well-attended prayer meetings.

III

The revival prospered dramatically in Aberdeen during the first three months of 1859. During this period, the movement was led principally by Radcliffe and was centred around Greyfriars Parish Church. However, by March Radcliffe's health was beginning to break down and he was forced to retire to the home of John Gordon at Parkhill. Radcliffe's departure marked the end of the first period of the revival.[64] Throughout the summer, a number of successful open-air rallies kept interest in the city movement alive, but it was upon Radcliffe's return to Aberdeen in the autumn that the revival entered a second period of intense activity. Crowded meetings were held for several months in the newly-opened Music Hall which was able to accommodate up to 3,000 people.[65] During this time, according to Professor Cowan of Aberdeen University writing in 1910, 'the whole community seemed to feel the influence at work . . . a feeling of solemnity seemed to pervade the life of the city'.[66] The city movement appears to have entered another period of suspension through the first quarter of 1860 while it raged uncontrollably along the Moray Firth. However, it returned for a third and final period of significant effect towards the end of the summer of 1860, having been injected with a fresh impetus by a two-day conference that had been held at Huntly in July. George Campbell, the minister of the Free North Church, reported in October how 'in the past six or seven weeks in Aberdeen we have seen a work of more power than we saw before. Since the Huntly meetings there seems to have been a new impulse given to the work . . . from the time of the Huntly meetings, it took a new start. The Spirit of the Lord seemed to come down upon the people as he had not come before'.[67] By the end of 1860 the fervour of the revival was beginning to abate once again. In May 1861, the *Aberdeen Free Press* reported that 'there have been few special religious services. The only meetings have been a series of nightly prayer meetings held in various places of worship, a week in a church at a time. Attendance varies depending on where they are held'.[68] Radcliffe and Richard Weaver, another evangelist, continued to conduct revival services during the summer of 1861 in Aberdeen, but the movement appears to have slowed down considerably. Although evangelists continued to visit the city and meetings were arranged until 1864, the dramatic scenes of revival had disappeared. The Aberdeen revival arose and receded over the course of two and a half years. This affirms the findings of Clifford Marrs who, in his post-graduate thesis, found that the revival had similar highs and lows in Glasgow.[69] After a period of preparation there was a two-year rotation that included three periods of expansion followed by decline. Clearly the revival ebbed and flowed as it surged through the city.

There are indications within the pattern of the Aberdeen revival that its appearance was affected by the patterns of work and rest that governed the lives of those who lived and worked in the city. The social and economic changes that accompanied the industrial developments at the start of the nineteenth century created a new urban environment where men and women worked long shifts in factories and other employments. A pamphlet, published in 1827 for example, referred to the 'system of working from six o'clock in the morning to six in the evening'.[70] This indicates the duration men and women were expected to work in the new industrial towns during the first quarter of the nineteenth century. According to W. H. Fraser, those who were involved in the building trade worked for sixty hours each week in the summer and forty seven hours during the winter, and payment was by the hour.[71] The situation for factory workers was similar. The 1844 Factory Act legislated that textiles workers should not work more than ten hours each day for six days each week.[72] Thus, although hours of work were curbed, they remained extensive. Significantly, the shift from task-orientated work, which the people had been previously accustomed to in rural areas, to timed labour was accompanied by a change in their apprehension of time. Time became currency that was no longer passed, but spent.[73] As men and women submitted themselves to the discipline of shift work in the mills and factories they began to value time in a new way, which affected how they spent their hours away from employment.

The shift towards a more regulated pattern of work afforded the townsfolk some time each day which they were able to spend as they pleased. Consequently a plethora of leisure and sporting activities emerged which began to fill this period away from labour. Undoubtedly the public house remained central to the social lives of the working classes, and Aberdeen continued to have a larger proportion of licences to the population than any other town in Scotland.[74] However sport was also an important pastime. The leisure revolution of the 1870s was not as sudden or unexpected as some have imagined, but was rather the culmination of the growth of a movement that had started at the end of the eighteenth century.[75] Sport was thriving in Aberdeen at the time of the revival. The working classes enjoyed various outdoor games such as quoiting, while the artisans and middle classes enjoyed horse racing and cricket.[76] William Carnie, a local journalist, recalled in his *Reporting Reminiscences* how during the 1850s 'in the summer afternoons and evenings there was a good deal of healthy, merry doings in the way of sport'. He described the Golf Club as 'steadily flourishing' and commented that 'cricket claimed a goodly number of active and earnest upholders . . . chiefly . . . law-clerks and university students'.[77] He also recounted the activities of the Aberdeen Musical Association, which was formed in 1853 and attracted between fifty and sixty lady and gentlemen members.[78] The theatre, whose season ran from September to March, provided another popular pastime.[79] Other opportunities for recreational activities were created by the opening of the local museum, art gallery and public libraries.[80] In addition, between 1839 and 1865 there were seventeen philanthropic and religious societies established in Aberdeen whose activities competed for the free time of the city person.[81] By far the most popular of these were the various local Temperance Societies which encouraged the cultivation of alternative social pursuits, such as the soiree, a Saturday evening gathering that included recitations and singing.[82] Finally, during 1859 the Volunteer Movement was started in Aberdeen. Stirred by Tennyson's stirring verses, 'Form, form, Riflemen, form', many young men, including a number of eager young clerks, were roused by the ominous threats of foreign invasion and decided to join the newly formed Rifle Corp.[83] Hence, there were a large number of social activities in Aberdeen around the middle of the nineteenth century that sought to attract the attention and occupy the new leisure time which the townsfolk had begun to enjoy.

Obviously these work patterns and leisure opportunities impinged upon the time which people could devote to religious activities. In rural and coastal areas, where work time was not strictly disciplined and where there were fewer recreational opportunities, the revival faced little or no challenge from other social events. By contrast, the city revival meetings had to compete against work, theatres, pubs and other organisations in a bid to draw the attendance of the urban dweller. For instance, a prayer meeting for the elders of the South Free Church was started on Thursdays at three o'clock in December 1859, but within two months the time of the gathering had been moved to ten o'clock on Sunday mornings 'for the greater convenience of the office bearers'.[84] Likewise, the kirk session of Belmont Street United Presbyterian Church, 'agreed that in consequence of the small attendance at sermon on the Monday forenoon that the service be held at seven o'clock evening'.[85] As a result the organisers of the revival vigorously targeted the free time of the city workers.

Summer evening open-air evangelistic meetings were an important feature of the movement. An enormous effort was made to conduct out-door services as widely as possible in Aberdeen.[86] Teams of young preachers positioned themselves at strategic positions all over the city and soon attracted crowds that were numbered in their hundreds.[87] George Campbell remarked how 'it was quite uncommon to have less than a thousand people who could be gathered in the thoroughfares' listening to the preachers.[88] Street preaching was a novelty in Aberdeen and so it attracted the curious attention of the people. Thus it targeted successfully the free time which the townsfolk enjoyed during the long summer evenings.

The Music Hall rallies that began in the autumn of 1859, and which marked the second major period of the revival, demonstrate further how its leaders sought to plan services that would suit the working and leisure lives of the people. This series of meetings was conducted on a Sunday evening. They were held during the only reasonable period during the week when everyone was not at work. As a result the first gathering, addressed by Radcliffe, attracted 9,000 people, only a third of whom were able to gain admittance.[89] There can be little doubt that the day and time of these meetings, carefully organised by the revivalists, accounted for their popularity. The final heightened period of the revival came towards the end of the summer of 1860. Once again it is clear that the coordinators of the revival planned a period of special meetings that would coincide with the local public holidays and thus target the city dwellers' free time. A large two-day open-air rally was held at the Links when the organisers anticipated that 'many people will naturally congregate, it being the evening of the Cattle Show'.[90] In particular, special services were arranged for the working classes on the Saturday afternoon, when 'most of them have the half holiday' and consequently they were 'present in great numbers'.[91] These huge, gatherings of the revival illustrate how it was meticulously planned by its leaders to suit the work and leisure habits of those who lived in the city.

This attention to organisation was also displayed in perhaps the defining features of the Aberdeen religious movement: the two daily prayer meetings which, above all, displayed how the revivalists planned their services to fit around the social patterns of the city. The first meeting was held between two and three o'clock and 'gathered together [people] from the drawing room, lowly hearth side, shop and office'.[92] This time suited those who worked in businesses or lived in the centre of the city. In order to accommodate those who laboured in factories and mills a second meeting, conducted between eight and nine pm, was arranged specifically 'for the convenience of the working people'.[93] The times of these gatherings and the specific audiences they targeted reveals how the labour and leisure patterns of the city influenced the appearance of this religious movement. The revivalists were anxious to find ways of attracting men and women to religious services. Hence, the movement was carefully planned in order to fit around the disciplined working routines of the townsfolk, and to target their free time.

IV

The movement was led principally by a group of laymen who, it appears, administered its course in the same way they would have conducted their business affairs. Their influence was clearly evidenced in all the activities associated with the revival. It was displayed, in the first instance, not only in the timing, but also by the manner in which the prayer meetings were conducted. When these meetings were started, the organisers experimented by having a period of 'open prayer' when anyone could take part. According to one observer, this quickly led to 'anarchy' and consequently they reverted to a simple prescribed pattern which left no room for any spontaneity. A hymn or psalm was sung, a passage of scripture was read and then a number of selected men, usually four, would lead in prayer.[94] Furthermore, these gatherings, modelled on the original North Dutch Church prayer meeting where the American revival began, were strictly limited to an hour in length.[95] The time-conscious Evangelicals organised their prayer meetings in a controlled manner.

Similarly, the main services and events of the city revival were managed closely by its lay leaders. Most of the movement's meetings were held in the evening and they tended to follow a standard prescription. During the first few months of the revival, when Radcliffe preached daily at Greyfriars Church, the services began at six o'clock. Usually there were two ordinary meetings that lasted for one hour, from six to seven, and from seven to eight during which Radcliffe would preach for forty five minutes. The *British Messenger* correspondent described how 'when one service was over, some went away, but their places were immediately filled by those rushing in at other doors'.[96] After a brief interval for refreshments a third, final meeting was held specifically for anxious inquirers. Perhaps more surprisingly, the open-air meetings that were held at the Links during the summer were also carefully stage-managed. They began promptly at seven o'clock and ended at nine o'clock so that there would be sufficient time for the anxious inquirers to attend their second special meeting in a nearby church.[97] It is noteworthy that although there were 'some who would gladly stay all night' these gatherings were not protracted beyond ten o'clock.[98] This reveals the discipline which the leaders exercised over the city movement.

This was an organised revival that was conducted in a highly ordered fashion.

The coordinated nature of the Aberdeen religious movement was further demonstrated by the systematic Bible and tract distribution, another important feature of the revival. At the annual meeting of the Aberdeen Bible Society, it was reported that during 1858 765 Bibles were sold at a reduced price, while fifty-six Bibles and fourteen New Testaments were given away free. The *Aberdeen Free Press* reported that, 'this was the largest local circulation that had been made since the commencement of the society forty seven years ago'.[99] The distribution of religious pamphlets expanded considerably during the revival. Gospel tracts were highly regarded as a means of furthering the cause of the movement and their circulation was undertaken by a large band of enthusiastic recent converts. The Young Men's Christian Association was chiefly responsible for dividing the city into districts and administering the dissemination of tracts. By 1863, approximately 12,380 copies of the *Monthly Visitor* were distributed in Aberdeen each month by 263 female and fifty-six male volunteers.[100] In addition to this systematic circulation, young converts regularly 'took their station night after night opposite the door of the theatre and distributed tracts'.[101] Radcliffe also described a lady friend who 'is the organiser for me in cutting up the map of Aberdeen, and sending a handbill, etc. to every house, by many Christians, all over the city'.[102] In this way areas of the city were systematically targeted to ensure widespread tract distribution. The efficient, well ordered manner of the diffusion of religious pamphlets and Bibles, not to mention the coordinated advertisement of the revival, illustrates further the organised nature of this movement.

The control and discipline exercised by the revivalists is perhaps best illustrated by the manner in which they dealt with those who wanted to be converted. Finney, the chief architect of modern religious movements, had prescribed the use of the 'anxious seat'. This was a special pew set aside at the front of a building where those who were spiritually anxious were invited to come and sit at the end of a service. Here, they would be exhorted and prayed over and they were expected to make a public confession of faith. These highly charged situations often aroused emotions that could explode uncontrollably.[103] Consequently, the Aberdeen revivalists avoided the use of the 'anxious seat' and dealt with inquirers in a more orderly manner. Grattan Guinness described how 'at the close of the public meetings we invite all those who have been awakened under the Word and are anxious about their souls . . . to remain to a second brief meeting [which] is made up of prayer, hymns of a certain character, and personal exhortation, and consists in praying for, labouring for, waiting for and expecting conversion on the spot'.[104] Following this meeting, those who remained were counselled privately by Christians. In this way the organisers of the Aberdeen revival abandoned Finney's techniques and employed the secondary 'inquiry meeting', an even more modern, respectable means of dealing with those who were spiritually anxious. Later, this became the preferred method used by Moody during the 1873 revival. The Aberdeen movement was characterised by being highly organised, and modern in the methods it employed to encourage conversion.

The absence of any manner of physical manifestation was another important distinguishing feature of the Aberdeen revival, which exhibits further the controlled character of this movement. The revivalists were anxious to distance themselves from the emotional, cruder excrescences that had characterised earlier religious movements. They remembered, with a degree of embarrassment, the excitement that had attended the meetings which William Burns had conducted in Aberdeen during the revival of 1840. They did not want a repetition of those undisciplined scenes which would have served to alienate the more respectable members of society whom they hoped to win as converts.[105] Consequently, they worked hard and succeeded in creating a more dignified, ordered revival. Several attempts were made by some to promote an excited atmosphere that might have engendered some form of physical manifestation, but they were wholly unsuccessful in arousing the emotions of the people of Aberdeen.[106] Significantly James Turner, the Methodist evangelist who created scenes of raw excitement along the Moray Firth, was considered 'neither convincing nor impressive' when he preached in Aberdeen.[107] On the contrary, Hamilton MacGill, the Home Secretary of the United Presbyterian Church, speaking at the 1860 annual conference of the Evangelical Alliance, reported that in Aberdeen, 'it cannot be said that any corporeal or unnatural affection accompanied the awakening in this city'.[108] Elsewhere it was recorded, 'there were no physical manifestations, such as were reported from Ireland, at those meetings, and there was no particular display of excitement, but a spirit of deep devotion and prayerfulness'.[109] Radcliffe claimed that 'our meetings are conducted without a sound, as still and orthodox as possible'.[110] Meanwhile the *British Messenger* added, 'there has been a total absence of exciting preaching, of noise or confusion. The addresses have been distinguished mainly by their perfect simplicity.'[111] The meetings in the city were designed to be calm and controlled. The absence of any form of physical manifestation during the Aberdeen revival separated it from other appearances of the same movement that were characterised by prostrations. Its restrained expression suggests further that it was a modern, respectable, organised revival.

There is no doubt that the manner of this movement was set by those who were charged with its leadership. It was coordinated chiefly by a group of Evangelical men who had not been trained to work in the church. John Gordon of Parkhill presided over the first union prayer meetings.[112] According to one eye-witness, 'the first thing that strikes us in looking at these leaders is that they are laymen. God has seen meet, in this awakening, to give the chief portion of the work into the hands of those who have enjoyed no regular training for the Christian ministry'.[113] Another observed 'so far as the workers were concerned, these were almost entirely confined to evangelical laymen'.[114] Indeed, ministers were conspicuous by their absence from the movement in the beginning. David Rait, a child convert of the revival, recalled in 1910 how 'one noticeable feature of the revival movement, however, was the fact that the majority of the ministers did not approve very much of the work of the revival at first, gave it very little encouragement'.[115] Also, a correspondent of the *British Evangelist* reporting on the union prayer meeting from Aberdeen in February 1859, said that 'only in one thing were we disappointed – the paucity of ministers in attendance – not of any one denomination in particular, but of all denominations'.[116] Within a few months, however, a number of city clergymen began to support the movement, but by then its leadership was firmly in the hands of the laymen. They approached the organisation of the revival in a business-like manner and employed all of their professional skills in its coordination. There is no doubt that their methods made an indelible impression upon the appearance of the movement in Aberdeen.

These laymen shared a large proportion of the responsibility for the work of the revival with the local Young Men's Christian Association. This group was established in Aberdeen at the start of July 1858 in the Bon Accord Free Church as a direct result of the American revival, by a group of young men who were anxious to participate in this religious movement.[117] Composed chiefly of 'young men engaged in business in town' it had attracted, within a year, seventy six members.[118] This group of enthusiastic Evangelicals provided much of the vision and energy upon which the revival flourished. Their motto was very clear and simple. They were engaged in 'a mission of converted young men to young men who are not yet Christians'.[119] The founder of the YMCA, George Williams, held a strong belief in the efficacy of modern revival techniques.[120] During the revival, one observer noticed that 'the Association became a centre to attract and stimulate young men, as well as others, while its members supplied many of those who carried out the details of the numerous meetings that followed'.[121] This role was noticed further by Peter Drummond who commented, 'Young Men's Christian Associations are likely to become very important as a basis for action, and the more of them we have, the better may evangelising efforts be expected to prosper'.[122] Half a century later Alexander Gammie, author of *The Churches of Aberdeen*, validated the prophecy. The YMCA, he said, 'has been the centre of many of the religious movements in the city and district within the last fifty years'.[123] The YMCA played a leading role in the administration of the revival and its influence, which was decidedly modern, was evident in all its activities.

However, the itinerant evangelists who conducted the revival services exercised perhaps the most profound effect upon the nature and course of this movement. It is noteworthy that at an open-air conference, held in September 1860, 'during the ordinary proceedings of the day, which were conducted principally by clergymen, the people, though quiet and attentive, seemed in a great measure unmoved'.[124] The evangelists, however, who belonged to the higher and educated classes, created a great deal of excitement when they appeared conducting religious meetings in Aberdeen. Firstly it was unusual to see a gentleman wearing a morning suit preaching in a church. Furthermore an eye-witness reported how

> They come to town with a great name; advertise themselves as about to preach, perhaps every day, sometimes twice a day, for a week or two; and then suddenly leave for some other sphere of labour. Somebody the other day compared them to comets, and I think the comparison a good one. They appear very suddenly and unexpectedly, shine with a bright lustre, strike the inhabitants with astonishment, and then disappear as suddenly as they come.[125]

Another noticed how 'they have been the means of creating considerable sensation here. Wherever they preach, the churches are crowded; multitudes unaccustomed to trouble the house of God much rush to hear them.'[126] Although their sincerity of purpose was never questioned, some critics judged that their style was more suited to the platform than to the pulpit.[127] Nevertheless, there is no doubt that the spectacle of a laymen preaching in a church accounted for some of the popularity of the revival. Much of the success of the revival lay in the presence of the evangelists who commanded a greater influence than the ministers over the people during this period.

V

The appearance of the evangelists provoked an unfortunate response from many of the city's clergymen. William Gauld, who studied at Aberdeen University during the revival, remembered how 'most of the ministers looked askance at the movement . . . it was then a comparatively new thing for a layman to preach in a church, and especially from the pulpit. The innovation was an unpalatable one.'[128] Another observer said it was unfortunate that 'there was not a better understanding between the lay preachers and the clergy . . . we do think that the laymen, being strangers, had a right to expect better entertainment and more cordial sympathy'.[129] Meanwhile, the anonymous author of *Times of Refreshing* commented, 'surely it is most unreasonable that ministers who have been specially set apart from other men for the advancement of the work of God, should so frequently prove the chief and almost the only hinderers of it'.[130] Radcliffe quickly discovered that his services were creating noticeable anxiety among ministers. In a letter written after he had been in the city for a week he said, 'I have to be careful. I find the Free Church ministers do not like Mr North going into the pulpit . . . His posters are now changed from 'preach' to 'address' like mine. In Bon Accord Church it was thought better that I should not go into the pulpit; and next week, unless specifically asked, I purpose always going into the lower desk.' Later he wrote that 'Professor Martin says that many ministers do not like, and only tolerate because they cannot stop this lay work'.[131] After several months Radcliffe commented again 'the work increases, and souls are continually added; but churches do not offer easily. Some few godly ministers and people come about us and help most heartily; but these are quite the exception.'[132] Even when ministers supported the revival, the elders of churches often created a hindrance. Hence, the kirk session of Greyfriars Parish Church, where James Smith was minister, resolved that Radcliffe would be permitted to 'address' a prayer meeting 'provided that he [Smith] or another minister of the church, assisted by an elder or communicant of the church conduct the services'.[133] The success of North and Radcliffe, two unordained laymen, was the cause of offence to many and ensured that a considerable proportion of Aberdeen's ministers remained distant from the revival.

Often the cause of the disparagement was insecurity. It is a significant revelation, for example, that Andrew Bonar, the minister at Finnieston and an enthusiastic supporter of the revival, struggled to deal with jealousy that was aroused by the ascendancy of lay preachers. In the entry in his diary on 23 September 1859 he confessed 'yet envy is in my heart, and today I have been seeking grace to rejoice exceedingly over the usefulness of others, even where it casts me into the shade. Lord, take this Achan from me.' Towards the end of October, he again acknowledged how he had 'found out more of my corruptions in the form of jealousy and envy when others are used and myself forgotten'.[134] Pride, it appears, may have prevented many ministers, who otherwise would have been sympathetic, from supporting the revival wholeheartedly. Yet the movement continued unabated with enormous success, led principally by the itinerant evangelists.

However, on other occasions, ministers were reluctant to endorse the work of the lay preachers because they disagreed with the theological bias of their sermons and their method of dealing with inquirers. The revivalists taught that conversion was an instantaneous event which depended upon an immediate act of the will. Indeed, there was no more characteristic element in Radcliffe's preaching than his insistence on the doctrine of instant salvation. According to his biographer 'such a practical and business-like presentation of the Gospel message went home to men's hearts almost with a power of a new revelation, by its contrast to the preaching prevalent at that period'.[135] Dr Gauld, who became a missionary in China, recalled his conversation with Radcliffe on the night he was converted: 'He came to me and asked me if I were saved. I said, 'No.' 'Why not?' he asked. 'Everything has been done for your salvation; Jesus has finished it all long ago for you, and you have only to believe.' ... it was a new idea to me – 'only to believe' in Jesus. It seemed very simple and easy'.[136] Ministers were afraid that conversion was becoming too effortless. They believed that conversion required a 'protracted law work'. In their opinion, a Christian needed to 'flounder amongst his convictions of sin, his doubts, fears, corruptions and repentance for months or years before he can consider himself fit to go to Christ for salvation'.[137] According to the *Aberdeen Journal* of August 1860, they judged that the leaders of the revival were 'too ready to accept a demonstrative sentiment for a vital conviction'.[138] Furthermore, they were anxious when they heard 'youths talking of going to be converted, as if conversion were but an evening's entertainment'.[139] Nevertheless, conversion continued to be presented by the evangelists as an instantaneous experience that simply awaited the decision of an individual's will.

Also it has been suggested that ministers were reluctant to support the revival because it included the singing of hymns to popular tunes which they found irreverent and distasteful. Andrew Drummond and James Bulloch have suggested that the 1859 revival 'did most to stimulate the demand for hymns' in the Victorian Scottish Church. They believe that the enthusiasm for hymn-singing was greatest where the movement was led by laymen, and that it was resisted by the Established and Free Churches.[140] Notwithstanding the prominent role played by itinerant evangelists in the Aberdeen revival, it does not appear that it was accompanied by a significant rise in the singing of religious words to fashionable tunes. An anonymous convert of the revival recalled the details of a typical service he attended during which the congregation 'sang four verses of a Psalm', listened to a Bible reading, and then sang '[an]other four verses of a Psalm'.[141] Meanwhile James Stark described how during the movement, 'having few hymns which they could use at such meetings in those days, they were never tired of singing over and over again the 126th Psalm and the 41st paraphrase'.[142] Hence it appears that Psalms and paraphrases were used principally during the Aberdeen revival, and thus the movement did not give rise to modern, popular hymn-singing in the city.

Nevertheless there remained considerable prejudice against the revival. Many people remembered the excesses that had accompanied the previous movement in 1840. The anonymous Omicron admitted that the very word 'revival' excited within the minds of many Aberdeen churchgoers 'only feelings of prejudice, scorn or disgust . . . holy fairs and raving speeches, and wild bodily and mental excitement'. Hence, he believed that calling the daily union prayer meeting a 'Revival Prayer Meeting' aroused the suspicions and fears of many good people.[143] However, much of the antagonism against the religious movement was created by local ministers. Some of them were envious of the success of the untrained evangelists who filled churches to overflowing with anxious listeners. Others disagreed with their theology or disliked their methods of dealing with anxious inquirers in after meetings. Undoubtedly many ministers of the city were uncomfortable with the manner and style of this religious movement.

The nature of the Aberdeen movement reveals that it was essentially a modern revival. Initially its origins lay in the American awakening that had started in New York in 1857. However, the disciplined working context in which it appeared meant that it had to be knitted neatly into an already busy situation. Consequently, the activities upon which the revival flourished were always highly organised, targeted events. Indeed, in all aspects of its implementation, the movement was supremely ordered and controlled. This was a reflection upon the character and habits of the businessmen who assumed responsibility for its leadership. Another significant influence upon the revival was the YMCA. The young clerks of this organisation, who undertook most of the practical organisation of the movement, were anxious to employ the modern revival techniques of Finney and others they had read and discussed together. In addition, the primary role played by Radcliffe and the other itinerant evangelists suggests further that this was a new religious movement. Moreover, their message of an instant conversion and the full assurance which they preached was also extremely contemporary. In some respects, particularly in its targeting and organisation, this movement resembled those which Finney sought to encourage. Yet upon closer inspection it appears that this revival had embraced even more advanced techniques of evangelism. Undoubtedly, therefore, the chief characteristics of the Aberdeen revival that started in 1858 demonstrate that it was a modern religious movement.

Notes

1. F. H. Groome, *Ordnance Gazeteer of Scotland: Volume One* (Edinburgh, 1882), p. 7.
2. H. MacKenzie (ed.), *The Third Statistical Account of Scotland: The City of Aberdeen* (Edinburgh, 1953), p. 45
3. *The New Statistical Account of Aberdeenshire* (Edinburgh, 1843), pp. 71-3.
4. Ibid., p. 60.
5. MacKenzie, *Statistical Account: Aberdeen*, p. 44.
6. 'A Short History of Aberdeen and Its People' (A Series of 48 Articles from the *Free Press*, printed from 12 July 1890), Article No. 39.
7. Ibid., Article No. 43.
8. J. S. Smith, D. Stevenson (ed.), *Aberdeen in the Nineteenth Century: The Making of the Modern City* (Aberdeen, 1988), p. 8.
9. 'History of Aberdeen and Its People', Article No. 42.
10. *New Statistical Account of Aberdeenshire*, p. 68.
11. 'History of Aberdeen and Its People', Article No. 36.
12. MacKenzie, *Statistical Account: Aberdeen*, p. 46.
13. R. Duncan, *Textiles and Toil: The Factory System and the Industrial Working Class in Early Nineteenth Century Aberdeen* (Aberdeen, 1984), p. 3.
14. MacKenzie, *Statistical Account: Aberdeen*, p. 47.
15. Smith, Stevenson, *Aberdeen in the Nineteenth Century*, p. 20.
16. Ibid.
17. A. Keith, *The North of Scotland Bank Limited 1836-1936* (Aberdeen, 1936), pp. 61, 66.
18. Ibid., p. 70.
19. Smith, Stevenson, *Aberdeen in the Nineteenth Century*, p. 2, MacKenzie, *Statistical Account: Aberdeen*, pp. 51-58.
20. Keith, *North of Scotland Bank Limited*, p. 70.
21. S. J. Brown, 'Thomas Chalmers and the Communal Ideal in Victorian Scot-

land' in T. C. Smout (ed.), *Victorian Values* (Oxford, 1992), pp. 69-71.
22. *B.Mr.*, No 47, (January 1857), p. 1.
23. J. Birkbeck, *Peter Drummond: Man of Conviction and Action* (Stirling, 1984), pp. 20-31,
    M. J. Cormack, *The Stirling Tract Enterprise and the Drummonds* (Stirling, 1984), p. 14.
24. *T.R.*, Vol 1, No 1, (30 July 1859), p. 3.
25. *B.Mr.*, No 52, (June 1857), p. 47.
26. *N.C.J.M.*, Vol 5, No 7, (1 July 1858), p. 174.
27. *B.Mr.*, No 63, (May 1858), p. 129.
28. *First Report of the General City Mission* (Aberdeen, 1854), p. 5.
29. St Clements Parish Church Kirk Session Minutes, December 1859
30. *First Report of the Aberdeen Evangelistic Association* (Aberdeen, 1861), np.
31. Ibid.
32. K. Moody-Stuart, *Brownlow North: Records and Recollections* (London, 1878), pp. 14, 16-17.
33. M. M. Gordon, *Hay MacDowall Grant of Arndilly: His Life, Labours and Teaching* (London, 1876), p. 39, 57.
34. *B.Mr.*, No 47, (January 1857), p. 3.
35. Ibid.
36. Ibid., No 71, (January 1859), p. 7.
37. Bon Accord Free Church Kirk Session Minutes, 12 December 1856, 11 March 1857
38. Peterculter Free Church Kirk Session Minutes, 27 August 1857
39. Maryculter Free Church Kirk Session Minutes, 25 January 1860
40. Woodside Free Church Kirk Session Minutes, 16 May 1859
41. South Free Church Kirk Session Minutes, 15 December 1859
42. George Street Congregational Church Minute Book of Church Meetings, 28 September 1859
43. *B.F.E.R.*, (October 1858), p. 911,
    B.E., Vol 1, No 1, (July 1858), p. 27,
    B.Mr., No 63, (May 1858), p. 134.
44. Free West Church Kirk Session Minutes, 17 May 1858
45. *B.E.*, Vol 1, No 6, (December 1858), p. 243.
46. *B.Mr.*, No 63, (May 1858), p. 129.
47. An Eye witness, *The Appearance of God's Work in the Chief Towns of Scotland: With Special Reference to Aberdeen and Dundee* (Aberdeen, 1859), p. 8.
48. *B.Mr.*, No 77, (July 1859), p. 243.
49. T. T. Matthews (ed.), *Reminiscences of the Revival of Fifty Nine and the Sixties* (Aberdeen, 1910), p. 6.
50. Ibid., p. 35.
51. Anon, *Times of Refreshing. Being Notices of Some of the Religious Awakenings which have taken place in the United Kingdom, with Special Reference to the Revival in Aberdeen* (Aberdeen, 1859), p. 12.
52. *A.J.*, (2 February 1859), p. 3.
53. *B.E.*, Vol 1, No 4, (October 1858), p. 146.
54. Matthews, *Reminiscences*, p. 36.
55. *B.Mr.*, No 75, (May 1859), p. 230.

56. Anon, *Times of Refreshing*, p. 12.
57. Ibid., p. 14.
58. *B.E.*, Vol 1, No (5, November 1858), p. 194.
59. Eye witness, *God's Work in the Chief Towns of Scotland*, p. 9.
60. *A.F.P.*, (26 August 1859), p. 8.
61. Eye witness, *God's Work in the Chief Towns of Scotland*, p. 10.
62. Anon, *Times of Refreshing*, p. 18.
63. J. Stark, *The Lights of the North* (Aberdeen, 1896), p. 309.
64. J. Radcliffe, *Recollections of Reginald Radcliffe* (London, nd), p. 54.
65. *T.R.*, Vol 1, No 17, (19 November 1859), p. 133.
66. Matthews, *Reminiscences*, p. 113.
67. *A.F.P.*, (12 October 1860), p. 6.
68. Ibid., (25 May 1861), p. 5.
69. C. J. Marrs, 'The 1859 Religious Revival in Scotland: A Review and Critique of the Movement with Particular Reference to the City of Glasgow', unpublished PhD thesis, University of Glasgow, 1995, pp. 213-322.
70. An Intelligent Emigrant at Philadelphia, *A Letter on the Present State of the Labouring Classes in America* (Bury, 1827) quoted by E. P. Thompson, 'Time, Work Discipline and Industrial Capitalism', *Past and Present*, 38, (1967), p. 85.
71. W. H. Fraser, *The Coming of the Mass Market 1850-1914* (London, 1981), p. 18.
72. E. J. Evans, *The Forging of the Modern State: Early Industrial Britain 1783-1870* (London, 1983), pp. 228-32.
73. Thompson, 'Time, Work Discipline and Industrial Capitalism', p. 56.
74. A. S. Cook, *Pen Sketches* (Aberdeen, 1901), p. 232.
75. D. Brailsford, *Sport, Time and Society: The British at Play* (London, 1991), p. 65.
76. W. Skene, *East Neuk Chronicles* (Aberdeen, 1905), p. 16.
77. W. Carnie, *Reporting Reminiscences: Volume One* (Aberdeen, 1902), pp. 34-5.
78. Ibid., p. 145.
79. Skene, *East Neuk*, pp. 16-22.
80. Fraser, *Coming of Mass Market*, pp. 208, 214.
81. *Aberdeen Almanac 1860* (Aberdeen, 1860), p. 241.
82. *Northern Temperance Record* (Aberdeen, 1841), np.
83. Carnie, *Reporting Reminiscences*, pp. 325-6.
84. South Free Church Kirk Session Minutes, 9 February 1860
85. Belmont Street United Presbyterian Church Kirk Session Minutes, 5 October 1861
86. *A.F.P.*, (13 April 1860), p. 6.
87. Ibid., (29 July 1859), p. 6.
88. Ibid., (13 January 1860), p. 6.
89. *B.J.*, (18 October 1859), p. 5.
90. *S.J.*, (28 July 1860), p. 3.
91. *P.S.*, (24 August 1860), p. 3.
92. Omicron, *Five Letters on the Religious Movement in Aberdeen: with an Appendix on the Nature, Probability and Necessity of a Religious Revival* (Aberdeen, 1859), p. 4.
93. *A.J.*, (2 February 1859), p. 3.
94. Omicron, *Five Letters*, p. 6.

95. *N.C.J.M.*, Vol 5, No 8, (2 August 1858), p. 201.
96. *B.Mr.*, No 74, (April 1859), p. 223.
97. *T.R.*, Vol 1, No 1, (30 July 1859), p. 6.
98. Radcliffe, *Recollections*, pp. 47, 53.
99. *A.F.P.*, (1 April 1859), p. 5.
100. *Sixth Annual Report of the Aberdeen Young Men's Christian Association* (Aberdeen, 1864), p. 5.
101. Eye witness, *God's work in the chief towns of Scotland*, p. 16.
102. Radcliffe, *Recollections*, p. 41.
103. R. Carwardine, *Transatlantic Revivalism: Popular Evangelicalism in Britain and America, 1790-1865* (Westport, Connecticut, 1978), p. 8.
104. *T.R.*, Vol 9, No 221, (15 October 1863), pp. 241-2.
105. *Evidence on the Subject of Revivals taken before a committee of the Presbytery of Aberdeen* (Aberdeen, 1841), pp. 5-7.
106. *A.H.*, (30 July 1859), p. 5.
107. Ibid., (16 June 1860), p. 6.
108. H. MacGill, *On the Present Revival of Religion in Scotland A paper read at the Annual Conference of the Evangelical Alliance in October 1860 at Nottingham* (London, 1860), p. 6.
109. Matthews, *Reminiscences*, p. 109.
110. Radcliffe, *Recollections*, p. 47.
111. *B.Mr.*, No 75, (May 1859), p. 230.
112. Anon, *Times of Refreshing*, p. 9.
113. Eye witness, *God's Work in the Chief Towns of Scotland*, p. 12.
114. Matthews, *Reminiscences*, p. 108.
115. Ibid.
116. *B.E.*, Vol 2, No 2, (February 1859), p. 41.
117. *Fourth Annual Report of the Aberdeen Young Men's Christian Association* (Aberdeen, 1862), np.
118. Ibid.
119. *First Annual Report of the Aberdeen Young Men's Christian Association* (Aberdeen, 1859), np.
120. C. Binfield, *George Williams and the YMCA: A Study in Victorian Social Attitudes* (London, 1973), pp. 17-21.
121. Matthews, *Reminiscences*, p. 52.
122. *B.Mr.*, No 70, (December 1858), p. 191.
123. A. Gammie, *The Churches of Aberdeen: Historical and Descriptive* (Aberdeen, 1909), pp. 363-70.
124. *T.R.*, Vol 3, No 59, (8 September 1860), p. 78.
125. Omicron, *Five letters*, p. 10.
126. Ibid., p. 11.
127. *A.H.*, (19 February 1859), p. 5.
128. Matthews, *Reminiscences*, p. 46.
129. Anon, *Times of Refreshing*, p. 44.
130. Ibid., p. 27
131. Radcliffe, *Recollections*, pp. 39, 44.
132. Ibid., p. 47.
133. Greyfriars Parish Church Kirk Session Minutes, 9 July 1859

134. M. Bonar, (ed.) *Andrew A. Bonar, DD.: Diary and Letters* (London, 1893), pp. 202-3.
135. Radcliffe, *Recollections*, p. 40.
136. Ibid., p. 63.
137. Anon, *Times of Refreshing*, p. 21.
138. *A.J.*, (22 August 1860), p. 8.
139. Omicron, *Five Letters*, p. 39.
140. A. L. Drummond, J. Bulloch, *The Church in Victorian Scotland 1843-1874* (Edinburgh, 1975), p. 187.
141. Matthews, *Reminiscences*, p. 90.
142. Stark, *Lights of the North*, p. 313.
143. Omicron, *Five Letters*, pp. 45-6.

CHAPTER 4

The Revival in Aberdeen

Analysis and Results

An important feature of modern religious movements as they appeared in America during the nineteenth century was the use of aggressive techniques that served to attract men. Female converts tended to outnumber males by about three to two. Nevertheless, these techniques led to an increase in the number of men attending religious services and served to redress the gender imbalance within the American churches.[1] Kathryn Long, in the most recent study of the American awakening that acted as the catalyst of the Aberdeen movement, has revealed that although men accounted for around forty per cent of the converts, this was principally a laymen's revival that led to a noteworthy rise of male piety within southern Evangelicalism.[2] The daughter of the American movement, the Aberdeen revival, was characterised by several features that suggest it was a modern religious movement. Hence, it is worthwhile to consider whether it attracted a large number of men and if it led to a shift in the gender balance of Aberdeen churches. Accordingly the composition of those who joined the city's congregations at the height of the revival will be examined in order to assess what section of society it affected most.

A feature of the movement in Aberdeen was the use of targeting. Special events were organised for certain groups of people, according to their occupation and lifestyle. Reginald Radcliffe, one of the main evangelists of the revival, described midnight meetings held for prostitutes. He also mentioned gatherings that were particularly suited to Sabbath School teachers and a weekly Saturday service that was for students.[3] The *Aberdeen Herald* published the following advertisement which demonstrates how the organisers of the revival planned special meetings for particular groups of people. It announced

> Open-air Meeting for WORKING MEN. A meeting will (D.V) be held on the Links of Aberdeen, on Saturday the 10th inst. (Today), at five o'clock.
>
> A MEETING for CHILDREN will be held in the Free South

Church, and, if necessary, in the East and West Churches on Wednesday evening, at half-past six o'clock.

It is hoped that a SPECIAL MEETING, for men exclusively will be held on Thursday evening, at eight o'clock, in St Nicholas Lane U. P. Church.

A MEETING for SAILORS, and those connected with the Shipping and Trade about the Harbour, will be held on Wednesday evening, at seven o'clock, at Weigh-House Square, or, in case of rain, in Free Union Church.[4]

At these gatherings, evangelists delivered addresses that were intended to have a certain psychological appeal for their specific audiences. According to the evangelist, Grattan Guinness, 'hymns of a certain character' were used that sought to evoke a response from those who were present.[5] In particular, the YMCA, which organised most of the meetings of the movement, worked towards the conversion of their peers, other young men engaged in business. Hence it is important to seek to identify those who were converted during the 1859 revival in order to discover whether the organisers were successful in their targeting of young men.

Notwithstanding the large amount of anecdotal evidence that describes the types of people affected by this movement, an exact study of the revival converts could be made only by undertaking a thorough examination of the records of Aberdeen churches for the period. There were fifty four places of religious worship in the city in 1859. This included seventeen congregations of the Free Church, eleven Parish Churches, five United Presbyterian Churches, four Congregational Chapels, three Baptist Chapels, two English and two Scottish Episcopal Churches, two Roman Catholic Chapels, a Methodist and an Evangelical Union Church, two mission churches at Gallowgate and Northfield, as well as several smaller independent religious groups that included the Unitarians, the Friends, the Glassites and a United Christian Church.[6] Documents belonging to the period of the revival were found for fourteen Free Churches, six Established Churches, two United Presbyterian Churches, two English Episcopal Chapels, a Congregational Chapel, a Baptist Chapel, and the Evangelical Union Church. However, the nature and detail of these records varies enormously. Detailed communion rolls and membership lists, which afford the greatest opportunity for useful analysis, were found for Holburn and Woodside Parishes Churches, Newhills and South Free Church, St Nicholas Lane United Presbyterian Church, George Street Congregational Chapel, St Paul Street Evangelical Union Church and Union Terrace Baptist Chapel. From these eight sources it was possible to identify 561 people who became members of these churches upon their first profession of faith during the period of the revival. They form the constituency of the examination.

I

The first observation that can be made from the church records that were examined is that a large proportion of the Aberdeen congregations appear to have been unaffected by this religious movement. The revival was not experienced in a universal manner across the city's churches. Indeed, throughout Scotland it was reported how

> a large proportion of the church going community has been outside this great work . . . many have scarcely wished it otherwise . . . the great proportion of our settled well to do congregations have been on the whole unmoved . . . so far from wishing a revival of God's work, many churchgoers have done their utmost to quench the first appearance of religious earnestness in their own homes.[7]

In May 1859 the *British Evangelist* reported from Aberdeen that 'out of about fifty four churches and chapels which the city and its suburbs contain, the doors of about eighteen have been thrown open to them, and five of these belong to the National Church'.[8] Therefore, it may be assumed that approximately one third of the congregations in the area were influenced by the revival. Seventeen of these churches have been successfully identified. They include Greyfriars, Holburn, John Knox and Woodside Parish Churches, the Bon Accord, East, Holburn, Newhills, North, South and West Free Churches, Belmont Street and St Nicholas Lane United Presbyterian Churches, Albion Street and George Street Congregational Churches, St Paul's Evangelical Union Church and Union Terrace Baptist Church.[9] It is noteworthy, given the often contradictory and doubtful nature of the Established Church's attitude towards the revival, particularly in Aberdeen, that five from eleven of the parish congregations in the city supported the movement. Also, in spite of the general impression that the Free Church championed the movement wholeheartedly, it is important to acknowledge that only seven out of seventeen of its congregations joined enthusiastically in the revival. Proportionally it appears that the smaller denominations, including the United Presbyterians, Congregationalists, Baptists and Evangelical Union Church, were more involved in the movement. Nevertheless, the first principal finding to be made from the church records that were examined is that only a third of Aberdeen's churches participated actively in the revival. This movement did not receive widespread support in the city.

There were certain churches, that included the independent and

Evangelical English Episcopal chapels, which might have been expected to be associated with the movement but were not. It appears that the congregation of St Paul's may have practised their religion more devoutly during the revival without having become directly involved with it. Although the two relevant documents of the church, a Minute Book and a series of annual addresses by the minister, Fred W. B. Bouverie, contain no direct reference to the revival, the latter did indicate that in 1858, when the congregation celebrated the Eucharist nine times each year, the average attendance at these services was only sixty seven. However, in 1859 when it was decided to administer the sacrament eighteen times a year, the average number of those who communicated rose to ninety three, before falling slightly to ninety one in 1860.[10] Clearly this at least demonstrates an increased attention to religious matters in this church which was probably aroused by the revival. However, St James, the other English Episcopal Church in Aberdeen, does not appear to have been affected by the revival, despite the evangelical nature of the congregation that is suggested from letters written when it was seeking to appoint a new minister. John Crombie, the Church's secretary, was anxious to inform prospective incumbents that 'what . . . [the congregation] need is the preaching of Christ as the lone way of salvation'. Indeed, he went on to comment that 'the congregation is not Tractarian, but the reverse'.[11] Nonetheless, in 1858 he was able to tell inquiring ministers that 'there are 600 sittings in St James Church of which 250 are at present let'.[12] Three years later, when the church became vacant again, and after the revival had affected Aberdeen he reported, 'there are about 500 sittings in St James Church, of which nearly 250 are at present let'.[13] Thus it seems that St James may have decreased in numerical strength through the period of the revival. Accordingly it seems that the Episcopalians in Aberdeen remained largely unaffected by this movement.

Perhaps more surprisingly, the Methodists did not become involved in the revival. At present records are not known to exist that reveal the history of their chapel at the time of the movement, but no references have been found within the local newspapers or other primary sources that suggest the Methodists participated in the movement. Rather, D. Wilson, an Aberdeen Methodist, writing in 1850, lamented the state and prospects of the denomination he represented within the city. He wrote '[Methodism's] future prospects are still more discouraging from the extraordinary decrease of male members, especially among the intelligent and useful class, as well as of the children of Methodists, which has taken place during the last twelve years.'[14] Moreover, women outnumbered men within the Church by four to one, 'a disparity' Wilson suggested, 'which effectively strikes at the hope of future stability or progress'.[15] He did not believe that the Arminian doctrinal basis of Methodism was the cause of its lack of success in Scotland, especially during this period, when he said, 'a great evangelical change has taken place in the Established and other churches; while within the last twelve years, a still greater change has taken place on the religious mind of this country'.[16] Alexander Gammie, author of a study on the churches of Aberdeen published in 1909, concluded his analysis of the Methodists in Aberdeen by saying, 'Methodism has never been numerically strong in Aberdeen ... since the Disruption of '43, the sympathies of Scotsmen of evangelical tendencies have turned more surely than ever towards one or other of their native denominations, and thus Methodism has lost many it might otherwise have gained.'[17] Indeed, although other denominations experienced increases in membership during this period, the membership of the Methodist Church in Aberdeen decreased steadily during the greater part of the nineteenth century. From having 370 members in 1819, the church roll fell to 318 by 1836, and declined further to 181 by 1867 and finally to 113 when the congregation moved from their Longacre chapel to Crown Terrace in 1873.[18] These statistics indicate that the Methodists were a dwindling presence in Aberdeen in the nineteenth century, and that they were, in all likelihood, unaffected by this revival.

Nevertheless, there remain eighteen churches which were influenced by this religious movement. Firstly the revival created an important impression within the Established Church. Between 1856 and 1863 Greyfriars Parish Church was clearly stirred by the movement. This congregation, which at the height of the movement was obliged to have seven services each Sunday, almost doubled its number of members within two years, from 103 in 1857 to 194 in 1859.

Table 4.1.

Greyfriars Parish Church: Communion rolls 1855-1864

Year	C' cants	Increase /Decrease
1856	141	
1857	103	-38
1858	137	+34
1859	194	+57
1860	179	-15
1861	183	+4
1862	165	-18
1863	159	-6

Source: Greyfriars Parish Church Communion Rolls 1848-1864

The congregation of Holburn Parish Church was also affected by the revival. The communion roll book of this church for the years 1859-1861 lists twenty five young communicants, new members who were admitted upon the first profession of their faith, the majority of whom joined in 1861.

Table 4.2.

Holburn Parish Church: Young communicants 1859-1861

Year	Male	Female	Total	Annual Total
April 1859	0	0	0	
Oct 1859	1	1	2	2
April 1860	0	0	0	
Oct 1860	1	1	2	2
April 1861	4	8	12	
Oct 1861	5	4	9	21

Source: Holburn Parish Church Communion Rolls 1859-1861

Woodside Parish Church, located just beyond the boundaries of the city in a suburb of manufacturing mills, was another Established Church clearly affected by the revival. The table below reveals how between October 1859 and October 1861 156 people joined the church upon their first profession of faith, while, during the same length of period, between April 1862 and April 1864, only eighty eight people were admitted to the congregation.

Table 4.3.

Woodside Parish Church: Young communicants 1859-1864

Year	Male	Female	Total	Annual Total
Oct 1859	10	12	22	
April 1860	15	23	38	
Oct 1860	20	5	25	63
April 1861	13	18	31	
Oct 1861	20	20	40	71
April 1862	6	9	15	
Oct 1862	7	9	16	31
April 1863	13	11	24	
Oct 1863	4	7	11	35
April 1864	10	12	22	

Source: Woodside Parish Church Communion Rolls 1859-1868

Therefore, in spite of the somewhat lukewarm, and at times ambivalent, attitude which the Aberdeen Established Presbytery displayed towards the revival, these records demonstrate how at least three parish churches were affected by this awakening.

The Free Church was popularly considered as the chief protagonist of the city movement. The *Aberdeen Herald*, for example, complained bitterly in July 1859 about how this denomination seemed 'to have appropriated to itself the exclusive task of converting the heathen and ungodly portion of our community; they invite no congregations to aid them, neither do they seem to wish any other sect to take part in the good work'.[19] Notwithstanding this criticism, the Free Church was the largest single denomination represented among those that supported the awakening. The Free West Church experienced growth through the revival. Between 1858 and 1862 there were on average eleven new members added at each communion season, but at the October 1860 celebration of the sacrament, when the revival was at its height, twenty one people joined the church.[20] The church's historian, J. Ogilvie Skea, is in no doubt that the revival 'had a profound influence on the members of the Free West' and he cites, as evidence, the increased giving of the congregation at this time.[21] Also it was recognised that 'no church in the city was so greatly blessed as the Free North Church'.[22] According to Gammie, 'in the revival movement, which stirred Aberdeen in the early 1860s, Mr [George] Campbell stood in the forefront, and the Free North became for the time the recognised evangelical centre for the whole city.. [as] crowds thronged to the church . . . the membership increased until the accommodation was quite insufficient'.[23] This congregation welcomed the movement and experienced its dramatic effect.

The Free South Church also embraced and benefited from the

revival. The kirk session of this congregation minuted that 'a greater than usual interest in Divine things was apparent and a good number, especially among the young, appeared to be in a hopeful state'.[24] This 'greater than usual interest' was manifested in a rise in the number of new communicants who joined the church at this time, which almost doubled at the height of the movement.

Table 4.4.

Free South Church: Young communicants 1857-1863

Year	Male	Female	Total	Annual Total
Mar 57	6	13	19	
Sep 57	7	7	14	33
Mar 58	10	14	24	
Sep 58	5	9	14	38
Mar 59	8	24	32	
Sep 59	13	19	32	64
Mar 60	14	13	27	
Sep 60	2	12	14	41
Mar 61	7	13	20	
Sep 61	6	15	21	41
Mar 62	8	17	25	
Oct 62	7	12	19	44
Mar 63	8	10	18	
Oct 63	3	2	5	23

Source: South Free Kirk Session Minutes 1855-71

Newhills Free Church, located just beyond the boundaries of the town, was widely acclaimed as another centre of the religious movement. On 15 November 1859 'the session agreed to record their thankfulness to the God of all grace for a marked and growing interest in eternal things over the part of a considerable number of the people'.[25] In 1860 twenty one young communicants were added to the church's roll, which was around twice the usual number.

Table 4.5.

Newhills Free Church: Young communicants 1858-1862

Year	Male	Female	Total	Annual Total
July 1858	3	1	4	
Dec 1858	2	3	5	9
July 1859	5	2	7	
Dec 1859	0	4	4	11
July 1860	4	5	9	
Dec 1860	4	8	12	21
July 1861	2	6	8	
Dec 1861	0	5	5	13
July 1862	3	2	5	
Dec 1862	2	0	2	7

Source: Newhills Free Church Communion Rolls 1852-1860
Newhills Free Church Kirk Session Minutes 1844-1878

Although approximately only two fifths of Aberdeen's Free Churches embraced the revival, the members of this denomination emerged as the chief supporters of the movement.

Beyond the two larger denominations, the revival flourished among the other churches in Aberdeen. The Managers' Minutes of St Nicholas Lane United Presbyterian Church contain a list of members admitted to its fellowship by profession of faith for the first time. This church grew significantly through the period of the revival, with membership increasing threefold between 1860 and 1862.

Table 4.6.

St Nicholas Lane United Presbyterian Church: Young communicants 1857-1864

Year	Male	Female	Annual Total
1857	4	3	7
1858	3	4	7
1859	5	5	10
1860	17	26	43
1861	13	8	21
1862	18	12	30
1863	8	8	16
1864	8	3	11

Source: St Nicholas Lane United Presbyterian Church Kirk Session Minutes 1842-1865

The Albion Street Congregational Church was one of the leading pioneers of this religious movement. James Wilson, its minister until 1859, was a founder of the union prayer meeting.[26] It was at the forefront of the evangelistic crusades held during the autumn of 1858 and it provided the hall wherein the revival began when Radcliffe addressed a group of children. Built in 1849, enlarged in 1854, the church was altered again in 1862 when a gallery was erected to accommodate the growing crowds that attended its services.[27] The George Street Congregational Church also prospered during the revival. The Minute Book of the Church Meetings revealed that the number of new members welcomed at this time upon their first profession of faith in this congregation increased by a third between 1859 and 1862.

Table 4.7.

George Street Congregational Church: New members 1857-62

Year	Male	Female	Annual Total
1857	8	9	17
1858	7	9	16
1859	9	12	21
1860	14	21	35
1861	14	14	28
1862	10	19	29

Source: George Street Congregational Church Minute Book of Church Meetings 1797-1862

In addition, Aberdeen's Evangelical Union Church, which met at St Paul Street, appears to have benefited from the revival. The Communicants' Roll Book of this congregation revealed a large increase in the number of people who joined the church upon their first profession of faith during the period of the movement. Thirty four men and women became members in 1859, which was twice the number that were admitted the previous year.

Table 4.8.

St Paul Street Evangelical Union Church: New members 1855-62

Year	Male	Female	Annual Total
1855	4	7	11
1856	3	4	7
1857	6	15	21
1858	8	9	17
1859	10	24	34
1860	6	12	18
1861	5	7	12
1862	2	6	8

Source: St Paul Street Evangelical Union Church Communicants Roll Book 1846-1872

Finally, despite Allan MacLaren's judgment that the Baptists were a 'dwindling force' in Aberdeen around the middle of the century, the membership lists of the Union Terrace congregation's Minute Book, appear to indicate that this fellowship grew at an above average rate through the time of the revival.[28] The number of those who were admitted to the congregation by baptism increased from one in 1857 to thirteen in 1859 and eighteen in 1861.

Table 4.9.

Union Terrace Baptist Church: New Members 1857-1863

Year	Male	Female	Annual Total
1857	-	1	1
1858	7	6	13
1859	7	6	13
1860	2	3	5
1861	10	8	18
1862	3	2	5
1863	1	-	1

Source: Union Terrace Baptist Church Minute Book 1821-1868

Although the revival did not affect every congregation in Aberdeen, examination of communicants' roll books and kirk session minutes show clearly how it heralded an increase in the growth of a number of the city's churches that belonged to a variety of the main denominations.

It is noteworthy that a number of these congregations shared at least two common characteristics. In the first instance, twelve of the seventeen revival churches identified were less than thirty years old in 1859. The seven Free Churches were established in 1843, St Paul's Evangelical Union Church emerged in 1846, and the Albion Street Congregational Chapel, where the revival began, was formed in 1848.[29] It is particularly significant that three of the five Established Churches that embraced the revival, Woodside, John Knox and Holburn were built as Chapels of Ease in 1830, 1835 and 1836 respectively, and that the movement did not affect any of the older, traditional parish churches, apart from Greyfriars.[30] Clearly the revival flourished among young congregations.

Secondly, the greater proportion of the ministers of these churches were young men and many of them were in their first charge. John Duncan, who succeeded James Wilson as minister of Albion Street Congregational Church in 1859, was thirty two years old.[31] William Keay was thirty one years old when he was ordained as minister of Woodside Parish Church in August 1859.[32] Meanwhile, John Milne, minister of Holburn Parish Church, was thirty nine years old when the revival began.[33] Charles Ross was thirty three years of age at the time of the movement and had been minister of Bon Accord Free Church since 1854.[34] George Campbell, ordained into the charge of the Free North Church in 1859, was born in 1833.[35]

John Adam was born in 1818 and inducted into the Free South Church in 1849, while James Macphail was thirty nine years old in 1859 and had been minister of the Free East Church since his ordination ten years previously.[36] Finally John Craven was born in 1817 and received the charge of Newhills Free Church in 1847.[37] Hence eight of the ministers who championed the revival and have been successfully identified were between thirty one and forty two years old when the movement began. They were all within their first charge and had less than twelve years' experience of parish ministry. Indeed three of them had been ordained for less than a year when the movement began. This suggests strongly that the revival prospered under the leadership of young men who entered the ministry after the struggles of the Disruption years and who had been educated from the late 1840s when urban mission was becoming increasingly important in the life of the church.[38]

II

Nevertheless, it remains more significant to ascertain the nature of the church growth and to examine the composition of the people who joined these congregations at the height of the revival. Then it will be possible to determine whether the targeting of the revivalists was successful and if this movement affected a disproportionate number of young men. There are a number of studies to be made of the people who joined the Aberdeen churches at the height of the revival. Firstly, it is necessary to consider whether they were preceded into church membership by another member of their family. This will tend to suggest the nature of the influences that were operating upon them at this time. W. B. Sprague, in his *Lectures on Revivals* published in 1832 which reflected upon traditional religious movements, commented, 'if it be asked, whence come the greatest number of the subjects of our revivals, we answer, from our Sabbath schools, and Bible classes, and from families in which the parental influence is decidedly religious'.[39] Long-established religious movements operated most successfully through the network of family relationships. Hence if a large proportion of Aberdeen's new church members followed a mother or a father into church membership, this would imply that the revival operated in a traditional manner. By contrast, if a considerable number joined a congregation without having been preceded by another family member, this would indicate that the revival had successfully targeted and attracted the irreligious who had no previous church connection. Given the nature of the communion rolls and membership lists used to identify the new church members it was possible to analyse the religious backgrounds of only those who joined Holburn and Woodside Parish Churches.

Table 4.10.

Holburn Parish Church: The religious background of young communicants in 1861

	Total	Percentage
Preceded	5	24 %
Unpreceded	13	62 %
Unknown	3	14 %

Source: Holburn Parish Church Communion Rolls 1859-1861

Table 4.11.

Woodside Parish Church: The religious background of young communicants between 1859 and 1861

	Total	Percentage
Preceded	10	17 %
Unpreceded	24	41.5 %
Unknown	24	41.5 %

Source: Woodside Parish Church Communion Rolls 1859-1868

Notwithstanding the third of young communicants from Holburn and Woodside Parish Churches whose religious background is unknown, the statistics demonstrate that the majority of those who joined these congregations at the height of the revival did not follow a father or a mother into the fellowship. Among those whose religious background is known, more than two thirds became new church members without the influence of another family member. This suggests that the impulses of this revival were operating outwith the accustomed channels, and that converts had been successfully targeted by the leaders of this movement.

The geographical distribution of the revival converts will also be considered in an attempt to discover whether this movement affected particular areas of the city of Aberdeen, which will in turn suggest which class was especially touched by the movement. (See Map 4.1., on p.88 based upon a copy of the *Keith and Gibbs Map of the Cities of Aberdeen*, published in 1862.) The parish boundaries have been identified because they help to determine the social composition of various parts of the city. Generally the West parish was the most wealthy, followed by the South and the East. St Clement's parish, 'within the city but apart from it', was made up predominantly of fisherfolk and seafarers, while the North and lower part of

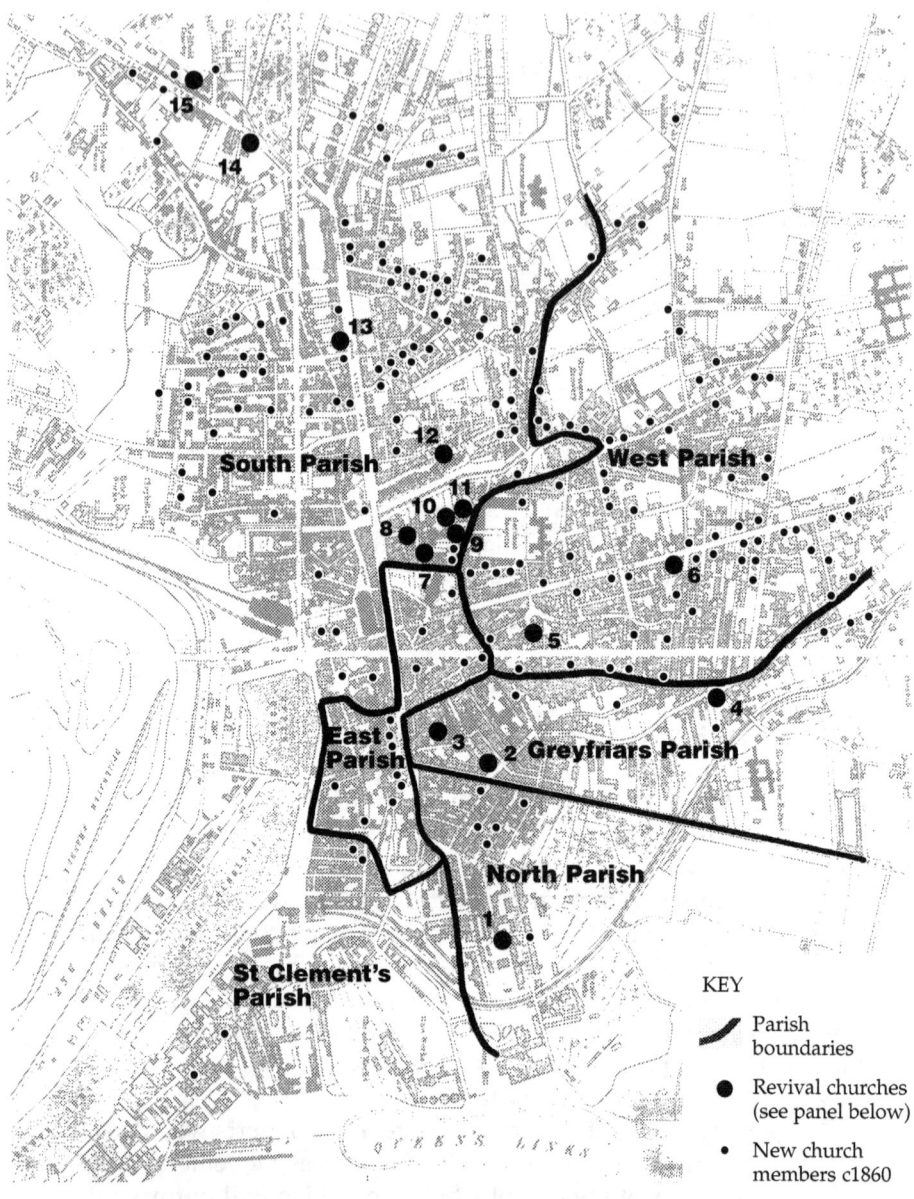

REVIVAL CHURCHES

1. Albion Street Congregational Church
2. Free North Church
3. Greyfriars Parish Church
4. John Knox Parish Church
5. St Paul's Evangelical Church
6. George Street Congregational Church
7. St Nicholas Lane United Presbyterian Church
8. Belmont Street United Presbyterian Church
9. Free East Church
10. Free West Church
11. Free South Church
12. Union Terrace Baptist Church
13. Bon Accord Free Church
14. Holburn Parish Church
15. Holburn Free Church

Map 4.1. The Aberdeen churches that embraced the revival and the homes of some of those who joined these congregations at the height of the religious movement

Greyfriars parish, within which the most densely populated working-class slum areas of the city existed, were the poorest. The area between the Gallowgate and King Street was widely recognised as the most destitute part of Aberdeen.[40] Indeed after the Disruption those who withdrew from the Established Church deserted this part of the town and erected the new Greyfriars Free Church in the more fashionable Crown Street.[41] Captain Shepherd of Kirkville, Skene, criticised 'their own ambition [which] drove them to the west end among the gentry'.[42] Within the South parish lay the suburbs of Gilcomston and Holburn that were inhabited by 'small communities of working people . . . [who] had found the rents and taxes lower than in the city'.[43] This district of Aberdeen became a haven for skilled artisans, such as shoemakers and tailors. Indicated on the map are the seventeen churches which have been identified as those which participated in the religious movement. Also the location of the homes of the new church members shown on the map provide an important indicator of the social composition of those who were most likely affected by the revival.

The distribution of these people reveals a division in the city between two distinct areas, but a comment is required before immediate observations lead to presumptuous judgments. The Greyfriars Parish and the Free North Churches, which lay within the poorest part of Aberdeen, were widely recognised as those affected most significantly by this movement. There are no records in existence that can determine the increase in the membership of the North Church, but it has been discovered that the number of communicant members of Greyfriars rose by fifty seven in 1859. However it was not possible to locate where these people lived because their names but not their addresses appeared in the church's list of members. It cannot be assumed that those who joined these churches lived within their parishes. Indeed, given the random distribution, displayed on the map, of those who joined the other congregations, it may be likely that a considerable proportion lived elsewhere in Aberdeen and that Greyfriars and the Free North attracted a gathered congregation from a wide area. Certainly their location within the poorest district of the city does not necessarily mean that the revival flourished among the lower orders of society. The map also reveals that none of the new members of the other churches lived in the poorest district of Aberdeen between Gallowgate and King Street, and that only a few resided in the North and St Clement's parish. Clearly the city was divided in two. Less than ten per cent of those identified as new church members were located in the three poorer parishes, while forty four per cent were found within the West Parish and thirty eight per cent in the South Parish, areas that were generally regarded as the wealthier parts of the town. There are no other discernible patterns of distribution as the people appear to have been scattered randomly across the city. Therefore the map suggests that this movement did not affect the poorest areas of this urban community. It appears rather to have prospered among the skilled working and the middle classes. However, this proposition requires confirmation from a more detailed analysis of the class composition of the new church members.

Accordingly an analysis of the occupations of those who joined the Aberdeen churches during the revival is required in order to ascertain which social class was most affected by this movement. Several historians have argued that the working classes were alienated from the churches in the nineteenth century. In particular, MacLaren has suggested that the Aberdeen Free Churches failed to attract working-class members. Rather he says it 'increasingly became a Church catering for the prosperous middle classes'.[44] Indeed he goes on to assert that 'there was a general recognition [during the mid nineteenth century] that it was the working class who were not the regular attenders', the cause of which he explains as 'the class conscious nature of the Presbyterian churches'.[45] More recently however, Callum Brown, P. L. M. Hillis and Linda Jeffrey have revealed that working people were attracted to the Scottish churches during the nineteenth century. They have found that the skilled working class was consistently the largest single social group in churches in Glasgow and Stirling.[46] Hence the social composition of the Aberdeen revival converts is of particular interest.

Scholars have sought also to discover the class composition of converts of other religious movements. T. C. Smout has made a detailed analysis of the occupations of those who were affected by the Cambuslang revival of 1742, using the records that were made by William M'Culloch, the parish minister. Cambuslang, which lay on the outskirts of Glasgow, developed quickly from a small, rural hamlet into a bustling weaving centre in the 1730s so that by the time of the revival almost half of the inhabitants of the parish were employed in the cloth industry.[47] Although it is anachronistic to use nineteenth century terms to describe those who lived and worked one hundred years previously, it was decided to judge the Cambuslang converts using the social classification created by Hillis. This revealed that five per cent were drawn from the upper middle classes and that eight per cent were from the lower middle classes. Thus about an eighth of the converts were members of the middling orders. Furthermore, forty six per cent of those affected were skilled artisans and forty per cent were from the unskilled working class. Only a fifth of those from the unskilled workers, that is eight per cent of the total affected, were men. These statistics show that the Cambuslang revival produced its chief effect among the working classes. However, the number of artisans was greater than that of the unskilled working people, and men were noticeably poorly represented among the latter group.[48] Marguerite Van Die, in her study of the Brantford revivals in Ontario during the 1870s and 1880s, found similar trends among the male Methodist converts. In 1875 only nine per cent, and in 1882 a mere eleven per cent, of those affected by these awakenings were labourers or unskilled workers.[49] It is noteworthy that although these revivals produced their main effect among the working classes, unskilled men were conspicuously under-represented among the converts of these movements.

The criterion for measuring the social class of the men and women affected by the Aberdeen revival was their occupation. The classification system used was that devised by Hillis in his examination of nineteenth-century Glasgow churches, and amended by Jeffrey in her study of Stirling churches in the same period. (See Appendix 2) The class of women was determined according to the occupation of their husbands if they were married, and of their fathers if they were unmarried. Particular care was taken over the categorisation of female domestic servants who accounted for a significant proportion, eighteen per cent, of the new church members. Jeffrey, in her analysis of the role of women in the churches of Stirling in the nineteenth century, estimated that approximately twenty per cent of female domestic servants were skilled, while the remaining eighty per cent were unskilled.[50] The same proportion was found upon an examination of domestic servants in Aberdeen. Thus the ratio of 1:4 of skilled and unskilled was used for the classification of female domestic servants. Using this criterion, the class composition of 188 new church members, who were successfully identified in the 1861 city census, was established and examined.

Table 4.12.

The class composition of 188 people who joined Aberdeen churches at the height of the revival

Status	N' hills	South	W' side	H' burn	Un Pres	Cong	Ev Un	Bapt
MC (H)								
Male	2	1	0	0	0	3	0	0
Female	0	1	0	1	1	5	0	0
MC (L)								
Male	0	3	0	1	2	2	2	1
Female	0	3	0	0	3	2	4	0
WCA								
Male	5	10	2	2	3	15	13	5
Female	0	6	0	1	4	9	6	1
WCU								
Male	0	0	5	2	1	1	1	1
Female	7	0	1	1	1	4	8	1
WCD (Female)	2	8	3	3	5	10	4	1

Sources: Holburn Parish Church Communion Rolls 1859-1861
Woodside Parish Church Communion Rolls 1859-1868
Newhills Free Church Communion Rolls 1852-1860
South Free Church Kirk Session Minutes 1855-1871
St Nicholas Lane U P Church Kirk Session Minutes 1842-1865
George Street Congregational Church Minute Book of Church Meetings 1797-1862
St Paul Street Evangelical Union Church Communicants Roll Book 1846-1872
Union Terrace Baptist Church Minute Book 1821-68
1861 Census, Aberdeen, Aberdeenshire

Key: MC (H): Upper Middle Class
MC (L): Lower Middle Class
WCA: Skilled Working Class
WCU: Unskilled Working Class
WCD: Female Domestic Servants

Table 4.13.

The distribution of new church members in each congregation according to class

Status	N' hills	South	W' side	H' burn	Un Pres	Cong	Ev Un	Bapt
MC (H)	12 %	6 %	0 %	9 %	5 %	16 %	0 %	0 %
MC (L)	0 %	19 %	0 %	9 %	25 %	8 %	16 %	10 %
WCA	32 %	56 %	27 %	36 %	40 %	51 %	53 %	60 %
WCU	56 %	19 %	73 %	46 %	30 %	25 %	31 %	30 %

Notwithstanding the variations among the seven churches of the proportion of new church members whose occupation was identified, there are nevertheless some startling patterns. It is clear that the Free South, United Presbyterian and Congregational churches attracted the largest number of people from the middle classes. Between twenty four and thirty per cent of those who joined these churches were from this section of society. Furthermore these congregations drew a great proportion of their members from the artisan class and had correspondingly fewer people from the unskilled working classes. Indeed less than a fifth of those who joined the Free South Church were from this section of society. The Evangelical Union and Baptist Churches commanded a broader social appeal. About an eighth of their new members were from the middle classes, just over half were artisans and about a third were unskilled working people. Clearly Newhills Free, Holburn and Woodside Parish Churches possessed a greater attraction for working people than any of the other churches. Almost all of their new members were drawn from among this class. In particular, they had a considerable number of unskilled men and women. Between a half and three quarters of those who joined were from among the lowest orders of society. The obvious explanation for the distribution of these people is the location of each of the churches. The Free South, United Presbyterian and Congregationalist Churches were city centre churches which drew members from every social class represented in Aberdeen. Holburn Parish Church was located in a strongly working-class district of the town, while Woodside Parish and Newhills Free Churches were very near to manufacturing mills and factories, from where a large proportion of their new members came. The situation of the eight churches examined exercised an important influence upon the composition of the members they attracted.

The overall distribution of those who joined these churches during the revival according to their occupation is also critical because the statistics provide several insights into the class composition of the converts of the Aberdeen revival of 1859.

Table 4.14.

An analysis of the class composition of the new churchmembers during the Aberdeen revival

Status	Men	Women	% Men	% Women	Total
Middle Class (H)	6	8	3 %	4 %	7 %
Middle Class (L)	10	12	5 %	6 %	11 %
Working Class Skilled	56	34	30 %	18 %	48 %
Working Class Unskilled	11	52	6 %	28 %	34 %

Firstly a substantial proportion came from the higher echelons of society. Altogether just less than one in five were drawn from the middle classes. However, the revival produced its main effect among the working classes. Within this broad community the most interesting observations can be made. The greater proportion, two thirds, of the skilled working-class members were men. Almost seventy per cent of all the men belonged to this class. Indeed they constituted almost a third of all those who joined churches in Aberdeen during this period. Clearly, skilled working-class men were especially sensitive to the appeal of the evangelist in 1859. Unskilled working men appear to have been less affected by this revival. Less than a fifth of the unskilled were men, and only an eighth of all the male new church members belonged to this class. Overall they accounted for only six per cent of the whole sample. Notwithstanding the success of individual churches such as Woodside in attracting these men, in general they appear to have made up a small proportion of the revival converts. An Aberdeen correspondent of *The British Messenger* commented in April 1859 that 'some have said that Mr Radcliffe should have confined himself to the lower classes . . . but I am of opinion that he is doing far more good as he is presently employed'.[51] This suggests that the evangelist concentrated his efforts and became most successful in reaching the male artisans of Aberdeen. However, it appears that he failed to address and win the confidence of the unskilled working men of the city.

Yet almost paradoxically the revival exercised its greatest attraction among the women of the unskilled working class. Almost one third of all who joined the church in the course of this revival belonged to this class. This group was dominated by two particular occupations, domestic servants and mill workers. The former, many of whom originated from the countryside and who made up over forty per cent of the occupied female work force in Aberdeen, constituted fourteen per cent, that is one in seven, of new church members during this movement.[52] The mill workers, on the other hand, most of whom were unmarried, young females in their teens, accounted for ten per cent of the additions to the churches' rolls.[53] They formed a particularly close knit, homogeneous group. W. M. Walker, writing about Dundee's mill girls in the second half of the nineteenth century, described them as 'gang workers' who followed a common style of life.[54] It appears that, once infected with religious enthusiasm, these mills produced a large number of converts. An elder, remembering revival meetings in the Bon Accord Free Church, described 'one peculiarity of these meetings we have never observed in other gatherings of the kind.. It was . . . crowds of young women without bonnets or caps, but with little shawls about their shoulders, which they put on their heads when they left church'.[55] These groups of young women, bound together within a tightly knit community, were foremost among those who were influenced by the movement. It remains that the Aberdeen revival of 1859 exercised a peculiar appeal to certain sections of the city's working classes. The skilled male artisans, the unskilled domestic servants and mill girls were among those who were principally affected by this religious movement.

The marital status of those who were admitted into membership of the Aberdeen churches during the period of the revival is also illuminating. From his studies of the Cambuslang converts, Smout found that sixty of the eighty two people, that is almost three quarters of those whose marital status he could determine, were unmarried. Women accounted for more than ninety per cent of these converts. Indeed overall, unmarried women constituted sixty eight per cent of the total number of people awakened during that revival. Twenty two per cent of the men and women were married, but it was not possible for Smout to ascertain how many of them were couples. A considerable weakness of his analysis was that the marital status of seventy seven per cent of the men was not identified. Nevertheless it remains clear that the Cambuslang revival's greatest influence lay amongst unmarried women.[56] Van Die has commented upon the high proportion of men and women who joined the Brantford churches as married couples during periods of revival. Between 1856 and 1859 thirty three per cent of the Congregational converts, thirty seven per cent of the Methodists, thirty four per cent of the Presbyterians, and twenty six per cent of the Baptists were married couples. It appears that almost a third of these revival converts were husbands and wives. This is a particularly high proportion which reflected the demographic circumstances of this town, when a fifth of its population were aged between twenty and twenty-nine and at a stage in life when marriage commitments were being made.[57] Accordingly there are variations between the marital status of the Cambuslang and the Brantford revival converts. The Scottish eighteenth-century movement affected more unmarried people, while the Canadian nineteenth-century revival was, proportionally, more popular among married couples.

In Aberdeen the marital status of 256 men and women who joined the churches at the height of the revival was discovered. However one particular problem emerged. A gender imbalance arose because the marital status of eighty nine men remains unknown. They could not be found in the census. This suggests they were socially mobile during the period, which would indicate that they were most likely unmarried and young. Their absence from the study is an unfortunate omission and as a consequence women are over-represented in the analysis. Nevertheless, the findings provide a useful insight into the marital status of those affected by the revival.

Table 4.15.

The marital status of 256 people who joined Aberdeen churches at the height of the revival

M/S	W'side	H'burn	South	Un Pres	Cong	Ev Un	Bapt
Marr Couples							
Male	1	2	1	5	9	4	1
Female	1	2	1	5	9	4	1
Marr Individ.							
Male	5	1	1	0	5	4	3
Female	4	0	0	2	10	7	3
Unmarried							
Male	2	3	12	4	7	2	4
Female	12	9	18	11	32	24	15
Widow							
Male	0	0	0	0	1	0	0
Female	3	1	0	2	2	0	1

Sources: Holburn Parish Church Communion Rolls 1859-1861
Woodside Parish Church Communion Rolls 1859-1868
Newhills Free Church Communion Rolls 1852-1860
South Free Church Kirk Session Minutes 1855-1871
St Nicholas Lane U P Church Kirk Session Minutes 1842-1865
George Street Congregational Church Minute Book of Church Meetings 1797-186
St Paul Street Evangelical Union Church Communicants Roll Book 1846-1872
Union Terrace Baptist Church Minute Book 1821-68
1861 Census, Aberdeen, Aberdeenshire

Table 4.16.

The distribution of new church members in each congregation according to their marital status

M/S	W'side	H'burn	South	Un Pres	Cong	Ev Un	Bapt
M C	7 %	22 %	6 %	34 %	24 %	18 %	7 %
M I	32 %	6 %	3 %	7 %	20 %	24 %	21 %
Unm	50 %	66 %	91 %	52 %	52 %	58 %	68 %
W	11 %	6 %	0 %	7 %	4 %	0 %	4 %

Key: M / S: Marital Status
M C: Married Couples
M I: Married Individuals
Unm: Unmarried
W: Widows and Widowers

The churches can be divided into three groups according to the marital status of the new members they attracted during the revival. Firstly the Free South Church emerges distinctly as a congregation which drew a very large number of unmarried people. More than ninety per cent of those who joined this church between 1859 and 1860, and could be successfully identified in the census, were single men and women. Holburn Parish and Union Terrace Baptist Church make up the second group of churches. At least two thirds of their

The Revival in Aberdeen

new members were unmarried, while only twenty eight per cent were married. The remaining four churches had a much greater proportion of married people and fewer single men and women among their new members. This indicates further how each church attracted different types of people. Clearly the Free South was especially popular among young, unmarried people, while the Congregational Church, forty four per cent of whose new members were married, attracted more older people. It is apparent therefore, that the churches appealed to different sections of the community.

The marital status of all those who joined the Aberdeen churches during the revival enables three observations to be made.

Table 4.17.

An analysis of the marital status of new church members during the Aberdeen revival

Marital Status	Men	Women	% Men	% Women	Total
Married Couples	23	23	9 %	9 %	18 %
Married Individ	19	26	8 %	10 %	18 %
Unmarried	34	121	13 %	47 %	60 %
Widow	1	9	.5 %	3.5 %	4 %

It is perhaps unremarkable given the different life expectancy of men and women that nine tenths of those whose spouse had died when they joined the church were female. Nevertheless, this suggests that among older people the revival was more successful among women than men. Also it was found that a large proportion, thirty six per cent, of the new church members were married. Half of them were couples, while the others were single married people. The largest number of new church members were unmarried. Indeed sixty per cent of those who joined the church during the revival were single, and if the marital status of the large company of unidentified men had been discovered it is likely that this figure would have risen even further. Even though at least two thirds of Aberdeen's new communicants during the revival were unmarried, this revival attracted almost twice as many husbands and wives as the Cambuslang movement of 1742, and around the same proportion of married people that were affected in Brantford. This suggests that nineteenth-century religious movements may have affected a greater number of married, and older people.

Hence it is it is necessary to examine the age at which women and men joined these Aberdeen churches at the height of the revival. Several studies have been conducted that have sought to identify the ages at which people were converted during the course of the nineteenth century. M. R. Watts, in his study of 607 people who experienced an evangelical conversion between 1780 and 1850, found that half were 'born again' between the ages of fourteen and twenty, and that three quarters had been 'awakened' before they were twenty six.[58] D. W. Bebbington has studied the conversion accounts of 140 people who became Christians during the period from 1740 to 1850. Ninety one of them were 'born again' in the half century around 1800 and sixty three were recorded as having been converted at a particular age. Twenty two per cent were less than fifteen years old, sixty eight per cent were less than twenty years old, and eighty two per cent were less than twenty five years old when they were awakened.[59] K. D. Brown has examined the age at which 581 nonconformist ministers were converted in the nineteenth century. He found that forty per cent were less than fifteen years old, eighty per cent were less than nineteen years old, and ninety seven per cent were less than twenty five years old when they were 'born again'.[60] Brown also cites the findings of a postgraduate thesis by Clive Field that analysed conversion ages of Wesleyan ministers between 1841 and 1900. Field found that forty five per cent were less than fifteen years of age and that ninety six per cent were less than twenty one years of age when they were awakened.[61] Each of these studies show that a high proportion of those who experienced an Evangelical conversion in the nineteenth century were young people. At least three quarters were less than twenty years of age.

Other scholars have examined the age at which people were converted at the height of various religious movements. T. C. Smout has identified the age of 105 men and women who were affected by the Cambuslang revival. He discovered that twenty two per cent were less than twenty years old and that seventy five per cent were less than thirty years old when they were awakened. He calculated that the mean age of the male and female converts was twenty eight and twenty five years respectively.[62] Watts has discovered that several late eighteenth-century Methodist revivals were experienced largely by young people. At Bala, in 1791 for instance, most of the converts were children and young people, from eight or ten to thirty years of age, and at Hull in 1794 many were believed to be less than fourteen years of age. After a meeting at Armley, the evangelist, John Allen, admitted sixty people to the church's fellowship, fifty of whom, that is eighty three per cent, were under twenty.[63] A minor revival affected Aberdeen towards the end of 1840 during the visit of the evangelist, W. C. Burns. David Mitchell, an advocate, who led a class for some of the converts, gave a detailed account of ten young women whom he taught, and their average age was seventeen.[64] The 1857 American revival, the precursor of the Aberdeen movement, also appears to have affected a large number of young people. In May

1858 *The United Presbyterian Magazine* produced an account of 113 people who were converted and joined the Presbyterian Church on Thirteenth Street, New York. It revealed that fifty six per cent were less than twenty and that ninety per cent were less than thirty years old when they were awakened. It also disclosed that the average age of the converts was just twenty two.[65] This illustrates that between seventy three and ninety per cent of those who were 'born again' during these religious movements in the eighteenth and nineteenth centuries were less than thirty years of age.

Unfortunately a serious and regrettable omission from the survey of the ages of those who joined Aberdeen churches at the height of the 1859 revival is the considerable number of children who were affected by this movement. This revival began among the young people who gathered to hear Radcliffe lead services at the Albion Street Congregational Chapel, and the interest of adults in the awakening was initially aroused by the perceptible religious changes that had overcome their children.[66] Regular revival children's meetings were held in Marywell Street School each Monday and Saturday by Radcliffe. These attracted large crowds of boys, 'upwards of sixty younger lads, ranging from about ten to fourteen years of age, in which the Spirit of God is remarkably manifested'.[67] In a letter written at the beginning of 1859 to Mrs Reginald Radcliffe, the celebrated evangelist, Hay MacDowall Grant of Arndilly, remarked how, 'the conversion work at this time in Aberdeen was largely carried on amongst children from eight to fourteen years of age.'[68] In April the Aberdeen Free Church Synod observed that 'the movement pervades different classes. The young however are principally the subjects of it'.[69] Later during May *The British Messenger* described how 'the greatest number of the awakened and converted are found among children and young men and women'.[70] A young convert of the revival, W. B., recalled 'I would be then thirteen to fourteen years of age. Some of those round me, and under the same influence of grace, were even younger; some were two or three years older. We ranged from twelve to eighteen years of age, and there were a goodly number of us. To my knowledge there were fifty or sixty boys such as myself who all regarded ourselves as converted'.[71] Unfortunately the analysis of revival converts in Aberdeen has been unable to include these children among the new church members because no records have been found which provide any personal details of these young people, and furthermore the city's congregations did not usually admit to membership those who were younger than sixteen years of age. A very tentative indication of the proportion of children among those affected by the revival arises from a comment made by Radcliffe, when he observed 'I have never had so many on the Sabbath before as on last Sabbath – three thousand fully, counting about five hundred children'.[72] Although exact statistics cannot be examined, it is obvious that children were very well represented among the converts of the Aberdeen movement.

Nevertheless an attempt was made to find each person listed in the communion rolls and membership lists within the 1861 census of Aberdeen. However, this was hindered because people regularly moved after joining a church in 1859 and 1860 and before the census was undertaken. This suggests there was considerable mobility amongst those who joined the churches, which in turn implies that many of them were probably young people. Also it is clear that the proportion of those whose age was identified varied considerably amongst the congregations. Nonetheless the gender ratio overall of those whose age was discovered corresponds to the general proportion of revival converts. Therefore there is no inherent gender imbalance within the age analysis. The ages of 142 people provide a fairly representative cross section of the new church members that have been found and they will comprise the sample which will be examined.

Table 4.18.

The ages of 142 people who joined Aberdeen churches at the height of the revival

Age	W'side		H'burn		South		Un Pres		Congreg		Ev Un		Baptist	
	M	F	M	F	M	F	M	F	M	F	M	F	M	F
15 – 20	1	3	3	4	12	16	1	6	1	1	2	6	2	1
21 – 30	4	0	1	2	2	1	5	6	8	13	1	2	2	1
31 – 40	1	1	1	0	0	1	0	0	3	3	4	2	2	0
41 – 50	1	0	0	0	0	0	0	1	0	2	0	1	1	0
51 – 60	0	2	0	0	0	0	0	0	3	1	0	0	0	1
60 +	0	0	0	0	0	0	0	1	1	2	0	0	0	0

Sources: Holburn Parish Church Communion Rolls 1859-1861
Woodside Parish Church Communion Rolls 1859-1868
South Free Church Kirk Session Minutes 1855-1871
St Nicholas Lane U P Church Kirk Session Minutes 1842-1865
George Street Congregational Church Minute Book of Church Meetings 1797-1862
St Paul Street Evangelical Union Church Communicants Roll Book 1846-1872
Union Terrace Baptist Church Minute Book 1821-68
1861 Census, Aberdeen, Aberdeenshire

Table 4.19.

The distribution of new church members in each congregation according to their age

Age	W'side	H'burn	South	Un Pres	Congr	Ev Un	Bapt
15 – 20	31 %	64 %	88 %	35 %	5 %	44 %	30 %
21 – 30	31 %	27 %	9 %	55 %	55 %	17 %	30 %
31 – 40	15 %	9 %	3 %	0 %	16 %	33 %	20 %
41 – 50	8 %	0 %	0 %	5 %	5 %	6 %	10 %
51 – 60	15 %	0 %	0 %	0 %	11 %	0 %	10 %
60 +	0 %	0 %	0 %	5 %	8 %	0 %	0 %

The Free South Church attracted the greatest proportion of young people. Almost ninety per cent were less than twenty years of age. Holburn Parish and St Nicholas Lane United Presbyterian also appear to have been particularly popular among the younger generation. At least ninety per cent of those who joined these churches at the height of the revival were less than thirty years of age. The age structure of the new members of the four remaining churches is quite similar. Approximately sixty per cent of their additions were under thirty years of age. Nevertheless it is significant that it was possible to identify a larger proportion of the new members of the first three churches than of the other four. This suggests that they provide a more exact representation of those who were affected by the revival. In so doing they indicate that this religious movement thrived abundantly amongst teenagers and those in their twenties.

Table 4.20.

An analysis of the ages of new church members during the Aberdeen revival

Age	Men	Women	% Men	% Women	Total
15 – 20	22	37	15	26	41 %
21 – 30	23	25	16	18	34 %
31 – 40	11	7	8	5	13 %
41 – 50	2	4	1	3	4 %
51 – 60	3	4	2	3	5 %
60 +	1	3	1	2	3 %
Mean Age	26.82	26.36			

There are two principal observations to be made concerning the ages of those affected by the Aberdeen revival of 1859. Firstly the non-inclusion of the younger teenage and child converts in the church records, not to mention the problems encountered in trying to identify within the census young people who were socially mobile, has distorted the true mean age of those affected by the 1859 revival in Aberdeen. There can be no doubt they were considerably younger than the age that these findings suggest. Indeed it may be estimated that the true average age of those who were converted during the revival was between five and seven years less than that which has been calculated.

Nonetheless, secondly, there are important observations to be made from the correlation between age and gender. Most noticeable is the high proportion of females who joined the church between the ages of fifteen and twenty. This suggests that within this age group almost two thirds of those who were affected by this movement were female. This is a substantial disproportion which indicates that amongst teenagers this revival appears to have been more popular among girls than boys. However, the imbalance virtually disappears amongst those aged between twenty one and thirty. Among these people the ratio of men and women is almost equal. Furthermore, the earlier disproportion is reversed amongst the thirty one to forty year olds. Within this group, almost two thirds were male and a third were female. Men represent the higher proportion of those aged between twenty one and forty who became church members during the course of this revival. A possible explanation for the decline in the number of female members among those aged between twenty one and forty may be that women, who generally married younger than men, were more preoccupied with domestic and family matters, which prevented them from attending revival meetings and being converted. In addition, seventeen people, out of the survey of 142, were discovered to be more than forty one years of age when they joined a church, and two thirds of them were women. Accordingly a general pattern of the ages of the men and women affected by the revival begins to emerge. Among the teenagers and those more than forty years of age it seems the movement affected twice as many women as it did men. However, within the twenty one to forty age group the revival appears to have affected more men than women. Therefore, teenage and older women, and young and middle aged men were among those who were most likely to be converted during this religious movement in Aberdeen.

Finally the gender balance of the new church members will be examined. It appears that throughout Britain in the nineteenth century women attended church in larger numbers than men. C. D. Field has examined samples of English Wesleyan, Baptist and Congregational churches between 1751 and 1850. He found that females accounted for fifty seven per cent of 62,235 Wesleyans, sixty five per cent of 11,398 Baptists and sixty per cent of 3,623 Congregationalists he examined. Thus the approximate ratio of female to male membership of English Nonconformist churches in the first half of the nineteenth century was three fifths and two fifths.[73] R. E. Chadwick's study of churches in Bradford between 1880 and 1914 found a disproportionately lower number of church members who were men. In the Baptist and Congregational churches only twenty five per cent were male, while this figure rose to thirty four per cent in two Wesleyan chapels she examined.[74] Hence it appears that the predominance of female members was a marked characteristic of nineteenth-century church life.

Evidence also suggests that revival converts have been more likely to be women than men. If the 110 converts whom M'Culloch interviewed were a fair representation of those who were 'born again' during the 1742 Cambuslang revival, it may be assumed that approximately two-thirds of these people were women.[75] Also it appears that the 1840 revival that affected Aberdeen was distinctly predominated by women. According to the Procurator Fiscal of the period, William Simpson, one meeting which he attended was occupied 'almost wholly with women, composed chiefly of girls from fifteen to eighteen, and of women upwards of fifty; a few men and boys interspersed, but very few'.[76] Although James Reid, a joiner, led one class of nineteen young converted men, another meeting was composed solely of seventy factory girls who had been influenced by the awakening.[77] Van Die, in her gender studies of the Brantford revivals has found that these movements did not lead to a greater gender parity within the church. On the contrary it widened the gap by 2%. She calculated the gender ratio of revival converts to be sixty per cent female and forty per cent male.[78] Finally, during the Billy Graham crusade in Scotland during 1955 at the Kelvin Hall, Ibrox and Hampden stadiums, it was calculated that of the 19,835 people who responded as 'inquirers' 14,016 or 71%, were women and 5,819, or 29%, were men.[79] Therefore, it appears that women have usually accounted for between at least sixty and seventy per cent of revival converts.

During this period Aberdeen was noted for the gender imbalance in its population as a whole. From the end of the eighteenth century the higher proportion of women living in the city was created by the number of females who were employed in the textiles industries and domestic service. It was observed as early as the beginning of the nineteenth century how 'many of our young men emigrate ... in quest of lucrative employment'.[80] Employment patterns in the city affected the gender imbalance of its population, with the result that the city had a disproportionately large number of single women between the ages of fifteen and twenty five. It is acknowledged how this pattern was repeated throughout urban Scotland. Nevertheless it was more exaggerated in Aberdeen. For instance, in

1861 there were 118 females to 100 males in the burghs of Scotland, while in Aberdeen there were 122 to 100.[81] This helps to explain why the 1840 revival in the city was dominated by women. Accordingly it was even more likely, given the gender imbalance of the city's population, that the greater proportion of the 1859 Aberdeen revival converts would be women.

Examination of the communicants' roll books and kirk session minutes enables the gender ratios of those who joined the Aberdeen churches during the period immediately before and after the 1859 religious movement to be compared with those who became members at the height of the revival.

Table 4.21.

The gender status of those who joined Aberdeen churches before, during and after the revival

Church	Year	Male	Female	Ratio M / F (%)
Holburn	Before / after Revival	25	43	37 / 63
	During the Revival	14	11	56 / 44
W' side	Before / after Revival	50	60	45 / 55
	During the Revival	68	66	51 / 49
Newhills	Before / after Revival	21	24	47 / 53
	During the Revival	10	19	34 / 66
Free Sth	Before / after Revival	74	144	34 / 66
	During the Revival	35	56	38 / 62
Un Pres	Before / after Revival	36	32	53 / 47
	During the Revival	48	46	51 / 49
Congr	Before / after Revival	41	70	37 / 63
	During the Revival	38	54	41 / 59
Evan Un	Before / after Revival	31	53	37 / 63
	During Revival	16	36	31 / 69
Bapt	Before / after Revival	23	32	42 / 58
	During Revival	24	20	55 / 45

Sources: Holburn Parish Church Communion Rolls 1859-1861
Woodside Parish Church Communion Rolls 1859-1868
Newhills Free Church Communion Rolls 1852-1860
South Free Church Kirk Session Minutes 1855-1871
St Nicholas Lane U P Church Kirk Session Minutes 1842-1865
George Street Congregational Church Minute Book of Church Meetings 1797-1862
St Paul Street Evangelical Union Church Communicants Roll Book 1846-1872
Union Terrace Baptist Church Minute Book 1821-68

Variations among the gender distribution of the congregations require closer scrutiny. In the first instance, there was a large shift in the gender balance of those who joined Newhills Free Church. During the revival the proportion of new female members rose from fifty three to sixty six per cent, a noteworthy shift of thirteen per cent. This is accounted for by the considerable number of female mill workers who joined the church during the revival. Almost one third of the congregation's new members were women who worked in the mills that were situated close to the church. Secondly, there was another substantial shift in the gender balance of Holburn Parish Church and Union Terrace Baptist Chapel. Here the proportion of new male members rose by nineteen and thirteen per cent respectively. Once more it appears that the geographical location of these churches accounted for the particular gender of the people they attracted. Both of these churches were found at the centre of Aberdeen's artisan community, and hence during the revival they drew many of their new members from this section of the city's population. Each of the remaining five churches experienced less noteworthy shifts in the gender balance of their new members through the revival. The United Presbyterian and Evangelical Union churches increased their proportion of female members, while Woodside Parish, the Free South and the Congregational Church had a greater ratio of men who joined. Nevertheless, the dissimilar gender balances demonstrate further that these congregations attracted different groups of men and women, and how their location was an important factor that accounts for the composition of the people who became their members.

The overall gender balance of those who became members of churches in Aberdeen before and after, and during the revival is also revealing.

Table 4.22.

An analysis of the gender status of those who joined Aberdeen churches before, during and after the revival

		No	Percent
Before and after the Revival	Male	301	40%
	Female	458	60 %
During the Revival			
	Male	253	45 %
	Female	308	55 %

During the period immediately before and after the revival the gender ratio of new church members in Aberdeen was forty per cent male and sixty per cent female. This correlation corresponds to the pattern which Field found among English Nonconformist churches during the nineteenth century. However, at the height of the revival forty five per cent of the city's new church members were male and fifty five per cent were female. Hence it is demonstrated that the gender balance of church membership in Aberdeen in the mid nineteenth century was affected as a result of the 1859 revival. This also shows that this religious movement produced a greater proportion of male converts than both previous and subsequent revivals. Almost half of those who were awakened during the course of this movement were male. Clearly it held a particular attraction for men. This is an important deviation from the typical gender composition of revival converts which requires explanation.

A considerable body of anecdotal testimony points to the attraction this revival held for the young men of Aberdeen. James Smith, minister of Greyfriars Parish Church, commenting in *The Revival* in July 1859, said, 'many young men in shops, many young women from the factories . . . have been added to the church'.[82] Another correspondent remarked, 'most of those who gave evidence, however, were young men engaged in business, or as mechanics'.[83] Meanwhile *The British Messenger* in July 1859 described how 'a large number of shopkeepers and apprentices have been remarkably awakened'.[84] Those who attended the churches also remarked on the attraction the revival held for men. One enthusiastic teacher commented upon 'such numbers of promising young men', while a Free Church minister described how, 'quite a host of young men lately came over to the Lord's side, chiefly shopkeepers, to the number, I suppose, of fifty or sixty'.[85] Another eye-witness remarked how 'the awakening extended to all classes, but was specially marked in the case of assistants in banks and solicitors' offices, in the numerous drapery and other establishments . . . scarcely a shop could be found in the whole length of Union Street without at least one young man who had come under the influence of the revival'.[86] Other observers commented upon the effect on the shops of the city saying, 'another marked feature of the work was the great number of commercial young men who were converted; in the many shops and warehouses all over the city, converted young men were to be found'.[87] David Rait, a young boy at the time of the revival, remembered 'a most gracious work amongst the young men, amongst students, and young men in business, and practically every large establishment in town had some young men who had been influenced for good by the revival'.[88] The movement also spread quickly through the University, affecting students in both King's and Marischal Colleges.[89] J. B. Sturrock, who later became a Free Church minister at Paisley, remembered large gatherings with fellow students at Greyfriars Church, which was situated at the entrance to Marischal College, and listening to Reginald Radcliffe, whose style of address, he recalled, 'told upon all classes, but particularly upon the students'.[90] Young men, it appears, were especially susceptible to the influence of this revival.

There are at least three factors that serve to explain the particular attraction this movement held for males. Firstly women, specifically mothers, played a crucial role in the conversion of male family members. Van Die has highlighted how women's concern for the moral welfare of their menfolk acted as the stimulus of the 1853 Brantford revival.[91] Kathryn Long, in her study of the 1857 American revival, has emphasised the important role women played within families in the spread of revivalistic fervour.[92] Similarly, although the role of women in this movement was largely ignored by the newspapers and pamphlets that recorded its public progress, they exercised considerable influence over the course of the Aberdeen revival. The reminiscences of a revival prayer meeting demonstrate how men were the focus of petitions offered by mothers and wives, and how often these prayers were answered. One observer recalled how

> A woman requests prayer for a scoffing husband, and on returning to her house she finds the scoffer on his knees. A wandering youth, long lost to sight, is prayed for, and shortly afterwards the prodigal is converted in a foreign hospital, and reappears at home a new man. A widow asks for prayer on behalf of her son at sea, and one night the sailor lad as he paces the deck is suddenly seized with the pangs of conviction, and then and there he gives himself to Christ. Prayer is offered for a notorious drunkard, and to the amazement of the community he is suddenly arrested in his evil course, and becomes a miracle of grace.[93]

Many of the revival converts had a praying mother or wife. The movement enveloped Aberdeen through small house meetings that met in hundreds of homes across the city. In a letter written to *The Revival* from Aberdeen, Duncan Matheson comments that 'another striking thing is, that few have found Christ themselves, but they have been instrumental in the awakening of others. Many instances of this have come under my notice.'[94] Within these unremarkable and hidden contexts, wherein the strength of the movement lay, women prayed with and counselled husbands and sons anxious about their conversion. Their selfless prayers and evangelistic work, both within their immediate families and throughout the wider community, help to explain how this movement had such an effect upon their husbands and sons, the men of the city.

Another important factor that serves to explain the potency of this movement among young men was the role played by the members of the aggressively evangelistic Young Men's Christian Association. They were chiefly responsible for inviting the evangelists who came to Aberdeen during the autumn of 1858 and made the necessary arrangements for their stay, organising the times and venues of the meetings.[95] Also they coordinated the first series of open-air evangelistic meetings in the spring of 1859. Indeed it was acknowledged that it was their efforts that 'led to the out door preaching of the gospel throughout the city'.[96] Throughout the course of the revival these young men were responsible for the organisation of many of its principal meetings at the Music Hall, including that of Charles Spurgeon in 1861.[97] In addition, they undertook the organisation of Christian outreach work in some of the most destitute parts of the city and arranged the monthly distribution of 10,000 religious tracts.[98] There can be no doubt that this group of young men, who organised and resourced the revival, had a profound influence upon its nature and course. Chiefly responsible for the planning of many of its meetings, they relentlessly targeted their peers and were successful in their efforts. This serves to explain why the 1859 revival became so popular among young men in Aberdeen.

Thirdly it seems this particular revival, from its origins in America, was predominantly a man's affair. James Douglas, a writer for the *British and Foreign Evangelical Review*, had observed in the American revival of 1857 that 'there is a larger proportion of males and adults among the converts than in former revivals'.[99] Across the Atlantic it was beginning to appear that religious movements were becoming more masculine.[100] One of the most distinguishing features of the Aberdeen revival was the prominent role played by laymen. They exercised a large influence over its organisation.[101] In addition, most of the evangelistic meetings, upon which the revival flourished, were conducted by itinerant male evangelists. The revival, and in particular its stress on lay activity, created the conditions within which the work of female evangelists later began to flourish.[102] Aberdeen was visited by several women preachers, including Miss Graham, Miss Armstrong, and Miss MacFarlane in January 1865.[103] However, the movement that affected the city between 1859 and 1862 was led and dominated by laymen, and therein lay much of its appeal to the young artisans of the city. Religious and philanthropic activities were becoming a popular and respectable recreational pursuit for gentlemen and young, upwardly mobile shop assistants and clerks were anxious to become part of this new, modern, fashionable movement.

Examination of those who joined Aberdeen churches around 1859 has suggested the type of person who was affected by this revival. In the first instance it appears to have attracted a large number of men and women who were not preceded into church membership by another family member, which suggests they had been targeted successfully by the organisers of the movement. However, it appears to have failed to reach into the most destitute areas of the city. The chief proportion of those who were affected included skilled working-class men, domestic servants and female factory workers who lived in the suburbs of the city. Also most of the new church members were either unmarried teenage girls or married men in their twenties and thirties. Perhaps of most significance, notwithstanding the greater number of young, unmarried women who lived and worked in Aberdeen, it appears the 1859 revival in Aberdeen affected many young men. The composition of Aberdeen's new church members during the revival demonstrates that it attracted a disproportionate number of young men. This shows that the targeting undertaken by the organisers of this modern religious movement was successful.

Notes

1. T. Bilhartz, 'Sex and the Second Great Awakening: The Feminisation of American Religion Reconsidered' in P. Vandermeer, R. Swierenga (ed.), *Belief and Behaviour: Essays in the New Religious History* (New Brunswick, NJ, 1991), pp. 122, 127-8.
2. K. T. Long, *The Revival of 1857-58: Interpreting an American Religious Awakening* (New York, 1998), pp. 69-71, 90.
3. J. Radcliffe, *Recollections of Reginald Radcliffe* (London, nd), p. 41, 46.
4. A.H., (10 August 1861), p. 4.
5. T.R., Vol 9, No 221, (15 October 1863), p. 241.
6. *Aberdeen Almanac 1859* (Aberdeen, 1859), pp. 121-5.
7. W.J., No 30, (21 April 1860), p. 236.
8. B.E., Vol 2, No (5, May 1859), p. 191.
9. T. T. Matthews (ed.), *Reminiscences of the Revival of Fifty-Nine and the Sixties* (Aberdeen, 1910).
10. F. W. B. Bouverie, *The Pastor to His Flock* (Aberdeen, 1860), np.
11. John Crombie to Rev William Stewart, 30 July 1858, St James Episcopal Church Copy Letter Book of Manager's Secretary including letters from John Avery 1854-1858 and John Crombie 1858-1880
12. Ibid.
13. John Crombie to Rev Samuel Wainwright, 21 January 1861, St James Episcopal Church Copy Letter Book of Manager's Secretary including letters from John Avery 1854-1858 and John Crombie 1858-1880
14. D. Wilson, *Methodism in Scotland* (Aberdeen, 1850), p. 14.
15. Ibid.
16. Ibid., p. 23.
17. A. Gammie, *The Churches of Aberdeen* (Aberdeen, 1909), p. 327.
18. C. Diack, *Sketches of Methodism in Aberdeen* (Aberdeen, 1901), p. 14, 25, 27.
19. A.H., 30 (July 1859), p. 2.

20. Free West Church Kirk Session Minutes, 1858-1862
21. J. Ogilvie Skea, *The Free West: A Record of the West Church of St Andrew, Aberdeen 1843-1961* (Aberdeen, 1963), p. 33.
22. Matthews, *Reminiscences*, p. 105.
23. Gammie, *Churches of Aberdeen*, pp. 157-61.
24. Free South Church Kirk Session Minutes, 15 December 1859
25. Newhills Free Church Kirk Session Minutes, 15 November 1859
26. Anon, *Times of Refreshing: Being Notices of Some of the Religious Awakenings which have taken place in the UK, With Special Reference to the Revival in Aberdeen* (Aberdeen, 1859), p. 9.
27. Gammie, *Churches of Aberdeen*, pp. 238-41.
28. A. A. MacLaren, *Religion and Social Class* (London, 1974), p. 41.
29. Gammie, *Churches of Aberdeen*, pp. 238-41, 252-6.
30. Ibid., pp. 29-35, 81-4.
31. W. D. McNaughton, *The Scottish Congregational Ministry 1794-1993* (Glasgow, 1993), p. 40.
32. H. Scott, *Fasti Ecclesiae Scoticanne: The Succession of Ministers in the Church of Scotland from the Reformation: Volume 6* (Edinburgh, 1926), p. 43.
33. Ibid., p. 10.
34. W. Ewing (ed.), *Annals of the Free Church of Scotland 1849-1900* (Edinburgh, 1914), p. 304.
35. Ibid., p. 114.
36. Ibid., pp. 77, 254.
37. Ibid., p. 128.
38. S. J. Brown, 'Thomas Chalmers and the Communal Ideal in Victorian Scotland' in T. C. Smout (ed.), *Victorian Values* (Oxford, 1992), pp. 69-71.
39. W. B. Sprague, *Lectures on Revivals of Religion [1832]* (London, 1959), pp. 144-5.
40. MacLaren, *Religion and Social Class*, pp. 6, 52-4, 87.
41. Ibid., p. 60.
42. Gammie, *Churches of Aberdeen*, p. 131.
43. Ibid., p. 17.
44. MacLaren, *Religion and Social Class*, p. 113.
45. Ibid., p. 126, 138.
46. C. J. Brown, *The Social History of Religion in Scotland since 1730* (London, 1987), pp. 155-8,
    P. L. M. Hillis, 'Presbyterianism and Social Class in Mid-Nineteenth-Century Glasgow: A Study of Nine Churches', *Journal of Ecclesiastical History*, 32, (1981), pp. 48-9,
    L. Jeffrey, 'Women in the Churches of Nineteenth Century Stirling', unpublished M.Litt thesis, University of Stirling, 1996, p. 112.
47. N. Landsman, 'Evangelists and their Hearers: Popular Interpretation of Revivalist Preaching in Eighteenth-Century Scotland', *Journal of British Studies*, 28, (April 1989), p. 124.
48. T. C. Smout, 'Born Again at Cambuslang: New Evidence on Popular Religion and Literacy in Scotland', *Past and Present*, 97, (1982), p. 117.
49. M. Van Die, 'The Marks of a Genuine Revival: Religion, Social Change, Gender and Community in Mid Victorian Brantford, Ontario', *The Canadi-*

an *Historical Review*, 79, (1998), p. 528, 555.
50. Jeffrey, 'Women in Churches of Stirling', pp. 103-6.
51. *B.Mr.*, No 74, (April 1859), p. 223.
52. W.H. Fraser, C.H. Lee (ed.), *Aberdeen 1800-2000 A New History* (East Linton, 2000), pp. 156-62.
53. Ibid.
54. W. M. Walker, *Jutepolis: Dundee and the Textile Workers 1885-1923* (Edinburgh, 1979), p. 37.
55. W. Robbie, *Bon Accord Free Church, Aberdeen: A Retrospect 1828-1878* (Aberdeen, 1887), p. 121.
56. Smout, 'Born Again at Cambuslang', p. 116.
57. Van Die, 'Marks of a Genuine Revival', pp. 534-5.
58. M. R. Watts, *The Dissenters: Volume 2, The Expansion of Evangelical Nonconformity* (Oxford, 1995), p. 57.
59. D. W. Bebbington, 'Evangelical Conversion, c1740-1850', North Atlantic Missiology Project, Position Paper Number 21, University of Cambridge, 1996, pp. 7-9.
60. K. D. Brown, *A Social History of the Nonconformist Ministry in England and Wales 1800-1930* (Oxford, 1988), p. 54.
61. C. D. Field, 'Methodism in Metropolitan Liverpool', unpublished D.Phil thesis, Oxford University, 1974, p. 232 quoted by Brown, *Social History of the Nonconformist Ministry*, p. 54.
62. Smout, 'Born Again at Cambuslang', p. 116.
63. Watts, *Dissenters*, pp. 64-67.
64. *Evidence on the Subject of Revivals taken before a Committee of the Presbytery of Aberdeen* (Aberdeen, 1841), pp. 46-48.
65. *U.P.M.*, (May 1858), p. 238.
66. Radcliffe, *Recollections*, p. 60.
67. Anon, *Times of Refreshing*, pp. 52-3.
68. H. Sprange, *Kingdom Kids: Children in Revival* (Fearn, Ross shire, 1994), p. 169.
69. Minutes of the Aberdeen Free Church Synod, April 1859
70. *B.Mr.*, No 75, (May 1859), p. 230.
71. Matthew, *Reminiscences*, p. 136.
72. Radcliffe, *Recollections*, p. 49.
73. C. D. Field, 'Adam and Eve: Gender in the English Free Church Constituency', *Journal of Ecclesiastical History*, 44, (1993), pp. 63-5, 75, 78.
74. R. E. Chadwick, 'Church and People in Bradford and District, 1880- 1914: The Protestant Churches in an Urban Industrial Environment', unpublished D. Phil thesis, University of Oxford, (1986), pp. 144-6, 165-8, quoted by Jeffrey, 'Women in Churches of Stirling', pp. 43-4.
75. Smout, 'Born Again at Cambuslang', p. 116.
76. *Evidence on the subject of Revivals*, p. 17.
77. Ibid., pp. 32, 51.
78. Van Die, 'The Marks of a Genuine Revival', p. 536.
79. T. Allan (ed.), *Crusade in Scotland: Billy Graham* (London, 1955), p. 108.
80. J. Sinclair (ed.), *The Statistical Account of Scotland, 1791-1799: Kincardineshire and South and West Aberdeenshire* (Edinburgh, 1982), p. 293.

81. J. Valentine, *Aberdeen as It Was and Is* (Aberdeen, 1871), p. 21.
82. *T.R.*, Vol 1, No 1, (30 July 1859), p. 3.
83. Ibid., Vol 1, No 23, (31 December 1859), p. 182.
84. *B.Mr.*, No 77, (July 1859), p. 243.
85. Anon, *Times of Refreshing*, pp. 48-50.
86. Matthews, *Reminiscences*, p. 48.
87. Ibid., p. 119.
88. Ibid., p. 108.
89. Anon, *Times of Refreshing*, p. 62.
90. Matthews, *Reminiscences*, 126.
91. Van Die, 'Marks of Genuine Revival', p. 535.
92. Long, *Revival of 1857-58*, p. 57.
93. Matthews, *Reminiscences*, pp. 64-65.
94. *T.R.*, Vol 1, No 7, (10 September 1859), p. 53.
95. *B.E.*, (November 1858), p. 194.
96. *First Annual Report of the Aberdeen YMCA* (Aberdeen, 1859), np.
97. Matthews, *Reminiscences*, p. 52.
98. *Second Annual Report of the Aberdeen YMCA* (Aberdeen, 1860), np.
99. *B.F.E.R.*, (Edinburgh, 1858), No 26, October 1858, p. 916.
100. Long, *Revival of 1857-58*, p. 68.
101. Omicron, *Five Letters on the Religious Movement in Aberdeen: With an Appendix on the Nature, Probability and Necessity of a Religious Revival* (Aberdeen, 1859), p. 4.
102. O. Anderson, 'Women Preachers in mid-Victorian Britain: Some Reflections on Feminism, Popular Religion and Social Change', *The Historical Journal*, 12, p. 475.
103. *T.R.*, Vol 12, No 285, (5 January 1865), p. 10.

CHAPTER 5

The Revival in the Rural Hinterland

Timing and Manner

After a few months, when the initial burst of religious enthusiasm that accompanied the revival had begun to wane in Aberdeen, the movement started to emerge within the agricultural hinterland that surrounded the city, before spreading across the north east of Scotland. An eye-witness recalled how 'in the spring of 1859 the flow of the movement rather lessened in the town, and was more manifest in the country districts'.[1] An explanation of how and why the farming communities in Aberdeenshire were affected by the revival from the spring of 1859 is necessary to appreciate the influence and nature of the movement in the north east of Scotland. To ascertain the factors that influenced its timing, the pattern of the revival will be considered, before the process by which it was diffused through the region is described. In addition, the importance of the main characters involved in the revival and the influence they commanded upon the distinctive expression of the movement will be discussed. Finally, the manner in which it was assimilated into the affected towns and villages and its main features will be examined. In this way the different character the revival displayed in the surrounding districts from the city movement will be highlighted, and the singular rural experience of the 1859 awakening will be revealed.

I

Among the circumstances scholars have suggested as the principal factors which influence the timing of revivals are social and economic factors. There is no doubt the rural community of north east Scotland underwent a period of unprecedented change between 1780 and 1840. In the mid-eighteenth century much of the arable land lay unenclosed, usually near the coast or in river valleys in small patches, and was worked in runrig, the heavily manured land bearing mostly corn crops repeatedly with no rotation. Meanwhile, rough grazing was carried on between the specks of arable land.[2] In the 1790s several modernising landowners, such as Sir Archibald Grant of Monymusk, began to enclose large areas of land and consolidate previously scattered holdings. As a result, the landscape of the region was radically altered. Many of the farming townships, which had appeared on a local survey undertaken by William Roy in 1749, were broken up and dispersed among the newly enclosed fields.[3] The drastic failure of the 1782 harvest encouraged the development of these improvements so that by 1811 extensive changes had taken place. They included the introduction of threshing machines, a more efficient plough and a new system of turnip husbandry.[4] Robert Mieklejohn described the changes that affected the parish of Strathdon where he served as minister. He recalled 'the vast improvement of the century by reclaiming and planting of waste lands, the drainage and the enclosure of fields and general introduction of the improving system of husbandry'.[5] Upon a visit to the north east in 1838 Lord Cockburn remarked, 'I know of no part of Scotland so much, and so visibly, improved within thirty years as Aberdeenshire. At that time the country between Keith and Stonehaven was little less than a hopeless region of stone and moss.'[6] Hence noteworthy changes affected the rural landscape of Aberdeenshire during the first third of the nineteenth century.

The economy of north east Scotland was also transformed between 1780 and 1840. In the first instance, the weaving of woollen cloth and the knitting of worsted stockings, which had been the principal rural domestic industries in the eighteenth century, began to decline. This was a result of the war with France from 1793 which had destroyed overseas markets, and the rise of the frame-made stocking industry, centred at Hawick. In 1811 George Keith estimated that 41,000, or just over 30% of the population of rural Aberdeenshire, was employed in the home textiles industry. By 1851 this number had fallen to 8,000, which represented only 3.6% of the population.[7] The expansion of factories around Aberdeen served further to kill off these home-based industries. In this way a staple industry of the rural economy of north east Scotland dwindled in the first half of the nineteenth century with the result that people were forced to move in the search for new employment.

Yet around the same time developments in the cattle trade, initiated by a steep rise in the demand for beef during the Napoleonic Wars, and assisted in 1828 by the introduction of a regular steam ship service to London, began to create new wealth in other areas. By 1837 Aberdeen was the leading port on the east coast of Scotland for the export of live cattle. In 1847, 15,634 beasts and 750 tons of dead meat, the equivalent of 1,800 cattle, were exported. The arrival of the railway stimulated further dramatic growth. By 1865 these figures had risen so that Aberdeen's export of beef totalled 13,589 live animals and 10,135 tons of meat, representing 24,363 cattle, an increase of 118 per cent in less than thirty years.[8] Beef became such a lucrative industry that farmers moved quickly to capitalise upon these new opportunities. At the same time the fast-growing population of Aberdeen led to an increased demand for agricultural products, including milk and vegetables, while the Crimean War in the 1850s encouraged a rise in grain prices which stimulated further growth in the rural economy.[9] Altogether these circumstances led the agricultural industry in the north east of Scotland into what Ian Carter has described as the 'golden summer of mid-Victorian high farming'.[10] Hence, inspite of the decline of the home-based industries, the changes that accompanied the 'improvements' appear to have encouraged the growth of the rural economy in Aberdeenshire during the first half of the nineteenth century.

However the north east of Scotland experienced exceptionally poor harvests in 1860 and 1861 and they may have influenced the timing of the religious movement. Aberdeenshire suffered a tremendous storm in October 1860 which devastated farms and villages in the region. The *Aberdeen Free Press* gathered a series of reports from various places, each of which testified to the catastrophic damage that the high winds had caused to trees, crops and homes. At Fintray, for instance, it was estimated that in some cases up to two thirds of the crop had been lost.[11] There is no doubt the harvest of 1860 was greatly affected by this storm and that considerable poverty was experienced in the area as a consequence. The north east of Scotland endured another poor harvest during the following year of 1861. The *North British Agriculturist* recorded that it had been less than bountiful. The last quarter before the harvest was characterised by high winds and an abundance of rain with the result that, although the grain crops produced a good yield, half the potatoes and turnips were lost to disease.[12] For two successive years, at the height of the revival, the farming people of Aberdeenshire experienced particularly poor harvests. Although a direct correlation has not been found between the affliction caused by these storms and the religious movement, it is probable that the hardship created by the loss of the crops was a contributory factor, among others, which serves to explain the timing of the revival.

II

Notwithstanding the possible influence of this external circumstance, there are other factors which clearly had a more definite bearing upon the timing of the revival. Firstly between five and ten years before the movement began, the Free Church in rural Aberdeenshire began to grapple seriously with its responsibility for evangelism in what was becoming an increasingly irreligious society. George Bain, the Free Church minister of Chapel of Garioch, for example, recalled a conversation he shared with Henry Williamson, Free Church minister of Huntly, in 1857 about the 'dead and low spiritual state of the Church' and their opinion that 'if we did not get a revival we would, in ten years, be in a very poor condition'.[13] Ministers were beginning to recognise that a generation of young farming people was becoming alienated from the church. This view was confirmed by J. Alexander who, in a prize essay on the condition of farm servants published in 1852, remarked that 'while there has been a steady and rapid improvement going on almost in every operation connected with agriculture, there appears to have been a corresponding deterioration going on in the moral and social habits of agricultural labourers'.[14] Meanwhile Alexander Fraser, in another essay printed in 1859, said that despite the many improvements in the rural economy there had been 'a steady deterioration going on in the moral and social habits of the labouring class'.[15] Consequently the Aberdeen Synod of the Free Church established a committee, under the leadership of Robert Reid, minister at Banchory, to examine means by which this farm servant class could be evangelised. They reported their findings in 1859 and recommended that ministers ought to take a more active interest in this group of young people. They were urged to preach on the duties of masters and servants once a year, visit all farm servants at least twice a year and 'to use all means in their power for the religious instruction of young persons in farm service and for preventing these from careless and irreligious habits'.[16] Accordingly it appears that the Free Church in Aberdeenshire was becoming more aware of its need for a revival. Conscious that it was losing a generation of young people to unbelief, it had begun to seek the means by which they might be brought back within the influence of the church.

Around the same time, as was mentioned previously, a group of lay, itinerant evangelists began leading religious campaigns in Aberdeenshire. These men, who included Duncan Matheson, Brownlow North, Hay MacDowall Grant of Arndilly, Lord Kintore, John Gordon of Parkhill and Gordon Forlong served a crucial function as they conducted missions across the north east of Scotland from 1855. In particular, they raised a sense of anticipation of revival in the area. The nature of their work is illustrated by several extracts from the diary of Grant of Arndilly. At the end of 1856 he recorded, 'I have been led to speak earnestly and privately to 212 persons about the state of their souls, and the necessity of seeking forgiveness of their sins. Of these, sixty one have professed to find peace. Of the remaining 151, thirty remain earnestly seeking; fifty remain in doubt; ten are old converts; and the rest are careless.'[17] At the end of 1857 he reported that 'the work of the Lord, which was commenced twenty months ago, has gone on increasing in an extraordinary manner'.[18] This reveals that a preparatory work of evangelism in rural Aberdeenshire preceded the revival. Alexander Reid, the Free Church minister at Portsoy, was convinced of the importance of these endeavours. In January 1860 he commented that 'in all the places where a revival had been taking place, there had been a previous preparation, when, through the instrumentality, for instance, of such as Mr Radcliffe and Mr North, this gradual preparation had been developed by leading many to make earnest inquiry'.[19] Clearly this band of lay evangelists, through their unstinting efforts from 1855, exercised an important influence upon the timing of the revival. They were responsible, through the services they led, for creating a spiritual climate that was conducive to an awakening.

The religious journals that had begun to appear around the middle of the 1850s which promoted revival also served an important role by creating the anticipation of a religious movement. The north east of Scotland was one of the most literate regions in the country where newspapers were read widely and carefully.[20] Articles began to appear regularly which highlighted the nation's need for a reawakening of religion. There is no doubt they had a decided effect upon those who read them. Indeed David Henry, the Free Church minister at New Marnoch, commenting upon the various factors that precipitated the revival, said in 1860 that 'among other means for good, it may be mentioned that about a thousand tracts have been distributed monthly for the last fourteen years, by about forty distributors. The *British Messenger* has also been extensively read.'[21] Meanwhile, in the same year, Robert McCombie, Free Church minister at Leslie and Premnay, described how prior to the movement 'religious periodical publications began to be sought for with avidity, and extensively circulated'.[22] It is clear that the diffusion of revival information across parts of Aberdeenshire by these religious journals aroused the expectation of the people for a similar 'work of God'.

This was stimulated further by reports of religious movements that had begun to appear in America in 1857 and Ulster in 1859. Repeatedly ministers who experienced the revival referred to the influence of this news which they read at prayer meetings. Many regarded it as the catalyst of the movement in their parishes. William Ker, the Free Church minister at Deskford, for example, constantly drew his congregation's attention to the religious movements that had spread across these lands, and as a result, he said, 'those truly seeking the Lord were led to expect an outpouring of the Spirit'.[23] George Bain recalled how in Chapel of Garioch

> the good news of the revival in America tended greatly to cheer us, and mention was frequently made of that good work in our Sabbath services, and prayer-meetings . . . when the news of God's great work in Ireland reached us, we thought we could see 'his glorious marching' towards us, and we set ourselves accordingly to welcome and receive him. We opened an additional prayer-meeting – and that in the Church – feeling confident that the school, where our prayer-meeting had till then been held, could not long contain us . . . The Lord was pleased to honour our enlarged expectation.[24]

John Manson, Free Church minister at Fyvie, said that 'in regard to what, under God, has led to . . . [revival], I believe that, besides the ordinary services of the sanctuary, the reports of the American and Irish Revivals materially conduced to it. I was anxious to get one who had witnessed the work in Ireland to give an account of it to my people. At my request, Mr Bain of Chapel of Garioch kindly did so, and, after his visit, the interest increased.'[25] This atmosphere of expectation, created by news of the American revival and recharged by the Irish movement, enveloped the church in the agricultural hinterland of the north east of Scotland. The excited spirit of anticipation initiated by these events had a profound influence upon the timing of the revival.

As a result, by 1859 religious awakenings had become a popular and fashionable subject. However, interest had not simply been aroused, but rather desire had been created that Scotland should experience a similar 'season of grace'. At Huntly United Presbyterian Church, on 23 June 1858, 'a series of religious exercises were conducted with a view to obtain a revival of religion in the congregation'.[26] Just over a month later, James Mailler, the minister, appointed 4 August as 'a day of humiliation and prayer in the congregation in consequence of past shortcomings and that God may grant the outpouring of the Holy Spirit and shew more evident tokens of his favour and presence in the midst of the people'.[27] Meanwhile in the State of Religion report of Fordyce Free Presbytery, delivered in September 1858, the moderator of the Presbytery discussed 'the necessity, practicability and means of a revival'.[28] In this way a yearning for an awakening appears to have been aroused within the lives of a number of ministers and churches across the rural hinterland of Aberdeenshire.

Perhaps the clearest expression of a sense of anticipation and desire for a religious movement was demonstrated by the number of prayer gatherings that appeared in the farming communities of the north east of Scotland. This is indicated by their predominance in kirk session minutes which repeatedly describe the remarkable spirit of prayerfulness that overcame rural congregations. The elders of the High Free Church at Elgin, a rural market town, for example, recorded in March 1859 their proposal 'to observe this year the usual season for united prayer for a revival of religion . . . from the 14th till the 21st current'.[29] At Ardclach in June the Free Church minister, Henry McLeod, called a meeting of his elders in order to 'submit to them the propriety and desirableness of having a weekly prayer meeting in addition to the monthly meeting with this great end in view, the revival of God's work'.[30] At Forgue Free Church, the elders met in July 1859 and 'spent some time in conference on the state of religion in the congregation . . . [and made it] a matter of urgent prayer that the Lord would bless his own work in the congregation that there may be a revival of religion among us'.[31] In some cases, prayer meetings were established because of the desire of large numbers of people. For instance, in September 1859, Insch Free Church, 'owing to the greater interest felt taken in spiritual things and the means of grace by the people in general, at present, the Session resolved to establish, for some time, a weekly prayer meeting in the village, and to afford similar opportunities as far as possible, throughout the district'.[32] Others were encouraged by the activity of neighbouring parishes. In October 1859 the Kirk Session of Clola Free Church, for instance, 'having had their attention called to the interesting movements which are presently going forward in various parts of the land connected with the revival of religion resolved that their next meeting should be devoted specially to prayer and conference with a view to the revival of the Lord's work in this congregation'.[33] Meanwhile the elders of Old Deer Free Church in November 'resumed conference with regard to the state of religion in the congregation and special prayer for revival was offered up'.[34] Hence, during 1859 the elders of a number of congregations, particularly in the Free Church, established many meetings across the rural hinterland that gathered to pray specifically for revival.

These gatherings attracted the interest of the farming people and they grew quickly. At Culsamond Free Church, in November 1859, the elders 'resolved to endeavour to establish weekly prayer meetings under the supervision of elders in those districts where they do not already exist'.[35] The following January it was minuted that nine district prayer meetings, each attended by up to thirty five people, had been established.[36] In January 1860 the Kirk Session of Oyne

Free Church also recorded that 'prayer meetings have been multiplied, there being now four held during the week, some of these being very numerously attended'.[37] Similarly eleven prayer meetings arose within Rothiemay Free Church.[38] Meanwhile David Henry reported that 'the weekly attendance at the congregational prayer-meeting is nearly tenfold what it used to be' at New Marnoch.[39] Henry Williamson, astounded by the enthusiasm for corporate prayer that was generated at Huntly, commented,

> The desire to pray seems somewhat remarkable. I can scarcely tell you the number of prayer meetings. In my own congregation alone, about six prayer meetings among the young men, about the same number among the boys, say from ten to fourteen years of age, three or four among the girls and some among the young women. The thirst for prayer is wonderful.[40]

Across the north east of Scotland in countless parishes, men and women gathered in homes and barns, indeed wherever they could find room to meet together, and prayed earnestly for revival. It was within these groups that their desire and expectation of a religious movement grew.

Subsequently, after the revival had begun, the ministers were in no doubt of the essential role that had been played by these meetings for prayer. Archibald Gardner, the Free Church minister from New Deer, testified to how 'the work now going on had been preceded by much prayer'.[41] Further north, the effects of prayer were also noted. In 1860 Donald Fraser, Free Church minister at Inverness, said 'as in other places, the roots of this movement have been in prayer'.[42] Meanwhile Alexander M'Kenzie, the Free Church minister at Nairn, said, 'I believe it is the experience of all ministers that this work has originated in connection with prayer.'[43] Alexander Reid also recognised the importance of the preparatory meetings stating that 'there had been a preparation for it, shown in the increased number of prayer-meetings'.[44] In January 1860 William Ker also commented, 'there was a gradual preparation . . . it was long prayed for and expected'.[45] There was no doubt in the minds of the ministers who led the rural revival, that it was inherently related to the growth of prayer meetings in the area. They believed that the movement was conceived within these gatherings. The correlation between the location of prayer meetings and incidents of the awakening is displayed on map 5.1., on p. 121.

It is remarkable how the desire to meet and pray for a revival appears to have seized the imagination and will of so many farming people. Quite simply they grew to believe that a religious movement would begin amongst them and they expressed this sense of anticipation by gathering together to pray. The influence exercised

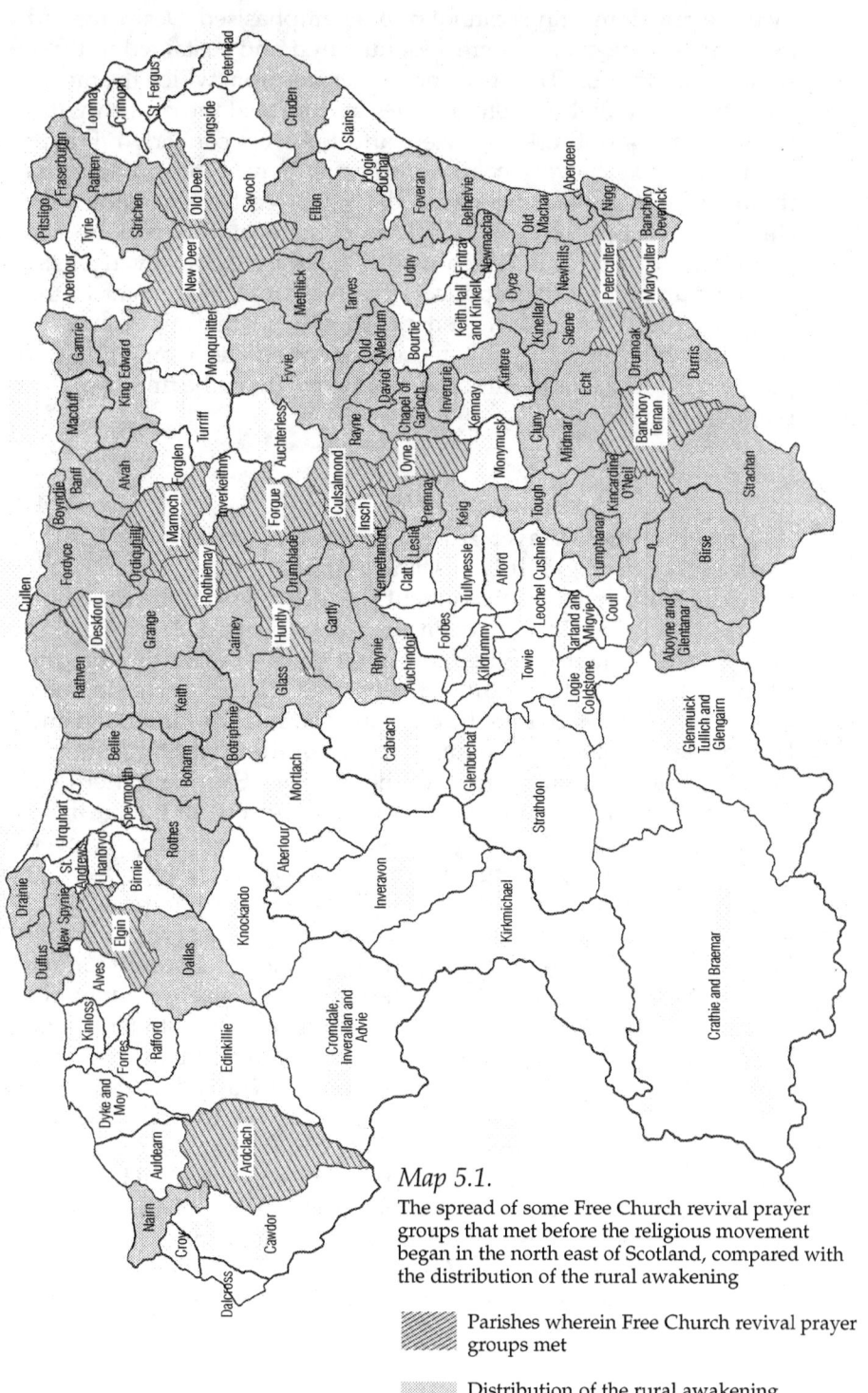

Map 5.1.

The spread of some Free Church revival prayer groups that met before the religious movement began in the north east of Scotland, compared with the distribution of the rural awakening

Parishes wherein Free Church revival prayer groups met

Distribution of the rural awakening

by these prayer meetings cannot be over emphasised. Desire for and expectancy of revival was created, nurtured and sustained in these small house groups. They became the centres from which the movement permeated whole communities and formed the context within which many of those who were affected were converted. Prayer meetings lay at the very heart of the rural revival. Accordingly, the timing of the movement across the north east of Scotland was chiefly determined by the religious climate of this region. The expectancy of a revival, which was initiated by the lay evangelists, and encouraged by the reports of the American movement in the religious press, but manifested principally in the appearance of these humble gatherings where ordinary men and women met to pray, exercised the most important influence upon the timing of this religious movement.

III

As a result of these prayer groups, the revival broke out across the north east of Scotland. It is possible to identify three main sources from which the religious movement was diffused into the rural hinterland. They are illustrated on map 5.2., on p. 123. In the first instance the influence of the movement spread outwards from the city of Aberdeen. This diffusion occurred in two ways. Initially groups of young men from the city travelled into the hinterland and led revival meetings in farming communities. Gordon Gray, a divinity student in 1859, recalled how 'every Saturday afternoon found several of us young men setting out for one of the northern parishes to address meetings in schoolrooms, workshops, even barns'.[46] Meanwhile, during the same year, *The Revival* reported that 'the people of God in . . . [Premnay] were very much refreshed and stirred up by a recent visit from a number of the Aberdeen Young Men's Missionary Union (an association which . . . is doing much good in the destitute localities in the city of Aberdeen)'.[47] Similarly, Robert McCombe described how a young medical student, who was a member of his congregation of Leslie and Premnay, was converted at a revival service conducted by Reginald Radcliffe in Aberdeen. He went on to tell how upon his return home the students began holding prayer meetings in various parts of the district and as a result many young people were converted.[48] Hence the influence of the revival entered the rural hinterland through the enthusiastic endeavours of students and young men who had been affected by the movement in Aberdeen.

It was spread through the rural areas also by farming people who had travelled into Aberdeen and were converted at religious servic-

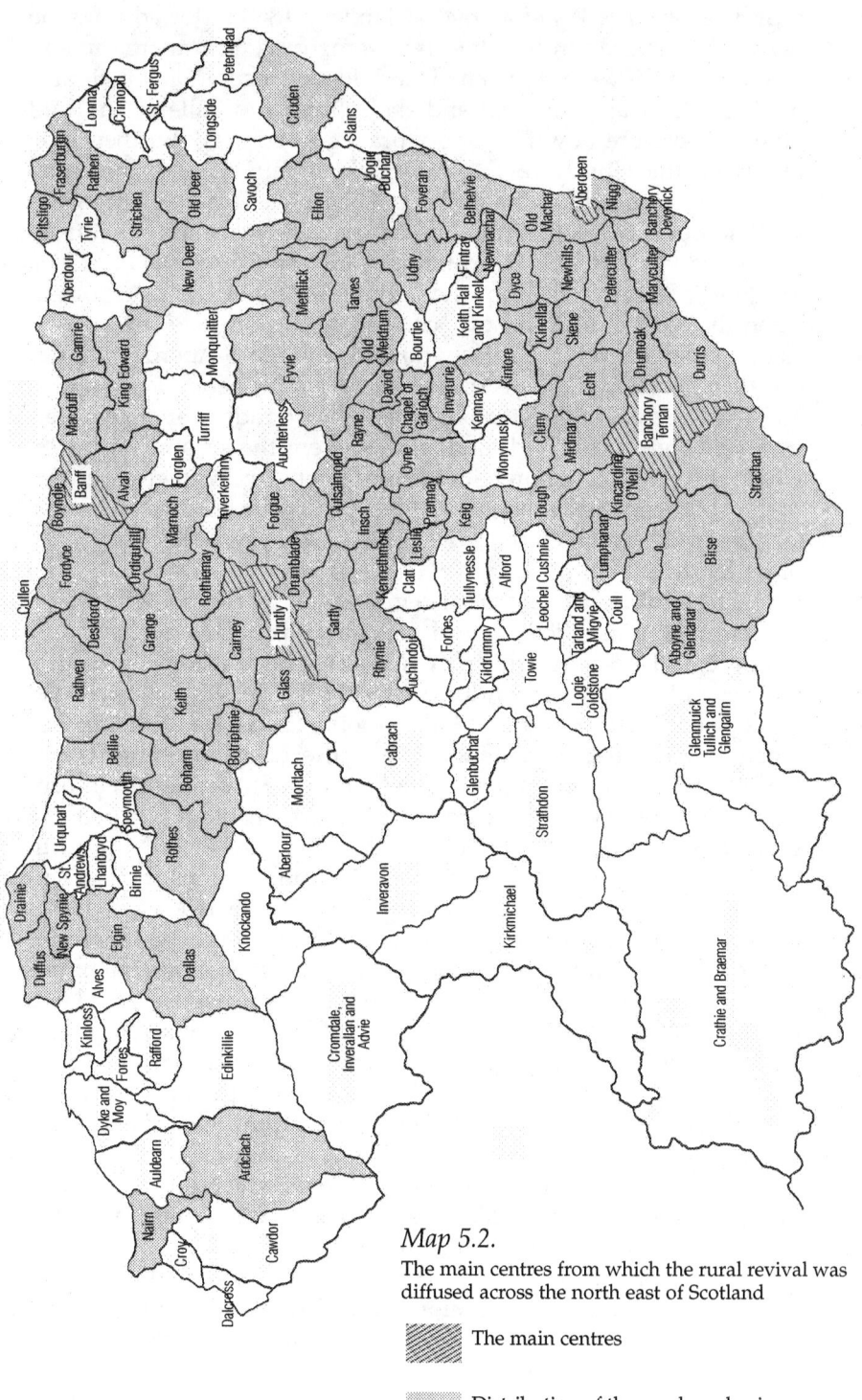

Map 5.2.

The main centres from which the rural revival was diffused across the north east of Scotland

The main centres

Distribution of the rural awakening

es in the city. *The Wynd Journal* of January 1860 reported how the revival had started in Ballater after 'some girls from there came to Aberdeen and were awakened and found Jesus. One invited a mother who was converted and she returned to Ballater and told others. There are now five or six prayer meetings.'[49] Furthermore, following the Huntly revival rally held in July 1860, a three-day conference was held at the Links in Aberdeen. This event attracted such numbers of people from the surrounding rural areas that facilities were 'afforded by the different Railway Companies to those wishing to be present from the country'.[50] Robert Reid, reporting upon the revival in Banchory, commented upon how 'there were cases of conversion in parties who had come into Aberdeen under serious impressions'.[51] This reveals how country people were affected by the revival in the city. Fermfolk who attended religious meetings and were converted in Aberdeen were the second means by which the movement spread into rural towns and villages. Accordingly Aberdeen, the capital city of the north east, became an important centre from which the awakening spread into the agricultural hinterland.

The fermfolk's revival was also influenced by contact with several fishing communities along the Moray Firth. This occurred, for example, in Deskford, which lay five miles inland from the coastal villages of Portknockie, Findochty and Portessie, where the revival manifested itself in a particularly emotional fashion. William Ker recounted how the movement began to affect Deskford during September 1859 in an undramatic, quiet manner. Subsequently, in February 1860, the revival appeared in the nearby fishing villages in an excited fashion which had not hitherto been manifested in the north east of Scotland. Sceptical of the physical prostrations that accompanied it, Ker visited these villages. He conducted a service at Portessie during which a woman fell prostrate. This experience produced a more sympathetic attitude within Ker towards such outward physical signs of repentance. Upon his return to Deskford two people were 'struck down' during one of his Sunday services, and he was obliged to conduct several 'protracted meetings', including one which was carried on until 4.30 am.[52] Ker's experience of revival in a nearby fishing village affected his attitude towards physical manifestations which subsequently began to appear in his rural parish. The religious movement in Deskford, which previously was quite unemotional, was affected quite radically by contact with the revival experience of the local fisherfolk.

Further along the Moray coast, Banff became a centre from which the movement was diffused along the eastern stretch of the Firth, and into the local agricultural hinterland. Thomas Baxter, the United Presbyterian minister, described in September 1860 how young converts of the fishing revival did not 'confine their labours to the spread of the Gospel in the town, but also sent deputations, composed of four to five of their number, to the rural districts around, to conduct meetings for prayer'.[53] Boyndie, Castleton and other parts of King Edward parish were frequently visited, while two deputations made a 'considerable impression' at Millseat.[54] Meanwhile in other districts 'little meetings in outlying country districts were established in rooms, farmhouses and barns for Christian fellowship and mutual exhortation' by Banff converts.[55] This suggests that currents of religious enthusiasm spread inland from the seaboard communities. In this way, the revival spread from the fishing villages along the Moray Firth into the rural hamlets that lay within walking distant of the coast.

However, the most significant nuclei from which the movement was dispersed across north east Scotland were the agricultural towns of Huntly and Banchory which became centres of the revival. Huntly began to experience the awakening in January 1859, Henry Williamson became recognised as a principal leader of the revival.[56] The Duchess of Gordon, who also gave wholehearted support to the movement, lived in the town, and it was within the grounds of her estate that great rallies were held. These gatherings had a very noteworthy effect upon the progress of the revival. They served to refocus the vision of the movement and to strengthen those who laboured within it. Letters were frequently received by ministers in Huntly requesting prayer for the movement in other areas which indicates how this town was considered by many as one of the regional headquarters of the revival.[57] Meanwhile Banchory, which lay in the south of Aberdeenshire, was the second major rural centre of religious enthusiasm. The revival began here at the beginning of May 1859. According to the clergyman William Dower, Banchory became important principally because of the work of Robert Reid. 'Reid of Banchory', he said, 'became the man of the hour, became the inspiration of the revival movement from the city as far west as Braemar.'[58] Dower went on to say, 'the village of Banchory Ternan became a kind of transmitting centre to the regions beyond and the parishes around. Certainly from it, more than any other of the Deeside villages, the word sounded out and the gracious influence spread abroad.'[59] Therefore Huntly and Banchory became the most important centres of religious fervour from which the 1859 revival was diffused into neighbouring rural towns and villages.

IV

There were three groups of people, each of whom fulfilled different functions, who were responsible for the dissemination of the revival across the agricultural hinterland of north east Scotland. The greater share of the work was undertaken by its converts. In many respects the success or failure of the revival lay within the response of ordinary people. In most areas they reacted positively and became the chief means of its propagation through the rural communities. They achieved this in two ways. Firstly the startling and often remarkable changes that accompanied their spiritual awakening arrested the attention of their families, friends and neighbours to such an extent that many of them were consequently converted as well.[60] In 1860 Robert Reid described how 'God had made those who were awakened and changed the means of awakening others, and turning them to the Lord. He knew the case of a young woman, notorious for her levity, who had been led to think seriously by meeting on the road a companion who had undergone a saving change.'[61] Similarly William Ker traced the origins of the revival at Deskford in 1859 to the remarkable conversion two years previously 'of a man looked upon as perfectly hopeless – a drunkard'.[62] This man possessed enormous influence in the parish and consequently his life came under close inspection throughout a large district. After a period, during which his profession of faith remained strong, local people began to question how he had changed. When this man engaged earnestly in the revival his witness 'had an important influence upon the work generally'.[63] Subsequently a group of people from Grange, attracted by accounts of the revival in neighbouring Deskford, walked eight miles to attend a revival meeting and 'went home with a blessing, and so the work was carried into the neighbouring parish'.[64] Accordingly the testimony of changed local lives exercised an important influence upon the course of the revival.

In addition the revival converts assumed responsibility for conducting meetings in their homes and farms, outwith the church, wherein the movement thrived. William Smith, Free Church minister of Keig and Tough, was amazed by the number of prayer meetings that sprang up spontaneously in his parish. He spoke about how these meetings were conducted 'either wholly or in part, by the people themselves'.[65] Henry Williamson reported upon several interesting revival gatherings that were conducted by local people in Strathbogie. He described 'a farmer addressing, on a Sabbath evening, about a hundred people gathered in a mill loft . . . At another, he found, on a week evening, a quarrier's prayer meeting assembled in the smithy belonging to the work, surely a most gratifying sight. This prayer meeting, moreover, was originated entirely by the workmen, and is usually conducted by them.'[66] In this way, the revival progressed in rural communities under the direction of local people as groups of friends and relatives met to discuss religious matters and personal spiritual concerns in one another's homes. It is clear that ordinary men and women exerted considerable influence upon this popular movement as it spread through the farming communities of rural Aberdeenshire.

The second group that acted as a stimulus of the revival in many places were itinerant evangelists. Attitudes towards these gentlemen varied considerably across the north east of Scotland. There were parts of Aberdeenshire which embraced the revival, but did not appear to welcome the evangelists warmly. At Culsamond, for example, the Kirk Session of the Free Church remarked how 'no men of public note have been employed to arouse the people. All has been brought about in the use of the ordinary means of grace'.[67] Meanwhile George Archibald, the Free Church minister of Udny, reported proudly how the revival had flourished in the Presbytery of Ellon inspite of the fact that itinerant evangelists had not visited any of the parishes in that area. On the contrary he boasted how 'God has been blessing the ordinary ministrations of the pulpit'.[68] However it is significant that the revival does not appear to have affected those parishes where ministers categorically opposed the work of these laymen. For instance, the movement did not appear in Alves in Morayshire where the Free Church minister, Alexander Gentle, had said 'the immediate effects of lay preaching is to lower the character of the whole Church – to lower the character of the ministry in the estimation of the people'.[69] Consequently, no lay preaching occurred in his parish and no revival was experienced. Hence the movement does not appear to have flourished in some areas as it did in other places where the lay preachers were received more gladly.

Indeed the evangelists were the means by which the movement prospered in many towns and villages across Aberdeenshire. In several situations they served to release the religious enthusiasm that had been built up in congregations over a period of many months by local ministers. William Ingram, Free Church minister at Rothiemay described how 'there was a smouldering anxiety among the people for a considerable time, which was very remarkably manifested in the visits of Mr Radcliffe'.[70] Similarly, Alexander Reid described how 'after this preparation, a visit from Mr Radcliffe had been much blessed in awakening a spirit of anxious inquiry' at Portsoy.[71] Also William Leslie, minister of the Free Church at Macduff, said that for a period there were signs of an increased spiritual concern amongst members of his congregation. This, he said, was most evidenced in the rise in the number of prayer meetings and increased attendance at Sunday worship. Nevertheless he acknowledged that 'the special work of God' did not begin until Reginald Radcliffe visited and spoke at his church. He describes how 'there was evidently much power with the word spoken, and many were deeply impressed'.[72] Likewise George Bain attributed the beginnings of revival in his parish to the influence of Radcliffe's preaching. Bain visited scenes of the Irish revival for two weeks at the end of July 1859 and arranged that Radcliffe would conduct worship in the church during his absence. When he was in Ireland Bain sought the prayer support of friends in Coleraine and Belfast. They prayed particularly for the first meeting Radcliffe was to conduct on a Thursday evening and when he returned Bain discovered that a great awakening had occurred within his church that very same night.[73] Despite Bain's preparatory work, revival did not occur until an itinerant evangelist had spoken to his congregation. Unordained, travelling preachers, and in particular Reginald Radcliffe, possessed an extraordinary ability to arouse whole communities to a consideration of spiritual matters in 1859. The itinerant evangelists acted as the chief spurs of the movement in many parishes in the north east of Scotland.

Notwithstanding the importance of the roles played by the converts and these laymen, the leadership of the rural revival was undertaken largely by a number of Free Church ministers. There were four in particular who emerged as the key organisers: Robert Reid of Banchory, William Ker of Deskford, Henry Williamson of Huntly and Archibald Gardner at New Deer. These men, placed in strategic parishes in the north east, acted as the spiritual directors of the revival. It is interesting to consider their common characteristics. Each of them, except Reid who was forty eight, was aged between twenty seven and thirty six at the time of the revival and they had been ordained into their first charges between 1852 and 1856.[74] Hence they were young men who had become ministers during an exciting period when active evangelism was becoming increasingly important in the Free Church.[75] Of greater significance they assumed responsibility for directing the rural revival and as a consequence these young ministers exercised enormous influence upon its manner and course. Certainly they were responsible for the reporting of the movement in the secular and religious press. As a result it was always presented as an orderly, controlled revival because they generally abhorred physical manifestations of religious excitement.[76] Their authority was certainly reflected in the expression of the rural movement which differed appreciably, as we shall see, from that experienced in Aberdeen. Indeed the guidance of these ministers exercised the most significant influence upon the manifestation of the revival in the rural areas of north east Scotland.

V

An indication of the tone of the rural revival may be speculatively inferred from the contents of Robert Reid's library, which were auctioned, after his death, in Aberdeen in 1894. Among his books for sale were *Revivals of the Eighteenth Century and Sermons* by George Whitefield, *McCheyne's Memoirs* and *Nettleton and his Labours* both by Andrew Bonar, as well as several other volumes by Richard Baxter, William Couper and Matthew Henry. These books create a distinct impression about Reid's theological persuasion which imply that his sympathies lay with Whitefield and Nettleton, who advocated and practised long-established revival means. Despite being fashionable and highly regarded authorities on religious movements around the middle of the nineteenth century, Finney and Colton, who encouraged the use of more modern revival techniques, were conspicuous by their absence from among Reid's collection of books.[77] This may suggest that Reid, a principal architect of the rural revival, brought a traditional influence to bear upon this manifestation of the movement.

The authority which Free Church ministers exercised over the revival in Aberdeenshire is demonstrated more clearly by the manner in which conversion appears to have been understood and experienced. These men were, on the whole, staunch Calvinists. Accordingly they believed that conversion was, most often, a gradual awakening which was preceded by what they described as 'a work of the law'. During this unspecified period they held that men and women became first of all distressed in their conscience by the weight of their sinfulness. Only after this time did they judge that people were comforted by God's gift of faith. Then people were enabled to repent and be converted. Repeatedly in the accounts and reports which they wrote, the impression is created that people experienced gradually before conversion a 'growing feeling of earnestness and solemnity' towards religious matters.[78] Robert Reid said 'he had seen several in such a state of distress that they could not sleep by night, nor take their food, nor attend to their usual duties in the world', such was the anxiety they felt about their relationship towards God.[79] Donaldson Rose, the Free Church minister at Kinnethmont, also noticed these symptoms. He recounted the conversion experience of those who came under his notice. He said that 'when awakened, they were found by us in deep trouble of mind from conviction of sin, which had often been going on long before any outward signs appeared. When it does break out, it is in tears and sighs, and solemn confessions of sin'.[80] This suggests that feelings of guilt affected the lives of people for a period before they were converted. George Bain, commenting upon the response made after services which he and Reginald Radcliffe had conducted, said of the awakened, 'of these persons the great majority obtained peace in waiting on the Lord Jesus in the course of from one to four weeks'.[81] Hence it appears, according to these minister's accounts, the fermfolk did not experience conversion as a spontaneous, immediate act of their own will during the excitement of a religious service. Certainly special meetings held after revival services for anxious inquirers were not a feature of the rural movement as they were in Aberdeen. On the contrary, at Culsamond, regular opportunities were provided 'every Lord's Day after divine service for anxious persons to remain for prayer and consultation as to the way of salvation'.[82] Accordingly it appears the farming people understood the 'new birth' in a traditional, Calvinist manner, to be a protracted, agonising ordeal that could last for weeks and even months. The nature of conversion in the rural revival reflected not only the character of the people amongst whom it was felt, but also the theological persuasion of the ministers who led and controlled the movement.

There were several, isolated incidents of prostration that accompanied the conversion of some of the fermfolk during the revival. Two were recorded by Archibald Gardner, who had become accustomed to scenes of prostration during his visit to Ireland. On one occasion he described an aged woman who, distressed by her sin, cried loudly at a service conducted in his church, while another concerned a young woman who attended a Bible Class meeting during which she was 'awakened' by a remark made by the preacher. According to Gardner 'she was so much affected that she could not leave, and he was obliged to give her over to the care of two young persons of her own age to speak with her'.[83] The kirk session minutes of Culsamond Free Church describe 'several remarkable cases of spiritual concern'. Yet the most public exhibition was that a woman 'prayed one Sabbath after Divine service in the Church without being asked. She stated she could not restrain it.'[84] Given that such an outburst drew this attention it becomes clear that the fermfolk were not accustomed to unusual, spontaneous outbursts of religious enthusiasm in their churches. William Leslie reported that only two accounts of prostration had come under his notice in Macduff. And both of these had occurred in people's homes and not at public meetings.[85] Also, William Ker recounted the story of how a quiet, respectable, religious middle aged gentleman was arrested by a physical prostration in his home in Deskford. One evening this man prayed earnestly before he went to bed 'that he might be really brought to Christ as a sinner'.[86] Ker described how 'he tried to sleep, but a trembling seized him so that the bed shook under him, and he was forced to his knees to cry for mercy, so loud that all in the house heard him'.[87] Once again the manifestation seized the man when he was at home, and not at a public service of worship. These accounts demonstrate that physical prostrations accompanied the conversion experience of only a few individuals who were 'born again' in the course of the rural revival. Manifestations that appeared at public meetings were relatively quiet and not infectious, but more often the fermfolk were affected in their homes. The sober manner of these prostrations reveals how the character of the fermfolk, and the guidance of their ministers, influenced the undemonstrative nature of this religious movement.

Indeed it often appears that Free Church ministers sought to prevent physical manifestations from appearing among their parishioners altogether. They seem to have been anxious that the revival appeared in an orderly manner. Robert Reid, for instance, boasted 'there had been no great public excitement' at Banchory Ternan.[88] Meanwhile William Ingram reported 'there was nothing of extravagance – nothing of enthusiasm in an offensive sense; all was sober, ardent, deep, calm' at Rothiemay.[89] Furthermore, Archibald Gardner remarked how 'there had not been many very extraordinary circumstances connected with the conversion of anyone' during the revival at New Deer.[90] Also a judgment made by the Kirk Session of the Huntly United Presbyterian Church, after a service was conducted in the building by the excitable itinerant Methodist evangelist, James Turner, confirms further the control which ministers and elders sought to exercise over the rural revival. Turner, who was responsible for generating highly emotional scenes amongst the fisherfolk along the Moray Firth, led a meeting at Huntly, after which the elders discussed whether the use of their church should on any future occasion be granted to him again. According to their minutes 'after consultation it was agreed that he should be admitted but that diligent care should be exercised that nothing take place which might make the cause of God to be evil spoken of'.[91] This demonstrates further how the leaders of the religious movement among the fermfolk were anxious that it should be conducted in a controlled and disciplined manner. Consequently physical manifestations did not tend to accompany the conversion experience of most farming people.

VI

The fermfolk's daily lives also had an effect upon the assimilation of the revival into the rural hinterland of north east Scotland. Although some farm workers, most notably the horsemen, worked long hours, most people did not adhere to a rigid work pattern in the countryside.[92] On the contrary their tasks each day followed a somewhat natural, unregimented rhythm. Their work unfolded as it followed the seasons of the year. According to David Kerr Cameron, a local author, 'the calendar on the kitchen wall was an irrelevance; it had no dominance in their lives'.[93] He continued, 'they could not alter . . . the hallowed cycle of the year itself. The turn of the seasons imposed their own order on the lives of the folk of the farmtouns . . . the grieve might order the farmtoun day but God and the soil itself set the rhythm of the year.'[94] However, there were particular periods of intense industry and of rest in the course of each year. The Farmer's and Grazier's Calendar in the *Aberdeen Almanac* of 1860 said that September 'may be considered the harvest month. Engage plenty of assisting hands for this important season.'[95] Clearly this was a busy period during the agricultural year. In the winter, however, there was a greater amount of time for rest. Cameron describes how 'for six weeks together, and maybe for longer, the ploughs would be rested as the year turned . . . horsemen unyoked from the plough and unsettled by idleness moved cautiously in the silence of the winter wrapped toun cowled in cornbags, like monks in a cloister'.[96] A clear seasonal pattern governed the daily lives of the fermfolk. The late summer was their busiest period, while the winter afforded more time to rest.

These annual rhythms of work and rest that directed the lives of rural communities had an important influence upon their religious practices. For example, in September 1859, the elders of Insch Parish Church 'considering that the third Sunday in August is rather late in the season for the dispensation of the sacrament of the Lord's Supper, as the days for public worship connected with the sacrament do occasionally interfere with the operations of the harvest, unanimously resolved to appoint, and hereby do appoint the sacrament to be dispensed in future on the first Sabbath of July'.[97] The rural pattern of work also affected the timing and appearance of the revival. Henry McCleod summoned his elders at Ardclach in November 1859 in order to 'submit to them the propriety of resuming the weekly [revival] prayer meeting as harvest work was brought to a close'.[98] Similarly David Henry recorded how revival 'meetings were renewed after harvest, and extremely well attended, and followed by a similar good effect' at New Marnoch.[99] The revival began to appear in some rural areas in the spring of 1859, but some ministers described how it abated during the summer, before resuming with greater effect during the following autumn.[100] Meanwhile, according to other reports gathered in religious journals, the most significant period of the movement among the fermfolk in Aberdeenshire lasted from October 1859 to February 1860.[101] Accordingly the rural revival flourished during the period when the fermfolk were not consumed with work and had more free time to devote their attention towards religious concerns.

This is further illustrated by the appearance of the movement during the principal holidays in the agricultural calendar. The biannual feeing markets, at which agricultural workers hired themselves to local farmers, were held during the terms of Whitsunday and Martinmas. These were great farming public festivals which attracted large crowds of people.[102] Regularly they were frowned upon on account of 'the very serious moral mischiefs and dangers' that accompanied them.[103] Nevertheless the revivalists seized the opportunity which these markets afforded and used them to address enormous crowds on more than one occasion. Donaldson Rose described his experience at the Huntly feeing market in 1859 as 'one of the most remarkable days in my life – perhaps one of the most remarkable days I will ever see in this world'.[104] He reported how he saw 'old men, and young lads, and intelligent tradesmen – all assembled together, and the room crowded over and over again by the anxious, many of whom had been arrested in the market . . . those solemn meetings and solemn dealings will never be forgotten'.[105] A correspondent of *The Wynd Journal* reported how

> Two houses were opened in the Square to receive inquirers; the Court House, with different rooms for men, and four rooms on different floors for women, where there were hundreds during the day under deep conviction. Several ladies were at work all day with tracts; and Mr Radcliffe, Mr Williamson and others, were engaged in addresses publicly and privately. Such a day has not been seen here before.[106]

Meanwhile the Duchess of Gordon described how 'the market at Insch was something wonderful; so different from former years. The eagerness to hear of Jesus was most earnest, the solemnity great, with the warm pressure of the hand of all around. The hall taken to speak to anxious ones was filled all day. The greatest wonder is that they did not see one intoxicated person, nor hear one bad word.'[107] Thomas Baxter also described remarkable scenes of a feeing market held at Banff. Services were held from two to ten o' clock in his church, while open air meetings were conducted amidst the very throng of the market 'with very marked success'.[108] Lastly, the

Aberdeen Free Press, commenting upon the feeing market conducted at Potarch in May 1861, described how it 'never saw a market pass with so little disturbance. Formerly there used to be fighting and terrible rows at public houses, but there has been nothing of that kind tonight.'[109] The association between the feeing markets and the revival demonstrates how the latter appeared and prospered within the rural community when the fermfolk were relatively free from the demands of work.

However, a more noteworthy feature of the rural revival was its association with the traditional communion season. These long-established five-day religious festivals acted, frequently, as the occasion of the rural movement, and became the means by which it prospered and was sustained. Robert Reid described how 'in regard to the commencement of the work, he might state that it seemed to begin the week after their Spring Communion, on the first Sabbath of May, which not a few had felt to be a very solemn season to their souls'.[110] Alexander Thomson, a local gentleman from Banchory, recalled 'we never had apparently so solemn a communion; we had forty more than ever before'.[111] In June of that year, Reid 'submitted to the consideration of the Session whether it might not by the blessing of God have a beneficial effect and serve to advance the Lord's work in our midst that the Lord's Supper should be dispensed towards the end of next month'.[112] As a result an extraordinary shortened communion season, lasting only two days, was held at the beginning of August. George Bain also recognised the potential of the communion season to serve the purposes of the revival. He recorded how he 'had asked for the assistance of the most godly ministers I could get, especially at our communions, – which solemn seasons we endeavoured further to improve by meetings for prayer, with appropriate addresses, every evening of the preceding week, and on that of the Monday following'.[113] In December 1859 his elders, 'took into consideration the propriety of holding a special communion in connection with the blessed revival'.[114] The following month, after the specially arranged celebration of the sacrament, the kirk session minutes recorded 'there has been a truly wonderful awakening . . . on the occasion of a special communion . . . there were more communicants added to the roll than there was during the whole past nine years of the minister's incumbency'.[115] Bain wrote in his personal reports, 'last Sabbath, which was the first day of the year, we had the Lord's Supper dispensed specially in connection with the blessed work. We had about fifty communicants added to our roll.'[116] Clearly, the traditional communion season, which was knitted into the annual rhythms of the farming calendar, had a profound influence upon the timing and manner in which the revival appeared in Aberdeenshire. Regularly the high points of the movement coincided with these great rural religious festivals.

Furthermore, the open-air field services, which became perhaps the most important feature of the revival among the fermfolk, were often planned in order to coincide with the local communion seasons.[117] These gatherings resembled the outdoor meetings that became popular during the eighteenth-century revivals in America. Essentially they were employed as an instrument of evangelism in rural situations.[118] Although they began to disappear at the start of the nineteenth century, despite the efforts of Lorenzo Dow, the 'camp meeting' was used with enormous effect in the agricultural villages and small towns during the Ulster revival.[119] It appears that upon their return from visiting scenes of the Irish revival that ministers from Aberdeenshire began to use these outdoor meetings in their parishes. During the autumn of 1859 they were held almost every evening in the principal agricultural towns of the north east. The *Banffshire Journal*, for instance, described a typical summer's evening open air service held at New Pitsligo. It reported how 'it is something impressive to hear the earnest voice of the preacher and romantic to behold large groups of women with babies in their arms, and workmen, in working dress, seated around him in the grass sward, on our village square, devoutly listening to the word of truth'.[120] Following the 1860 Huntly revival rally, which appears to have injected fresh enthusiasm into the religious movement, open-air revival meetings became even more popular in the north east of Scotland. One thousand people attended a gathering at Chapel of Garioch, some of whom had walked up to twelve miles in order to attend.[121] Similarly approximately 1,600 attended a gathering at Skene, 3,000 met together at Banchory Lodge, the home of Colonel Ramsay and between three and four hundred attended an open-air service at Durris.[122] During the early summer of 1861 another series of open-air revival services were held in the rural towns of the north east, including New Pitsligo, Banchory Ternan, Chapel of Garioch, Aboyne and Fyvie.[123] It is significant that this manifestation of the 1859 revival flourished at open-air religious services that were held in fields. This indicates how the means and manner of the fermfolk's movement were influenced by the setting within which it appeared. It also reveals how the rural revival employed traditional methods of outreach.

The expression of the 1859 religious movement that spread across the north east of Scotland was clearly different from that which affected Aberdeen. However, there is no doubt, that both appearances of the revival were preceded by a climate of desire and expectation that was created by news of the American revival and displayed in the profusion of prayer meetings. Nevertheless, the means, manner and expression of the farming movement were different from those that were manifest elsewhere. In the first instance, this was a regional campaign that was diffused over a wide area. Consequently, and despite the noteworthy role played by the converts and itinerant evangelists, it relied upon the leadership offered by a number of local clergymen, the greater proportion of whom belonged to the Free Church. These men dominated and exercised a profound influence upon the course of the revival. The steady and undramatic unfolding of the movement displayed by the absence of religious excitement and the anxious, protracted conversion experiences were evidence of their guidance of events. Yet these features also demonstrated how the rural revival was fundamentally conditioned by the context within which it arose. They reflected the character of the places and people who were involved. This was exhibited even more clearly by the manner in which the awakening was assimilated into the farming communities, moulded around their patterns of work and holiday and appearing during the long established communion seasons. It seems the rural revival belonged to an older tradition of religious movements, and this is confirmed by its frequent use of the time-honoured open-air field meeting. Accordingly, moulded intrinsically by the context within which it appeared, the rural manifestation of the 1859 revival was a traditional religious movement.

Notes

1. T. T. Matthews (ed.), *Reminiscences of the Revival of Fifty Nine and the Sixties* (Aberdeen, 1910), p. 54.
2. I. Carter, *Farm Life in North East Scotland, 1840-1914* (Edinburgh, 1979), p. 15.
3. J. S. Smith, D. Stevenson (ed.), *Fermfolk and Fisherfolk: Rural Life in Northern Scotland in the Eighteenth and Nineteenth Centuries* (Aberdeen, 1989), pp. 1-9.
4. A. A. MacLaren, *Religion and Social Class: The Disruption Years in Aberdeen* (London, 1974), p. 9.
5. D. K. Cameron, *The Cornkister Days: Portrait of a Land and its Rituals* (London, 1984), p. 26.
6. A. Keith, *The North of Scotland Bank Limited* (Aberdeen, 1936), p. 11.
7. Smith, Stevenson (ed.), *Fermfolk and Fisherfolk*, pp. 63-80.
8. Carter, *Farm Life*, p. 33
9. Ibid., p. 21.
10. Ibid., p. 40.
11. *A.F.P.*, (5 October 1860), p. 5.
12. Ibid., (4 October 1861), p. 7.
13. *A Report of a Conference on the State of Religion and Public Meeting, held in the*

Free Church, Huntly, January 5, 1860 (Huntly, 1860), p. 26.
14. J. Alexander, *Prize Essay on the Present Condition of Farm Servants in Scotland, with Means to be Adopted for its Amelioration* (Aberdeen, 1852), p. 4.
15. A. Fraser, *First Prize Essay on the Condition of the Agricultural Population and the Best Means of Ameliorating their Condition, Morally and Socially* (Edinburgh, 1859), p. 14.
16. A.F.P., (15 April 1859), p. 5.
17. M. M. Gordon, *Hay MacDowall Grant of Arndilly: His Life, Labours and Teaching* (London, 1876), p. 68.
18. Ibid., p. 89.
19. W.J., No 17, (21 January 1860), p. 134.
20. Carter, *Farm Life*, p. 2.
21. *Conference on State of Religion*, Huntly, p. 32.
22. Ibid., p. 36.
23. Ibid., pp. 16-18.
24. Ibid., pp. 26-7.
25. Ibid., p. 35.
26. Huntly United Presbyterian Church Kirk Session Minutes, 23 June 1858
27. Ibid., 18 July 1858
28. Fordyce Free Church Presbytery Minutes, September 1858
29. Elgin High Free Church Kirk Session Minutes, 4 March 1859
30. Ardclach Free Church Kirk Session Minutes, 6 June 1859
31. Forgue Free Church Kirk Session Minutes, 21 July 1859
32. Insch Free Church Kirk Session Minutes, September 1859
33. Clola Free Church Kirk Session Minutes, 20 October 1859
34. Old Deer Free Church Kirk Session Minutes, 9 November 1859
35. Culsamond Free Church Kirk Session Minutes, 16 November 1859
36. Culsamond Free Church Kirk Session Minutes, 30 January 1860
37. Oyne Free Church Kirk Session Minutes, 9 January 1860
38. *Conference on State of Religion*, Huntly, p. 33.
39. Ibid., p. 32.
40. A.F.P., (8 July 1859), p. 8.
41. Ibid., (13 January 1860), p. 6.
42. *Conference on State of Religion*, Huntly, p. 9.
43. Ibid., p. 14.
44. Ibid., p. 11.
45. W.J., No 17, (21 January 1860), p. 134.
46. Matthews, *Reminiscences*, p. 37.
47. T.R., Vol 1, No 5, (27 August 1859), p. 37.
48. *Conference on State of Religion*, Huntly, p. 36.
49. W.J., No 15, (7 January 1860), p. 114.
50. A.F.P., (10 August 1860), p. 5.
51. Ibid., (15 April 1859), p. 6.
52. A.J., (11 April 1860), p. 9.
53. M.R.UP.C., (September 1860), Vol 15, p. 167.
54. W.J., No 40, (30 June 1860), p. 317.
55. Matthews, *Reminiscences*, p. 74.
56. *Conference on State of Religion*, Huntly, p. 30.

57. *F.A.*, (25 November 1859), p. 2.
58. Matthews, *Reminiscences*, p. 119.
59. Ibid.
60. *Conference on State of Religion*, Huntly, p. 8.
61. Ibid.
62. *A.F.P.*, (13 April 1860), p. 6.
63. *W.J.*, No 30, (21 April 1860), p. 235.
64. Ibid.
65. *Conference on State of Religion*, Huntly, p. 38.
66. Anon, *The Appearance of God's Work in the Chief Towns of Scotland: With special reference to Aberdeen and Dundee* (Aberdeen, 1859), p. 40.
67. Culsamond Free Church Kirk Session Minutes, 30 January 1860
68. *A.F.P.*, (13 April 1860), p. 6.
69. *N.T.*, (4 May 1859), p. 3.
70. *Conference on State of Religion*, Huntly, p. 33.
71. Ibid., p. 11.
72. Ibid., p. 39.
73. Ibid., p. 28.
74. W. Ewing (ed.), *Annals of the Free Church of Scotland 1849-1900* (Edinburgh, 1914), pp. 122, 165, 199, 296, 356.
75. S. J. Brown, 'Thomas Chalmers and the Communal Ideal in Victorian Scotland' in T. C. Smout (ed.), *Victorian Values* (Oxford, 1992), p. 71.
76. *Conference on State of Religion*, Huntly, pp. 7, 33. *A.F.P.*, (13 January 186)0, p. 6.
77. *Catalogue of a collection of books being portions of the libraries of the late Rev Robert Reid, Banchory, and others, to be sold by auction, by the Aberdeen Auction Company Limited within their rooms, 120 Union Street, Aberdeen, on successive evenings, commencing 28 February 1894. Sale at 6.30 pm each evening. John F Smyth, Auctioneer* (Aberdeen, 1894), pp. 1-12
78. Inverurie Free Church Kirk Session Minutes, 12 January 1860, Oyne Free Church Kirk Session Minutes, 7 February 1860
79. *Conference on State of Religion*, Huntly, p. 8.
80. Ibid., p. 20.
81. Ibid., p. 29.
82. Culsamond Free Church Kirk Session Minutes, 30 January 1860
83. *A.F.P.*, (13 January 1860), p. 6.
84. Culsamond Free Church Kirk Session Minutes, 30 January 1860
85. *Conference on State of Religion*, Huntly, pp. 38-9.
86. Ibid., p. 17.
87. Ibid.
88. Ibid., p. 7.
89. Ibid., p. 33.
90. *A.F.P.*, (13 January 1860), p. 6.
91. Huntly United Presbyterian Church Kirk Session Minutes, 10 December 1860
92. Carter, *Farm Life*, p. 112.
93. Cameron, *Cornkister Days*, p. 54.
94. D. K. Cameron, *The Ballad and the Plough* (London, 1978), p. 35.

95. *Aberdeen Almanac 1860* (Aberdeen, 1860), p. 13.
96. Cameron, *Cornkister Days*, p. 75.
97. Inch Parish Church Kirk Session Minutes, 10 September 1859
98. Ardclach Free Church Kirk Session Minutes, 7 November 1859
99. *Conference on State of Religion*, Huntly, p. 32.
100. Ibid., p. 33.
101. *T.R.*, Vol 1, No 18, (26 November 1859), p. 139, *W.J.*, No 17, (21 January 1860), p. 123.
102. W. Alexander, *Rural Life in Victorian Aberdeenshire* [I. Carter ed.], (Edinburgh, 1992), p. 50.
103. *A.F.P.*, (20 May 1859), p. 4.
104. Ibid., (13 January 1860), p. 6.
105. *Conference on State of Religion*, Huntly, p. 21.
106. *W.J.*, No 10, (3 December 1859), p. 75.
107. G. Gordon, *The Last Dukes of Gordon and their Consorts, 1743-1865* (Aberdeen, nd), p. 217.
108. *M.R.UP.C.*, Vol (15, Sept 1860), p. 167.
109. *A.F.P.*, 17 May 1861, p. 5
110. *Conference on State of Religion*, Huntly, p. 7.
111. G. Smeaton, *Memoir of Alexander Thomson of Banchory* (Edinburgh, 1869), p. 427.
112. Banchory Ternan Free Church Kirk Session Minutes, 1 June 1859
113. *Conference on State of Religion*, Huntly, p. 26.
114. Chapel of Garioch Free Church Kirk Session Minutes, 18 December 1859
115. Ibid., 30 January 1860
116. *Conference on State of Religion*, Huntly, p. 29.
117. *A.F.P.*, (9 August 1861), p. 5.
118. R. Carwardine, *Transatlantic Revivalism: Popular Evangelicalism in Britain and America, 1790-1865* (Westport, Connecticut, 1978), p. 106.
119. Ibid., p. 172.
120. *B.J.*, (13 December 1859), p. 6.
121. *A.F.P.*, (17 August 1860), p. 5.
122. Ibid., (7 September 1860,) p. 8; 14 September 1860, p. 5; 21 September 1860, p. 5.
123. Ibid., (12 July 1861), p. 8; 26 July 1861, p. 6.

CHAPTER 6

The Revival in the Rural Hinterland

Analysis and Results

The manner and expression of the revival among the farming people of Aberdeenshire suggest it was deeply indebted to tradition. This impression is strengthened when the principal effects of the movement are considered. An examination of the influence which the revival commanded over the main denominations represented in the area, and the factors which determined the geographical distribution of the movement indicate it was a long established awakening. This interpretation is confirmed by an analysis of the composition of those who joined rural churches during this period. A survey of these results of the agrarian religious movement will confirm the conviction already created, that it resembled the traditional, Presbyterian revivals of the seventeenth and eighteenth centuries.

I

There were 296 churches and chapels in the rural hinterland of north east Scotland in 1859. They included 130 Church of Scotland, ninety two Free Church, thirty nine Episcopal, twenty one United Presbyterian, twelve Congregational and two Baptist congregations.[1] An examination was made of the records of sixty of these churches, which included sixteen Church of Scotland congregations, thirty seven from the Free Church, four United Presbyterian and four Episcopal churches. This sample of churches studied was restricted by the nature of some documents and the non-existence of others. For instance, unfortunately no documents that related to this region and period were found for the Congregational and Baptist churches. Also, Episcopal documents were often difficult to locate, while the usefulness of the information they contained varied considerably. Nevertheless, two sets of records in particular presented illuminating results. It was found that the Established Church kirk session minutes dealt almost exclusively with cases of discipline around the middle of the nineteenth century and none of those examined made a single reference to the revival. Parish communion rolls, however, provided more useful information and as a result, all those that remain in existence, eleven in total, were investigated. Free Church kirk session minutes, on the other hand, regularly contained accounts of the revival and its effect upon congregations. Hence all of the documents that belong to the Free Church in the north east of Scotland during the period of the revival which are held in the National Archives of Scotland were analysed. Similarly, the United Presbyterian church records provided helpful descriptions of the revival and all those that remain were studied. The records that were examined have produced some noteworthy results. In the first instance they reveal the extent to which the various denominations were affected by the revival.

Given that the Church of Scotland kirk session minutes appeared to deal almost exclusively with cases of discipline, it was decided to examine a selection of parishes where it had been discovered that the revival had had a decided effect. Hence the minutes for Banchory Ternan, Chapel of Garioch, Culsamond, Echt, Insch, Inverurie and Oyne Parish Churches were examined. No single reference to the revival was found in any of these records.[2] In addition, the communion rolls of five Established congregations, those at Aberlour, Ellon, Inch, Oldmeldrum and Savoch, revealed that the number of new communicants added to their rolls and the total number of those who celebrated the sacrament in these churches during the revival did not increase, but rather in some instances fell.[3] This evidence, along with the silence of the session minutes, appeared to confirm the impression, created by the absence of any reference to a parish church or its minister in any of the religious or secular reports of the movement, that the Church of Scotland remained largely unaffected by the rural awakening.

However the findings from four other parish communion rolls suggest that in some quarters the Established Church was stirred by this movement. The Communion Roll Book of Millbrex Parish Church lists those who joined the congregation upon their first profession of faith from 1862 to 1866. It does not cover the early years of the revival, yet nevertheless shows that forty six men and women, almost four times as many who joined in subsequent years, were admitted into the congregation in 1862. This suggests it was influenced by the religious movement.

Table 6.1.

Millbrex Parish Church: Young communicants 1862-66

Date	YC
17 July 1862	46
26 April 1863	12
30 August 1863	15
24 April 1864	12
28 August 1864	6
30 April 1865	10
22 April 1866	13

Source: Millbrex Parish Church Communion Rolls 1862-66

The number of young communicants who joined Cluny Church of Scotland from 1857 to 1864 varied between twelve and seventeen, which gave no indication that the religious movement had affected this congregation. However, the number of people celebrating the sacrament rose in 1860. It increased by thirty two: a marked contrast to the previous and subsequent years when the rate of attendances fell. This implies that the revival acted upon this congregation too.

Table 6.2.

Cluny Parish Church: Communion rolls 1857-63

Year	C' cants	Increase / Decrease
1857	372	
1858	388	+16
1859	378	- 10
1860	410	+32
1861	386	-24
1862	403	+17
1863	371	-32

Source: Cluny Parish Church Communion Rolls, 1857-63

A similar situation is apparent from the number of people who joined Daviot Parish Church between 1857 and 1863. Admissions to the church rose markedly in 1859, by more than sixty per cent, which suggests this congregation was affected positively by the revival.

Table 6.3.

Daviot Parish Church: Young communicants 1857-63

Year	YC
1857	13
1858	13
1859	22
1860	7
1861	9
1862	11
1863	12

Source: Daviot Parish Church Communion Rolls 1829-1873

The total number of people who celebrated the Lord's Supper and the number of young communicants who joined Rhynie Parish Church from 1858 to 1864 also shows an increase. The statistics indicate clearly that the parish church of Rhynie flourished during the period of the revival, particularly in 1859. For instance, there were twenty seven young communicants added to the church roll during that year, which represented almost a tenth of the total congregation. Also, the number of communicants rose by fifty six, an increase of twenty five per cent of the total who celebrated the sacrament the previous year.

Table 6.4.

Rhynie Parish Church: Communion rolls 1858-64

Year	YC	C' cants	Increase / Decrease
1858	11	226	
1859	27	282	+ 56
1860	15	306	+ 24
1861	18	319	+ 13
1862	24	340	+ 21
1863	15	347	+ 7
1864	13	335	- 12

Source: Rhynie Parish Church Communion Rolls 1857-58, 1859-72

The communion rolls of these four parish churches suggest that certain congregations of the Established Church in the north east of Scotland experienced considerable growth during the course of this movement. Notwithstanding the silence of the Parish Church's kirk session minutes and the absence of its ministers from reports of the movement, it seems that the Church of Scotland did, in some quarters, participate in and benefit from this 'season of grace'.

However, the impression created from accounts of the revival is that its greatest supporter in the rural hinterland was the Free Church. Consequently it was surprising to find a number of congregational records which made no reference to the movement. The kirk session minutes of Aberlour, Auchendoir, Kirkmichael, Mortlach, Knockando, Rafford and Strachan Free Church congregations, for example, made no mention to the revival at all.[4] Meanwhile the communion rolls of Botriphinie, Inveravon, Longside and Lumphanan Free Churches revealed that the number of new communicants and the total number of people celebrating the sacrament in these congregations did not not grow during the period of the revival, which suggests they were unaffected by the movement.[5] Accordingly eleven of the thirty seven rural Free Churches examined do not appear to have participated in the revival. This is quite a large minority which reveals that the Free Church was not universally influenced by this movement in this region of Scotland.

Nonetheless there were a number of Free Church congregations that were involved in the revival. The following extracts from a number of kirk session minutes indicate this clearly. Firstly the elders of Skene Free Church were anxious to 'record their devout gratitude to God for the outpouring of his Spirit, and the blessed fruits and effects thereof, in the awakening and conversion of souls and in the quickening and reviving of God's people'.[6] Braemar Free Church kirk session also recorded the significance of the movement in July 1861 when they expressed 'their gratitude for the revival with which He [God] has blessed the congregation during the past six months'.[7] As well as adding new members to the churches' rolls, the movement also changed the spiritual life of congregations. Thomas Gray, the minister of Inverurie Free Church, for example, described 'a growing feeling of earnestness and solemnity in the congregation . . . tokens of the Spirit's power and presence . . . such as have not been seen or felt for years past'.[8] Each of these brief extracts represents only a small sample from a large number of minutes that contain similar descriptions. They demonstrate how this revival had a significant effect upon the lives of a number of Free Church congregations in rural Aberdeenshire.

The extent to which these churches were affected by the movement is perhaps more clearly demonstrated by some of the communion rolls that have remained. The first of these belongs to Insch Free Church. The minister, William Emslie, recorded in September 1859 a 'greater interest taken in spiritual things' within his congregation.[9] This was shown by the increased number of young communicants who joined the church. 1858-1861 were particularly important years of growth when fifty eight people were added to the church's roll.

Table 6.5.

Insch Free Church: Young communicants 1856-1865

Year	YC
1856	6
1857	5
1858	15
1859	17
1860	14
1861	12
1862	9
1863	10
1864	5
1865	6

Source: Insch Free Church Kirk Session Minutes 1843-1923

The communion roll of Banchory Ternan Free Church also reveals growth in the congregation at the time of the revival. In June 1859 Robert Reid, recorded 'the pleasing fact that there were at present some symptoms of an increased liveliness in spiritual things on the part of not a few in this neighbourhood'.[10] Unfortunately the communion roll of an extraordinary celebration of the sacrament held in August 1859, when the revival was at its height, has been lost. However, the following table reveals the rise in the number of young communicants and in the total number of people celebrating the sacrament during the movement.

Table 6.6.

Banchory Ternan Free Church: Communion rolls 1856-61

Year	YC	C' cants	Increase / Decrease
1856	17	619	
1857	13	616	- 3
1858	29	639	+ 23
1859	22+?	654	+ 15
1860	18	643	- 11
1861	17	653	+ 10

Source: Banchory Ternan Free Church Communion Rolls 1853-68

Alexander Robb, the minister of Pluscarden Free Church, was also pleased to comment in his annual state of religion report in 1861 that 'the attendance at the church, the prayer meeting and the sabbath school has increased during the last year, that there appears a greater seriousness among old and young in regard to divine things'.[11] This was again demonstrated by the rise in the number of young communicants who joined this church during the revival. In 1858 there were no young communicants, while between 1859 and 1862 a total of fifty nine people professed faith for the first time and

The Revival in the Rural Hinterland 147

were added to the church's roll.

Table 6.7.

Pluscarden Free Church: Young communicants 1858-66

Year	YC
1858	0
1859	14
1860	19
1861	15
1862	11
1863	9
1864	8
1865	5
1866	3

Source: Pluscarden Free Church Communion Rolls 1858-66

Finally, the table below displays the number of young communicants who became members of Elgin High Free Church between 1857 and 1863. It shows a rise in the number of young people who joined the congregation between 1859 and 1862, which suggests it was also influenced by the revival. The average annual number of young communicants before and after the revival was twelve. However, during the movement this rose to twenty five. Therefore the number of people who professed faith for the first time and joined the church doubled through the period of the awakening.

Table 6.8.

Elgin High Free Church: Young communicants 1858-66

Year	YC	Annual Total
April 1858	15	
Oct 1858	11	26
April 1859	8	
Nov 1859	22	30
May 1860	31	
Nov 1860	15	46
May 1861	29	
Nov 1861	30	59
May 1862	20	
Oct 1862	12	32
April 1863	14	
Oct 1863	12	26

Source: Elgin High Free Church Kirk Session Minutes, 1852-61, 1861-78

The statistics clearly show that the rate at which young communicants joined a number of Free Church congregations in the north east of Scotland rose appreciably during the revival, which demonstrates the positive effect the movement had upon this denomination in Aberdeenshire.

The United Presbyterian Church also increased its membership base through the period of the revival. Communion rolls and kirk session minutes were found for four United Presbyterian Churches, and each indicates how they prospered during the awakening. It is unfortunate that the kirk session minutes of Huntly United Presbyterian Church did not record the number of admissions to the church's roll between 1860 and 1862. Nevertheless, the increase in the number of new members during 1859 was fifteen, three times the number that joined in 1857.

Table 6.9.

Huntly United Presbyterian Church: Young communicants 1856-63

Year	YC
1856	7
1857	5
1858	10
1859	15
1860	-
1861	-
1862	-
1863	14

Source: Huntly United Presbyterian Church Kirk Session Minutes 1849-79

The New Deer United Presbyterian Church also experienced growth during the revival. Within seven years, from November 1856 to January 1863, its membership grew from eighty eight to 141, an increase of sixty per cent.

Table 6.10.

New Deer United Presbyterian Church: Young communicants 1856-63

Year	YC	Total Membership
1856	4	88
1857	7	-
1858	9	-
1859	8	-
1860	*14*	-
1861	7	-
1862	8	-
1863	3	141

Source: New Deer United Presbyterian Church Communion Rolls 1856-1907

A similar table reveals the expansion of the Craigdam United Presbyterian Church during the same period. It shows a surge in growth when the revival began. The annual average number of young communicants before and after the movement was five, while fourteen people joined the congregation in 1859.

Table 6.11.

Craigdam United Presbyterian Church: Young communicants 1857-63

Year	YC
1857	2
1858	6
1859	14
1860	8
1861	3
1862	8
1863	2

Source: Craigdam United Presbyterian Church Kirk Session Minutes 1848-1863

The following returns of Shiels United Presbyterian Church reveal the familiar pattern of growth through the period of the revival. The first table shows how the rate at which new members joined the congregation rose between 1857 and 1864, from fifty eight to 101, an increase of sixty per cent, before beginning to decline from the end of the 1870s.

Table 6.12.

Shiels United Presbyterian Church: Total membership 1857-97

Year	Total M 'ship	Increase / Decrease
1857	58	
1861	94	+ 36
1864	101	+ 7
1868	107	+ 6
1873	97	- 10
1888	70	- 27
1897	68	- 2

Source: Shiels United Presbyterian Church Congregational Roll Book 1857-1898

The second table displays the increased rate of growth the congregation enjoyed during the movement. The church added thirty two members between 1861 and 1862. This was an exceptional rate of growth, of around thirty three per cent, within a very short period.

Table 6.13.

Shiels United Presbyterian Church: Young communicants 1859-63

Year	YC
April 1859	5
August 1859	6
April 1860	2
August 1860	*10*
April 1861	*12*
August 1861	5
April 1862	*12*
August 1862	3
April 1863	2

Source: Shiels United Presbyterian Church Congregational Roll Book 1857-1898

The four United Presbyterian Churches whose records have been examined were comparatively small. Each had around one hundred members. Despite this, the tables above establish that they grew at a higher than average rate during the time of the revival. It appears the United Presbyterian Church in rural Aberdeenshire benefited considerably from this religious movement.

Finally, statistical church records were found for two Episcopal churches in the north east of Scotland that illuminate their congregational life at the time of the awakening. The first set belong to St James Chapel at Cruden. The table below illustrates the number of individuals confirmed in this congregation between 1853 and 1865. It reveals that the number of young people professing faith for the first time and being confirmed rose dramatically in 1859, almost doubling from thirty eight to sixty.

Table 6.14.

St James Episcopal Chapel, Cruden: Confirmations 1853-65

Year	Confirmations	Increase / Decrease
1853	39	- 6
1856	38	- 1
1859	*60*	*+22*
1862	40	- 20
1865	37	- 3

Source: St James Episcopal Chapel, Cruden, List of Confirmations, 1850-65

The second table displays the number of people who celebrated the sacrament from 1853 to 1865, and indicates an increase in the number of people communicating in 1861. Indeed, during a period of declining attendances, the number rose by six per cent from 591 to 631 in 1860. These statistics suggest that this church prospered during the revival.

Table 6.15.

St James Episcopal Chapel, Cruden: Communicants 1859-63

Year	C' cants	Increase / Decrease
1859	604	
1860	591	- 13
1861	631	+ 40
1862	630	- 1
1863	623	- 7

Source: St James Episcopal Chapel, Cruden, List of Communicants, 1844-69

St Ternan's Episcopal chapel at Banchory provided another list of communicants, which illuminated the degree of church attendance during the revival. Despite gaps that appeared in the roll during 1859, it was possible to calculate the average number of people receiving the sacrament at the church by dividing the total sum of communicants by the number of occasions when the Lord's Supper was celebrated. This reveals that between 1859 and 1861 more people attended the chapel than previously and subsequently, which suggests a greater devotion to religious practice by the Banchory Episcopalians during the revival.

Table 6.16.

St Ternan's Episcopal Chapel, Banchory Ternan: Communicants 1857-62

Year	C' cants	Cel'ns	Ave Attendance
1857	251	25	10.14
1858	306	25	12.24
1859	228	15	15.2
1860	485	28	17.32
1861	371	22	16.86
1862	304	25	12.16

Source: St Ternan's Episcopal Chapel Banchory, Ternan. List of Communicants, 1856-68

The communicants' list also contained, for three years, the names of young people who joined the congregation. In 1857 there were three new members, in 1858 there were four, while in 1860 there were seven.[12] Scant and incomplete as these records are, they warrant the suggestion that the Episcopalians at Banchory were influenced by this movement, which is unsurprising because the town was a major centre of revival activity. Given the general interpretation that denied the Episcopalians any involvement in this movement, it is noteworthy to demonstrate that at Cruden and Banchory, at least, they appear to have been touched by the revival.

The communion rolls and kirk session minutes that have been analysed reveal how the main denominations in the north east of Scotland were stirred by this revival. Although it seemed from reports of the movement and the records of their elders' meetings that the Established Church remained aloof from the awakening, it is significant that at least four communion rolls have demonstrated that some parish churches did embrace the movement. It is also notable that although the Free Church was the most influential supporter of the revival, there appears to have been a number of its congregations that were untouched by the movement. By contrast, all of the United Presbyterian churches examined revealed signs that they participated in the revival. Finally, it is important to acknowledge that the movement made an impression upon at least several Episcopal chapels. Accordingly it appears each of the main denominations represented in the rural hinterland was affected, in varying degrees, by the 1859 revival. This indicates that the agrarian movement commanded a broad appeal which suggests that it operated in a traditional rather than a modern manner.

II

The location of the rural churches influenced by this religious movement enables an examination to be made of the agricultural hinterland which was affected by this awakening. It is unfortunate that the absence of congregational and presbytery records for the district around Turiff has prevented an analysis of the movement's effect in this region. Nevertheless, there are at least eight factors which serve to explain why particular areas of the north east of Scotland were brought under the influence of this revival. James Obelkevich, in his study of religion and rural society in South Lindsey, found that parishes which had dispersed settlements tended to favour the growth of Methodism.[13] Likewise Alan Everitt, in his study of the pattern of rural dissent during the nineteenth century, found that it flourished in regions of dispersed settlement, while the Established Church was stronger in areas with nucleated communities.[14] The landscape of the north east of Scotland appears to have been particularly scattered in certain places. The table below, which compares the sizes of farms in Aberdeenshire and East Lothian in 1885, shows how the north east of Scotland had a relatively large number of small, separate farms. Indeed eighty two per cent of all the farms in Aberdeenshire, around the middle of the nineteenth century, were less than one hundred acres.

Table 6.17.

The comparative size of farms in Aberdeenshire and East Lothian, c 1885

Size of farms	Aberdeenshire	East Lothian
1 – 20 acres	46 %	27 %
20 – 100 acres	36 %	15 %
100 + acres	18 %	58 %

Source: I. Carter, 'Social Differentiation in the Aberdeenshire Peasantry, 1696-1870', *Journal of Peasant Studies*, 5, 1977, p. 51.

Consequently the north east became known as the 'poor man's country', because it had a greater number of smaller holdings than other areas.[15] Indeed the valuation roll of the county of Aberdeen in 1867 shows that of 11,422 holdings, 8,022, or seventy per cent, had a rental of less than £50, and of this number 5,525, or almost half, had rentals of between £4 and £20. The north east of Scotland remained through the middle of the nineteenth century a region of small farms and crofts, while other regions became areas of nucleated settlement. The distribution of these land holdings in Aberdeenshire compared with the spread of the rural revival is illustrated on map 6.1., on p. 156.[16] It shows how the pattern created by the scattering of these small farming communities is similar to that of the awakening. The movement flourished towards the east of the region where they were more dense and failed to prosper towards the west where there were fewer hamlets. The dispersed nature of the rural landscape of north east Scotland appears to help to explain why certain areas of Aberdeenshire were particularly susceptible to the impulses of this religious movement.

Another particular feature of the rural landscape of north east Scotland was the planned village. Again Everitt believes that dissent emerged 'in communities of very early origin or in areas of very late settlement', that is within the new planned villages of the eighteenth and nineteenth century.[17] T. C. Smout has identified twenty five such villages that were built in the north east of Scotland between 1730 and 1830 as a response to the changes that were affecting the rural economy at this time. Within this region there were more planned villages than anywhere else in Scotland. Some, including those built in the first quarter of the nineteenth century, were fishing villages, but the majority, erected between 1750 and 1770, appeared in the inland districts. Several notable landowners joined enthusiastically in the work of building these new villages, including the Dukes of Gordon who built two of their own.[18] One of these was Huntly. Built in 1765, it grew quickly and within fifty years became one of the finest villages in the north east. Another was Deskford which was built in 1760.[19] These villages became two

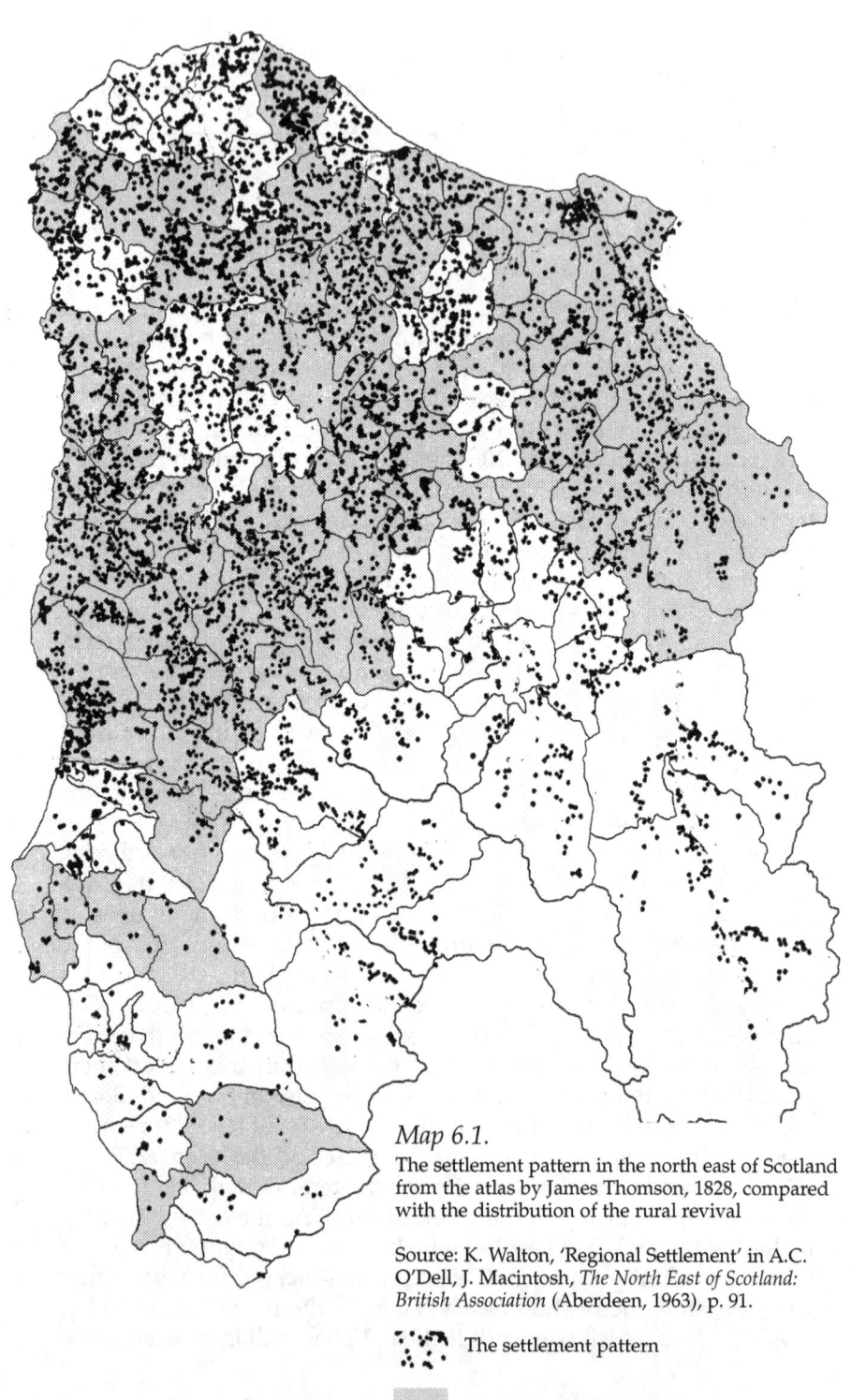

Map 6.1.
The settlement pattern in the north east of Scotland from the atlas by James Thomson, 1828, compared with the distribution of the rural revival

Source: K. Walton, 'Regional Settlement' in A.C. O'Dell, J. Macintosh, *The North East of Scotland: British Association* (Aberdeen, 1963), p. 91.

The settlement pattern

Distribution of the rural awakening

of the major centres of the religious movement, and were planted in areas that subsequently enjoyed some of the most celebrated scenes of the revival. (See Map 6.2., on p. 158.) They predominated in the central northern region of the north east of Scotland which was one of the areas of Aberdeenshire most affected by this movement. Hence it emerges that the 1859 revival flourished in the north east in the places where most of the new planned villages were found.

It also appears the revival prospered in parts of the north east of Scotland where the population was growing. Callum Brown, from his analysis of the 1851 religious census, suggested that many small dissenting sects 'had a greater appeal in small communities which had experienced recent growth of population'.[20] Meanwhile Alan Gilbert describes how the Anglican Church was unable to respond to the demands that were created by the growth of many rural parishes in England and how dissenting churches filled the void which had been created.[21] Similarly Heather Rowe, in an undergraduate dissertation on the geographical distribution of non-established Protestant churches in Stirlingshire and Clackmannanshire in the mid-nineteenth century, found that Falkirk, which experienced the most rapid population growth between 1755 and 1851 in this region, had the highest number of dissenting religious bodies, while parishes which declined during the period had a lower number of churches.[22] The changes to the rural economy in the north east of Scotland did not lead to universal population growth. In some situations there was decline as smallholdings were absorbed into larger farms, but in other places where land reclamation was encouraged there was a redistribution of the population, and on some occasions growth.[23] The revival did not appear in those parts of Aberdeenshire where the population fell during the first half of the nineteenth century. They included Strathdon, for instance, where the number of inhabited houses decreased during the 1840s from 344 to 290.[24] Similarly in Clatt, 'where clusters of cottages at one time flourished, there scarcely now remain any vestiges to point to their former site', the movement made no impression.[25] The relationship between the movement and demographic change is perhaps more clearly displayed in the following table and map. (See Map 6.3., on p. 158.) They show the growth and decline of a number of parishes in the north east of Scotland which were known to have been affected and unaffected by the revival.

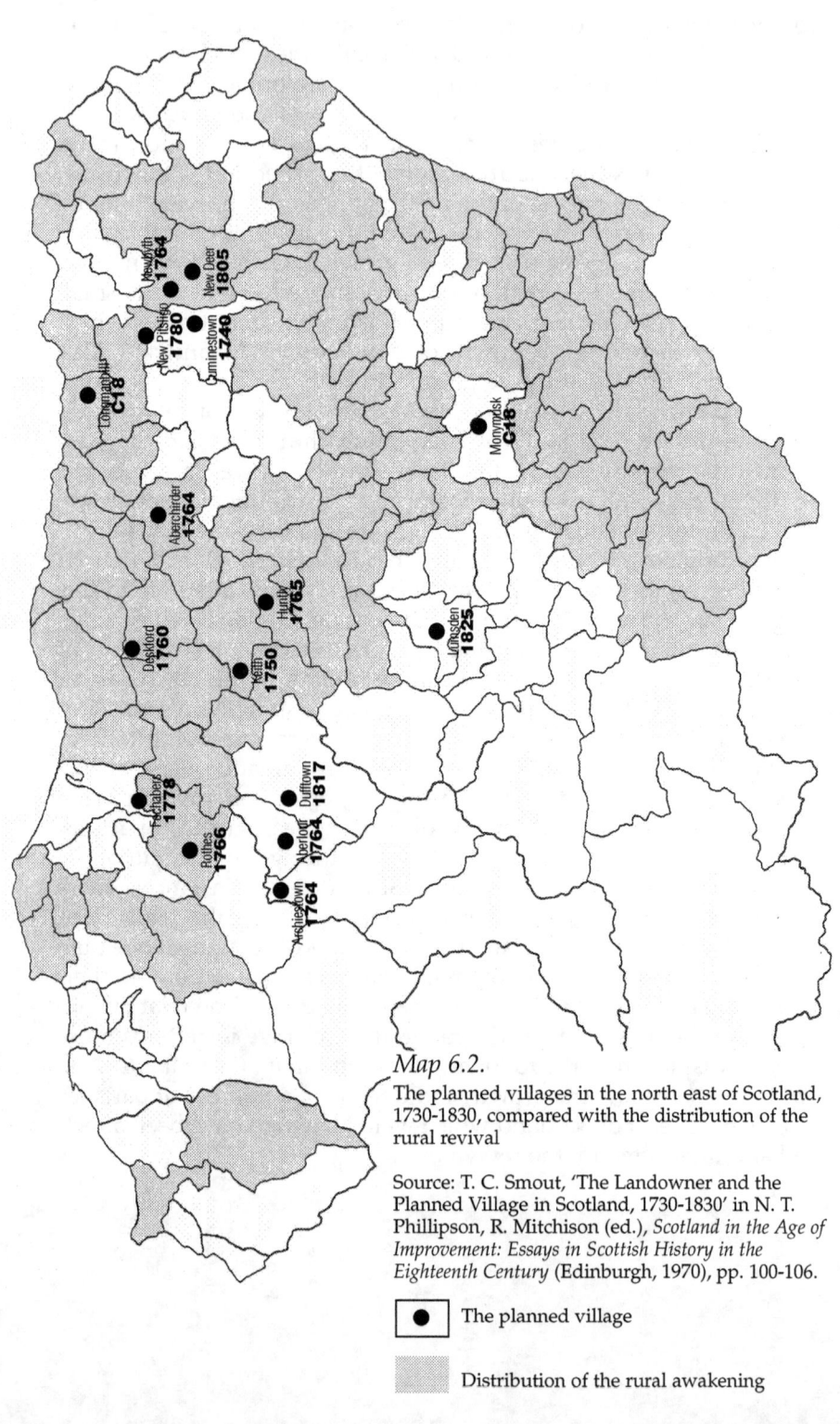

Map 6.2.
The planned villages in the north east of Scotland, 1730-1830, compared with the distribution of the rural revival

Source: T. C. Smout, 'The Landowner and the Planned Village in Scotland, 1730-1830' in N. T. Phillipson, R. Mitchison (ed.), *Scotland in the Age of Improvement: Essays in Scottish History in the Eighteenth Century* (Edinburgh, 1970), pp. 100-106.

● The planned village

▨ Distribution of the rural awakening

Table 6.18.

The demographic pattern of parishes unaffected by the revival

Parish	Popn 1851	Popn 1861	Difference 1851 / 1861
Glenmuick	1,984	1,668	- 316
Inveravon	2,552	2,487	- 65
Kirkmichael	1,558	1,511	- 47
Knockando	1,771	1,736	- 35

Source: *Census of Scotland, 1861: Population Tables and Report* (Edinburgh, 1862), pp. 22-32.

Table 6.19.

The demographic pattern of parishes affected by the revival

Parish	Popn 1851	Popn 1861	Difference 1851 / 1861
Banchory Ternan	2,462	2,947	+ 485
Deskford	917	1,031	+ 114
Huntly	3,131	3,448	+ 317
Inverurie	2,084	2,232	+ 148

Source: *Census of Scotland, 1861: Population Tables and Report* (Edinburgh, 1862), pp. 22-32.

Table 18 and Map 6.3. demonstrate that the population of a number of parishes where the revival did not appear fell between 1851 and 1861. Meanwhile, the number of people living in Huntly and Banchory, which became the two major centres of the rural revival, grew by ten and twenty per cent respectively between 1851 and 1861. Therefore it seems the population was growing where the movement flourished, and communities were in a state of decline where it failed to appear.

Another feature of the westerly parishes that were unaffected by the revival was their uninhabited, mountainous topography. (See Map 6.4., on p. 160.) A large proportion of this land was dominated by hills and consequently sparsely populated and difficult to access. In addition many of these parishes did not have a village or market town. The parish of Glenmuick, Tullich and Glengairn, for instance, described as 'mountainous and hilly', encompassed 180 square miles. Within this area 3,643 acres were cultivated, while 108,372 acres were left uncultivated.[26] Similarly along the west of Logie Coldstone parish there was a 'range of steep and high hills [which] runs the whole distance'.[27] The parish of Strathdon was also described as 'mountainous', and there was 'no village in the parish, unless nine cottages at Heugh-head may be called one'.[28] The New Statistical Account of Aberdeenshire of 1843 recorded that the area of Glenbucket parish was ten miles by two and a half miles that was mostly mountainous, within which six miles by one mile was used for arable farming.[29] Towie was another comparatively small parish

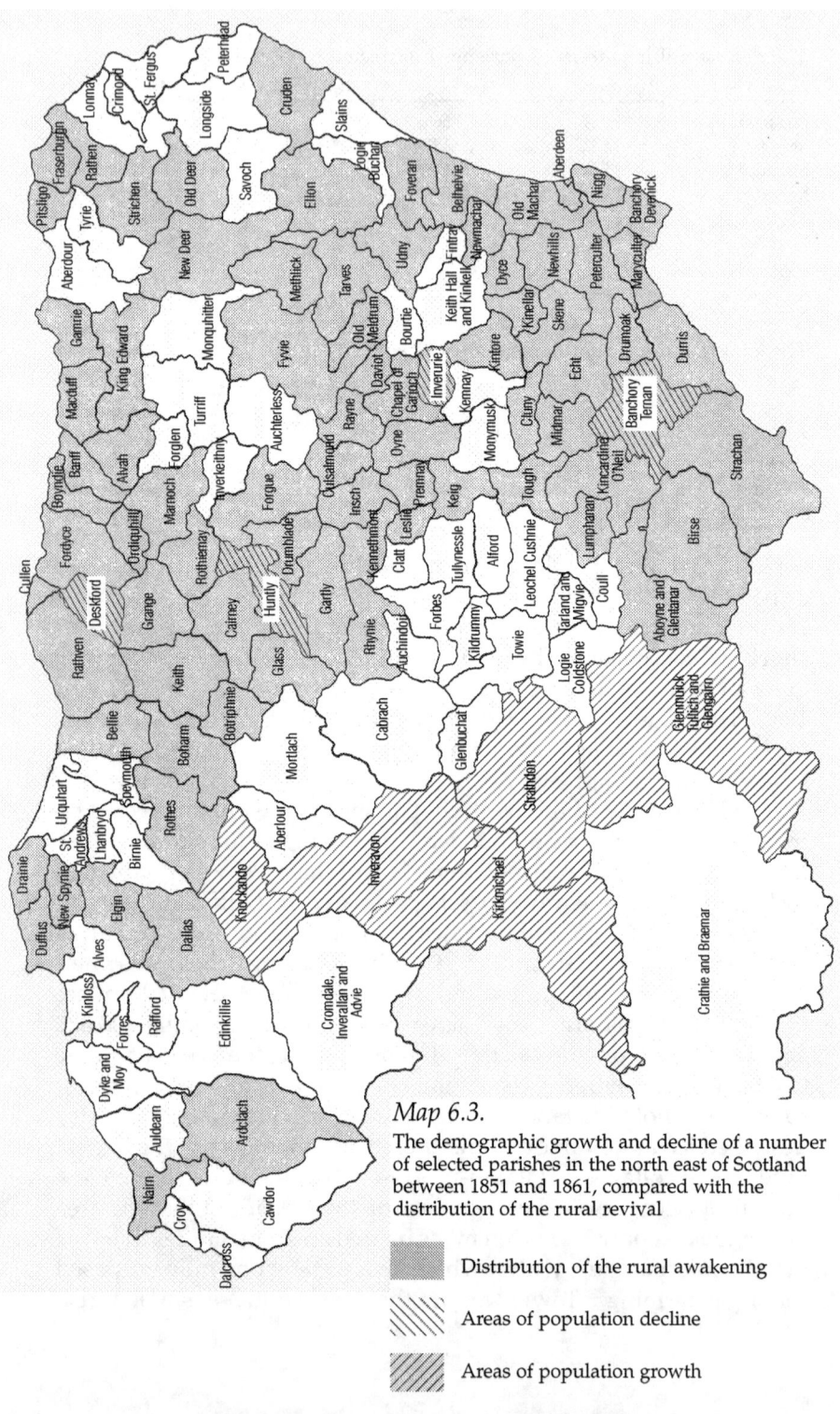

Map 6.3.
The demographic growth and decline of a number of selected parishes in the north east of Scotland between 1851 and 1861, compared with the distribution of the rural revival

Distribution of the rural awakening

Areas of population decline

Areas of population growth

that measured ten by five miles, but was inhabited within only four by two and a half miles of this area because of its inaccessibility.[30] Rough terrain also prevented much of Kirkmichael parish from being populated. It stretched for thirty miles, but it was recorded in 1843 that 'only about eighteen miles of its length is inhabited'.[31] Likewise Inveraven, which had no towns or villages, was made up 'by much the larger proportion of moorland and mountains' which gave the parish 'a bleak and barren appearance'.[32] Each of these descriptions reveal how the western area of Aberdeenshire was quite desolate. Large tracks of this region were mountainous and therefore largely uninhabited. As a result access to these isolated communities was not easy. Their remoteness among the mountains may be another factor which explains why the influences of the revival did not penetrate these places.

In addition they were strongholds of the Roman Catholic Church, which was unaffected by the awakening. (See Map 6.5., on p. 163.) In the parish of Kirkmichael in the 1840s, for instance, the average number of communicants of the parish church was 293, while there were 485 worshippers at the Roman Catholic chapel.[33] Meanwhile the Inveravon report in *The New Statistical Account* recorded that 'in Glenlivet . . . about three fifths of the people are of the Roman Catholic persuasion'.[34] The parish of Mortlach boasted a 'handsome Catholic chapel' and according to the parish minister 'of late years . . . their numbers have increased and amount at present to 170'. At the same time he mentioned that 'there are no dissenting meeting houses, nor any society for religious purposes in the parish'.[35] Similarly in Glenbucket there were between twenty and thirty Roman Catholics in the parish and 'no Dissenters of any denomination from the Established Presbyterian Church'.[36] Likewise, in Strathdon, there were twenty three Roman Catholics and only one Free Church family who had migrated from Aberdeen.[37] Lastly, in the parish of Glenmuick, Tullich and Glengairn at the start of the 1840s there were 'no chapels of ease, Government churches, catechists, dissenting, Seceding nor Episcopalian chapels'. Rather the religious needs of the people were served by an Established Church, which had 1919 people on its roll, and a Roman Catholic chapel, which attracted 360 worshippers.[38] The western region of Morayshire, that had the largest Roman Catholic community in the whole of north east Scotland and no dissent, was unstirred by the revival. Accordingly, it appears that the movement did not flourish in those parts of Aberdeenshire that were predominantly Roman Catholic.

A further important factor which serves to explain why certain parishes were unaffected by the revival was the absence of religious dissent in these areas. Some parishes in the north east of Scotland

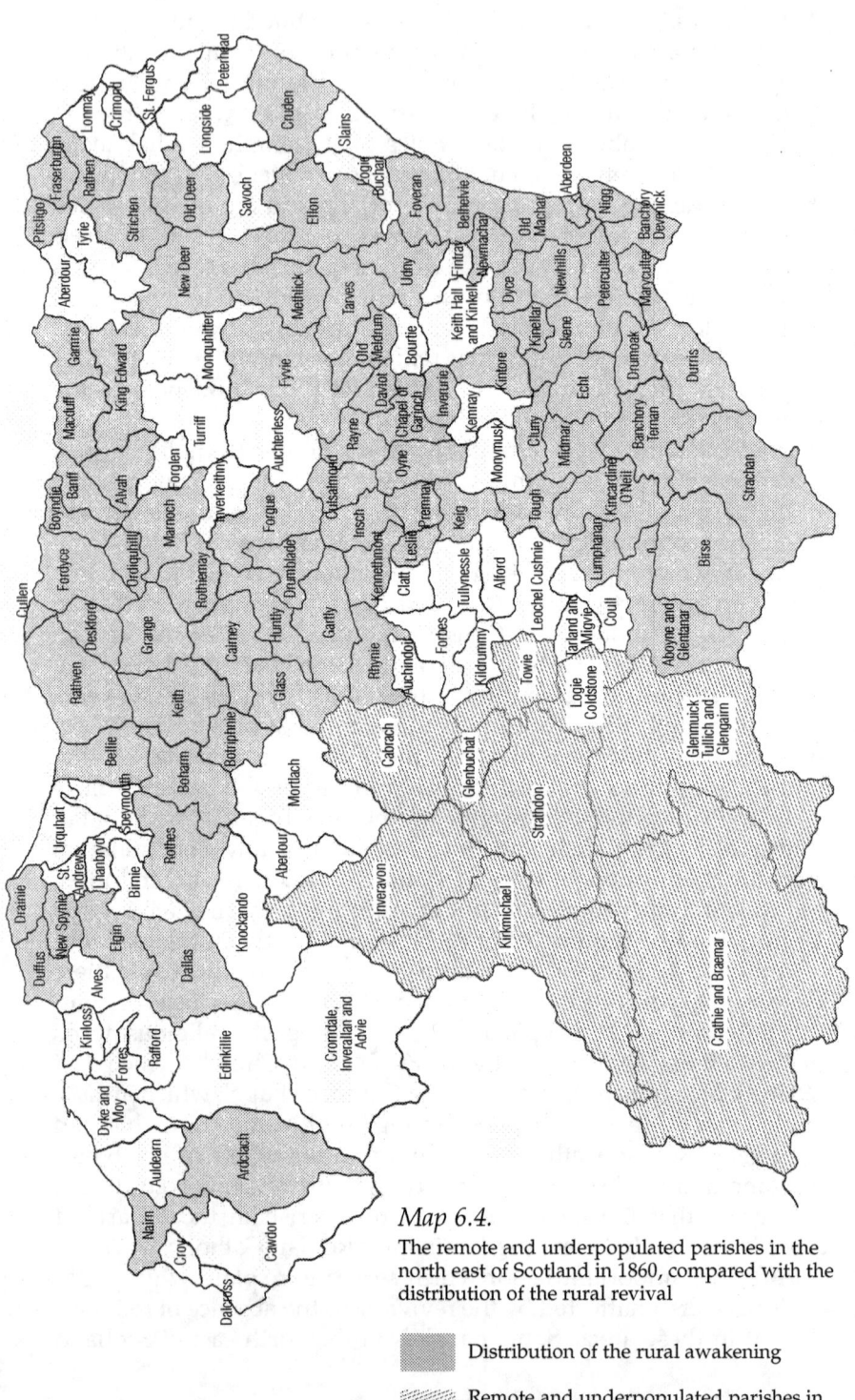

Map 6.4.

The remote and underpopulated parishes in the north east of Scotland in 1860, compared with the distribution of the rural revival

Distribution of the rural awakening

Remote and underpopulated parishes in Aberdeenshire in 1860

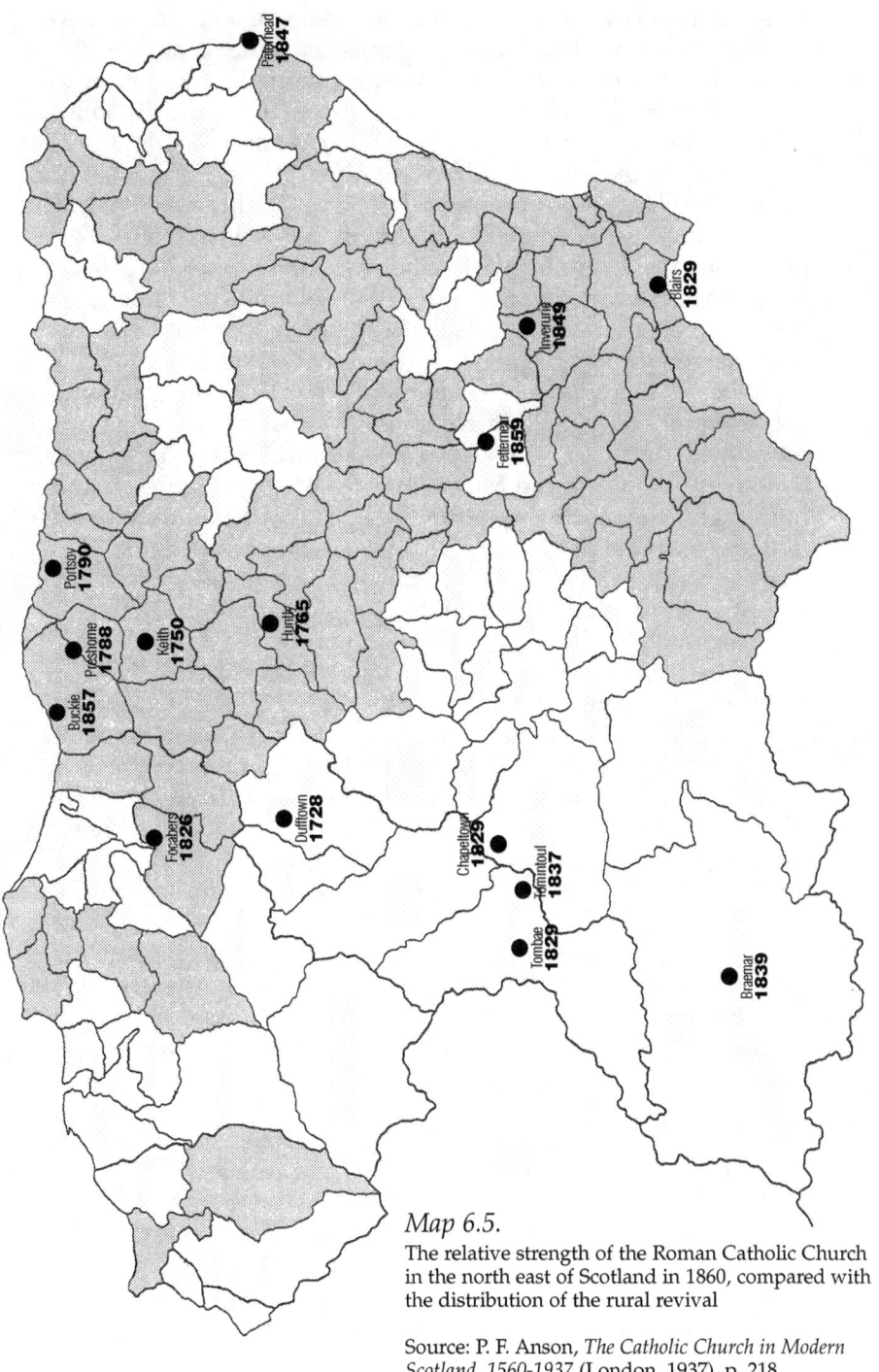

Map 6.5.

The relative strength of the Roman Catholic Church in the north east of Scotland in 1860, compared with the distribution of the rural revival

Source: P. F. Anson, *The Catholic Church in Modern Scotland, 1560-1937* (London, 1937), p. 218.

Distribution of the rural awakening

were occupied by the Church of Scotland alone and did not have a Free Church or other religious presence. Others, however, had churches apart from the parish congregation. There were at least thirty eight parishes that were monopolised by the Established Church. Only five of these parishes, that is about an eighth, were influenced by the revival. They were Birse, Daviot, Drumoak, Durris and Rhynie. However, more than seventy five per cent of the parishes that were dominated by the Established church and bereft of dissent were untouched by the movement. (See Map 6.6., on p. 163.) This shows how the revival did not affect the large proportion of parishes where the Established Church operated alone, without a neighbouring congregation of another denomination.

However, there were other parts of Aberdeenshire where there was a strong Free Church presence that were also unaffected by the movement. There were fourteen Free Church presbyteries in the Synods of Aberdeen and Moray in the north east of Scotland. The minutes for the meetings during the revival of ten of these presbyteries were found and analysed. Seven, those of Aberdeen, Kincardine O'Neil, Alford, Garioch, Ellon, Fordyce and Strathbogie, described in considerable detail the progress of the movement, but three, belonging to the Deer, Aberlour and Forres presbyteries, did not make a single reference to the revival.[39] The area of these presbyteries correspond to parts of north east Scotland that were not influenced by the movement. (See Map 6.7., on p. 164.) This demonstrates that despite its apparent wholehearted support of the movement, there remained pockets of the Free Church, in the west of Aberdeenshire, that appear to have been untouched by the revival.

Moreover it is noteworthy that the awakening arose in regions of north east Scotland that were traditionally Evangelical bastions and failed to penetrate those areas that were associated with Moderatism. George Booth Robertson produced in his postgraduate thesis that discussed the 'Spiritual Awakening in the North East of Scotland and the Disruption of the Church in 1843' a map, based upon his research, which illustrated the relative strength of the Evangelicals and Moderates in Aberdeenshire between 1822 and 1842.[40] It showed that Evangelicals were well represented in Fordyce and Turiff, relatively strong in Garioch, Deer and Kincardine, but noticeably weak in Alford and Ellon. It is clear that the revival flourished in those areas where Robertson had found the Evangelicals to be most strongly represented, and did not emerge in those places where the Moderates predominated. (See Map 6.8., on p. 166.) Hence the theological heritage of particular districts seems to have influenced the course of this religious movement.

Perhaps the single most important factor which explains the dif-

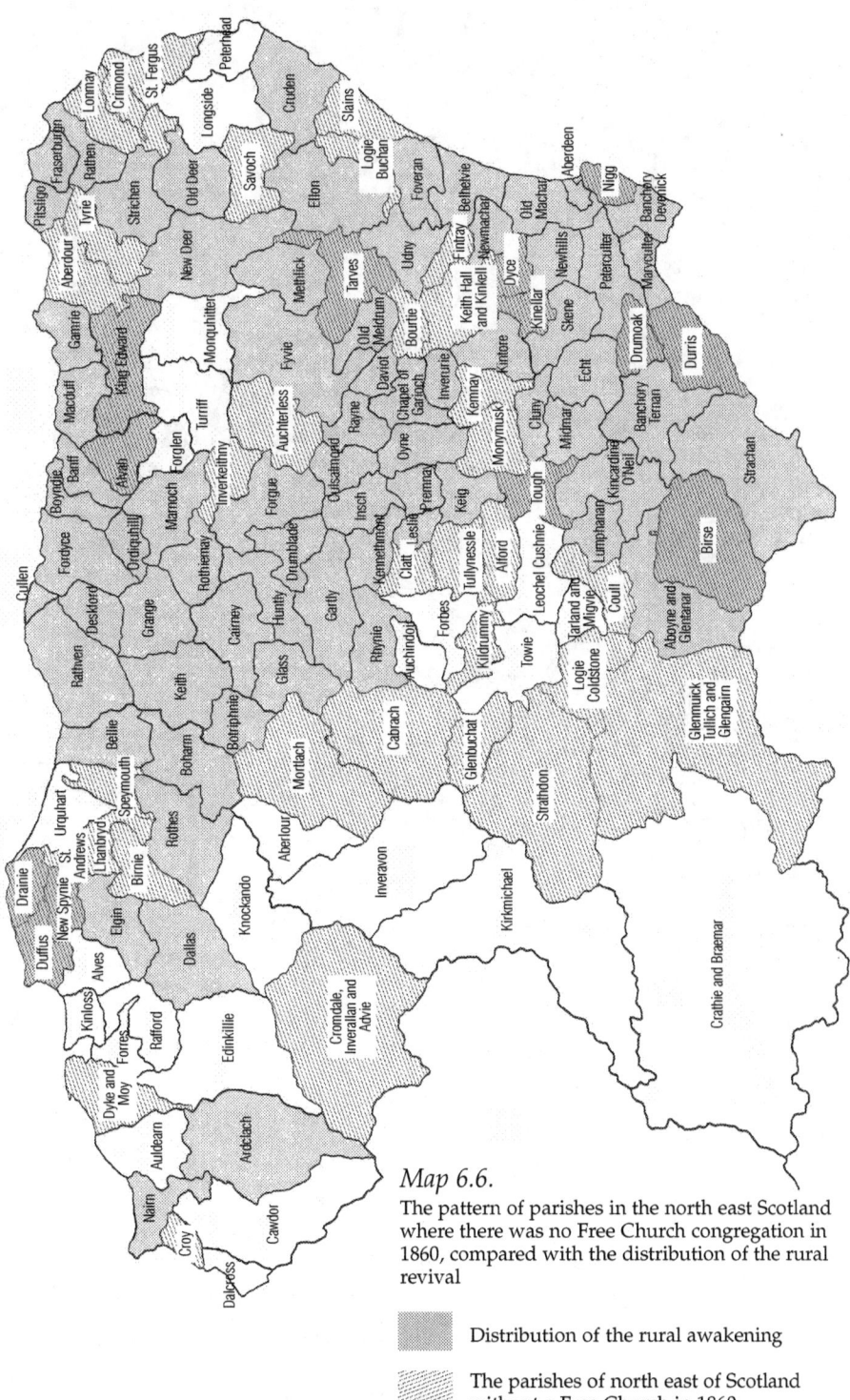

Map 6.6.
The pattern of parishes in the north east Scotland where there was no Free Church congregation in 1860, compared with the distribution of the rural revival

Distribution of the rural awakening

The parishes of north east of Scotland without a Free Church in 1860

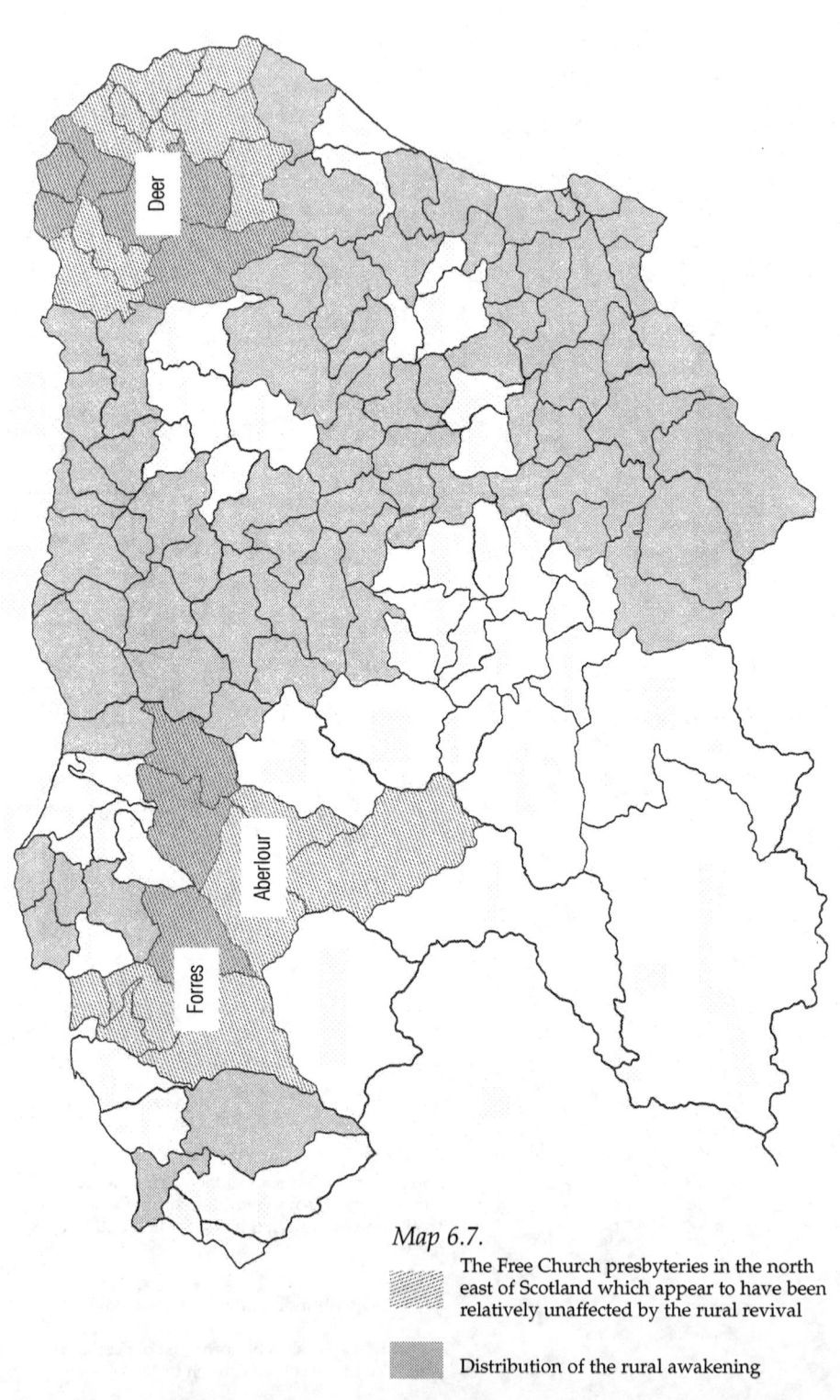

Map 6.7.
The Free Church presbyteries in the north east of Scotland which appear to have been relatively unaffected by the rural revival

Distribution of the rural awakening

fusion of the revival in the north east of Scotland is the modern, efficient communications network that had been established in some of the area in the years immediately before 1859. The increase in the cattle trade led to progressive road building projects in Aberdeenshire. By 1850 there were more than 766 miles of turnpike roads and 2,815 miles of secondary roads in the five counties of the north east of Scotland.[41] This led the parish minister of Daviot to comment in 1843 how 'the roads in the parish also have undergone a great improvement since the date of the last Statistical Account'.[42] However, it was the new railway, which, according to one journalist, 'wrought a complete revolution in all our travelling arrangements', that greatly facilitated the spread of the revival.[43] The Deeside Railway line reached Banchory in September 1853 and the Northern Railway line arrived at Huntly in September 1854.[44] The map that displayed the line of the Great North of Scotland Railway, published in 1881, shows how it ran through the area that was affected by the revival. (See Map 6.9., on p. 167.) Gordon Gray, a student at Aberdeen in 1859, described how the movement spread outwards along the northern and western railway lines. He said,

> When the interest spread from the city to the country districts, requests began to come to us to hold services here and there, and especially along the main line of the railway to the north . . . I could name twenty different centres along the Great North of Scotland Railway as far as Huntly, along the Deeside Railway from Aberdeen to Banchory . . . where there were many brought to a saving knowledge of the truth.[45]

The stations that serviced the line from Aberdeen to Huntly included Dyce, Kintore, Inverurie, Pitcaple, Oyne, Insch, Wardhouse, Kinnethmont and Gartly. Each of these places was affected by the revival. Similarly all the villages on the railway line from Aberdeen to Banchory, which included Cults, Murtle, Milltimber, Culter, Drum, Park and Crathes were influenced by the movement.[46] The new communication network, introduced by the arrival of the train, had a profound effect upon the diffusion of the revival. By transporting evangelists and anxious inquirers to religious meetings across the region, the train served a crucial role in the expansion of this movement. The railway line, above all, explains the spread of the 1859 revival as it was dispersed across the north east of Scotland.

III

Beyond discussing the factors that account for the geographical spread of the movement, it is necessary to return to the kirk session

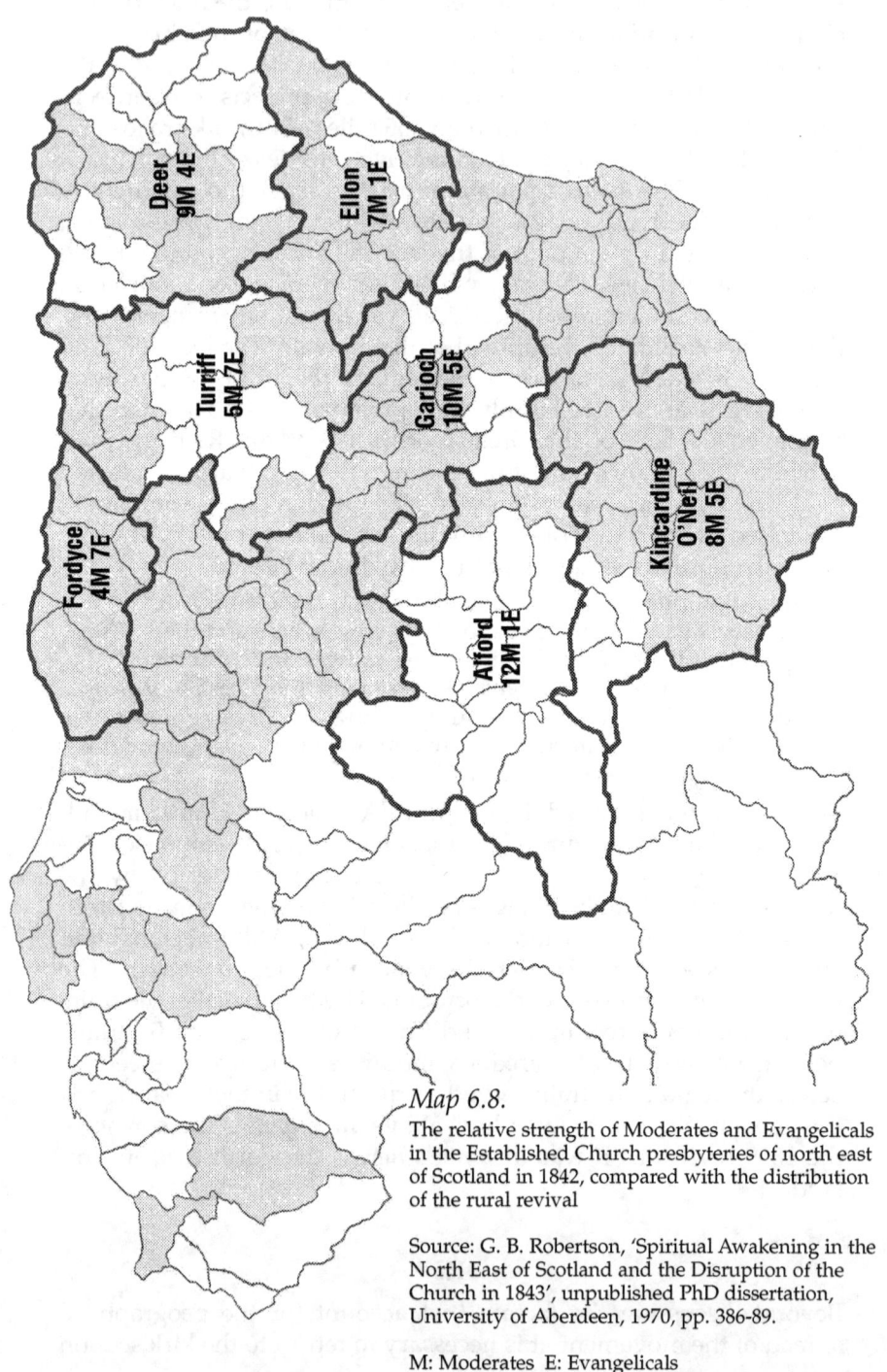

Map 6.8.
The relative strength of Moderates and Evangelicals in the Established Church presbyteries of north east of Scotland in 1842, compared with the distribution of the rural revival

Source: G. B. Robertson, 'Spiritual Awakening in the North East of Scotland and the Disruption of the Church in 1843', unpublished PhD dissertation, University of Aberdeen, 1970, pp. 386-89.

M: Moderates E: Evangelicals

Distribution of the rural awakening

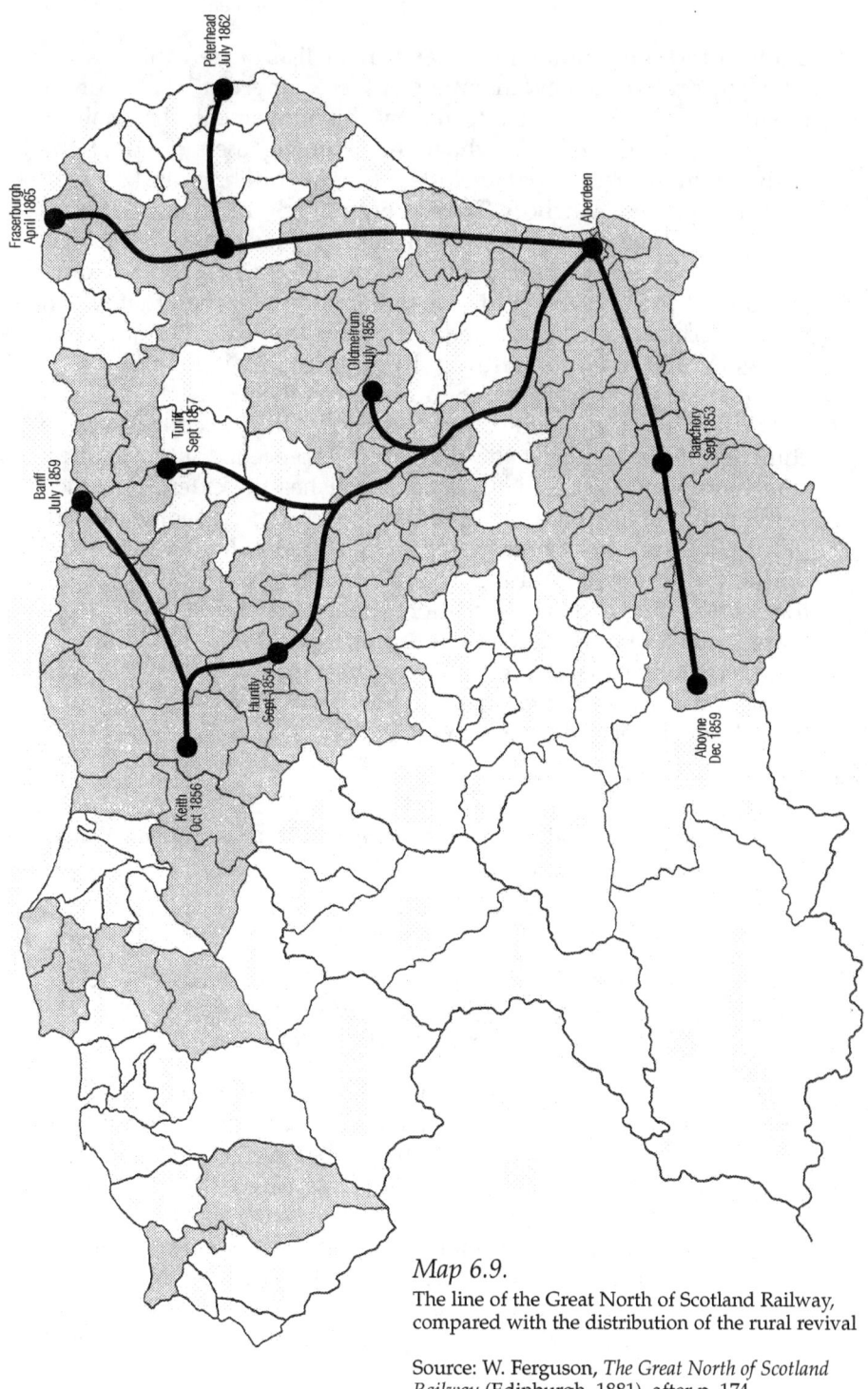

Map 6.9.

The line of the Great North of Scotland Railway, compared with the distribution of the rural revival

Source: W. Ferguson, *The Great North of Scotland Railway* (Edinburgh, 1881), after p. 174.

Distribution of the rural awakening

minutes and communion rolls that provide lists of men and women who constituted the new members of these congregations, in order to study those who were affected by this movement. An analysis was made of 471 people who joined, during the period of the revival, ten churches that included Daviot, Millbrex and Rhynie Parish Churches, Banchory Ternan, Elgin High, Insch and Pluscarden Free Churches, together with Huntly, New Deer and Shiels United Presbyterian Churches. (See Map 6.10., on p. 169.) The examination of the rural new church members is briefer than that which was undertaken for those who joined Aberdeen churches and does not generally include returns from individual congregations because disparities were not found between them.

The first inquiry considers whether those who joined the various churches at the height of the revival were preceded into membership by other close relatives. This establishes the extent to which familial influences were brought to bear upon these people, which, in turn, indicates the character of the movement. If a large proportion followed a near relative into church membership, it suggests the revival operated in a traditional manner, while if there were more who had no religious background, it would imply that it was a modern, religious movement. Given the nature of the sources consulted it was possible to undertake this study for only seventy two people who belonged to two congregations.

Table 6.20.

The religious background of those who joined Millbrex and Rhynie Parish Churches during the revival

	Total	*Percentage*
Preceded	43	45 %
Unpreceded	29	30 %
Unknown	24	25 %

Sources: Millbrex Parish Church Communion Rolls 1862-66
           Rhynie Parish Church Communion Rolls 1857-58, 1859-72

The statistics reveal that three fifths of the sample who joined a rural congregation during the revival, whose background is known, had followed a close relation into church membership. This suggests the religious movement was experienced principally within the family networks of those who were already within the influence of the church. Indeed it seems that many of the converts were the children of church members and were already regular attenders of religious services before they joined the church. Hence the revival served to build these congregations amongst those previously gathered rather than with those who were outwith the religious community.

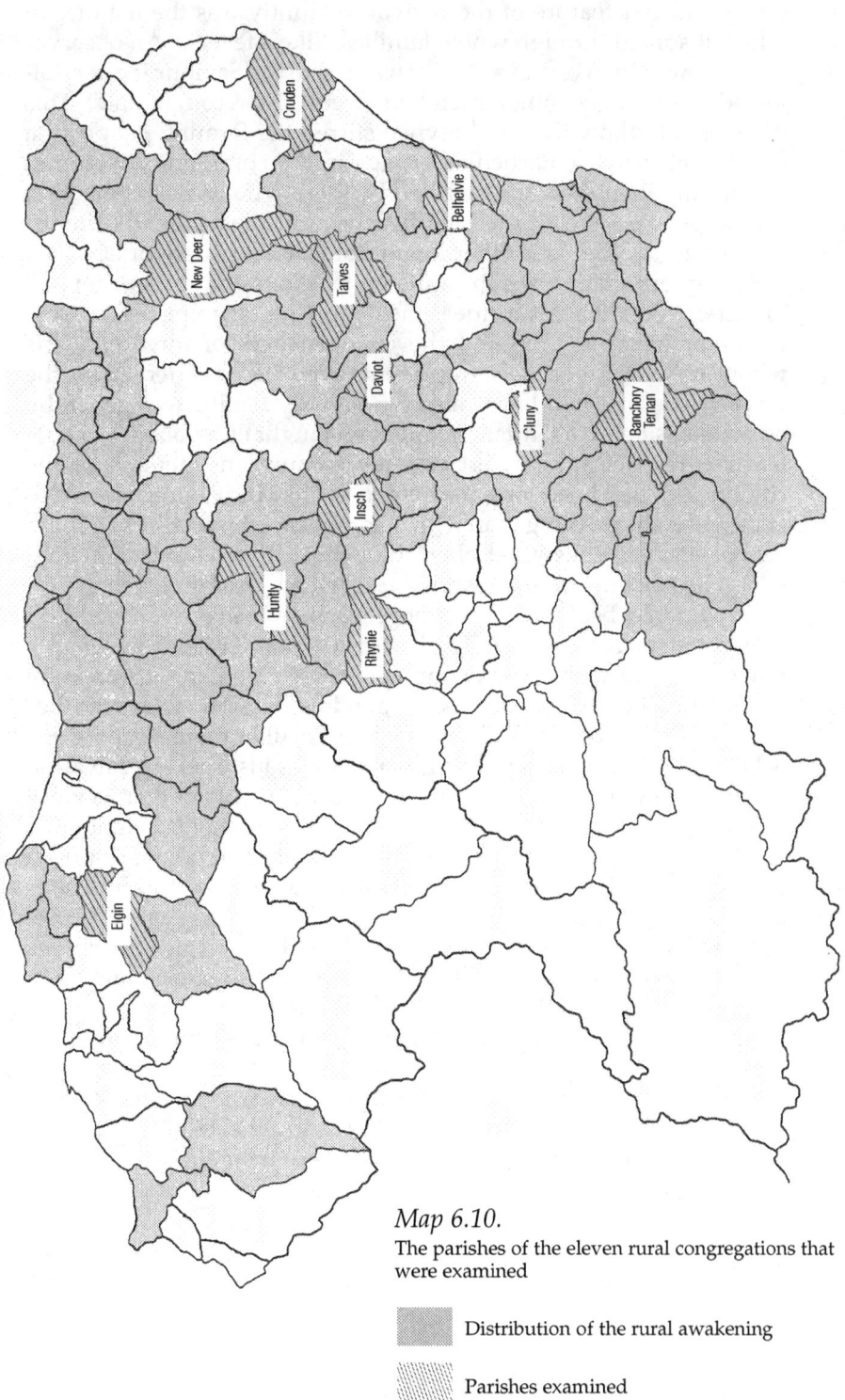

Map 6.10.
The parishes of the eleven rural congregations that were examined

Distribution of the rural awakening

Parishes examined

One particular feature of the revival in Huntly was the manner in which it spread through whole families, 'like a fever'.[47] An observer noted how, 'when one in a family was led to the Saviour it often followed that all the other members were also brought in'.[48] This demonstrates how the rural revival stirred the farming people in a traditional manner. Particular groups in the community were not specifically identified and targeted by those who were anxious that certain people were affected. Rather the movement spread primarily through families and other long-established kin networks.

This interpretation is substantiated by the testimonies of several ministers. Archibald Gardner, the Free Church minister at New Deer, for instance, recorded the circumstances of three converts whom he considered to be representative of those affected by the revival. The first had been raised in a godly family, was generally regarded as being a Christian and even taught as a Sabbath School teacher. The second convert was a communicant member of the church and 'had been long the subject of the Spirit's gracious influences'. The third young man who was awakened was also a Sabbath School teacher.[49] Likewise Robert Reid, Free Church minister at Banchory, described 'two interesting cases [which] had occurred of persons who had been Sabbath school teachers being awakened and brought to the Saviour'.[50] In Deskford, William Ker, the Free Church minister, recalled the conversion of 'one old woman, a professing Christian, who had tried to be as good as possible, who read her Bible and good books, and was very particular about keeping the Sabbath, had been made to feel that she was just seeking salvation in her own righteousness'. He narrated the story of another convert, 'a quiet and respectable man, of good repute among his neighbours, and regarded as truly a Christian', who at first said he did not need the revival until one night, after hearing a sermon on blind Bartimeus, could not sleep, and was consequently 'born again'.[51] These converts were typical of those affected by the revival. Therefore it would appear this movement was felt strongly amongst many who were already within the influence of the church.

The class composition of those who joined the rural churches at the height of the movement constitutes the second inquiry. The occupation of ninety eight men and women who became church members around 1859 was discovered using the 1861 census. The table below charts these people according to their class.

The Revival in the Rural Hinterland

Table 6.21.

The class composition of those who joined a number of rural churches during the revival

Status	Men	Women	% Men	% Women	Total
Middle Class (H)	9	12	9 %	12 %	21 %
Middle Class (L)	1	1	1 %	1 %	2 %
Working Class					
Skilled	31	19	32 %	19 %	51 %
Unskilled	7	18	7 %	19 %	26 %

Sources: Banchory Ternan Free Church Communion Rolls 1853-68
Daviot Parish Church Communion Rolls 1829-1873
Huntly United Presbyterian Church Kirk Session Minutes 1849-79
Millbrex Parish Church Communion Rolls 1862-66
New Deer United Presbyterian Church Communion Rolls 1856-1907
Rhynie Parish Church Communion Rolls 1857-58, 1859-72
Shiels United Presbyterian Church Congregational Roll Book 1857-1898
1861 Census, Banchory Ternan, Kincardineshire
1861 Census, Daviot, Aberdeenshire
1861 Census, New Deer, Aberdeenshire
1861 Census, Rhynie, Aberdeenshire

It emerges from the table that quite a considerable proportion of the new church members were drawn from the middle classes. For example twenty one per cent of those who joined rural churches during the revival were from the upper middle class. This has appeared because according to the categorisation used farmers belonged to the rentier group of the upper middle class. Quite a few of those who became members of rural congregations during the revival were sons and daughters of such farmers. Nonetheless the clear majority of new church members, more than three quarters, were from the working classes. However, there was a gender imbalance among these groups of people. Just over half of the total involved were from the skilled working class, and two thirds of them were men. A large number were ploughmen and cattlemen. This serves to confirm the observation of a correspondent of *The Wynd Journal* in January 1860 who reported that 'at Inverurie there has been much awakening among farm servants'.[52] In addition almost three quarters of the unskilled people who joined the church were women. Only seven per cent of the total number were unskilled working men. All the women belonging to this class were domestic servants. Hence a fifth of all who joined the rural church, at the time of this movement, were female house workers. Nevertheless it remains that the greater number of new church members, almost one third, were drawn from the artisan class of men. This suggests how they were among the section of the rural community that was most affected by the 1859 revival.

The marital status of those who joined rural churches in Aberdeenshire during the revival is the third aspect of the analysis. Three hundred and forty one people from nine churches made up this cross section to be examined.

Table 6.22.

The marital status of those who joined a number of rural churches during the revival

Marital Status	Men	Women	% Men	% Women	Total
Married Couples	37	37	11 %	11 %	22 %
Married Individ	6	29	2 %	8 %	10 %
Unmarried	84	148	25 %	43 %	68 %
Widow	0	0	0 %	0 %	0%

Sources: Banchory Ternan Free Church Communion Rolls 1853-68
Daviot Parish Church Communion Rolls 1829-1873
Elgin High Free Church Kirk Session Minutes 1852-61, 1861-78
Huntly United Presbyterian Church Kirk Session Minutes 1849-79
Millbrex Parish Church Communion Rolls 1862-66
New Deer United Presbyterian Church Communion Rolls 1856-1907
Pluscarden Free Church Communion Rolls 1843-71
Rhynie Parish Church Communion Rolls 1857-58, 1859-72
Shiels United Presbyterian Church Congregational Roll Book 1857-1898
1861 Census, Banchory Ternan, Kincardineshire
1861 Census, Daviot, Aberdeenshire
1861 Census, New Deer, Aberdeenshire
1861 Census, Rhynie, Aberdeenshire

The statistics indicate that just less than one third, thirty two per cent, of those who joined rural churches during the revival were married. Within this group seventy four, or twenty two per cent, were couples, while thirty five, or ten per cent, were single married people. However the greater balance of new church members, sixty eight per cent, were unmarried. Slightly more than a third were men, while the greater proportion, sixty four per cent, were women. Hence it appears that the largest group of those who were affected by the agrarian revival were young women, particularly those who were unmarried.

This is confirmed by the fourth study which examines the age at which men and women joined these rural congregations at the height of the awakening. Unfortunately, the absence of exact addresses on communion rolls proved problematic and limited the extent of the analysis. However, it was possible to identify the precise age of fifty eight farming people who became church members during this period.

Table 6.23.

The ages of those who joined a number of rural churches during the revival

Age	Men	Women	% Men	% Women	Total
15 – 20	10	25	17	43	60%
21 – 30	9	9	15.5	15.5	31%
31 – 40	3	1	5	2	7%
41 – 50	-	-	-	-	-
51 – 60	1	-	2	-	2%
60 +	-	-	-	-	-
Mean Age	24.13	18.88			

Sources: Banchory Ternan Free Church Communion Rolls 1853-68
Daviot Parish Church Communion Rolls 1829-1873
New Deer United Presbyterian Church Communion Rolls 1856-1907
Rhynie Parish Church Communion Rolls 1857-58, 1859-72
1861 Census, Banchory Ternan, Kincardineshire
1861 Census, Daviot, Aberdeenshire
1861 Census, New Deer, Aberdeenshire
1861 Census, Rhynie, Aberdeenshire

This table reveals some very important results. It shows that sixty per cent of those who joined the rural churches at the height of the revival were between the ages of fifteen and twenty, and that more than ninety per cent were less than thirty years of age. Teenagers made up the greater proportion of new church members during the time of this movement. In addition there are interesting observations to be made from the ages of the new members according to gender. Firstly almost three quarters of the teenagers were girls. Also men and women were equally represented among the twenty to twenty nine age group, while males accounted for more than three quarters of those who were more than thirty years of age. This suggests that the revival, among the teenagers, was more popular among girls, but that it touched a greater number of men among those who were more than twenty. Nonetheless, clearly teenage girls were, by far, among those who were most affected by this revival.

Regrettably, as at Aberdeen, young people influenced by the movement who were less than sixteen years of age are impossible to trace because the churches did not usually admit them into membership. As a result a considerable number of children and teenagers who were converted during the revival do not appear to have been added to the communion rolls of congregations, and because they are unrepresented in official records they cannot be precisely accounted for. Nevertheless there is an abundance of testimony that describes how children were affected by this movement.[53] They were clearly a significant group of revival converts. Indeed the movement began in several agricultural towns and villages, as it had started in Aberdeen, among children. On at least several occasions the conversion of boys and girls arrested the people's attention and acted as the stimulus of the increased religious activity. For example, Robert Reid recorded that the first conversion, which he associated with the revival at Banchory, was of a boy of fourteen years of age.[54] George Bain also attributed the start of the revival in Chapel of Garioch to the awakening of a group of young girls at the local school.[55] The conversion of young people often provoked the beginning of the revival. Other ministers reported the progress of the movement among the young. Alexander Reid, Free Church minister at Portsoy, for instance, commented 'I have had particular encouragement with regard to the young'.[56] Also, Alexander M'Kenzie, Free Church minister at Nairn, said 'he could mention interesting cases of children putting their parents up during the night to pray for them', while William Ker described several instances of 'little children [who] had been converted' at Deskford.[57] The 1859 rural revival influenced children in large numbers. In view of the findings of the ages of rural new church members and the testimonies of the ministers whose congregations were affected, it appears that children, teenagers and young adults formed, by far, the largest group among the converts of this rural religious movement.

The final inquiry to be made about those who joined rural churches in the north east of Scotland at the height of the 1859 revival concerns gender. The male female ratio of those who became church members during the revival has been compared against the same figure for the period immediately preceding and succeeding the movement.

The Revival in the Rural Hinterland 175

Table 6.24.

The gender status of those who joined a number of rural churches before, during and after the revival

Church	Year	Male	Female	Ratio M / F (%)
Banchory	Before / after Revival	94	117	45 / 55
	During the Revival	22	28	44 / 56
Daviot	Before / after Revival	103	92	53 / 47
	During the Revival	9	13	41 / 59
Elgin	Before / after Revival	41	53	44 / 56
	During the Revival	51	96	35 / 65
Huntly	Before / after Revival	11	16	41 / 59
	During the Revival	5	9	36 / 54
Millbrex	Before / after Revival	38	30	56 / 44
	During the Revival	21	25	46 / 54
New Deer	Before / after Revival	26	32	45 / 55
	During the Revival	5	9	36 / 64
Pluscarden	Before / after Revival	14	22	39 / 61
	During the Revival	15	33	31 / 69

Sources: Banchory Ternan Free Church Communion Rolls 1853-68
Daviot Parish Church Communion Rolls 1829-1873
Elgin High Free Church Kirk Session Minutes 1852-61, 1861-78
Huntly United Presbyterian Church Kirk Session Minutes 1849-79
Millbrex Parish Church Communion Rolls 1862-66
New Deer United Presbyterian Church Communion Rolls 1856-1907
Pluscarden Free Church Communion Rolls 1843-71

Table 6.25.

An analysis of the gender status of those who joined a number of rural churches before, during and after the revival

		No	Percent
Before and after the Revival	Male	327	47 %
	Female	362	53 %
During the Revival			
	Male	128	38 %
	Female	213	62 %

With the exception of Daviot and Millbrex parish churches, where females made up forty seven and forty three per cent of new church members before and after the revival, in most churches women accounted for between fifty five and sixty one per cent of new members during this period. Hence overall women made up fifty three per cent and men constituted forty seven per cent of new members before and after the revival. However there was a clear shift in the gender composition of new church members during the revival. It was quite small at Banchory Free Church, but in the remaining six congregations the ratio of male and female members was altered by between five and twelve per cent. As a result, overall, sixty two per cent of those who joined this group of rural churches during the revival were women, while only thirty eight per cent were men. This represents a noteworthy change in the gender composition of rural churches. During the religious movement it was altered by nine per cent in favour of women, which suggests that the rural revival commanded its greater influence among females.

The analysis of the people who joined rural churches at the height of the 1859 revival suggests this was a traditional religious movement. The greater proportion were preceded into the church by a near relative which reveals how the revival operated principally through the network of family kinship. Almost seventy per cent were unmarried, while more than ninety per cent were less than twenty nine years old. Finally almost two thirds were women. The archetypal convert was the unmarried, teenage, sabbath-school attending daughter of a church member. Hence the new rural church members in 1859 bore a close resemblance to those who were affected by the Cambuslang revival in 1742. Accordingly it appears that the movement among the farming people, on the basis of those it influenced, resembled the traditional Presbyterian revivals of the seventeenth and eighteenth centuries.

There are a number of conclusions to be drawn from the manifestation of the 1859 revival among the fermfolk of Aberdeenshire. The church records that were examined shed light upon the extent to which various denominations were involved within this movement. Having appeared, from contemporary reports, to be quite unaffected by the revival, it is important to acknowledge that a number of Established congregations were influenced by the movement. It was noteworthy also to discover that, despite creating the impression of having championed the revival, the Free Church did not universally participate in the movement. Indeed there were some congregations of this denomination that were clearly not willing to embrace it. Perhaps the most interesting revelation was that more than one Episcopal chapel appears to have prospered as a consequence of this religious movement. Secondly the revival affected a considerable area of the north east of Scotland. It appeared among scattered communities and within new planned villages. It emerged where the population was growing, but failed to arise in those places that were in a state of terminal decline. The religious nature of parishes also influenced the course of the movement. Generally it flourished in places where there were non-established, dissenting, Evangelical congregations, but failed to prosper in areas that were dominated by the National and Roman Catholic Churches. Above all the revival prevailed over those parts of north east Scotland that were reasonably accessible from Aberdeen by rail, but did not affect those regions that were more remote. In this way the movement was felt most strongly in the eastern and central northern regions of Aberdeenshire, while it produced an insignificant effect upon the parishes in the west of the county. The study into the composition of those who joined churches during the movement also produced some interesting results. It revealed that most of them were preceded into the church by a close relation. Moreover it showed that the majority were unmarried and young, the greater proportion were probably in their teens. Most importantly, the inquiry displayed that a disproportionate number were women. This, above all, demonstrates that the rural revival bore a closer resemblance to the traditional religious movement than to the modern evangelistic campaign. Accordingly these findings confirm that the 1859 revival, as it was experienced in the rural hinterland of the north east of Scotland, belonged to an older tradition of awakenings.

Notes

1. *Aberdeen Almanac 1860* (Aberdeen, 1860), pp. 157-87.
2. Banchory Ternan Parish Church Kirk Session Minutes 1857-60
   Chapel of Garioch Parish Church Kirk Session Minutes 1843-67
   Culsamond Parish Church Kirk Session Minutes 1853-1900
   Echt Parish Church Kirk Session Minutes 1851-1908
   Insch Parish Church Kirk Session Minutes 1856-77
   Inverurie Parish Church Kirk Session Minutes 1845-70
   Oyne Parish Church Kirk Session Minutes 1841-88
3. Aberlour Parish Church Communion Roll 1843-71
   Ellon Parish Church Communion Roll 1860-70
   Inch Parish Church Communion Roll 1836-61
   Oldmeldrum Parish Church Communion Roll 1856-61
   Savoch Parish Church Communion Roll 1858-64
4. Aberlour Free Church Kirk Session Minutes 1848-96
   Auchendoir Free Church Kirk Session Minutes 1843-88
   Kirkmichael Free Church Kirk Session Minutes 1843-1907
   Mortlach Free Church Kirk Session Minutes 1846-96
   Knockando Free Church Kirk Session Minutes 1844-1915
   Rafford Free Church Kirk Session Minutes 1855-1936
   Strachan Free Church Kirk Session Minutes 1843-1914
5. Botriphinie Free Church Communion Roll 1857-1930
   Botriphinie Free Church Kirk Session Minutes 1841-79
   Inveravon Free Church Kirk Session Minutes 1845-1904
   Longside Free Church Communion Roll 1852-1929
   Longside Free Church Kirk Session Minutes 1845-1929
   Lumphanan Free Church Kirk Session Minutes 1845-65
6. Skene Free Church Kirk Session Minutes, 22 November 1859

7. Braemar Free Church Kirk Session Minutes, 11 July 1861
8. Inverurie Free Church Kirk Session Minutes, 12 January 1860
9. Insch Free Church Kirk Session Minutes, September 1859
10. Banchory Ternan Free Church Kirk Session Minutes, 1 June 1859
11. Pluscarden Free Church Kirk Session Minutes, 3 April 1861
12. St Ternan's Episcopal Chapel, Banchory, List of Communicants, 1856-68
13. J. Obelkevich, *Religion and Rural Society: South Lindsey 1825-75* (Oxford, 1976), p. 9.
14. A. Everitt, *The Patterns of Rural Dissent: The Nineteenth Century* (Leicester, 1972), p. 41.
15. M. Gray, 'The Regions and Their Issues: Scotland' in G. E. Mingay (ed.), *The Victorian Countryside: Volume 1* (London, 1981), p. 87.
16. K. Walton, 'Regional Settlement' in A. C. O' Dell, J. Macintosh (ed.), *The North East of Scotland: British Association* (Aberdeen, 1963), pp. 91, 94.
17. Everitt, *Patterns of Rural Dissent*, p. 44.
18. T. C. Smout, 'The Landowner and the Planned Village in Scotland 1700-1830' in N. T. Phillipson, R. Mitchison (ed.), *Scotland in the Age of Improvement: Essays in Scottish History in the Eighteenth Century* (Edinburgh, 1970), pp. 75, 84.
19. Ibid., pp. 76-77, 101.
20. C. G. Brown, *The Social History of Religion in Scotland* (London, 1987), p. 72.
21. A. D. Gilbert, *Religion and Society in Industrial England: Church, Chapel and Social Change 1740-1914* (London, 1988), p. 106.
22. H. J. Rowe, 'The Geographical Distribution of Non-Established Protestant Churches in Stirlingshire and Clackmannanshire in the mid nineteenth century', undergraduate dissertation, University of Stirling, 1998, pp. 36-7.
23. A. A. MacLaren, *Religion and Social Class: The Disruption Years in Aberdeen* (London, 1974), pp. 8-9.
24. *The New Statistical Account of Aberdeenshire* (Edinburgh, 1843), pp. 547-8.
25. Ibid., p. 852.
26. Ibid., pp. 773-9.
27. Ibid., p. 1071.
28. Ibid., pp. 525, 553.
29. Ibid., p. 436.
30. Ibid., p. 415.
31. *The New Statistical Account of Scotland: Volume 13*, Banff, Elgin, Nairn (Edinburgh, 1845), p. 296.
32. Ibid., 123.
33. *New Statistical Account of Scotland: Banff, Elgin, Nairn*, p. 308.
34. Ibid., p. 140.
35. *The New Statistical Account of Banffshire* (Edinburgh, 1842), p. 108.
36. *New Statistical Account of Aberdeenshire*, p. 438.
37. Ibid., p. 555.
38. Ibid., p. 283.
39. Aberdeen Free Church Presbytery Minutes 1853-69
    Aberlour Free Church Presbytery Minutes 1854-60
    Alford Free Church Presbytery Minutes 1843-64
    Deer Free Church Presbytery Minutes 1843-70

Ellon Free Church Presbytery Minutes 1856-85
Fordyce Free Church Presbytery Minutes 1857-84
Forres Free Church Presbytery Minutes 1843-73
Garioch Free Church Presbytery Minutes 1843-66
Kincardine O' Neil Free Church Presbytery Minutes 1851-76
Strathbogie Free Church Presbytery Minutes 1847-64

40. G. B. Robertson, 'Spiritual Awakening in the North-East of Scotland and the Disruption in 1843', unpublished PhD thesis, University of Aberdeen, 1970, pp. 386-9.
41. I. Carter, *Farm Life in North East Scotland* (Edinburgh, 1979), p. 22.
42. *New Statistical Account of Aberdeenshire*, p. 830.
43. 'A Short History of Aberdeen and its People' (A series of 48 articles from the *Free Press*, printed from 12 July 1890), Article 42.
44. Ibid.
45. T. T. Matthews (ed.), *Reminiscences of the Revival of Fifty Nine and the Sixties* (Aberdeen, 1910), pp. 37, 39.
46. M. Barclay-Harvey, *A History of the Great North of Scotland Railway* (London, nd), p. 225.
47. Matthews, *Reminiscences*, p. 97.
48. Ibid.
49. *A Report of a Conference on the State of Religion and Public Meeting, held in the Free Church, Huntly, January 5, 1860* (Huntly, 1860), p. 13.
50. Ibid., p. 8.
51. Ibid., p. 17.
52. *W.J.*, No 15 (7 January 1860) p. 114.
53. H. Sprange, *Kingdom Kids* (Fearn, Ross shire, 1994), pp. 161-76.
54. *Conference on State of Religion*, Huntly, p. 8.
55. Ibid., p. 27.
56. Ibid., p. 11
57. Ibid., pp. 15, 17.

CHAPTER 7

The Revival in the Fishing Villages

Timing and Manner

Around the middle of the nineteenth century the Moray Firth did not, on the whole, enjoy a wholesome reputation. Most of the fishing villages were more renowned for their smuggling and excessive drinking than their spiritual fervour. However, in 1860 this stretch of the north east coast of Scotland was overcome by an extraordinary tide of religious excitement that fundamentally transformed its communities. This chapter seeks to understand how and why the Moray Firth was overwhelmed by this revival of religion in 1860. It will begin by considering the moral and spiritual climate of the area before the movement began and asks how significant this was for the latter's assimilation. Then it will look at several unique characteristics of these fishing villages that predisposed them towards Evangelical religion. The timing of the revival will also be examined in an attempt to understand why it occurred in 1860, before the manner in which this movement was successfully integrated into the local culture is analysed. Finally, two key characteristics of these fishing villages will be examined to determine why the Moray Firth was affected so remarkably by this awakening.

I

There were some nineteenth-century commentators who propounded a favourable view of the fishing people's religiosity. Several Church of Scotland ministers who wrote the Moray Firth parish profiles for the *New Statistical Account* published in 1843, for example, were positive about the moral well-being of the communities in which they worked. Francis Grant, the parish minister of Banff, describing his parishioners, said 'the intellectual, moral and religious character of the people deserves to be favourably mentioned.'[1] James Gardiner, in his report for Rathven parish that included the villages of Portknockie, Findochty and Portessie where the revival began, considered the fishermen under his pastoral care as 'a sober, hard working race of men'.[2] Meanwhile, George Henderson believed the people of Cullen to be 'in general, intelligent, moral, peaceable, and industrious'.[3] Writing about the village of Whitehills, the parish minister described 'twenty to thirty men, who can conceive and utter an extempore prayer with no less fluency, and with little less propriety, than most educated ministers'.[4] Clearly the Church of Scotland ministers of Moray Firth parishes in 1843 were generally content with the moral and religious tone of the towns and villages for which they were responsible.

However, the credibility of these reports is called into question as a different picture emerges of these villages from the dissenting ministers who worked within them. Thomas Baxter, the United Presbyterian minister at Banff, described how 'the moral and spiritual condition of our town has been long a matter of reproach; one intelligent observer of society says, that a few years ago there was scarcely a young man who was not addicted to intemperance, and the vices too commonly associated with it'.[5] He judged Portknockie, Findochty, Portessie and Portgordon as having a 'deplorable moral and spiritual condition' which had been 'notorious for generations'. Apparently 'few of that people made any profession of religion', while on the contrary 'strife, jealousy, malice, blasphemy, Sabbath-breaking, drunkenness, and almost every form of vice and sin prevailed'.[6] Another dissenting minister of religion, who had previous experience of working in several mining, manufacturing and agricultural parishes, spent some months along the Moray Firth. He commented that 'he had never met with any ignorance equal to the ignorance of saving truth he met within this fishing district'.[7] Hence some of the non-conformist ministers who served the fishing villages had a negative view of the religious and moral well-being of those they served.

Their appreciation of the spiritual climate of this coastline was affirmed by the admissions of several local people. A correspondent of *The Revival*, reporting from Findochty in 1860, commented that 'no villages were more destitute of spirituality prior to this change. According to the admission of the people themselves, they were deplorably careless of divine things.'[8] John McGibbon, a local historian writing towards the end of the nineteenth century, confessed on behalf of the people of Buckie that before the revival, 'we were very conservative and self centred . . . a more unlikely place for a revival of religion did not exist'.[9] Indeed the local factors which precipitated the closure of the Methodist Chapel in Buckie in 1834 illustrate the general character of the fisherfolk before the revival. Wesley Swift explained that drunkenness and smuggling, which were prevalent, led to many expulsions, a decrease in the number of members and eventual closure.[10] Accordingly a less positive image emerges, and the irreligiosity of the Moray Firth fisherfolk in the years immediately before the revival becomes apparent.

Perhaps of greater significance, beyond the conflicting accounts of the moral and spiritual nature of these villages, is that many of these communities had been 'neglected' by the church for a considerable period of time. Writing in a Methodist magazine in 1877, George Findlay commented on how around the middle of the century 'the large fishing population along the [Moray Firth] coast seemed to be left . . . pretty much to its own devices. An occasional sermon from a Methodist preacher or Independent missionary was about all the evangelical teaching it then enjoyed.'[11] It is noteworthy that among the villages of Portknockie, Findochty, Portessie and Portgordon, where the revival was most keenly experienced, there was a preaching station only in Portknockie. 'Organised religion' was not present at all in the remaining three villages.[12] The *British Messenger* commented in April 1860, 'with the exception of Buckie, none of these villages has a stated ministry in it, the churches being situated at some distance from them'.[13] It is important that the Church of Scotland and Free Church had not considered it a priority to establish active congregations in these villages that latterly became the centre of the revival. The enthusiasm with which the fishing people received this religious movement was, in part, a reaction to the years of having been neglected by the Presbyterian churches. Paradoxically, the absence of the church had created the fertile ground upon which the revival flourished.

II

In addition the church's apparent indifference towards these communities meant that it possessed a negligible hold over the imagination and emotions of the fisherfolk. This provided the opportunity for the rise of superstitions, which also, in a seemingly contradictory manner, served to incline them towards revivalist religion. A strange concoction of popular beliefs and religion combined to govern the lives of the north east fisherfolk. Peter Anson, in 1930, described how 'the Scottish fisherfolk possess an inborn sense of the supernatural . . . extraordinary superstitions, beliefs, and practices, ruled the daily lives of the fishing communities'. He discussed how fishermen considered that it was unlucky to meet, on the way to their boats, either a red-haired person, anyone flat-footed, someone who was 'ill-fitted', a dog, or a minister, and they would refuse to sail if they found a hare, a rabbit, or a salmon on board their vessels.[14] Often their popularly held beliefs were infused with elements of religious faith. H. G. Graham described how 'superstition grew up side by side with the most austere belief of orthodox religion, like flowers and weeds springing up in an ill kept garden. Each was held with equal tenacity in the same mind, unconscious of any incongruity.'[15] John Cranna, Fraserburgh's local historian at the beginning of this century, recorded fisherfolk superstitions that involved the rites of baptism and marriage. If two or more children were baptised during a church service fisherfolk believed that the first to be baptised would enjoy a charmed life. As a result parents often came to blows at such services over the issue of precedence. Also church weddings often involved several couples and fishing people believed that the first to leave the church after a multiple ceremony would be lucky. Hence several unpleasant incidents, which are recorded in kirk session minutes, arose at the end of wedding services at Fraserburgh's parish church.[16] The fisherfolk of north east Scotland were a highly superstitious people.

The central and most important figure in the revival along the Moray Firth was a Methodist lay preacher called James Turner, who possessed an acute sense of the supernatural. In recalling the circumstances of his conversion he described how four days after he was 'born again' he 'heard a voice say, "Did I not tell you before that God could not save you?"' His response was, 'I knew that this was Satan'.[17] His vivid imagination of an eternal world that was close at hand is illustrated by the following extract of a sermon he preached during the revival. 'People', he said, 'may have the ordinances and go down to hell with them . . . The Lord stands tonight, and He bids you lay hold on eternal life. Do you think you will be in a fitter state tomorrow? No; you will be in a much worse state, much darker, much blacker, much nearer the pit. Never in your life will you be nearer eternal life than tonight, tonight, tonight.'[18] According to one of his biographers, Elizabeth McHardie, Turner 'with a bold grasp himself of the horrors of an eternal hell, . . . held them up before the vision of his hearers' souls, its hopeless agony, careless blasphemy, the lurid glare of its quenchless flames, the myriad stings of the deathless worm that prevails for ever in its gloomy regions'.[19] After his premature death in February 1863, William Ker, Free Church minister at Deskford, commented that 'it appeared that his emotional faculties predominated over his intellectual powers, and that his vivid perception of the spiritual prevented the full exercise of a discriminating judgment'.[20] There can be no doubt that Turner's enthusiastic belief in the supernatural endeared him to the fisherfolk among whom he preached, and that their common popular beliefs created the perfect context for this type of revival to flourish.

Another feature of the fishermen's life, which helps to explain why they received this religious movement wholeheartedly, was the constant physical danger they encountered every day. John McGibbon described the precarious nature of the fishing industry. When the boats left each day those who remained onshore did not know how or when their husbands, sons or fathers would return.[21] A writer in the *Old Statistical Account* maintained that, before the safety which harbours afforded in bad weather, deaths at sea exceeded those from natural causes.[22] Indeed even in the 1860s Sir J. S. Forbes, who addressed the annual general meeting of the North East Coast Mission, remarked that 'about a thousand lives are lost yearly on an average on our coast by shipwreck and it is calculated that eleven out of every sixteen seafaring men die by drowning'.[23] From an analysis made of the 1861 census it was calculated that an eighth of all the women living in Portessie were widows of fishermen.[24] This was a considerable proportion which displays the dangerous nature of the fishermen's lives. Interestingly provident institutions and friendly societies did not prosper among the fishing people around the middle of the nineteenth century. Francis Grant, parish minister of Banff, commented in the *New Statistical Account*, that these institutions 'have gradually been suffering decay' and that more than half 'have all been dissolved within the last few years'. He went on, 'in this, as in most other things, there is a fashion; and here the fashion has declined'.[25] It appears that instead of inclining them towards life insurance, the perils of their occupation turned the fishermen towards a combination of religious and superstitious beliefs.

Furthermore, the deaths of fishermen had a profound effect upon the communities from which they came and often led to revival. Firstly, a boating accident led to the deaths of four men at Footdee, a fishing village adjacent to Aberdeen, in January 1860 which left fifteen children orphaned. 'The scene on the pier at the time', reported the *Aberdeen Journal*, 'where the whole community of Footdee were congregated, was indeed heart rending to witness.'[26] Shortly afterwards this village was enveloped by the religious movement. In addition, George Calder and Alexander Dundas were drowned crossing Dunnet Bay in June 1860. Within a week revival had begun at two local villages, Burnhaven and Buchanhaven.[27] In 1863 *The Revival* reported how a fishing accident near Peterhead acted as the spur of another outbreak of revival. It stated that 'the loss of three fishermen by the upsetting of a boat, first produced a deep impression on the villages. Frequent religious services, to which all gathered out, were immediately held, and in connection with them the awakening appeared.'[28] Elizabeth McHardie asked a woman who had been 'born again' during the revival at Inverallochy about the circumstances of her conversion. She answered, 'My uncle's sudden death, five weeks ago, made me feel the necessity of being ready. He was one of the men that was lost in the first boat.'[29] Danger was the constant companion of the fishermen. Their sudden and untimely deaths produced an enormous effect upon the small close-knit communities from which they came and often acted as the stimulus of revival.

III

In addition to the particular characteristics of the fishing communities that inclined them towards the revival, there were several specific reasons that explain why this movement appeared along the Moray Firth in late January 1860. In the first instance economic circumstances emerge as an important factor. The prosperity of the villages scattered along the Moray Firth in 1859 was wholly dependent upon the success of the fishing seasons.[30] Some fishermen used sailing boats which depended upon the wind and were less expensive to maintain. Others owned drifters which used coal and involved a greater amount of outlay. Several poor seasons could plunge the owner of a drifter irreparably into debt and often fishermen were forced to sell their boats and homes in order to repay their loans.[31] The following table shows that the total catch of the herring fishing industry in 1859, the season before the revival appeared, was particularly poor.

Table 7.1

The relative success of the herring fishing industry along the Moray Firth between 1850 and 1861

Annual Total Catch, in crans

1850	225,000.	1854	275,327.	1858	246,201.
1851	274,066.	1855	320,612.	*1859*	*190,515.*
1852	214,752.	1856	270,167.	1860	252,075.
1853	338,740.	1857	227,465.	1861	267,078.

Source: *Fraserburgh Advertiser*, 20 September 1861, p. 4.

The average number of crans of herring caught each year during this period was 258,499. The harvest of 1859 was the poorest during this time and represents a catch that was 26% less than the average over the twelve-year span. In October 1859, the *Peterhead Sentinel* reported gloomily that, 'the result of this season is most unsatisfactory, and the shortcoming will be severely felt by all classes of the community'.[32] The revival began in the fishing villages in January 1860 following this disastrous year and before the upturn of the

1860 herring season which started in July. The recession of 1859 created considerable despair and hardship among the fishing communities, and this predisposed them towards the consolation and hope offered by religion.

It is equally significant that the poor herring season lay behind James Turner's decision to embark upon an evangelistic tour of the Moray Firth in 1860 which acted as the catalyst of the awakening. Turner was a fish-curer. His busiest period of the year was during the summer and autumn months, while he spent the winter preparing barrels for the following season. As a result of having had a large number of barrels left over at the end of the poor year, Turner found himself virtually redundant. He wrote, 'The fishing in 1859 being low, we kept all our stock and lost about £300. This laid us idle for about three months, so I thought it would be well for one of us to go along the east and west coasts and hold meetings in all the fishing towns. My brother not being well, I left him at home and took the first turn myself.'[33] 'Providence', said William Robbie, another of Turner's biographers, 'opened up a door of usefulness for him, which, if success in business had continued, might have remained closed for ever.'[34] Turner began his expedition on 6 December 1859 at St Combs and preached with great effect in Fraserburgh and every village around the coast as far as Rosehearty before returning to Peterhead quite exhausted at the end of the month. However, it was during a second tour, beginning at Portknockie at the end of January, that the revival appeared in a dramatic, unprecedented manner.[35] (See Map 7.1., on p.190.) Turner's meetings were the primary and principal occasions of the Moray Firth revival. Clearly then, the poor herring season of 1859 was a vital factor in the timing of this movement.

Notwithstanding the importance of the economic factor, there were other local, national and international factors that had a greater influence upon the timing of this movement. Firstly the news of the American revival created the desire and expectancy that a religious movement would occur. Francis Grant reported in 1843 how 'from the increased diffusion of newspapers and cheap popular prints, a taste for reading has sprung up to a considerable extent'.[36] Quickly Christian publishers established a large circulation of tracts and cheap religious newspapers which carried accounts of the American movement. Turner recalled how 'before entering on the coast I spent a few days spreading the *British Messenger* in St Fergus, Crimond and Lonmay'.[37] The *Peterhead Sentinel* of January 1859 described how news of the transatlantic revival had affected earnest ministers, 'stirring them up to greater faithfulness and zeal, . . . true Christians everywhere among us have been quick-

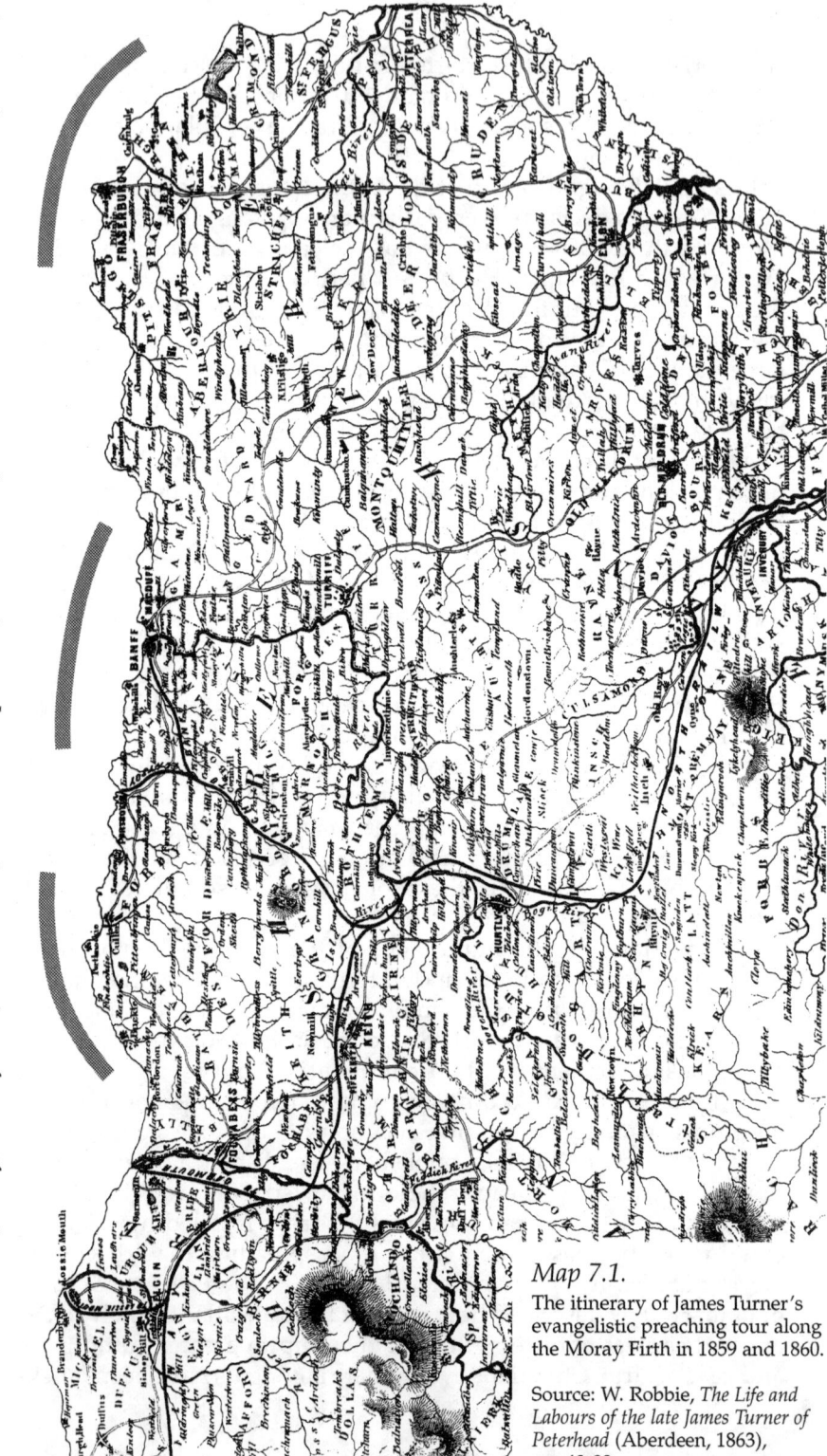

Leg 1 of the tour
December 1859 (successful)

Leg 3 of the tour
March/April 1860 (more successful)

Leg 2 of the tour
January/February 1860 (most successful)

Map 7.1.
The itinerary of James Turner's evangelistic preaching tour along the Moray Firth in 1859 and 1860.

Source: W. Robbie, *The Life and Labours of the late James Turner of Peterhead* (Aberdeen, 1863), pp. 49-89.

ened in consequence in their inner life, and stimulated at the same time to increased usefulness and activity'.[38] Furthermore, John Munro, the United Presbyterian minister at Gardenstown, in an article printed in the *Fraserburgh Advertiser*, remarked, 'I may mention, as another cause of the revival in this village, the reading at the prayer meeting from time to time accounts of the work of revival in America, in Ireland, and latterly in our own country.'[39] The news of the American revival arrived in Findochty after a local fisherman returned from Bo'ness where he had read an edition of *The Revival*.[40] Accordingly the heightened sense of anticipation and expectancy which appeared among Evangelicals along the north east coast was created by news of the 1857 American revival.

However, accounts of the Irish revival, which began to appear in all the regional newspapers in June 1859, were more significant as they increased further the sense of anticipation that a movement was imminent. They stirred the imagination of local Christians with such comments as 'there has been nothing like it, we are told, and have some reason to believe, in its nature or effective influences and power since the days of the Apostles'.[41] By the autumn of 1859 public meetings were held each week in towns and villages along the coast which were addressed by ministers who had made tours of Ireland to visit scenes of the awakening during the summer.[42] Throughout 1859 Mr Porteous, a deputy from the Scottish Reformation Society, toured along the Moray Firth addressing interested congregations in an enthusiastic manner about the Ulster revival.[43] Also several Irish ministers, including Samuel Moore, who led the revival in Ballymena, close to where the movement began in Ulster, preached at special services at Portsoy in April 1860.[44] Interest in the subject of religious movements grew quickly and intensified the atmosphere of anticipation that a revival would soon occur.

Principally news of the American and Irish awakenings gave rise to a number of local prayer meetings which had the most notable effect upon the timing of the revival. The *Peterhead Sentinel* commented, in January 1859, 'It is, however, in the springing up of prayer meetings, and in the large attendance on them, that we notice the most striking effect of the revival in America'.[45] Thomas Baxter, described how at Banff

> the public mind had been for some time preparing for a revival ... a union prayer meeting had existed for more than a year and a half, and the spirit of prayer had continued to deepen, and the attendance rather to increase. At the beginning of the present year, a short series of services, with the view to the revival of religion, was conducted ... the interest continued to deepen.[46]

Prayer meetings were also conducted every night at eight o'clock throughout the winter of 1860 at Banff Free Church in anticipation of an awakening.[47] When Turner arrived in Portknockie to begin his revival services it was reported that 'he immediately took the lead in the prayer meetings that had been held throughout the winter months'.[48] Likewise at Hopeman, when the movement began in March 1860, it was recorded how 'some time ago, district prayer-meetings, on week nights, had been established in private houses in the village, under the superintendence of office-bearers of the Free Church'.[49] Notwithstanding the neglect of the fishing communities by the Established Church, and the relative disregard displayed by the Free Church in particular places, it is clear there was an Evangelical presence along the coast of north east Scotland in certain towns and villages that was waiting for a revival. These meetings, that were specifically constituted for the purpose of praying for an awakening, served to create a heightened sense of anticipation of a revival. The local atmosphere of desire and expectancy engendered by these gatherings was perhaps the major determining factor, as it was in Aberdeen and the rural hinterland, of the timing of the 1860 religious movement.

IV

The popularity of the revival among the fisherfolk lay in the manner in which it was integrated into the local, daily circumstances of their village life. There were a number of particular features of the movement that facilitated its comfortable assimilation within these communities. Firstly the revivalist's gospel message was well adapted to suit the culture of these fishing villages. Images and metaphors were used which made sermons and hymns readily accessible to the audiences. Indeed Mason, the probationary minister at the Portknockie Free Church preaching station in 1860, was unsympathetic towards the revival for several reasons which included the manner in which converts of the movement sang spiritual words to contemporary, popular tunes. At a meeting of the Free Church Presbytery of Fordyce he remarked indignantly,

Most people have heard a song sung in the streets, beginning:
There was once a ship,
And a very valiant ship,
 Hey diddle dee for the Lowlands Low;
And she has met in
With a roving French gallee,
 And she sailed for the Lowlands low.'

I heard a young man singing to the same tune a hymn ending:

'We have laid down the cross,
And we've taken up the crown,
Hallelujah &c.'

It had the same clink, and it was not very agreeable to me.[50]

In August 1861, the *Peterhead Sentinel* criticised several hymns used during the awakening that treated solemn subjects, in their judgment, almost blasphemously. The offending hymn which was printed used sea-faring metaphors in an imaginative way to communicate the gospel message. It read

You are all invited
With Christ to embark
On board his rich ship
The old Noah's ark.

God's love, so amazing,
Is still her main sail;
She's planked with salvation
Quite down to the keel.

From her bow to her stern
She's strongly secured;
Her cargo is wealthy,
And wisely insured.[51]

Through sermons, hymns and testimonies, which contained sea-faring allegories, the evangelists contextualised their message in a manner which was directly relevant to the everyday experiences of the fisherfolk and their community.[52] Indigenous spiritual songs were an important feature of this manifestation of the revival. This helps to explain how the religious movement was successfully integrated into the fishing communities of the Moray Firth.

Also the conversion of several well-known and infamous infidels had an effect upon the progress of the revival amongst the closely knit fisherfolk. According to the *British Messenger* of April 1860, 'many remarkable wicked characters were the subject of an entire revolution of nature and character'.[53] One particular woman, who was considered to be the most profane person in Portknockie, went to a revival meeting in order to ridicule those who were taking part. However, she suddenly 'came under the influence of conviction of sin, and was discovered outside the door on her knees, among the snow, pouring forth her soul in prayer'.[54] Such was her notoriety that many people flocked to see her, astonished that she had been 'born again'. The fame of her conversion arrested the attention of local people and attracted them to the revival meetings. Similarly at Portgordon, where opposition to the revival was at first rather strong, the movement progressed after 'a very powerful man from the neighbourhood, who came to scoff and ridicule the work, was visited with conviction of sin'. The following evening, after his conversion, 'he stood up in the midst of the crowded school-room and confessed his sin, and asked them to join him in rendering thanksgiving to God for the mercy He had bestowed in pardoning his sins'.[55] Such remarkable scenes gripped the attention of local communities as men and women, well-known for their irreligiosity, were suddenly changed. Undoubtedly, these local conversions propelled the momentum of this movement among the fishing people.

A further factor that explains how the revival was readily absorbed by the fishing people was the background and character of its principal evangelist, James Turner. The revival did not affect the smaller fishing villages of the Moray Firth until the arrival of Turner at Portknockie on 28 January 1860. In March, the *Banffshire Journal* described how 'the position of matters was considerably altered by the appearance of Mr Turner'.[56] His addresses were of 'a rather loose and declamatory style' but they produced a powerful effect upon the fisherfolk. One reporter commented 'though very far from being a cultivated speaker, yet the very novelty of the language used, so different from the 'cut and dry' style of ordinary pulpit addresses, and the direct, forcible, and almost rude appeals to the consciences of his audience, coupled with the deep apparent earnestness of the speaker, produced a manifest impression'.[57] James Turner, by addressing the people plainly in their local dialect, attracted enormous audiences and aroused whole communities to a serious contemplation of spiritual matters. Without doubt, Turner was the chief personality of this remarkable revival. It is noteworthy that Reginald Radcliffe, the Liverpool lawyer turned itinerant evangelist, who played a primary role in the Aberdeen and rural revivals, did not produce the same effect among the fisherfolk.[58] Rather, the popular strength of the Moray Firth movement was due to the leadership of a local fishcurer.

Perhaps of greatest significance, the 1860 revival was readily accepted by the fishing villages of the Moray Firth because its origins were local, and it was principally led and diffused by Turner and other native men and women. The Moray Firth revival was three almost concurrent movements. The first of these began at the end of January 1860. It started in Portknockie before spreading to Findochty, Portessie, Buckie and Portgordon.[59] The second and third waves of the movement began simultaneously. Revival broke out spontaneously at Hopeman, during an ordinary house prayer meeting conducted by a Mr Sclater, a local Free Church elder, from where it was diffused to Burghead and Lossiemouth The *Elgin and Morayshire Courier* of March 1860 reported how on that night, at the conclusion of the ordinary services . . . a hymn was sung; and immediately thereafter, those present, or the greater part of them, felt their minds seriously impressed. Instead of separating as usual, one after another engaged in praise and prayer; and this was kept up without intermission till three o' clock next morning. From this time, the excitement increased, and began to diffuse itself over the village . . . it is proper to state, that so far as we can learn, no attempts were made to 'get up' this movement. There were no special 'revival meetings', the movement seems to have been purely spontaneous.[60]

At the same time Turner had retraced his journey back to Banff. From this third centre the religious enthusiasm of the revival was diffused to Whitehills, Portsoy, Fordyce, Macduff and Gardenstown.[61] (See Map 7.2., on p. 196.) It is noteworthy that the religious movement that spread along the Moray Firth was not 'imported' from Aberdeen or the rural hinterland. On the contrary, the fisherfolk's revival was spontaneous and indigenous.

Furthermore, it was diffused by ordinary local fisherfolk who had been converted. At Portessie it was remarked that 'the awakening commenced here principally through the instrumentality of some of the villagers who had gone to the meeting at Findochty'.[62] Similarly at Burghead, 'the movement began with some people who went to Hopeman on Monday', while in Lossiemouth 'the movement was begun in the first of the week by three fishermen from Hopeman'.[63] John Munro reported that the immediate cause of the revival in the parish of Gardenstown was the visit of four fishermen from Portessie, one of whom had three sisters living in the former village.[64] The *News of the Churches and Journal of Mission* described how

> the missionary activity of the [fishing] converts is very remarkable. A few of them sometimes go to hold meetings in neighbouring villages, and tell the people there what God has done for them. At other times they have occasion in the prosecution of their ordinary business to visit other places in their boats. They have held their meetings in these boats, and been joined by many of the inhabitants. A party of fishermen having had occasion to visit Lybster, on the opposite coast of Caithness, were instrumental in commencing a similar work there.[65]

Lastly, the April 1860 edition of *The Revival* commented that 'no clerical agency, no missionary appeals, no lay harangues have been the origin of this extraordinary movement, and although it has been prevailing over this village [Portessie] for two or three days, none but the villagers themselves have guided it'.[66] This explains the tremendous success of the fisherfolk's revival: it was led and dif-

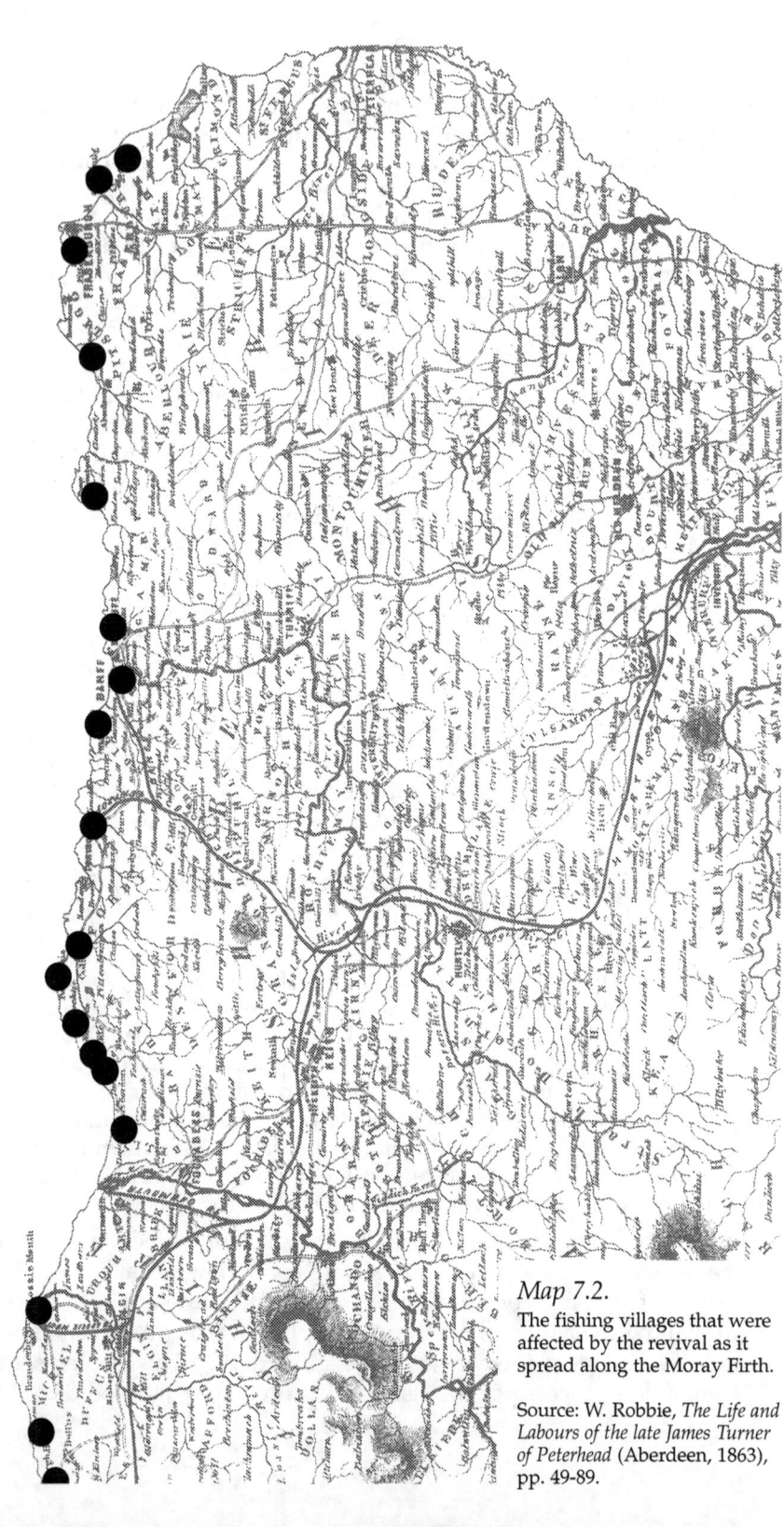

Map 7.2.
The fishing villages that were affected by the revival as it spread along the Moray Firth.

Source: W. Robbie, *The Life and Labours of the late James Turner of Peterhead* (Aberdeen, 1863), pp. 49-89.

fused by local people who were respected and trusted. It became a widespread popular religious movement principally because its origins lay amongst the indigenous people of these communities.

V

Without doubt the Moray Firth was affected by the 1860 revival in an exceptional manner. The fisherfolk's movement was indeed a singular experience. At the time it was recognised that these villages had had a more profound encounter of the awakening in 1860 than any other area in Scotland. A local observer noted how 'the fishing community have, more conspicuously than any other class, been brought under the power of the Gospel'.[67] Meanwhile the *Aberdeen Herald*, in March 1860, reported that, 'the excitement which has been prevalent in the coastline villages of the western district of Banffshire, for the last three weeks, has been . . . quite unequalled, it is believed, by anything which has yet taken place in Scotland in connection with the present revival movement'.[68] Clearly, the Moray Firth enjoyed an unrivalled experience of the 1859 revival.

It was without equal because its influence extended across whole communities. The *News of the Churches and Journal of Mission* described how 'a general awe has been diffused over the whole population, as in the days of the apostles, when "fear came upon every soul"'.[69] Meanwhile the reporter of the *British Messenger* wrote, 'At Findochty, I understand that, with but few exceptions, the whole village may be said to have found the truth. At Portessie, the majority of the people are rejoicing.'[70] Likewise at another unnamed fishing village 'they kept going on until every one of any age in the place had been "forritt" [converted]'.[71] Later, John McGibbon described how in a village near Peterhead, 'after the revivals the whole of the moral tone of our people was lifted up to a higher level, and many who made no profession of a religious regeneration left off their drinking habits, and their swearing, and other prominent sins'.[72] The fishing community of Footdee was also transformed beyond recognition as a result of the 1860 religious movement. A report written in the 1870s remarked upon how the whole village had become 'a picture of tidiness such as is seldom to be met with among classes of the population reckoned higher in the social scale'. It continued, 'this external order is only the index of a still more important change in the habits and character of our fisher town, the population of which has within the past few years undergone a remarkable change for the better in a moral point of view'.[73] Accordingly. the fisherfolk's revival was unparalleled because it affected the religious and moral appearance of entire villages along the north east coast.

There were two features of these communities that serve to explain why they were affected by the revival in such a remarkable manner. Firstly they were remote and secluded. The larger towns along the Moray Firth were better served by transport systems than the smaller villages that lay along the coast. For instance, by 1843 a daily stage coach operated from Banff to Aberdeen and Elgin, while an open car went from the town to Huntly each day.[74] Meanwhile the parish of Rathven, wherein lay Portknockie, Findochty, Portessie and Portgordon, four of the principal revival villages, was serviced only by one 'coach from Elgin to Banff [that] passes and repasses daily along this road'.[75] Also the major centres of the coastal shipping network were Fraserburgh and Peterhead which were a considerable distance from the smaller communities in which the revival flourished. Furthermore, the emergence of the railway network across the north east of Scotland, that began in the 1850s, offered quick and cheap communications with the result that traffic was attracted away from the roads of the region whose maintenance began to deteriorate as their revenue declined.[76] Although the railway reached Banff in June 1860, a line connecting the town to the fishing villages that lay to its west along the coast was not laid until the 1880s.[77] Hence the poor land communications network meant that smaller fishing communities along the Moray Firth were relatively cut-off from the inland rural areas and Aberdeen.

This comparative isolation had a noteworthy influence upon the manner of the revival as it affected these communities. One minister commented in the *Aberdeen Free Press* in 1860, about the unique nature of the revival amongst the fisherfolk. He suggested this was a result of their geographical isolation. He said,

> The remarkable awakening which seems to be extending along our coastline has a special significance from the character of the fishers. Their isolation in locality, but more in sympathy and interests from the agricultural and trading populations naturally tends to keep them untouched by those waves of religious excitement which are passing over the inland districts.[78]

There can be no doubt that the geographical isolation of the fishing villages and their separation from the culture and manners of a wider community was a principal reason that explains why these remote places experienced the revival in such a dramatic manner.

However, the kindred spirit that united fishing families together into tightly knit communities was perhaps the chief reason for their rare experience of the 1860 revival. Malcolm Gray, writing about the fishing industry in Scotland, has commented upon the close-knit nature of Moray Firth fishing communities and how they were visibly separate from the farming population that surrounded them.[79] Meanwhile the north east writer, John Allan, discussing the difference between fishers and farmers has said, 'We should think of fishers as people who of necessity make their homes on shore, but so mistrust the land that they build on the very edge of the waves and shun intercourse with the land dwellers.'[80] Even in the larger towns the fishing families lived apart in well defined areas that became known as the 'Seatowns'. The fisherfolk of Fraserburgh, for instance, lived in Broadsea, an area directly to the north of the town, and as a result were often regarded as an alien people.[81] The separate nature of the Moray Firth fishing villages was illustrated in the parish reports contained in the *New Statistical Account* of 1843, which invariably commented upon how the fisherfolk were 'a distinct class of society, with sentiments, sympathies and habits peculiar to themselves'.[82] Even later, in 1877, George Findlay commented, 'The population was separated, as the fishing class generally is, by sharp lines from the mere land folk.'[83] The social isolation of the fisherfolk in the nineteenth century was quite remarkable. They existed as detached groups of people with minimal contact with other people and this created a close-knit sense of community with an exclusive identity and separate way of life.

This deeply shared sense of community was encouraged further by at least six additional factors. Firstly the size and social composition of the villages created the ideal conditions wherein a sense of affinity could emerge among the people. In 1861 the population of the fishing settlements, illustrated in the following table, was relatively small.

Table 7.2.

The population of several Moray Firth fishing villages in 1860

Village	Population
Portessie	575
Findochty	393
Portgordon	630

Source: *Census of Scotland, 1861, Population Tables and Report* (Edinburgh, 1862), pp. 160-1.

Also the communities were made up predominantly of people whose work was related to the sea. In the village of Portessie in 1861 there were 143 working men and boys. One hundred and ten of them worked as whitefishermen, while a further fourteen were employed in ancillary trades related to the fishing industry. Only fourteen men were engaged in affairs not directly related to fishing. Accordingly eighty seven per cent of the male population of this village worked in the fishing industry.[84] Similarly, in the village of

Portknockie, seventy four per cent of the men had fishing-related jobs.[85] In the larger fishing town of Buckie, whose population was 3000 in 1860, only fifty two per cent of the male population worked at sea.[86] Clearly Buckie, although a sea-faring town and a scene of the revival, had a wider social composition than its smaller neighbouring villages. Meanwhile, it was within the more exclusive, smaller communities that the revival produced its most remarkable effects. Accordingly the size and narrow social base of the fishing villages created their strong sense of community, which affected the manner in which they experienced this religious movement.

Secondly, the fisherfolk's patterns of employment served to unite them closely to one another. Regularly fishing was pursued on a family basis as sons followed fathers and grandfathers into the industry in their early teens, when they became 'useful'. The men and women spent each day working alongside each other and this created close relationships of trust and support. After the men had set sail for the day, the women worked together baiting lines, curing and selling fish. These ties that bound them together were tightened by the patterns of employment and profit sharing of the period. Often landlords received a fixed rent in return for their provision of boats which allowed the fishermen to work as long and as hard as they wished.[87] The crews of each boat, between four and eight men, shared among themselves the expense of lines, the profits that were accumulated and the losses that were sustained. As a result a rough equality prevailed throughout the fishing villages of the Moray Firth.[88] Hence the work patterns of these communities served to strengthen a strong sense of community among the people.

As a result of working so closely together the fishermen became fiercely loyal towards one another. John McGibbon describes one of the finest features of their character as being the way they flocked to help a fellow fisherman in danger or distress. 'Men,' he says, 'will risk their lives for a neighbour and count it only their duty to that one.'[89] Also all of the fishermen wore identical clothes. When they were at sea they wore blue serge trousers, thick blue jerseys, a cloth cap and sea boots. When they were ashore they wore much the same each day, but on special occasions they wore their sabbath clothes, which consisted of blue serge trousers, a monkey jacket and a square peaked or a hairy storm cap.[90] This further engendered a strong sense of unity within the fishing communities. In addition, the fisherfolk lived in extremely close proximity to one another. The 'seatown' quarters of Moray Firth settlements had narrow streets and houses crowded closely together, which produced a very close knit community. James Bertram, a local author, collected statistics about the living conditions of the fishing village of Footdee in the

1870s that reveal how closely the fisherfolk of this community lived together. He wrote,

> In the south Square only three of the houses are occupied by single families, and in the North Square only three, the others being occupied by at least two families each, one room a piece, and four single rooms in North Street contain two families each. There are thirty six married couples and nineteen widows in the twenty eight houses, and the number of distinct families is fifty four.[91]

The confined physical structure of the villages within which the fisherfolk lived only served to heighten the sense of affinity among them.

Finally there was a very strict code within fishing villages that prohibited the young people from marrying anyone outwith their community. John McGibbon recorded that 'any attempt on a fisherman's part to "coort" a town's girl is met with stout resistance by his parents, so for peace sake he is obliged to look for a fisher lass to be his wife'.[92] Susan Baillie has calculated that between thirty four and forty four per cent of all marriages in Gardenstown in 1855 were between individuals who had lived less than one kilometre away from each other before they became husband and wife.[93] Hence George Henderson, the parish minister of Cullen, remarked how the fisherfolk's habit of intermarrying had 'the effect of rendering them a distinct class of society, with sentiments, sympathies and habits peculiar to themselves'. He went on to suggest that 'until some amalgamation shall take place between them and their brethren of *terra firma*, their advancement in the improvements of civilised life must necessarily be slow and partial'.[94] Each of these factors served to establish among the fishing villages along the Moray Firth an unparalleled social context. Such tightly knit communities created the perfect networks of relationships within which an infectious, excitable and spontaneous religious movement could flourish. The ethnic and cultural homogeneity of these mid- nineteenth century fishing villages explains why they experienced the revival in such a wholehearted and distinctive manner.

Before 1860 the small fishing villages along the Moray Firth would not have seemed to be a likely context in which a revival would prosper. They appeared to be, on the whole, an unchurched, irreligious group of strange communities. Yet the underlying features of these villages and the character of their inhabitants created an unequalled set of circumstances that were perfectly suited for the transmission of this religious movement. Notwithstanding the prayer societies that existed, the relative absence of organised religion, in a strange manner, served to create a fertile spiritual atmosphere for the revival. The daily danger and the constant threat of injury or death which confronted the fishermen, not to mention the popular beliefs and superstitions which this aroused, predisposed them towards the gospel, with its strong awareness of supernatural powers and beings. The appearance of the revival in January 1860 was clearly related to the economic depression experienced by the fishing people that winter. However, of greater significance for the timing of the movement was the climate of expectancy which had enveloped these villages following reception of the news of similar movements in America and Ireland. The manner with which the revival was integrated into the local culture was largely responsible for its popular success. The contextualised message, the conversion of well known, strong, local characters, the principal role played by James Turner and the work of many unknown local men and women helped the revival to become part of the lives of these villages. Finally two distinct features of the fishing communities, their geographical isolation and their ethnic and cultural homogeneity, created an unparalleled social context that was ideal for the diffusion of the revival's impulses. Herein lies the reason for the success of a popular religious movement in what at first appeared to be the most unlikely of circumstances.

Notes

1. *The New Statistical Account of Banffshire* (Edinburgh, 1842), p. 36.
2. Ibid., 256.
3. Ibid., p. 330.
4. Ibid., p. 240.
5. *M.R.UP.C.*, (September 1860), p. 165.
6. *B.Mr.*, No 86, (April 1860), p. 318.
7. *A.F.P.*, (3 February 1860), p. 8.
8. *T.R.*, Vol 2, No 38, (14 April 1860), p. 61.
9. J. McGibbon, *Fisherfolk of Buchan* (Edinburgh, nd), p. 89.
10. W. F. Swift, *The Romance of Banffshire Methodism* (Banff, 1927), pp. 35-6.
11. Ibid., p. 41.
12. *New Statistical Account of Banffshire*, p. 263.
13. *B.Mr.*, No 86, (April 1860), p. 318.
14. P. F. Anson, *Fishing Boats and Fisher Folk on the East Coast* (London, 1930), p. 37.
15. H. G. Graham, *The Social Life of Scotland in the Eighteenth Century* (London, 1906), p. 190.
16. J. Cranna, *Fraserburgh: Past and Present* (Aberdeen, 1914), p. 195.
17. E. McHardie, *James Turner; or, How to Reach the Masses* (Aberdeen, 1875), p. 2.

The Revival in the Fishing Villages

18. T.R., Vol 2, No 33, (10 March 1860), p. 77.
19. McHardie, *James Turner*, p. 16.
20. W. Robbie, *The Life and Labours of James Turner of Peterhead* (Aberdeen, 1863), p. 128.
21. McGibbon, *Fisherfolk of Buchan*, p. 39.
22. D. Amand (ed.), *The Moray Book* (Edinburgh, 1976), p. 243.
23. A.F.P., (3 February 1860), p. 8.
24. 1861 Census, Portessie, Banffshire
25. *New Statistical Account of Banffshire*, p. 57.
26. A.J., (1 February 1860), p. 4.
27. A.F.P., (8 June 1860), p. 8.
28. T.R., Vol 9, No 209, (23 July 1863), p. 53.
29. McHardie, *James Turner*, p. 55.
30. McGibbon, *Fisherfolk of Buchan*, p. 38.
31. J. R. Coull, 'The Scottish Herring Fishery: Development and Intensification of a Pattern of Resource Use', *Scottish Geographical Magazine*, 102, 1986, pp. 9-10.
32. P.S., (21 October 1859), p. 2.
33. MacHardie, *James Turner*, p. x.
34. Robbie, *James Turner*, p. 48.
35. Ibid., p. 51.
36. *New Statistical Account of Banffshire*, p. 37.
37. McHardie, *James Turner*, p. 21.
38. P.S., (21 January 1859), p. 3.
39. H. Sprange, *Kingdom Kids: Children in Revival* (Fearn, Ross-shire, 1994), p. 186.
40. MacHardie, *James Turner*, p. 116.
41. B.My., (7 October 1859), p. 7.
42. Ibid., (28 October 1859), p. 5.
43. F.A., (16 September 1859), p. 2.
44. B.J., (1 May 1860), p. 6.
45. P.S., (21 January 1859), p. 3.
46. M.R.U P.C., (September 1860), p. 165.
47. Banff Free Church Kirk Session Minutes 1843-66 (25 March 1860)
48. E.M.C., (2 March 1860), p. 6.
49. Ibid., (16 March 1860), p. 5.
50. S.J., (19 April 1860), p. 4.
51. P.S., (30 August 1861), p. 2.
52. D. E. Meek, '"Fishers of Men": The 1921 Religious Revival, Its Cause, Context and Transmission', *Scottish Bulletin of Evangelical Theology*, 17, 1999, pp. 40-54.
53. B.Mr., No 86, (April 1860), p. 318.
54. Ibid.
55. Ibid., No 87, (May 1860), p. 327.
56. B.J., (27 March 1860), p. 5.
57. P.S., (30 March 1860), p. 2.
58. A.F.P., (11 November 1859), p. 8.
59. B.Mr., No 87, (May 1860), p. 327.

60. E.M.C., (16 March 1860), p. 5.
61. Robbie, *James Turner*, pp. 75-90.
62. B.Mr., No 87, (May 1860), p. 327.
63. E.M.C., (16 March 1860), p. 5.
64. B.J., (10 April 1860), p. 5.
65. N.C.J.M., Vol 7, No 5, (1 May 1860), p. 119.
66. T.R., Vol 2, No 38, (14 April 1860), p. 60.
67. H. MacGill, *On the Present Revival of Religion in Scotland*, A paper read at the annual conference of the Evangelical Union held at Nottingham, October 1860 (London, 1860), p. 4.
68. A.H., (3 March 1860), p. 6.
69. N.C.J.M., Vol 7, No 5, (1 May 1860), p. 119.
70. B.Mr., No 86, (April 1860), p. 318.
71. McGibbon, *Fisherfolk*, p. 77.
72. Ibid., p. 75.
73. Anson, *Fishing Boats and Fisher Folk*, p. 142.
74. *New Statistical Account of Banffshire*, p. 46.
75. Ibid., p. 262
76. H. Hamilton (ed.), *The Third Statistical Account of Scotland: The County of Banff* (Glasgow, 1961), p. 135.
77. H. A. Vallance, *The Great North of Scotland Railway* (London, 1965), p. 173.
78. A.F.P., (3 February 1860), p. 8.
79. M. Gray, *The Fishing Industries of Scotland, 1790-1914* (Oxford, 1978), p. 12.
80. R. Smith, *One Foot in the Sea* (Edinburgh, 1991), p. 55.
81. Gray, *Fishing Industries*, p. 10.
82. Smith, *One Foot in the Sea*, p. 55.
83. Swift, *Banffshire Methodism*, p. 40.
84. 1861 Census, Portessie, Banffshire
85. 1861 Census, Portknockie, Banffshire
86. B.Mr., No 86, (April 1860), p. 318.
87. J.S. Smith, D. Stevenson (ed.), *Fermfolk and Fisherfolk: Rural Life in Northern Scotland in the Eighteenth and Nineteenth Centuries* (Aberdeen, 1989), p. 38.
88. Amand, *Moray Book*, p. 199.
89. McGibbon, *Fisherfolk of Buchan*, p. 35.
90. Ibid., p. 53.
91. P. F. Anson, *Scots Fisherfolk* (Banff, 1950), p. 15.
92. McGibbon, *Fisherfolk of Buchan*, p. 147.
93. Susan R. Baillie, 'The Structure of Population in Traditional Fishing Communities of North-East Scotland: Whitehills and Gardenstown', *Northern Scotland*, 6, 1984, p. 54.
94. *New Statistical Account of Banffshire*, p. 331.

CHAPTER 8

The Revival in the Fishing Villages

Analysis and Results

The culture of the Moray Firth fishing villages made a serious impression upon the way in which the 1860 revival affected their inhabitants. Indeed the indigenous environment of these mid-nineteenth-century fishing communities helped to fashion a distinct experience of awakening. This was created by the manner in which the movement was accommodated within the working lives of the fisherfolk, and it was displayed in the expression of the revival, in particular the physical phenomena, which were a peculiar feature of the awakening amongst these people. The involvement of the local churches, and the composition of those who were affected by the movement, reveal further the different nature of this manifestation of the revival. Finally the expansion of the dissenting churches and the establishment of new religious assemblies in the area demonstrate further the singular character of the fisherfolk's movement. This chapter will illustrate how the local circumstances of these communities profoundly shaped the exhibition and effects of the 1860 awakening along the Moray Firth.

I

In the first instance, the revival was knitted into the daily rhythm and annual pattern of work and leisure experienced by those involved in fishing in Aberdeenshire. The people were engaged in three main industries around the middle of the nineteenth century. The summer haddock season lasted from March to May. It was carried on in smaller boats, occupied by teams of four men and a boy.[1] This inshore fishing suited the smaller villages which lacked harbours, because only lighter crafts, which could be hauled over the beaches, were used. As a result fishermen rarely sailed more than an hour's journey from their village and returned home each night.[2]

The herring season, which provided a more lucrative occupation, constituted the most important commercial enterprise of fishermen. It began in June and lasted until the end of October when they 'followed' the herring and sailed to ports on the east coast of England where they continued to work.[3] Such employment could be undertaken successfully from only the larger fishing towns along the coast which had landing facilities for the greater boats that were used. Consequently most of the fishermen and women deserted their village homes during this period and spent the summer working out of the adjacent ports of Peterhead and Fraserburgh.[4] James Thomson has described the working habits of east-coast fishermen during this period in *The Scottish Fisheries*, which was published in 1849. He discovered that during the herring season, fishermen slept at home on Saturday and Sunday evenings, but throughout the rest of the week they worked day and night and slept for around two hours each afternoon. Also John McGibbon observed how 'fishermen have to be content with very few holidays during the [herring] fishing season . . . even funerals are so arranged as to take up as little time as possible, and are usually over in time to allow the men to sail to the fishing grounds, and shoot their nets, that night'.[5] Therefore, during the busy period of the herring season, between June and October, the fisherfolk lived away from their village homes in neighbouring, larger towns where they worked tirelessly and had little time to devote to social activities.

Once they returned from the herring season in November they spent the winter at home collecting bait and only occasionally did they go to sea.[6] In this period they had more time to relax during these shorter days when the demands of work were less onerous. Throughout this time it was anticipated that 'there will be no regular work for weeks. The boats and gear will be overhauled, and the nets spread out to air and dry in the fields . . . It will be a month of weddings. The lights will go out late, in some cases not till morning . . . they do not get up early in these days of semi-holiday.'[7] Consequently the leisure patterns of the fishing villages were closely related to the annual cycle of their working routines.[8] There was little time for leisure at the height of the herring season in the summer, while during the winter the village fishermen could afford to spend more time relaxing at home.

The timing of the fishing village revival demonstrates clearly how it was influenced by the work and rest habits of this people. One minister noticed in the winter of 1860 that 'during the inclement weather, an unusual listlessness and idleness and want, to some extent, prevailed among the fishing population, which predisposed them to turn their attention to whatever subject might be brought under their notice'.[9] The first signs of revival began to appear at St Combs on 6 December, but it was at Portknockie, from 28 January 1860, that the movement began in earnest before infecting every fishing village and town between Burghead and Gardenstown within the following few weeks.[10] During a second wave of revival that affected the Moray Firth at the beginning of 1863, the correspondent of *The Revival* remarked how 'in God's kind providence, the time for their special visitation was arranged when they were constantly at home, and thus able to unite together in a joyful reception of his blessing'.[11] Meanwhile later in the year another reporter of *The Revival* described how the fishing village revivals had 'taken place after much special prayer, two of them after severe afflictive dispensations, and singularly enough, all during the spring of each year'.[12] There is no doubt that the occasion of the religious movement among the fishing people was affected by the patterns of work and rest which governed their lives.

Also, the intense nature of the fisherfolk's experience of this revival was only possible because their order of work permitted them to devote whole days to religious concerns during the winter and spring. In March 1860, *The Wynd Journal* described how at Hopeman 'the nets [were left] on the shore, and the people, old and young, flocked to hear the Word of God'.[13] At Findochty a correspondent of *The Revival* reported how he had 'spoken to common fishermen who have for nearly three days and nights been praying and singing and exhorting their neighbours. Labour is totally suspended and has been during these five days. Even the cooking of victuals is much neglected.'[14] A local newspaper reported that many fisherfolk had 'not slept for two or three consecutive days, nor tasted food for the same period'.[15] Services were not planned and targeted for particular times. On the contrary they began spontaneously and were continued throughout days and nights for several weeks at a time. The *Forres, Nairn and Elgin Gazette* related that in Burghead 'their worldly employments are altogether given up; and the past week has been to them one long Sabbath, spent in religious exercises'.[16] Similarly it was reported from Findochty how 'work was almost entirely suspended' while the meetings 'continued for more than a week, night and day, with only a few hours of interval'.[17] The intense nature of this movement was only possible within a fishing community where, during this time of year, people could afford to suspend their labours indefinitely and devote their entire attention to spiritual matters.

However, by the third or fourth week of religious fervour a more normal pattern of life began to reassert itself after the intense enthusiasm began to wane. There are several factors that explain why the raw excitement of the fishing revival faded so suddenly. Firstly this was a result of the size of the communities within which it was felt. The demise of the revival was due, in many respects, to the emotional exhaustion it created among the fisherfolk. They were quite simply unable to sustain the level of activity and commitment which they demonstrated in the first few weeks of the movement. In addition after four weeks the revival had probably touched all those who were most likely to respond in these communities. The pool of potential converts had dried up.[18] Meanwhile, after ten weeks of incessant work, James Turner confessed that 'my body is not able to stand it until I rest a while'. Exhausted by his relentless efforts, he returned to Peterhead around the middle of April.[19] Upon his retreat the revival abated. Finally, around this time local ministers began to take responsibility for the leadership of the movement from the local people. At Lossiemouth, for instance, Charles Tulloch, the Free Church minister, became involved with the result that 'matters [began] . . . to assume a more methodical aspect . . . meetings [were] . . . conducted in a regular and systematic way'.[20] It is clear, therefore, that the brevity and fervency of the fishermen's revival were directly affected by the nature of these communities. Also the intense and brief nature of this awakening bore a close resemblance to the early nineteenth-century Methodist revivals in Cornwall which raged uncontrollably for up to eight weeks before ending abruptly.[21]

II

The distinct character of the fishing communities also affected the particular expression of its revival. The movement in these villages was accompanied by physical prostrations that were not experienced, to the same extent, among the main towns along the Moray Firth or elsewhere. The reporter of the *British Messenger* observed how 'there is a greater variety of character, creeds, knowledge, social position, trades, denominations' in Buckie than in Portknockie, Findochty and Portessie. He went on to remark that 'the greater proportion of the cases of conviction of sin, and joy in Christ, were of a much less demonstrative character' in Buckie than they were in its neighbouring villages.[22] Likewise, Thomas Baxter described how his church at Banff 'continued to be filled with persons apparently under deep religious emotion, although very few comparatively of them gave vent to their feelings by audible sounds . . . there were comparatively few in Banff who were struck down, when we consider the number of those under concern'.[23] It appears the relatively more cosmopolitan communities of the main towns were less inclined to indulge in public displays of religious emotionalism than the uncultivated fishing villages. As a result, physical manifestations in the 1860 revival were almost wholly restricted to the smaller fishing settlements.

There are a number of reasons why the village fisherfolk were afflicted in a more physical manner, than most of their town neighbours. Undoubtedly a vital factor was the emotional character of the fisherfolk, which was often described as unrestrained and excitable. Baxter remarked in the course of a sermon that 'the cases of physical prostration are chiefly confined to those who have never been accustomed to the usages of society, nor educated to restrain their feelings'.[24] This certainly applied to village fisherfolk. Also, women from these communities were affected by physical manifestations more than men. The greater proportion of cases cited in newspaper accounts concerned females. According to one reporter, 'instances were numerous of females fainting and falling quite helpless into the arms of those near them'.[25] Prostrations also regularly attended meetings that were conducted by young people. At several such gatherings held at Lossiemouth a reporter commented, 'we must be allowed to say that the scenes here were most irreverent'.[26] Indeed a great furore arose in Elgin one weekend when some young converts from Lossiemouth held a particularly excited religious meeting in the town, after which a member of the town's union revival prayer meeting disavowed any connection with the service.[27] It appears that physical manifestations were experienced almost exclusively by the village fisherfolk. Excitable women and young people, who were generally unaccustomed to regulating their behaviour before others in public, were the principal casualties of this emotional and religious distress.

Also, there were two specific situations that gave rise to a large number of the prostrations which further explain why they appeared almost exclusively among the fishing people. Firstly they appeared at revival meetings conducted by laymen. The manifestations that affected some men and women at Gardenstown occurred exclusively at gatherings conducted by four fishermen who had arrived from Portknockie. However, once they left, the prostrations ceased and there were no reports of physical manifestations at subsequent services conducted by the local United Presbyterian minister, John Munro.[28] Similarly prostrations accompanied the initial meetings at Hopeman that were conducted by fishermen, but once the local ministers assumed superintendence comparative order was immediately restored.[29] The *Elgin and Morayshire Courier* reported how 'the external excitement which prevailed during the previous week, has however, through the influence of the ministers, been completely allayed ... indecorous extravagance has now in a great measure been subdued'.[30] Following the outbursts of physical excitement that appeared at gatherings at Findochty addressed by

James Turner, it was reported that 'since that time the ministers of the various denominations have been holding services in this place and endeavouring to allay the excitement'.[31] In addition it is noteworthy that physical prostrations did not appear at revival meetings conducted by Turner when he preached in Banff, where he was assisted by a large number of local clergymen. The *Banffshire Journal* reported how 'from the different and improved character of the audiences, and the fact that there were always one or more clergymen present, there was a freedom from those extravagances that marked some of the meetings in the fishing villages on the coast'.[32] Indeed local ministers appear to have been anxious to stem the tide of religious enthusiasm as quickly as possible. At Garmouth, for instance, John Allan, the Free Church minister, 'at once came forward and took the direction of the meeting, so as to prevent any undue excitement or extravagance'.[33] Physical manifestations did not occur at every revival meeting that was conducted in the fishing villages and towns along the north east coast. They were actively discouraged by ministers of religion and as a consequence appeared only at gatherings that were presided over by local lay evangelists, and in particular James Turner.

Secondly physical prostrations occurred most frequently at what became perhaps the defining feature of the fisherfolk's revival, the crowded protracted meeting, that usually began in the early evening and was often carried on until between four and six o' clock in the morning. Representative of these gatherings was 'a meeting [at Portessie], which commenced on Friday evening at six o' clock, lasted till four o' clock next morning, and was resumed at ten am'.[34] John Forrester, the United Presbyterian minister at Keith, described how after revival meetings

> an utter impossibility exists of getting people to retire. In many instances, the benediction has been pronounced again and again, and the people peremptorily told to withdraw, but, in spite of all this, they would sit still, some anxious to have their burdened souls lightened, and some to hear more and yet more of those tidings that have made their hearts so strangely glad.[35]

Eventually crowds of people would leave the church and go to local schoolrooms, church halls and private homes where they continued to pray and sing in a less restrained manner. Reports often commented that 'there was comparatively little external excitement during the [church] service', while later 'in the schoolroom, there was a good deal of crying out, many were completely prostrated, and all appeared seriously impressed'.[36] The atmosphere at these extraordinary late-night gatherings was usually intensely hot and emotionally highly charged as a result of the crowds who squeezed into small rooms, and the excited preaching and praying of laymen which they attracted. The physical manifestations that accompanied the fisherfolk's revival generally appeared in the course of these protracted gatherings.

In March 1860, the *Aberdeen Herald* reported in detail the proceedings of one of these meetings that featured prostrations, held among the fisherfolk in Portgordon, which illustrates how the physical manifestations were generated. It described how 'the school got heated almost to suffocation by the people's breath, and in this state of atmosphere the meeting was kept up for nine and a half hours, many of the people remaining there the whole time without meat or drink'. Hymns and spiritual songs were repeated numerous times until 'the audience was quite in an excited state, boys and girls holding one another by the hands and rocking and rolling with their bodies, and even beating with their feet on the floor to the time of the music'. Then a series of prayers was offered by children and young men and women and as people's names were mentioned they shrieked, 'especially females, and commenced crying aloud, and throwing themselves into the arms of some of their neighbours'. Following this, James Turner addressed the congregation, telling them, 'every unconverted man and woman had a devil or devils in their breast, which must be plucked out before they could be saved. "Say to them tonight", he cried with violent gesticulations of his arms, "Devils begone, Devils begone, Devils begone"'. According to the report, this excited address was followed by several cases of physical prostration. However, the greatest commotion did not occur until around midnight when during a period of prayer a number of women shrieked loudly and then fell into an unconscious state. Finally the meeting began to draw to a close around 1.30 a.m., only because the lights were nearly all burnt out and the meeting place was beginning to get dark.[37] The detailed narrative of this specific revival meeting provides an insight into the nature and circumstances of the gatherings at which prostrations most commonly occurred along the north east coast. There is no doubt that the excitable character of the village fisherfolk and the nature of their gospel meetings were largely responsible for the physical phenomena which accompanied their experience of this movement. This particular expression of the awakening was identical to the 'scenes of wild excitement' that accompanied the revivals which affected the Methodist Cornish fishermen at the beginning of the nineteenth century.[38]

III

Although the 1860 revival affected to a greater or lesser extent every village and town along the Moray Firth between Burghead and Gardenstown, there was a variety of reactions from the congregations and ministers who served these communities towards the movement. It is revealing to consider their attitudes because they comment on the character of the revival. The temper of the main denominations towards the movement also had a serious effect upon the direction it took. Perhaps more importantly, the position of the churches had an important influence upon the revival's longer term consequences in these villages, and in particular the new religious landscape that emerged after 1859.

The Roman Catholic and Scottish Episcopal Churches did not foster or encourage the religious enthusiasm of the fisherfolk that accompanied this movement along the north east coast of Scotland. The Roman Catholic Church had four worshipping congregations where the revival flourished, at Banff, Portsoy, Buckie and Presholm around the middle of the nineteenth century. In 1843 the church at Banff comprised seventeen families, while the congregation at Portsoy had 112 members. Further to the west along the coast the church was stronger with both congregations at Buckie and Presholm enjoying an average attendance of 400 people each.[39] Notwithstanding its undoubted strength at Buckie, that was displayed in the erection of a considerable cathedral in 1857, the Roman Catholic Church remained a comparatively small denomination in this area. Peter (P. F.) Anson says that under James Kyle, the bishop from 1828-69, although 'nothing . . . of much consequence happened, . . . Catholicism in the northern district made slow but definite progress'.[40] However, there is no evidence that would suggest that its advance was associated with the revival.

Of even less numerical significance in this area was the Scottish Episcopal Church which had only two congregations in this region in 1860, one at Banff and the other at Portsoy. At Banff it had a membership of around 300 people, while approximately 100 men, women and children belonged to the congregation at Portsoy.[41] Unfortunately no records have survived that reveal the lives of these churches during the period of this revival. However, it is highly unlikely that either would have embraced the fisherfolk's revival. Certainly in all the newspaper reports and other sources that recorded the events of the movement there is not a single reference to any role played by, or effect upon, the Scottish Episcopal Church in this area. It is assumed, therefore, that this denomination did not become involved in the awakening.

The Established Church, across the whole of Scotland, adopted a somewhat ambivalent attitude towards this 'season of grace'. However, the ministers of the Moray Firth parish churches appear to have held a decidedly antagonistic attitude towards the movement. In all the press reports of the revival in this area there is no mention of the involvement of any parish minister. Indeed their absence from meetings of fellow town ministers who gathered to pray for the revival is conspicuous. For instance at Banff, William Barrowclough, the town's Methodist preacher, recounted how in 1859 'the dissenting ministers of the town met at each other's houses alternately on Friday afternoons' where they discussed 'the state of the work of God' and 'the best means of awakening the people to a due sense of spiritual things'.[42] Moreover, when James Turner arrived in Banff, he was assisted by Barrowclough, Thomas Baxter, the local United Presbyterian minister, the Free Church minister Alexander Smellie and John Murker, the Congregational pastor.[43] Similarly at Elgin, union prayer meetings were conducted, on a rota, by the ministers of the Free, United Presbyterian, Congregational and Baptist churches.[44] The glaring absence of the parish minister from these meetings suggests he did not endorse the revival.

In addition, all of the kirk session minutes of Moray Firth parish churches that remain in existence for the period of the revival, nine in total, were examined. Not one of them made a single reference to the revival. On the contrary, each was consumed with the details of confessions and absolutions of those who were charged with a breach of church discipline. Communion rolls also suggest the revival had no effect upon the Established Church in this area. In Drainy Parish Church, for example, the number of communicants who joined in 1860 was not greater than that in subsequent years. Consequently it is assumed that this congregation was not affected by the religious movement. Yet Lossiemouth, the main town of Drainy parish, was overcome with the religious enthusiasm of the revival in 1860 to such an extent that a new Baptist Church was founded there in 1861.[45]

Table 8.1.

Drainy Parish Church: Young communicants 1860-64

Year	YC
1860	10
1861	4
1862	5
1863	11
1864	12

Source: Drainy Parish Church Communion Rolls 1860-64

However, the Established Church appears to have been unable to accommodate the raw enthusiasm which this movement aroused amongst the fisherfolk. Clearly they did not affirm or champion the cause of this revival along the Moray Firth.

Meanwhile the majority of Free Church ministers and congregations appear to have had greater sympathy for the fisherfolk's movement. Twelve sets of kirk session minutes and four communion rolls of Free Church congregations between Nairn and Fraserburgh have survived and they were examined. Eight of the thirteen churches studied exhibited signs that revealed how they were affected positively by the movement. Those congregations influenced by the revival included Cullen Free Church whose minister, John Mackay, in March 1860 'resolved to record with gratitude to the God of all grace, that under the quickening influence of the Divine Spirit a deep and daily attending interest in the things of eternity has prevailed during the last five or six months'.[46] Subsequently in June he reported that 'as one result of the present religious awakening there were no fewer than five and forty to fifty applicants for admission to the communion of the church', all of whom were received with the result that the church roll grew by one third.[47] Similarly Murdoch M'Kay, minister of Fordyce Free Church, minuted that the kirk session agreed in September 1859 to meet each Sunday morning at half past ten 'to pray for a blessing on the services of the day and for a revival of the work of the Lord in the congregation and throughout the land'.[48] The following April he noted that 'during the past winter there has been an unusual spirit of inquiry among the people. The prayer meetings have been well attended in all parts of the parish. There is good reason to believe that not a few cases of conversion to God have occurred.'[49] These minutes of kirk sessions record the effect of the revival upon several Free Church congregations along the north east coast of Scotland.

The impression made by the revival is demonstrated further by the following tables which illustrate the growth of other Free Churches in the area during the movement. The Macduff Free Church kirk session's records of young communicants were found to be incomplete. Nevertheless they show that during the communion seasons of April and July 1860, when the revival was at its height, the church added twenty two new members, while the average number of young communicants professing faith for the first time at previous and subsequent services of the Lord's Supper was six.

Table 8.2.

Macduff Free Church: Young communicants 1857-61

Year	YC
April 57	5
Oct 57	6
April 58	13
Oct 58	7
April 59	4
Oct 59	-
April 60	10
July 60	12
Oct 60	4
April 61	-
July 61	-
Oct 61	5

Source: Macduff Free Church Kirk Session Minutes 1857-61

Also it is of particular interest that the church added an extra communion season, held in July, to its calendar in 1860 and 1861. As early as September 1859 William Leslie, the minister, recorded 'hopeful indications of a revived state of religion', while eighteen months later he described 'a very marked change in the tone of religious feeling generally, whilst not a few cases of what they believe to be saving conversion can be specified'.[50] Clearly this congregation was affected by the revival.

The third table illustrates the number of young communicants who joined Bellie Free Church, between 1857 and 1863. This reveals that the number of young people who became members of this church trebled during the period of the revival, which indicates clearly the effect produced by the religious movement upon this congregation.

Table 8.3.

Bellie Free Church: Young communicants 1857-63

Year	YC
1857	3
1858	4
1859	*9*
1860	*14*
1861	9
1862	3
1863	4

Source: Bellie Free Church Kirk Session Minutes 1857-63

The next table reveals the growth which Nairn Free Church experienced through the movement. During the six-month period from November 1859 to May 1860 forty six people joined this congregation, which represented more than three times the number that had been admitted during the previous year.

Table 8.4.

Nairn Free Church: Young communicants 1858-61

Year	YC
May 1858	4
Nov 1858	9
May 1859	4
Nov 1859	*19*
May 1860	*27*
Nov 1860	6
May 1861	12
Nov 1861	6

Source: Nairn Free Church Kirk Session Minutes 1858-61

There was also a noteworthy increase in the number of people who joined Portsoy Free Church upon their first profession of faith in 1860, and the communion roll of this congregation also expanded during the period of the revival. Indeed, between 1860 and 1861, forty four people were received into the church, representing more than double the number who joined during the previous three years. The minister of this congregation, Alexander Reid, recorded in February 1860 how 'the Lord has manifestly, for some time back, been owning and prospering his work in this place to a much larger extent than for many years before'.[51] His testimony and the figures testify to the considerable growth of the Free Church in Portsoy at this time.

Table 8.5.

Portsoy Free Church: Communion rolls 1857-62

Year	YC	C' cants	Increase / Decrease
1857	5	304	-1
1858	6	316	+12
1859	9	314	-2
1860	28	318	+4
1861	16	342	+24
1862	10	341	-1

Source: Portsoy Free Church Communion Rolls 1854-76.
Portsoy Free Church Kirk Session Minutes 1843-59.
Portsoy Free Church Kirk Session Minutes 1859-1911.

Banff Free Church also grew during the revival. The table below authenticates the minister's judgment recorded in March 1860 that 'there seems to be throughout the congregation an increased interest in religion ... that in a good many cases, and especially among

The Revival in the Fishing Villages 215

the young, there have of late been indications of an awakening at least and they trust also in some cases a real turning to the Lord'.[52] Indeed, in April 1860, at the height of the revival, thirty one young communicants joined the church, that was more than six times the number that were admitted at the same time during the previous year.

Table 8.6.

Banff Free Church: Young communicants 1859-1863

Year	YC
April 59	5
Oct 59	12
April 60	*31*
Oct 60	15
April 61	15
Oct 61	18
April 62	20
Oct 62	16
April 63	7

Source: Banff Free Church Kirk Session Minutes 1843-66

The rise in the number of young communicants joining the Free Church and the evidence drawn from kirk session minutes demonstrates how this denomination, along the Moray Firth, reaped considerable benefits from the revival.

Records remain for three of the six United Presbyterian Churches that lay along the Moray Firth during the mid-nineteenth century. There is no indication that the congregations at Buckie and Forres were influenced by the revival, but it is apparent that the church at Banff was affected in a positive manner. The minister of that congregation, Thomas Baxter, suggested at the end of February 1860 that 'a week be set apart to ask for a revival of religion in the congregation and neighbourhood and that the church be open every evening'.[53] Subsequently a series of services began in the church on 5 March. Shortly these meeting were infused by the excitement of the revival and many people began to be converted. As a result on 8 April Baxter reported that several people 'had applied for admission into the fellowship of the church, many of whom profess to have got good from the series of services held in the church during the month of March'.[54] They are represented in the following table.

Table 8.7.

Banff United Presbyterian Church: Young communicants 1858-63

Year	YC
1858	2
1859	1
1860	20
1861	10
1862	3
1863	0

Source: Banff United Presbyterian Church Communion Rolls 1850-1914

These statistics display a tremendous rate of growth in 1860 and 1861, when the number of people joining this congregation increased tenfold. It is clear that this church was affected by the awakening.

Finally there were a number of other comparatively smaller dissenting congregations, most notably the Congregationalists at Banff, the Baptists at Elgin and the Methodists at Buckie, who joined enthusiastically in the religious movement. Indeed these churches probably provided the strongest support and most effective leadership for this movement among the fishing people. John Murker was the Congregational minister at Banff. 'A careful observer and active agent in the revival' he admitted twenty five new members to his congregation during a six-month period at the height of the movement.[55] Through his endeavours new Congregational churches were begun at Portsoy and Macduff in the years immediately after the movement.[56] Thomas Vasey was the Baptist pastor at Elgin in 1859 who also took a 'prominent part' in the revival.[57] Indeed he was criticised in the local press for the leading role he played in house meetings held at Lossiemouth. The *Elgin and Morayshire Courier* complained that, 'without being thought uncharitable, we must say that we cannot on any account agree with him in tolerating extravagant demonstrations, which, as we have said before, have certainly nothing to do with true religion'.[58] Nevertheless, as a result of the support they afforded the fisherfolk during the revival, the Baptists planted a church at Lossiemouth, established a presence at Forres and strengthened their position at Peterhead and Fraserburgh.[59] However, it was the Methodists who, more than any other existing denomination, embraced and benefited from the revival among the fishing people. Before the awakening they had small, poorly attended chapels at Whitehills, Cullen and Banff. After the movement they planted new churches at Findochty, Portessie and Portgordon and reestablished another chapel at Buckie, and added new members at a prodigious rate. Wesley Swift judges this to have been 'a worthy

The Revival in the Fishing Villages

memorial to the work of this devoted servant of God', James Turner.[60] Although a considerable proportion of the revival converts along the coast joined the Free Church, it remains that among the existing denominations the Methodists probably gained most from the movement. Methodist revivals had tended to flourish among coastal communities, most notably in Cornwall.[61] Their particular style of worship, 'with the due place which it gives to emotion in moderation' was eminently more suited to the temperament of the village fishing people.[62] Accordingly, this was largely, by nature and expression, a Methodist awakening.

IV

The communion rolls and kirk session minutes also provide an insight into the individuals who were affected by this movement and became new church members in 1860. Unfortunately, given the limited details provided by some church records, it was possible to identify precisely only those people who joined the United Presbyterian and Free Church in Banff during the revival. These people represent a reasonable sample of those who were affected by the religious movement in a coastal town, but are atypical of the village converts. Nevertheless, in addition it was found that Elizabeth McHardie interviewed and recorded the details of 126 individuals who were converted in the fishing villages during the revival.[63] They provide some further useful insights into the composition of men and women whom this awakening influenced.

In the first instance the proportion of young communicants who were preceded into church membership by parents enables an examination to be made of the influence of family background in the lives of those affected by this movement. Unfortunately it was possible, given the nature of the church records, to discover the details of only twenty seven of the Free Church new members who joined the congregation at the communion season held in April 1860.

Table 8.8.

Banff Free Church: The religious background of young communicants in 1860

	Total	Percentage
Preceded	13	42 %
Unpreceded	14	45 %
Unknown	4	13 %

Source: Banff Free Church Communion Roll 1860

Forty two per cent of those who joined the Free Church, whose backgrounds could be ascertained, were preceded into church membership by another member of their family, almost one third by a parent. This is a considerable proportion, which suggests that a number of converts were drawn from families who were already members of the local church. This view is substantiated by John Murker who wrote in *The Scottish Congregational Magazine* in August 1860 that 'most of the converts were church-going people before [the revival]'. Indeed he goes on to say that 'most of them having been well trained in Sabbath schools and Bible classes, derive vast advantage now from their previous knowledge of the Scriptures'.[64] Likewise, in September Thomas Baxter commented that 'a great many of them had supposed they were Christians before the awakening commenced, and had passed for such among those who had made a profession of religion'.[65] Hence it appears that a substantial share of those affected by the revival in Banff were already within the influence of the church.

Furthermore McHardie's notes provide a detailed description of the lives of thirty three people before they were converted and indicate something of their background. They have been placed in a number of categories and are displayed in the table below.

Table 8.9.

The previous lives of a number of fishing village revival converts

Type of Life	Number
Church elder	4
Religious / Moral	7
Self righteous	3
Alcoholic	5
Scoffer	7
Curious	5
Wicked	1
Uninterested	1

Source: E. McHardie, James Turner; or, How to Reach the Masses (Aberdeen, 1875), pp. 40-258.

Undoubtedly the movement affected a variety of people from different circumstances. From McHardie's sample one in seven were alcoholics, while more than a fifth were scoffers, which demonstrates how the influence of the revival reached those who were clearly beyond the immediate reaches of the church. However, it seems that forty two per cent of those whom McHardie interviewed were made up of elders, the religious, the moral and the self righteous. They comprise the same proportion of Banff new church members who followed a near relative into church membership. Hence this suggests that even in the fishing villages a considerable

The Revival in the Fishing Villages 219

ratio of the revival converts still had a religious background.

Secondly the class composition of those who joined the churches in Banff during this movement displays the relative attraction of the revival for certain sections of this fishing town. The criteria used for measuring the social class of the men and women was the same as that which was applied to those who became church members in the Aberdeen and rural revivals during the same period.[66]

Table 8.10.

The class composition of Banff new church members during the revival

Status	Men	Women	% Men	% Women	Total
Middle Class (H)	1	1	2 %	2 %	4 %
Middle Class (L)	1	2	2 %	4 %	6 %
Working Class					
Skilled	19	15	36 %	29 %	65 %
Unskilled	2	11	4 %	21 %	25 %

Sources: Banff Free Church Communion Roll 1860
Banff United Presbyterian Church Communion Rolls 1860-61
1861 Census, Banff, Banffshire

A small proportion, only ten per cent, of the new church members belonged to the middle classes. Also, they were farmers from the rural hinterland and not Banff townsfolk. It is clear that these churches received their greatest support from the skilled working classes. Almost two thirds of those who joined the two congregations during the movement were drawn from this section of society. Three fifths of these people were men. A quarter of the new church members were unskilled working people, while eighty five per cent of them were women, all of whom were domestic servants. Indeed female house workers accounted for more than one fifth of the total number of those who were admitted into these two churches at the time of the revival. Only ten per cent of the sample who joined the two Banff congregations in 1860 were fisherfolk which shows how unrepresentative it was of those affected by the awakening in the smaller villages. Rather, the greater proportion were made up of bakers, shoemakers, cabinetmakers, carpenters and slaters, members of the traditional artisan class. Notwithstanding the female domestic servants, this section of the fishing town, it appears, was most affected by the revival.

McHardie recorded the occupational details of fifteen of the fishing village converts whom she interviewed.

Table 8.11.

The occupations of fifteen fishing village revival converts

Occupation	Number	Percentage
Fisherman	8	53 %
Domestic Servant	3	20 %
Minister of religion	2	13 %
Office worker	1	7 %
Joiner	1	7 %

Source: E. McHardie, *James Turner; or, How to Reach the Masses* (Aberdeen, 1875), pp. 40-258.

Although the extent to which those whom McHardie interviewed were representative of the number who were affected by the fishing villages during the revival may be questionable, they nonetheless provide a useful sample of converts. She probably held up the ministers as special cases of regeneration, but it is unlikely that over an eighth of those affected by the revival were religious professionals. However, it is noteworthy that a fifth of the fishing village converts were domestic servants. Clearly in Banff and within the smaller settlements stretched along the coast this particular class was especially influenced by the movement. However, there is a sharp contrast between Banff and the villages with regard to the proportion of fishermen affected by the revival. The ratio increased fivefold. It would seem that more than half of those McHardie met were fishermen. Along the coast in the smaller settlements these men were among those most influenced by this movement.

The marital status of those who joined the Banff Free and Banff United Presbyterian Churches during the revival constitutes the third investigation. The status of sixty four people was discovered.

Table 8.12.

The marital status of Banff new church members during the revival

Marital Status	Men	Women	% Men	% Women	Total
Married Couples	5	5	8	8	16 %
Married Individ	4	8	6	12	18 %
Unmarried	7	34	11	53	64 %
Widow	0	1	0	2	2 %

Source: Banff Free Church Communion Roll 1860
Banff United Presbyterian Church Communion Rolls 1860-61
1861 Census, Banff, Banffshire

The findings indicate that just over a third of those who became church members at the height of the movement were married. Approximately half of them, sixteen per cent, joined as couples, while eighteen per cent were individuals who joined the church

The Revival in the Fishing Villages 221

alone, but were nevertheless married. A small proportion, only two per cent, were widows. The greatest share, almost two thirds, were unmarried. Women accounted for more than four fifths of this group. It is unfortunate that the marital status of twelve men remain unknown. It is highly probable that most of them were unmarried. Had it been possible to determine this categorically, then the proportion of unmarried people would have risen to approximately seventy five per cent. Nonetheless it remains that the revival in Banff appears to have affected a large number of unmarried women.

McHardie mentions the relationships that existed between fifty one of the converts she met and interviewed.

Table 8.13.

The relationships that existed among fifty one of the fishing village revival converts

Relationship	Number	Percentage
Husband / Wife	12	24 %
Father / Mother	4	8 %
Son / Daughter	17	33 %
Brother / Sister	14	27 %
Friend / Other	4	8 %

Source: E. McHardie, *James Turner; or, How to Reach the Masses* (Aberdeen, 1875), pp. 40-258.

These statistics reveal how the influence of the fishing village revival was diffused primarily through the network of family relationships. It also appears to substantiate the findings that were drawn from those who joined the Banff churches during the revival. Clearly the husbands and wives, which made up twenty four per cent of the converts, were married. It is almost certain that the fathers and mothers were also espoused, which suggests that at least a third of the village revival converts were married. It may be conjectured that the sons, daughters, brothers and sisters were unmarried, and that most of the friends or others were also single. Then it would appear that two thirds of those affected by the movement in the smaller settlements were unmarried people. In any case it remains that the greater proportion of revival converts along the north east coast were single.

An examination of the age of the new church members when they joined the Banff congregations is also revealing. The table below classifies the age at which twenty seven people became members of these churches.

Table 8.14.

The ages of Banff new church members during the revival

Age	Men	Women	% Men	% Women	Total
15 – 20	3	8	11	29	40 %
21 – 30	6	6	22	22	44 %
31 – 40	1	1	4	4	8 %
41 – 50	1	1	4	4	8 %
51 – 60	0	0	0	0	0 %
60 +	0	0	0	0	0 %
Mean Age	26.18	23.75			

Sources: Banff Free Church Communion Roll 1860
Banff United Presbyterian Church Communion Rolls 1860-61
1861 Census, Banff, Banffshire

It reveals that two fifths of the new church members were less than twenty years of age, and that almost ninety per cent were younger than thirty when they joined these congregations during the revival. There are interesting gender differences in the various age bands. The ratio of male and female was equal in the twenty one to thirty, the thirty one to forty, and the forty one to fifty age groups. Yet among the teenagers girls outnumbered boys by more than two to one. Females were, on average, more than two years younger than men when they joined these churches. Accordingly the most important result of this analysis is that almost a third of the new church members were young women less than twenty years of age. Teenage girls, it would appear, were particularly susceptible to the influences of the revival in the town of Banff.

McHardie arranged her interviewees according to broad age categories which suggest how old they were when they were converted.

Table 8.15.

The 'age' at which fishing village people were converted during the revival

Group	Number	Percentage
Old men / women	3	2 %
Men / women	93	74 %
Young men / women	11	9 %
Boy / girl	19	15 %

Source: E. McHardie, *James Turner; or, How to Reach the Masses* (Aberdeen, 1875), pp. 40-258.

It is not possible to ascribe precise age brackets to the groups which McHardie has used to catalogue the converts. Nevertheless it may be suggested that the boys and girls were less than thirteen years of age, that the young men and women were aged from fourteen to nineteen, that the men and women were between twenty and thirty years of age, and that the older people were more than thirty. Accordingly it appears, from McHardie's notes, that a significant minority of the converts were children and young people, and that the greater proportion were less than thirty years of age.

In addition, there is an abundance of anecdotal evidence which describes how the fishing revival affected a large number of young people. Victorians regularly depicted children as 'potential recipients and bearers of grace' and certainly the latter appear to have captured the attention of journalists whose reports invariably carried accounts of child conversions and young people conducting religious services.[67] The *Banffshire Journal* of February 1860, for example, reported that at Portknockie 'the children, as in all the other villages were much affected, and could not be tired of praying and singing hymns'.[68] From Buckie a correspondent of *The Revival* reported that 'the Sabbath school in the United Presbyterian Church, Buckie, has increased from fifty to 200, at Portessie a Sabbath school has been opened with 180 children'.[69] The effect of the revival among young people also appeared in the kirk session minutes of Banff Free Church in March 1860. It recorded that within their congregation 'an increased interest in religion . . . especially among the young, there have of late been indications of an awakening'.[70] Meanwhile Thomas Baxter described how at Banff 'hundreds of neglected children are getting religious instruction at home and in the Sabbath school'.[71] It seems that child converts may have attracted a disproportionate amount of press attention during this revival. Nevertheless, given that the Banff churches did not generally admit to membership those who were less than sixteen years old, it may be estimated that the average age of those 'born again' along the north east coast was very probably about five years younger than that which has already been calculated. Above all it remains that the influence of the movement was probably felt most strongly by teenage girls.

The last investigation to be made into the composition of the Banff new church members during the revival concerns gender. A comparison can be made between the gender balance of those who joined several churches along the Moray Firth in the years immediately before and after the revival, and the proportion of men and women who became members of these congregations during the religious movement.

Table 8.16.

The gender status of Banff new church members before, during and after the revival

		No	Percent
Before and after the Revival	Male	134	34 %
	Female	264	66 %
During the Revival			
	Male	56	40 %
	Female	85	60 %

Sources:	Banff Free Church Communion Rolls 1850-63
	Banff United Presbyterian Church Communion Rolls 1855-67
	Bellie Free Church Kirk Session Minutes 1857-63
	Nairn Free Church Kirk Session Minutes 1858-61
	Portsoy Free Church Kirk Session Minutes 1857-62

Before and after the revival the ratio of men and women who joined these churches was clearly one to two, while at the height of the movement two fifths of the new church members were men and three fifths were women. This represents a substantial swing of six per cent. Nonetheless, these statistics suggest that the greater proportion of those affected by the revival were still women. This confirms the impression created by a report in the *Aberdeen Herald* of March 1860 describing a typical revival meeting held at Portgordon at the beginning of which there were fourteen men, fifty five women and about the same number of boys and girls present. Although the proportion of men increased, 'the great bulk of the meeting was made up of women and children'.[72] Accordingly a typical convert of the fishing revival emerges from the analysis. Jessie Allan, the unmarried nineteen-year-old daughter of the baker at Banff Alexander Allan, who was already a member of the Free Church, was the archetypal fishing town convert. Females, it seems, were more represented among the converts of the revival along the north east coast than men. Indeed, teenage girls constituted the single largest group of people affected.

V

Finally, among the most profound effects of the revival was the emergence of new religious groups, and in particular Brethren assemblies among the fisherfolk. (See Map 8.1., on p. 225.) This, above all, demonstrates how the character of these people affected the course and outcome of this religious movement. During this period Brethren thinking had begun to enter revivalism as a new attitude, indifferent towards denominational structures, began to arise.[73] The first Open fellowship in the north east of Scotland was

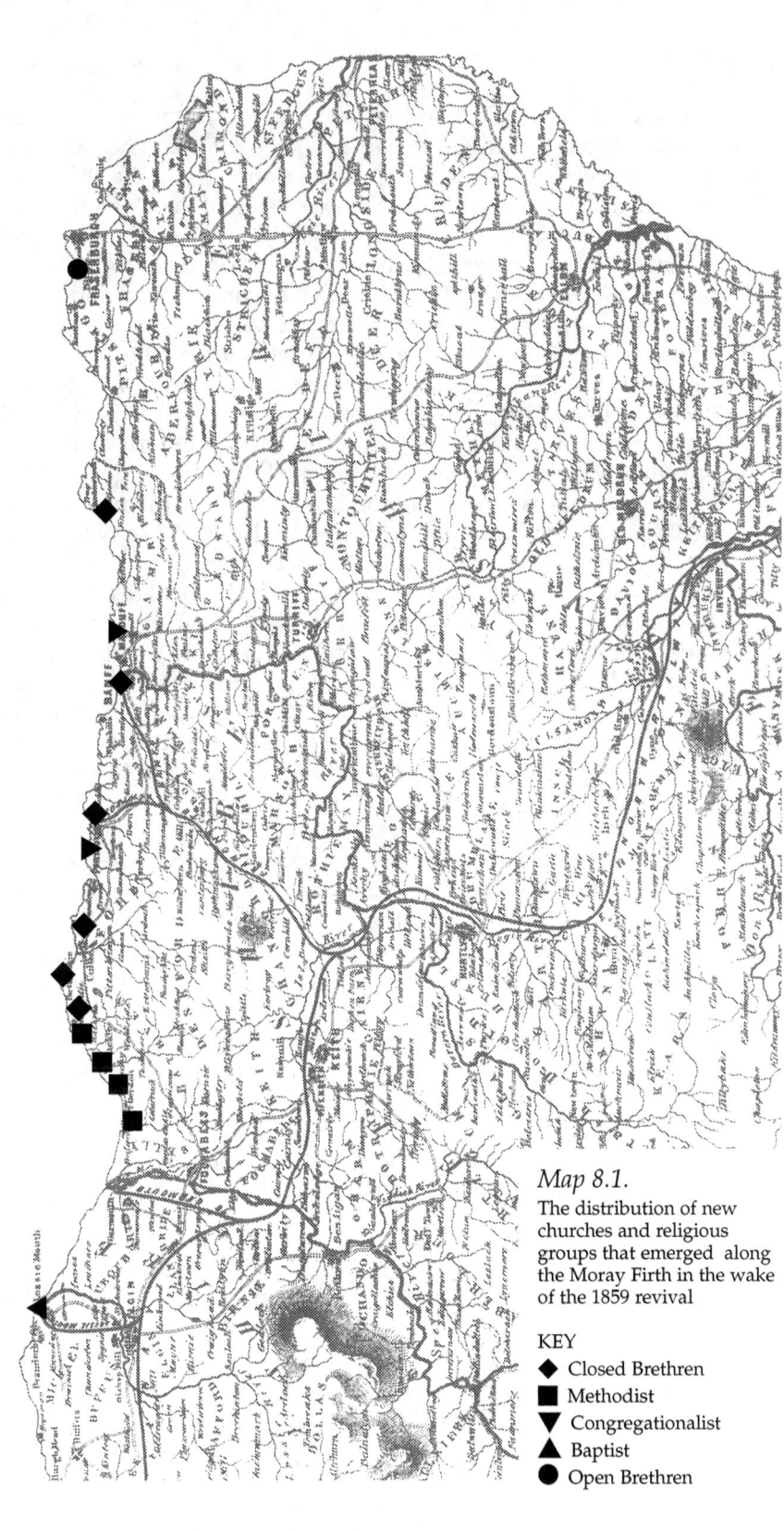

Map 8.1.
The distribution of new churches and religious groups that emerged along the Moray Firth in the wake of the 1859 revival

KEY
◆ Closed Brethren
■ Methodist
▼ Congregationalist
▲ Baptist
● Open Brethren

established in Aberdeen in 1867 and this was followed closely by an assembly founded in Peterhead in 1868 by William McLean. However, the work of Donald Ross, a chief evangelist of the 1859 revival, was primarily responsible for the expansion of the Open Brethren in the north east of Scotland. Dissatisfied by the careless manner in which the Free Church had begun to receive those whom he considered unconverted to the sacrament of communion, and by faults he identified in the way ministers dealt with converts, Ross became increasingly disenchanted by the church's unwillingness to continue its support of revivalism. Eventually, towards the end of the 1860s, he joined the small Brethren assembly in Aberdeen. Soon his example was followed by others who felt equally frustrated by the spiritual state of the churches to which they belonged, and who wanted to practise their religion uninhibited by the presence of an institutional denomination. Between 1871 and 1873 a network of at least twenty eight Open Brethren assemblies spanned Aberdeenshire.[74] However, only two Open assemblies, at Fraserburgh and Newburgh, were found on the coast. The Close Brethren, more sectarian in nature, had already proselytised the fisherfolk and established at least seven assemblies among them. By the 1870s Exclusive assemblies had been established in Crovie, Banff, Portsoy, Portknockie, Findochty, Cullen and Peterhead.[75] It was the 1860 revival that created the context within which the Open and Close Brethren Assemblies emerged and flourished amongst the fisherfolk along the Moray Firth.

A number of proposals have been suggested that attempt to explain why the Brethren movement prospered so remarkably along the Moray Firth in the wake of this revival. In the first instance the neglect of the larger denominations experienced by the fisherfolk before the awakening appears to have inclined them towards independent religious bodies. John Cranna, a local historian, observed how the fishing population of Fraserburgh despised the traditional churches and that they were very often favourably disposed towards new, dissenting churches. He writes,

> It has to be pointed out that the fisher people of this district have all along had a decided penchant for embracing every new form of religion that came round. It would almost seem that the more extreme the views from the standards of Old Zion, which at this time was a hated if not despised church, propounded by offshoot after offshoot, each one claiming greater spiritual perfection than the other, the greater attraction did they hold for the fisher people.[76]

The indifference and disregard displayed by the Church of Scotland towards the Moray Firth fisherfolk in the first half of the nineteenth century created an apathy towards organised, church religion within these villages. It was unsurprising therefore that after they were converted they distanced themselves from these institutional churches and joined more local, indigenous Christian fellowships.

Also, some of the village fisherfolk had previously felt alienated from the Presbyterian churches because they did not own any 'respectable' clothes. By contrast the services of the independent religious groups were popular among the poorer sections of the community because they created an atmosphere within which everyone felt accepted and included. John McGibbon described how many of the village fisherfolk.

> have got it into their heads that because they are clothed in rags and tatters they would not be allowed inside the kirks . . . they have a feeling that they count as some one at this [independent] meeting, and that they will not be despised because they have not the nice clothes of their better off neighbours.[77]

The fear of exclusion and rejection discouraged many of the people of the smaller settlements from attending the established congregations in the fishing towns. However, they did not experience concern or anxiety when they met in the inclusive and intimate atmosphere of a religious house group where they were received warmly. This serves to explain further why the Brethren assemblies became so popular among the fishing people.

Furthermore, these new assemblies conducted religious services in a fashion which were more suited to the character of the converted fisherfolk. Given the spontaneous nature of the revival meetings through which they became Christians, and the lay activity that was an integral aspect of the movement, it was unsurprising that the fishing people wanted to worship in a free, unconstrained manner. Presbyterian forms of worship were often considered cold and formal. Indeed Mr Manson, a Free Church probationer who was stationed at Portknockie, created considerable embarrassment and injury to the cause of his Church in that village during the revival by the manner in which he sought to discourage the excited scenes of the movement when they appeared among the fishing people.[78] Hence the unrestrained nature of the Brethren services, where anyone who cared to speak, sing or pray was permitted, was more suited to the temperament and experience of the fisherfolk than the more disciplined and liturgical forms of Presbyterian worship. Peter Anson described how 'it would seem that the greater number of those who are "converted" invariably go over to some other body where their emotional cravings will find satisfaction'.[79] The revival created a new generation of enthusiastic converts which the Presbyterian churches were not always able to accommodate. The attraction of the smaller churches to those affected by the religious movement lay in the opportunity they afforded to worship in a more open, uninhibited manner.

Lastly the independent and egalitarian nature of the Brethren assemblies was perhaps the principal reason why they attracted the fisherfolk converts of the revival. Their style of church government was eminently suited to the fisherfolk, a very autonomous group of people, who, as we have seen, shared the costs of their boats and divided their profits equally.[80] A correspondent of *The Revival*, writing in March 1863, described the fisherfolk's churchmanship, saying, 'they will not be bound or controlled by any man in regard to the ways, times and modes in which they choose to worship God'.[81] They joined the Free Church after the revival, but became increasingly dissatisfied with its system of church government and were more attracted to the lay-led Brethren meetings where there was more parity among the worshippers.[82] Indeed, the Methodists at Findochty, whose fellowship was established in 1860, worshipped without a minister until 1920, while those who met in Buckie waited until 1925 before accepting a professional leader.[83] Similarly the Baptists at Fraserburgh and Peterhead waited thirty eight and twenty seven years respectively before appointing their pastors.[84] The legacy of active lay participation in all aspects of church life and worship continued long after the revival had disappeared. The 1860 religious movement along the Moray Firth was dominated by James Turner, the Methodist fish curer from Peterhead. His enormous influence was exhibited by the men who followed him in subsequent generations to become the leaders of the new religious groups that were formed. The laity were liberated by this revival and therein lies the main reason for the explosive growth of the Brethren assemblies along the Moray Firth in the 1860s, that was perhaps the principal legacy of this movement in this region.

The 1860 Moray Firth revival was dissimilar to the movement which was simultaneously sweeping through the rest of the north east of Scotland. It appeared suddenly and led to an unprecedented six-week period of intense religious fervour among the fishing people. It totally disrupted patterns of work and consumed the attention of whole communities. A large proportion of those who were converted, especially women and children, experienced strange physical manifestations. As a result, many of the institutional churches considered the movement with mild disgust, while the Evangelical dissenting congregations thrived upon this spontaneous outbreak of zealous faith. Women and children outnumbered the men who were converted. Also it precipitated the growth of small dissenting denominations and the emergence of Brethren assemblies, which sought to satisfy the spiritual needs of a new generation of Christians. Each of the main features of this movement, including its length and expression, suggest strongly that it bore a close resemblance to the late eighteenth-century Methodist revivals. The reappearance of such a movement in 1860 was without doubt largely a result of the context within which it was conceived. Clearly the peculiar, distinctive circumstances and character of the Moray Firth fishing villages influenced fundamentally the course and outcome of their revival.

Notes

1. *The New Statistical Account of Aberdeenshire* (Edinburgh, 1843), p. 378. 2,
   John S. Smith, D. Stevenson (ed.), *Fermfolk and Fisherfolk: Rural Life in Northern Scotland in the Eighteenth and Nineteenth Centuries* (Aberdeen, 1989), p. 38.
3. J. McGibbon, *The Fisherfolk of Buchan* (Edinburgh, nd), p. 38.
4. M. Gray, *The Fishing Industries of Scotland, 1790-1914* (Oxford, 1978), p. 48.
5. McGibbon, *Fisherfolk of Buchan*, p. 141.
6. *New Statistical Account of Aberdeenshire*, p. 378.
7. J. Leatham, *Fisherfolk of the North East* (Turiff, 1930), p. 7.
8. P. F. Anson, *Scots Fisherfolk* (Banffshire, 1950), p. 13.
9. F.E.N.G., (24 April 1860), p. 3.
10. W. Robbie, *The Life and Labours of the late James Turner of Peterhead* (Aberdeen, 1863), p. 49, 51.
11. T.R., Vol 8, No 184, (29 January 1863), p. 53.
12. Ibid., Vol 9, No 209, (23 July 1863), p. 53.
13. W.J., No 26, (24 March 1860), p. 202.
14. T.R., Vol 2, No 38, (14 April 1860), p. 61.
15. E.M.C., (23 March 1860), p. 6.
16. F.E.N.G., (28 March 1860), p. 2.
17. B.Mr., No 87, (May 1860), p. 326.
18. R. J. Carwardine, 'American Religious Revivalism in Great Britain c1826-c1863', unpublished D.Phil thesis, University of Oxford, 1974, p. 423.
19. E. McHardie, *James Turner; or, How to Reach the Masses* (Aberdeen, 1875), p. 28.
20. E.M.C., (31 March 1860), p. 5.
21. T. Shaw, *A History of Cornish Methodism* (Truro, 1967), p. 65.
22. B.Mr., No 87, (May 1860), p. 327.
23. M.R.UP.C., (September 1860), pp. 165-6.
24. F.A., (9 March 1860), p. 2.
25. E.M.C., (2 March 1860), p. 6.
26. Ibid., (30 March 1860), p. 5
27. M.A., (28 March 1860), p. 4.
28. B.J., (10 April 1860), p. 5.
29. Ibid., (20 March 1860), p. 6.

30. E.M.C., (23 March 1860), p. 6.
31. Ibid., (2 March 1860), p. 6.
32. B.J., (13 March 1860), p. 5.
33. E.M.C., (13 April 1860), p. 5.
34. T.R., Vol 2, No 38, (14 April 1860), p. 60.
35. B.J., (27 March 1860), p. 5.
36. Ibid., (16 March 1860), p. 5.
37. A.H., (3 March 1860), p. 6.
38. Shaw, *Cornish Methodism*, p. 65.
39. *New Statistical Account of Aberdeenshire*, p. 48, 192, 262.
40. P. F. Anson, *The Catholic Church in Modern Scotland 1560-1937* (London, 1937), pp. 137-8, 140.
41. *New Statistical Account of Aberdeenshire*, pp. 48, 192.
42. J. Stark, *John Murker of Banff* (Banff, 1887), p. 169.
43. E.M.C., (16 March 1860), p. 6.
44. Ibid., (15 July 1859), p. 2.
45. G. Yuille, *History of the Baptists in Scotland* (Glasgow, 1926), p. 98.
46. Cullen Free Church Kirk Session Minutes, 27 March 1860
47. Ibid., 15 June 1860
48. Fordyce Free Church Kirk Session Minutes, 30 October 1859
49. Ibid., April 1860
50. Macduff Free Church Kirk Session Minutes, 9 August 1859; 25 March 1861
51. Portsoy Free Church Kirk Session Minutes, 26 February 1860
52. Banff Free Church Kirk Session Minutes, 25 March 1860
53. Banff United Presbyterian Church Kirk Session Minutes, 26 February 1860
54. Ibid., 8 April 1860
55. Stark, *John Murker*, p. 169, 171.
56. H. Escott, *A History of Scottish Congregationalism* (Aberdeen, 1960), pp. 260-1.
57. E.M.C., (15 July 1859), p. 2.
58. Ibid., (30 March 1860), p. 5.
59. D. W. Bebbington (ed.), *The Baptists in Scotland: A History* (Glasgow, 1988), pp. 266-7.
60. W. F. Swift, *The Romance of Banffshire Methodism* (Banff, 1927), p. 45.
61. Shaw, *Cornish Methodism*, pp. 64-66.
62. Ibid., p. 50, 60.
63. McHardie, *James Turner*, pp. 40-258.
64. S.C.M., (August 1860), pp. 267-8.
65. M.R.UP.C., (September 1860), p. 166.
66. See Appendix 2.
67. H. Sprange, Kingdom Kids (Fearn, Ross-shire, 1994), pp. 176-206, J. Sharp, 'Juvenile Holiness: Catholic Revivalism among Children in Victorian Britain', *Journal of Ecclesiastical History*, 35, (1984), p. 220.
68. B.J., (28 February 1860), p. 6.
69. T.R., Vol 2, No 36, (31 January 1860), p. 102.
70. Banff Free Church Kirk Session Minutes, 5 March 1860
71. McHardie, *James Turner*, p. 197.
72. A.H., (3 March 1860), p. 6.

73. D.W. Bebbington, *Evangelicalism in Modern Britain: A History from the 1730s to the 1980s* (London, 1989), p. 117.
74. N. Dickson, 'The History of the Open Brethren in Scotland 1838 – 1999', unpublished PhD thesis, University of Stirling, 2000, pp. 114-22.
75. N. Dickson, 'Open and Closed: Brethren and their Origins in the North East' in J. Porter (ed.), *After Columba, after Calvin: Religious Community in North East Scotland* (Aberdeen, 1999), pp. 154-5, 164.
76. J. Cranna, *Fraserburgh: Past and Present* (Aberdeen, 1914), p. 169.
77. McGibbon, *Fisherfolk of Buchan*, p. 130.
78. *B.J.*, (10 April 1860), p. 6.
79. P. F. Anson, *Fishing Boats and Fisherfolk on the East Coast* (London, 1930), p. 47.
80. Gray, *Fishing Industries of Scotland*, p. 22
81. *T.R.*, Vol 8, No 189, (5 March 1863), p. 110.
82. W. Chalmers, 'Brief History of the Testimony on the Moray Coast' (np, nd), p. 16.
83. Swift, *Banffshire Methodism*, pp. 57-8.
84. Yuille, *The Baptists in Scotland*, pp. 94, 99.

CHAPTER 9

The Relative Failure of the Revival to affect Peterhead

The revival began among the fishing villages and towns of the Moray Firth at St Combs on 6 December 1859. Quite spontaneously, during this first movement, entire villages that included St Combs, Charlestown, Inverallochy, Cairnbulg, Broadsea and the town of Fraserburgh attended religious gatherings and 'fell under deep conviction of sin.'[1] However, it was during a second wave of excitement, that began in February 1860, that the revival commenced in earnest. The awakening started in the villages of Portknockie, Findochty and Portessie and within several weeks it had spread along the Banffshire coast and engulfed every town and village between Burghead and Gardenstown.[2] Yet, the revival did not affect Peterhead. Despite appearing in the small fishing settlements that lay at either side of the town, it remained untouched by the waves of religious enthusiasm that swept over the Moray Firth in 1860. Hence it is necessary to examine why this religious movement, which appeared in every fishing settlement between Boddam and Buckie, did not emerge in Peterhead to the same extent or in a similar manner during this period.

I

Peterhead was becoming, by the middle of the nineteenth century, a fairly cosmopolitan, modern town. Erected into a burgh of barony by George Earl Marischall in 1593, its original inhabitants were fisherfolk. However, by the end of the eighteenth century this indigenous population had been removed to small settlements that encompassed the town. During the period between the first and the second Statistical Accounts, Peterhead grew significantly, so that by 1843 the ground occupied by the town extended to around seventy imperial acres. Noteworthy improvements had been made to the harbour with the result that during 1836 832 vessels entered the port with a combined weight of 48,136 tons. This indicated, according to William Donald, the parish minister, the 'importance these harbours are to the general trade and shipping interests of the country'. Indeed five boats were regularly employed in the London trading route. Peterhead also boasted a Savings Bank, which by 1837 had 295 depositors. Also it was noticed how 'the streets are now kept in good repair. Side paths with crib paving have been made', while the thoroughfares 'are now lighted with gas'.[3] In addition the town was, in the first half of the nineteenth century, a highly fashionable watering place and spa that was 'resorted to every season by hundreds of health and pleasure seekers and patronised by the flower of the Scottish nobility'. St Peter's Well, famous for the cures performed by its mineral waters, attracted ladies and gentlemen of all ranks and titles. As a result the appearance of the town changed considerably. Peat stacks and dunghills which used to stand on the principal streets disappeared and were replaced by hotels and grand houses, so that demand for building plots increased the annual rent of ground from a pound an acre to one hundred and fifty pounds an acre.[4] Hence Peterhead was, around the time of the awakening, an increasingly wealthy, popular, urbane Victorian town.

In 1859 there were a number of indications in Peterhead, similar to those that appeared in other towns that experienced the revival, which suggest that it ought to have been influenced by this movement. In the first instance, in response to the news of the American awakening, 'a number of prayer meetings' was organised in the various churches of the town.[5] Also, large groups of men and women met to listen to accounts of the Ulster revival. According to the report of a gathering addressed by Alexander Brand, a gentleman from Aberdeen, 'the hall was crowded, and all present seemed deeply interested in the statements that were made'.[6] Later Moir Porteous, an agent for the Scottish Reformation Society, addressed another meeting held in the Free Church about the progress of the Ulster revival, while James Stirling, a United Presbyterian minister from Aberdeen, spoke at a gathering in the Maiden Street Hall on the subject of religious movements.[7] Moreover, Gordon Forlong, an evangelist, in a letter addressed to *The Revival* in September 1859 reported upon how 'a united prayer meeting has been blessed here of the Lord. It began about a year ago, and above fifty persons have found peace whilst attending it. It has also quickened the church much.'[8] Accordingly there were signs that Peterhead was prepared to embrace the revival.

At the beginning of November 1859, Reginald Radcliffe, the itinerant evangelist who acted as the spur of the Aberdeen revival, visited Peterhead for three days. On Saturday, the day of his arrival, he conducted the daily union prayer meeting at the Windmill Street Congregational Chapel. He led worship there on the following Sunday morning, spoke in the Free Church in the afternoon, and addressed another congregation in the United Presbyterian Church in the evening. He devoted Monday to meetings with children and young people. It was observed that the ministers of the Free, the United Presbyterian and the Congregational Churches welcomed Radcliffe warmly and how the 'churches [were] filled to overflowing'.[9] The following January, in 1860, Peterhead was visited again by another evangelist, Gordon Forlong. He stayed for two days and led four meetings in the Congregational chapel. The *Aberdeen Free Press* reported that he 'was permitted to see some fruit'.[10] The planning and organisation of these meetings suggest that at this time at least there was a group of people in Peterhead who wanted and were waiting to experience revival.

Yet when the movement broke out with unprecedented influence along the coast between February and April 1860, there is no sign whatsoever that it appeared in Peterhead. The town is not referred to in a single report of the revival during this period. Rather, in March when the fishing towns and villages were quite literally ablaze with religious excitement, the Peterhead correspondent of the *Aberdeen Free Press* described the lack of enthusiasm in the town. He wrote that 'after the Greenland fleet sail, a season of dullness usually follows, and this year affords no exception to the general rule. The harbours are dull, so are the streets; the shops are dull and the continued wet weather has made the farmers dull also.'[11] During these months when the Moray Firth was overwhelmed with religious excitement with the result that normal patterns of life were temporarily suspended as whole communities were engaged with spiritual matters, Peterhead was described as having an indifferent, tiresome atmosphere. The town stands out as an anomaly. It appears as the only settlement along the coast of north east Scotland between Aberdeen and Inverness that did not embrace this religious movement.

The failure of the revival to affect Peterhead began to appear even more peculiar after the two small fishing villages of Buchanhaven and Burnhaven, which lay at either end of the town, became infected by the movement at the end of April 1860. The *Aberdeen Free Press* reported how

> among the fishing population on either side of this town [Peterhead], the Revival Movement has begun to manifest itself during the past month. At the fishing village of Burnhaven, a special prayer meeting for a Revival has been held for some time past in the Congregational Mission Chapel; and about four weeks ago, after sermon by the Rev R. H. Smith, the awakening commenced, and has since increased steadily and quietly. At Buchanhaven the work is more recent. About a fortnight ago, after

a week evening service by Mr Smith, a number were impressed and the work commenced.[12]

Robert Smith was the Congregational minister at Peterhead. He was thirty four years old when he was inducted into this charge in 1859 after having served three years as a minister in Dundee.[13] Accordingly, the only minister in Peterhead who became identified with the movement was a young man who had arrived recently in the town. Yet despite the appearance of the movement in these local villages that lay immediately beside Peterhead, there is no mention of it spreading from the smaller settlements into the churches in the larger town. Indeed after the summer it was reported how 'what is called the Union Prayer Meeting has on several occasions been almost entirely deserted'.[14] Interest in the movement appears to have quickly abated. Despite the revival's effect upon its neighbouring villages it failed to penetrate Peterhead during 1860.

Notwithstanding the impervious reaction of the town towards this religious movement, Peterhead finally became affected by another wave of revival towards the end of 1863, following the visit of a young female evangelist from Edinburgh, Miss Graham. She arrived around the start of October and immediately produced a remarkable effect upon the town. According to a correspondent of *The Revival* she inaugurated 'such a season of awakening as has never before been witnessed in Peterhead . . . every Sabbath night hundreds go away that cannot get in'.[15] Usually two meetings were held each evening of her campaign. First there was a public service of worship that was followed by a smaller gathering for 'anxious inquirers'. It was during this second meeting, 'held for conversation and prayer that we see the working of the Spirit'.[16] Perhaps most significantly it was reported how during the services 'there was no noise . . . all was done decently and in order'.[17] After Miss Graham left, at the end of the year, up to 400 people continued to meet each evening. However, she returned again in February 1864 and once again led gatherings that attracted a large response.[18] Although Peterhead did not participate in the revival that swept along the north east coast in 1860, it is noteworthy that it was overwhelmed by a second different religious movement that appeared three years later. Among other factors, the conventional and respectable nature of the more recent movement was, as we shall see, an important reason for its success in Peterhead.

Nevertheless, it remains that the town did not embrace the earlier outburst of revival. It appears that it had been prepared for it. Prayer meetings were established after news of the American and Ulster movements had been diffused and people began to be converted. Thereafter the town was visited by several well-known evangelists as the anticipation of the people seems to have been raised. Then abruptly, when the revival began to appear among the fishing villages in an excited, spontaneous manner, the interest of the town towards the movement seems to have faded. It is necessary, therefore, to consider the factors that explain how and why this awakening passed by Peterhead while it became manifest in the other fishing towns and villages along the Moray Firth.

II

There are three principal reasons why this town remained beyond the influence of the 1859 awakening. In the first instance, despite the meetings that were held to pray for the movement, the overwhelming spiritual climate of Peterhead created by the most influential churches appears to have been at least indifferent towards the revival. The Established and Episcopal Churches, which adopted at times an ambivalent and on other occasions an antagonistic attitude with regard to the movement, occupied a position of relative strength in Peterhead. This is illustrated by the returns of the 1851 census on religious worship and education in Scotland. The Church of Scotland, anxious about what it would reveal of the Scottish religious landscape, failed to return schedules from almost a quarter of its congregations. This allowed critics of the census to pour scorn on 'the unsatisfactory and untrustworthy nature of Mr Mann's report and tables'.[19] Nevertheless, the complete returns from Peterhead show that the Established Church remained the largest religious denomination in this town around the middle of the nineteenth century.

Table 9.1.

The 1851 Religious Census, Peterhead

Church	Attend	Morn	After	Even
Established		1860	180	1400
Free Church		850		800
Episcopal		550		450
Congregational		290	500	80
United Pres		208		
Methodist		137	130	163
Roman Catholic		40		

Source: *1851 Census Great Britain Reports and Tables on Education England and Wales and on Religious worship and Education Scotland* (Dublin, 1970), p. 539.

Given that a high proportion of those who attended services in the afternoon and evening had already been present at the morning act of worship, the relative strength of each denomination was estimated on the basis of the number who gathered at the first meeting of the congregation. Accordingly it was found that forty seven per cent of the town's worshipping community went to the Established Church on the Sunday morning of the census, twenty two per cent joined together at the Free Church, fourteen per cent met at the Episcopal Chapel, while the remainder were divided among the United Presbyterian, the Congregational, the Methodist and the Roman Catholic Churches. Hence more than three fifths of Peterhead's churchgoing population attended the Established and Episcopal Churches, which were not, in general, favourably disposed towards the revival.

Certainly in Peterhead they did not appear to embrace the movement. According to one local historian, 'Episcopacy has traditionally a strong hold in the villages of East Aberdeenshire, and Episcopacy and "corybantic religion" [Evangelicalism] (as Huxley called it) do not go together.'[20] Around a fifth of Peterhead's population in 1840 were thought to be adherents of the Episcopal Church. They were particularly well represented among the wealthier families, which placed them in positions of social influence and power.[21] As a result there is no doubt that their discouragement of any religious enthusiasm would have had an important effect upon the progress of the movement. It is noticeable that the other churches in the town welcomed Radcliffe and Forlong to preach in their buildings while the Established and Episcopal Churches did not.[22] It appears that these churches were reluctant to endorse the revival and, commanding perhaps the greatest religious influence in Peterhead, their unwillingness to embrace the movement helps to explain its relative failure in this town.

Also it seems that the dissenting denominations in Peterhead, which elsewhere championed the cause of the movement, failed to redress the indifferent attitude which the larger churches espoused towards the revival. Despite welcoming Radcliffe in November 1859, the Free Church, and its minister James Yuille, do not appear again in any reference to the movement. Meanwhile the Congregationalists appear to have been a dwindling force in Peterhead around the middle of the century. William Donald commented in his parish report for the New Statistical Account of 1843 that 'the number of persons belonging to this congregation has not been ascertained; but it is believed that it has rather been in the decrease of late'.[23] The chequered history of the Methodists highlights further the weakness of Evangelicalism in Peterhead. They established a presence in 1759, following the visit of the itinerant preacher Christopher Hopper, who came from Durham. In 1815 they bought

Topping's Hall in Chapel Street. However, the minister withdrew and, when the circuit collapsed in 1828, the church was sold to the Church of Scotland. They moved back into Topping's Hall in 1846 and by September 1852 had ninety-three members. Fourteen years later, after the revival, they had ninety-seven members.[24] This suggests that Methodism did not flourish in Peterhead in this period. Similarly the Evangelical Union, which was committed to revivalism, appeared in Peterhead in 1849, but 'terminated their efforts ... within five years of their first appearance on the scene.'[25] The apparent apathy of the local Free Church towards the revival, not to mention the distinct weakness of the other dissenting churches, explains further the failure of the movement to affect this town.

Indeed the only religious group in Peterhead that identified itself firmly with the cause of this revival was the Baptists. They had been meeting in the home of George Thorne at Longside, a village near Peterhead, since 1840.[26] They held their first service of public worship in the town in a hall in Maiden Street at the start of June 1859.[27] The Baptists were responsible for convening the first meetings that heard reports from those who had visited scenes of the revival in Ulster.[28] It is noteworthy that almost all the evangelistic meetings held in connection with the movement took place in the Hall which they occupied. Also the first open-air gatherings, held in front of the Town House during the summer of 1859, were conducted by two Baptist pastors, Peter Grant and Mr Beattie.[29] The Baptists appear to have been the only group of Christians that sought to further the work of the revival in Peterhead. However, they were a small church and, despite their wholehearted efforts, they did not command widespread influence in this town.

Therefore, it seems that the spiritual climate of Peterhead in 1859 is the first reason why it was not affected by the revival. J. Arbuthnot and P. Buchan, two local historians, commented upon the 'liberal ideas with regard to religion' which characterised the spiritual tone of the town.[30] Certainly the lack of interest of the Established and Episcopal Churches, as well as the failure of the other denominations to exercise any guidance in the religious affairs of the town, explain why the movement did not envelop this place. The Peterhead correspondent of the *Aberdeen Free Press* complained bitterly, following the departure of Donald Ross, the East Coast Mission's evangelist at the end of August 1859, that

> at a time when we have so many who do not attend any place of worship, special services of this nature are much needed . . . .. we only regret that none of our own clergymen have yet turned out. At a time when we have so many who do not attend any place of worship, special services of this nature are much needed.[31]

Also it is revealing that after a public meeting that launched the work of the East Coast Mission in Peterhead, it was remarked that 'the calls of the society for pecuniary assistance had been, in a marked degree, more warmly responded to at Fraserburgh than here'.[32] Peterhead was not an enthusiastic supporter of Evangelical ministries. The reluctance of the town's churches and ministers to lead wholeheartedly this religious movement is undoubtedly one of the major factors that explains its relative failure in this town. It is unlikely that ordinary people would have become affected by a religious movement that was ignored, if not roundly condemned, by those whom they trusted as their spiritual leaders. The antipathy of the local clergymen was an important cause of the apathetic religious climate that led to the revival's lack of success in Peterhead.

III

The second chief factor that explains the failure of the fisherfolk's revival to affect Peterhead was the heterogeneous nature of its community. The character of this town was very dissimilar to that found in the fishing villages where the movement flourished abundantly. Peterhead was considerably larger than the settlements dotted along the coast. In 1861 there were 9769 people who stayed in the parish, of whom 7541 resided in the town.[33] At the same time Burnhaven, the village immediately beside the town that experienced the revival in April 1860, had a population of 280.[34] Moreover, the settlements that lay at the centre of the Moray Firth revival, where it began in earnest and appeared in a very excited manner, Portessie, Findochty and Portgordon, had populations of 575, 393 and 630 respectively in 1861.[35] The movement also affected, albeit in a more restrained fashion, the larger towns of Banff and Fraserburgh whose populations in 1861 were 3719 and 3101.[36] Yet it failed to emerge in Peterhead. It is suggested that the size and therefore the diverse nature of the town's population was a vital factor that helps to explain why it did not experience the revival in the same manner as its more close-knit neighbouring towns and villages.

With a larger population, the economic base of Peterhead was more varied than that of the smaller villages. Besides being the principal fishing station on the north east coast of Scotland, the town also had a number of other industries and employers. There were three mills for manufacturing grain in the parish and two brick and tile works. There was a brewery that distilled whisky and a granite polishing works which prepared the stone that was mined at the quarry near the village of Stirling.[37] Also there was a woollen factory owned by Messrs Thomas Smith & Co which employed around

100 people in the manufacture of blankets, worsteds, kerseys and plaidings. In addition there were steam bone and saw mills belonging to Mr Murray and a large curing works, that undertook a large business in grain and artificial manures. There were several establishments for the manufacture of agricultural implements, iron founding and coach making as well as several ship building yards at Port Henry.[38] Finally there were upwards of forty one public houses and about thirty other people were licensed to sell spirits and ale.[39] None of these industries or manufacturers existed in the villages along the Moray Firth. Instead everyone, with the exception of the local artisans, was employed within the fishing trade. The basis of Peterhead's economy differed considerably from that of the smaller fishing settlements, and this had a serious effect upon the character of the town, which in turn serves to explain why it was not influenced by the revival.

As a result of its diversified economic base, the social composition of Peterhead was much more disparate than that of the close-knit fishing village communities. William Donald, in his report for the New Statistical Account of Peterhead, recorded the employment pattern of his parish.

Table 9.2.

Employment patterns in Peterhead, c 1840

Type of Employ	No of families	Percentage
Other	687	52 %
Trade, manufacturers	452	34 %
Fishing	167	13 %
Agriculture	12	1 %

Source: *The New Statistical Account of Aberdeenshire* (Edinburgh, 1843), p. 358, 382.

Donald found that more than a third of his town parishioners were employed in various trades and manufacturing industries, while only an eighth worked as fishermen. Meanwhile Thomas Wilson, the minister of Gamrie Parish, provided a very different social analysis of Gardenstown, a small fishing village, for the New Statistical Account.

Table 9.3.

Employment patterns in Gardenstown, c 1840

Type of Employ	No of Men	Percentage
Fishermen	45	62 %
Handicraftsmen	20	27 %
Retired Men	7	10 %
Merchants	1	1 %
Agriculturalists	0	0 %
Manufacturers	0	0 %

Source: *The New Statistical Account of Banffshire* (Edinburgh, 1842), p. 286.

This reveals that almost two thirds of the men of this village were fishermen, while just less than a third were traditional artisans. There was only one merchant in the village and no one was engaged in agriculture or manufacturing. This demonstrates that in 1840 the social structure of Peterhead was more varied than that of its neighbouring fishing villages.

This is illustrated further by a random sample that was taken of 220 people from the Peterhead census returns of 1861 who were examined in order to ascertain the broad composition of this town just after the revival. For the sake of comparison, the 137 working men who were listed in the Portessie census of 1861 were also studied. The criteria used for measuring the social status of the men and women was the same as that which was used in previous chapters to ascertain the class composition of those who joined the various churches during the revival.[40]

Table 9.4.

The class composition of a random selection of people living in Peterhead in 1861

Status	Men	Women	Percent
Middle Class (High)	9	3	5 %
Middle Class (Low)	31	19	23 %
Work Class (Artisan)	52	38	41 %
Work Class (Unskilled)	11	57	31 %

Source: 1861 Census, Peterhead, Aberdeenshire

Table 9.5.

The class composition of the inhabitants of Portessie in 1861

Status	Men	Women	Percent
Middle Class (High)	0	0	0 %
Middle Class (Low)	8	1	7 %
Work Class (Artisan)	102	9	81 %
Work Class (Unskilled)	1	16	12 %

Source: 1861 Census, Portessie, Banffshire

Peterhead had a fairly diversified population in 1861. Approximately one in twenty of the society belonged to the upper middle class, while a considerable proportion, one quarter, were members of the lower middle class. The largest section of the population belonged to the skilled working classes. Nevertheless, almost one third of the town were found to be amongst the unskilled working class. Decidedly Portessie, by comparison, was inhabited by a population that was more homogeneous. More than four out of every five men living in the village shared the same occupation. Indeed the only men living in the village who were not directly employed in the fishing industry were several shoemakers, a grocer and two teachers. It is clear that Peterhead had a highly assorted population, while Portessie was inhabited by a more uniform group of people. This is a weighty factor that will serve to explain why the revival was not manifested in Peterhead to the same extent or in a similar manner as it was in the fishing villages along the Moray Firth.

The greater diversity within the social composition of Peterhead's population meant that it did not share the features of the fishing villages which predisposed them towards the religious movement. There can be little doubt that Peterhead fishermen were as superstitious as those who lived in smaller fishing communities. However, the former were surrounded by other classes of people who would not have shared their beliefs and consequently these larger towns would not have been infused with superstition to the same extent as the villages. Consequently, Peterhead would not have been as inclined as the villages towards the supernatural aspects of revivalist religion that were presented by James Turner.[41] Also the village fishermen shared a relatively limited education and intellectual outlook, and consequently they possessed little social refinement. In addition their villages were bereft of an educated middle class which might have tempered this lack of social civility. By contrast, there was greater intellectual diversity among the people of Peterhead. There were a number of professional men, particularly within the churches. As a result, the excited religious ideas of the revivalists were not accepted as readily and uncritically in Peterhead as they were in the villages.[42] Lastly there was a higher incidence of death from drowning among the adult men in the villages.[43] Although it is probable that a similar proportion of the Peterhead fishermen died at sea, they would have constituted a smaller share of the overall working population in the town. Hence there were, relatively, more deaths of young men in the villages, which regularly acted as the occasion of the revival. Peterhead, by the nature of its broader social basis, did not exhibit the peculiar aspects of the fishing villages which prepared them to receive the revival in 1859, and this serves further to explain why the larger town was unvisited by this movement.

In addition, Peterhead had a greater number of recreational and sporting activities that occupied the free time of the townsfolk and competed against religious activities. George Henderson, parish minister of Cullen, described how during holidays at Halloween and Christmas the fisherfolk of the local villages 'resorted to the sands and links of the bay of Cullen, for the purpose of playing football, running foot races, throwing the hammer, playing bowls'.[44] Meanwhile Peterhead had a far wider range of leisure pursuits. Organised football and cricket were played regularly on the Links, while the local golf club, one of the oldest in Scotland, was instituted in 1841.[45] The town also had a licensed theatre from 1830 which operated in the Broad Street Hall, and 'for months on a stretch the local boards were held by stock companies of repute, who were able to draw big houses night after night'.[46] A Mutual Improvement Association was established in 1849, for 'the stimulation of general knowledge and literature'. Weekly meetings were enthusiastically attended, especially during the winter when courses of lectures were given by eminent speakers.[47] As a result the church had to compete for the attention and free time of those who lived in the town. Unlike the fishing villages, where a dearth of social activities permitted wholehearted attention to be devoted to religious matters during the revival, Peterhead offered more distractions from this movement.

The distinctive features of community-life in the fishing villages served to create a social context that was ideally suited to the transmission of the spontaneous religious enthusiasm of the 1859 revival. These aspects were not present in Peterhead. Their absence helps to explain why the movement did not appear in this town. Calvin Colton, the nineteenth-century American revivalist, remarked how traditional revivals of religion 'are not to be expected in a state of society where there is not a community of feeling'.[48] Peterhead, by the nature of its economic base and social composition, was a heterogeneous town. It did not possess the 'community of feeling' that existed within the fishing villages, and this is the second main factor that serves to account for the failure of the 1859 revival to affect this town.

Nevertheless, Aberdeen did not own the close-knit sense of community that characterised the fishing villages either and yet it was affected by the awakening. However, the movement that influenced Aberdeen was fundamentally different from that which appeared along the Moray Firth. It was a modern evangelistic campaign rather than a traditional, spontaneous revival. Moreover, Peterhead was relatively isolated from the capital city of the north east. The Great North of Scotland Railway Line from Aberdeen reached Banff in July 1859, but the route from Aberdeen to Peterhead was not officially opened until July 1862.[49] Hence it was, to some extent, cut off from the influences of the city during the period of the movement. It was closer to its neighbouring fishing villages. News from these smaller settlements was diffused more quickly through Peterhead. As a result the people of this town considered the revival according to their knowledge of it from the fishing villages, rather than from Aberdeen where the movement was more orderly and respectable. Although they might have wanted to become involved in the type of revival that affected Aberdeen, they did not want to embrace the form that was affecting the smaller fishing settlements.

IV

This leads to the final factor that explains the relative failure of the 1859 religious movement to affect Peterhead. This concerns the absence of a desire amongst its people for a traditional, spontaneous revival like the one that affected the fishing villages. The want of a longing for a religious movement in Peterhead is the principal reason why the revival did not affect this town. James Turner was said to have 'felt very much the indifference that pervaded in Peterhead, in regard to divine things, compared with the towns in which he had just been, and had a strong desire to see it otherwise'.[50] Later, on 24 May 1861, the *Peterhead Sentinel* commented that 'in no part of the country, we believe, has . . . [the revival] occupied less attention in its general aspects than in Peterhead, or has it been so generally looked upon with grave suspicion by the more intelligent and thinking portion of the community'.[51] Rather than wanting to become affected by this movement, the people of Peterhead came to adopt an apathetic, if not sceptical view of the revival. There are at least two causes that account for the misgivings of the townsfolk concerning the awakening.

In the first instance, the local newspaper, the *Peterhead Sentinel*, which would have exercised a considerable influence upon the formation of public opinion, adopted a negative attitude towards the revival after it appeared in an excited manner among the fishing villages. At first this newspaper carried positive reports of the American revival. On 21 January 1859 it printed a letter written by Alexander Shiras, a minister in Philadelphia who described 'a wonderful season in respect to spiritual influence in the United States'. He sought to reassure his readers by saying

> on your side of the water, many look with suspicion on such movements; but in this case everything has been so healthful and heavenly – so little of the wind, the earthquake and the fire; and so audible the sound of God's still, small voice – that even the most suspicious among us have had to acknowledge that the thing was God's doing.[52]

The paper also reported, in a favourable manner, upon the revival when it began to appear in Aberdeen. It printed accounts of the first meetings which Reginald Radcliffe addressed and commented 'if those that are to follow be conducted in the same manner, they may be productive of much good'.[53] In this way, during the first quarter of 1859, the *Peterhead Sentinel* adopted an affirmative attitude towards the revival.

However, there appears to have been a sudden shift in the approach of the newspaper towards the movement when it started to print accounts of its rather more exuberant manifestation in Ulster. It featured several pieces by George Gilfillan, a Dundee minister, who became a vociferous opponent of the movement when it was accompanied by physical prostrations, which he judged to be 'a work of the devil'. He said that 'there were . . . people who wished us to take a pattern from our Irish friends, but that he would tell his people to be on their guard'.[54] He also attacked the apparent instantaneous joy that accompanied the sudden conversions that attended revival services. 'True joy' he believed, 'was generally preceded by long and deep anxiety.'[55] The newspaper also printed the report of a lecture about the Ulster revival delivered by another minister, R. Stewart, who described the physical prostrations as 'unfavourable features of the movement'. He went on to say that 'he denied that these physical effects were produced through the direct agency of the Spirit of God . . . [but that they] were to be explained in accordance with natural principles'.[56] Accordingly the *Peterhead Sentinel* established itself as a critic of the Ulster revival on account of the physical prostrations that accompanied its appearance.

Similarly, the newspaper became a fierce antagonist of the religious movement when it appeared, in a rather dramatic fashion, along the Moray Firth at the end of January 1860. On 24 February it reported a meeting at Buckie where 'the speaker's voice was drowned by cries' and that 'when the cries for mercy broke out, . . . others fell down'. Later it said that 'many are struck down' before mentioning that 'the most prominent among the instruments in this work is Mr Turner'.[57] The following week it carried a report of a protracted meeting at Banff which Turner led and its effect upon those present in some detail. It reported how they were often conducted within a very heated and excitable atmosphere with the result that 'confusion was very great' as many people became victims of physical prostration. It described how 'one man was taken, by force of arm, into the vestry of the chapel, and while there his cries rung through the building' and how 'another intelligent young man got into a furious and insane state of mind . . . [that] the chapel had to be cleared before he could be quieted'. It went on to report how the congregation repeated incessantly for upwards of half an hour the phrase, 'I can, I will, I do believe that Jesus died for me'. It concluded with the disdainful comment, 'with the hearers it is a matter of feeling more than a matter of hearing and believing as in the former days'.[58] The *Peterhead Sentinel* poured considerable scorn upon the revival as it appeared among the fisherfolk and portrayed it as an orgy of ignorant, undisciplined religious fanaticism.

Yet towards the middle of 1861 it seems that the newspaper's approach towards the revival changed again and became positive once more. The reports it contained contrasted the manner in which the revival was now led with the way it had been directed previously. It criticised lay preachers, like Turner, who had spread erroneous doctrine, preaching the terrors of hell and the wrath of an angry Deity, and was glad to report that they were 'sinking to their proper level'. Meanwhile it praised 'the clergy . . . [who] are now taking cognizance of and lending a hand to the movement, regulating it in its details and checking the extravagances of its well meaning but mistaken leaders'. It welcomed their efforts 'to direct its force and power in the proper channel by the appointment of committees to regulate the movement'. Also it reported gladly how the physical manifestations 'are fast disappearing'.[59] Hence it appears that after the excited scenes of the fisherfolk's revival had abated and the movement became more ordered, the *Peterhead Sentinel* began to approve of it once again.

Nevertheless it remains that the newspaper was bitterly opposed to the traditional manifestation of the revival among the village fisherfolk. In particular it reported the physical prostrations in an alarmist, unsympathetic manner which served to arouse the fears of ordinary people. Its vitriolic slander of this particular appearance of the movement was, in a large measure, responsible for the grave suspicion and indifference that arose in Peterhead towards the revival. It was responsible for discrediting the awakening in this town and for creating the scepticism with which it was viewed. Accordingly, the manner in which the *Peterhead Sentinel* reported the revival was a vital reason why the town did not want to become affected by it. The absence of this desire explains why it remained untouched by this movement.

Perhaps more importantly, the people of Peterhead did not want to participate in a religious movement that was led by a local fishcurer and Methodist lay preacher. It seems that James Turner's personality and enthusiastic manner alienated a number of people who might otherwise have become involved in the revival. He was converted on Monday morning, 4 May 1840, at the age of twenty two. Seven years later, following a conversation with 'a godly old woman' he joined the Methodist Church. Then on Sunday evening, 5 March 1854, as two friends prayed for a special blessing upon Turner, he became 'completely prostrated under the mighty power of God' and received his 'second baptism of the Holy Spirit'.[60] As a result of these personal experiences, Turner believed that conversion was immediate and instantaneous, physical prostrations often accompanied the works of God's Spirit, and entire sanctification was an experience to be sought after. Turner's distinctly Wesleyan understanding of these matters would not have been widely embraced by the greater proportion of Peterhead's predominantly Presbyterian and Episcopalian religious population. Indeed these differences in theology created a considerable gulf between them. Hence many of the townsfolk were unwilling to participate in a religious movement that was led by an unordained, over-zealous fishcurer and underpinned by what they considered to be erroneous doctrine.

It also appears that Turner became quickly estranged from the Christians in Peterhead. Certainly he did not approach those who also wanted revival in a conciliatory manner. Rather he dealt with them in a very cursory way. Gordon Forlong provides the following account which demonstrates how Turner was adept at making himself unpopular among those whom he considered unconverted. Forlong described how

> some ministers . . . institute[d] a daily prayer meeting . . . Of course, Turner attended . . ., but to the horror of its originators, he prayed for those ministers and office-bearers whom he considered to be unconverted. This gave great offence. He was reproved, warned and exhorted. But James Turner got warmer and warmer, and preached on his knees in a way that made formalists tremble – and what did they do? They shut up the prayer meeting, closed

it altogether, and an unconverted office-bearer put the key in his pocket and thus stopped James Turner's public preaching in Peterhead.[61]

Shortly afterwards Turner began to experience 'determined opposition' against his evangelistic work in Peterhead, which 'never assumed the same importance as it had done in many other places'.[62] Indeed he received several hostile threats about the evening revival meetings he held with his brother in his cooperage in the town.[63] Forlong ventured to comment that, 'his natural field of work was Peterhead in Aberdeenshire; but Peterhead soon cast him out . . . Nature landed him in Peterhead; grace drove him forth to work elsewhere.'[64] Clearly Turner's evangelistic work was rather unwelcome in the town.

Certainly his flamboyant and excited style of preaching was not well received in Aberdeen. A local newspaper reported how

> he throws himself into all manners of contortions; howling, yelling, roaring, then becoming the plaintive and sad, all alternately; and were he not said to be under 'spiritual influence' he would naturally be regarded as a maniac . . . . In prayer, he kneels, his head is thrown back, his face upwards, his eyes open, his arms raised and his hands expanded, and always moving, and in this way he howls and evokes the outpouring of the Spirit almost in the loudest pitch his voice can reach.[65]

This manner of address was unsuited to the more discerning people of Aberdeen who had become accustomed to the earnest yet 'respectable' preaching of Radcliffe, the lawyer trained evangelist. It served to explain why Turner failed to repeat his evangelistic success in the city. The *Aberdeen Herald* went on to comment

> The Spirit is no less powerful in . . . [Aberdeen] than in . . . [Buckie], the Aberdonians are no less susceptible of receiving the Spirit than the Buckies. The reason simply is, the Buckies are less spiritual, more idiotical, and more susceptible of being played upon by Mr Turner than the Aberdonians are. This likewise explains why the epidemic has been almost invariably confined to the illiterate, the nervous and the weak minded.[66]

Turner, the hero of the fishing village revival, was considered a 'maniac' by the reporters of the larger towns and cities. There is little doubt that the discriminating men and women of Peterhead would have shared the Aberdonian's opinion of Turner. They considered him to be an uncontrolled religious fanatic. Even Thomas Baxter, who supported Turner's evangelistic labours faithfully, conceded that 'he erred sometimes in conduct and judgment'.[67] James Turner was a highly animated communicator and although his methods produced remarkable results in the fishing villages, they did not impress the more urbane sensibilities of those who lived in larger towns and cities.

Peterhead was not infused with a spirit that regarded the 1859 revival as a movement to be desired or eagerly anticipated. On the contrary, public opinion in this town appears to have considered the revival with sceptical indifference. The local newspaper informed and thus helped to create this climate of feeling. Nonetheless, the peculiar, traditional manifestation of the movement within the villages, that was influenced largely by James Turner, was poorly suited to the social context of Peterhead. The Yale professor, Chauncey A. Goodrich, commented around the middle of the nineteenth century, 'If I were asked why revivals are so frequent in America, and so rare in Europe, my first answer would be, that Christians on one side of the Atlantic expect them, and on the other side they do not expect them.'[68] The principal factor that explains the failure of the 1859 religious movement to appear in Peterhead was the absence of a spirit of excited expectancy that considered revival as something to be desired.

There was a large number of Christians in Britain in 1859 who were more content to expect a revival than they were to experience one. This particular religious movement did on occasions, and in certain situations, manifest itself in a spontaneous fashion that included the appearance of physical manifestations. Order and sobriety were often sacrificed on the altar of raw and intense spiritual excitement. This served to alienate many respectable Evangelicals from the awakening. It appears, from the numbers who attended the first Union prayer meetings in Peterhead, that before the revival emerged in such a dramatic manner amongst the fishing villages along the Moray Firth, many people in the town were anxious to become part of this religious movement. However, it seems that these desires faded once the revival began to affect the neighbouring villages, because the respectable, educated Christian townsfolk were unable to accept the teaching of James Turner and the physical phenomena that accompanied this movement. This Methodist type of revival was not agreeable to the culture of this town. The nature of the Peterhead community and its rejection of the particular manifestation of this awakening among the fishing villages explains why it did not enjoy a 'season of grace' in 1860.

Notes

1. W. Robbie, *The Life and Labours of the late James Turner of Peterhead* (Aberdeen, 1863), p. 49.
2. Ibid., pp. 51-91.
3. *The Statistical Account of Aberdeenshire* (Edinburgh, 1843), pp. 368-96.
4. J. T. Findlay, *A History of Peterhead* (Peterhead, 1933), pp. 200-9.
5. *P.S.*, (1 April 1859), p. 2.
6. *A.F.P.*, (12 August 1859), p. 8.
7. Ibid., (23 September 1859), p. 8.
8. *T.R.*, Vol 1, No 8, (17 September 1859), p. 60.
9. *P.S.*, (4 November 1859), p. 2. *A.F.P.*, (11 November 1859), p. 8.
10. *A.F.P.*, (13 January 1860), p. 8.
11. Ibid., (30 March 1860), p. 8.
12. Ibid., (8 June 1860), p. 8.
13. W. D. McNaughton, *The Scottish Congregational Ministry 1794-1993* (Glasgow, 1993), p. 150.
14. *A.F.P.*, (5 October 1860), p. 8.
15. *T.R.*, Vol 9, No 222, (22 October 1863), p. 259
    Ibid., Vol 9, No 230, (17 December 1863), p. 395.
16. Ibid., Vol 9, No 225, (12 November 1863), p. 310.
17. Ibid., Vol 9, No 222, (22 October 1863), p. 259.
18. Ibid., Vol 10, No 249, (28 April 1864), p. 265.
19. *Church of Scotland Magazine and Review, September / October 1854* (Edinburgh, 1854), p. 3 quoted by D. J. Withrington, 'The 1851 Census of Religious Worship and Education: With a Note on Church Accommodation in Mid-Nineteenth-Century Scotland', *Records of the Scottish Church History Society*, 18, (1973), pp. 134-5.
20. J. Leatham, *Fisherfolk of the North East* (Turriff, 1930), pp. 19-20.
21. J. T. Findlay, 'A History of Peterhead' (published in the *Buchan Observer* in 54 parts from 3 March 1896 to 16 March 1897), Article 24.
22. *A.F.P.*, (11 November 1859), p. 8.
23. *Statistical Account of Aberdeenshire*, p. 382.
24. F. M. Duthie, *Peterhead Methodist Church: Centenary Souvenir Programme* (Peterhead, 1966), np.
25. Findlay, *History of Peterhead*, p. 180.
26. G. Yuille (ed.), *History of the Baptists in Scotland* (Glasgow, 1926), p. 99.
27. *P.S.*, (10 June 1859), p. 2.
28. Ibid., (12 August 1859), p. 3.
29. Ibid.
30. J. Arbuthnot, *An Historical Account of Peterhead* (Aberdeen, 1815), p. 59, P. Buchan, *Annals of Peterhead* (Peterhead, 1819), p. 87.
31. *A.F.P.*, (2 September 1859), p. 8.
32. Ibid., (23 November 1860), p. 8.
33. *Census of Scotland, 1861, Population Tables and Report* (Edinburgh, 1862), pp. 30-1
34. A. Smith (ed.), *A New History of Aberdeenshire* (Aberdeen, 1875), p. 1135.
35. *Census of Scotland, 1861, Tables and Report*, pp. 160-1.

36. Ibid., pp. 24-5, 28-9.
37. Smith, *New History of Aberdeenshire*, p. 1127.
38. Ibid., p. 1137.
39. Ibid., p. 1138.
40. See Appendix 2.
41. J. McGibbon, *The Fisherfolk of Buchan* (Edinburgh, nd), pp. 51-2.
42. Findlay, 'A History of Peterhead', Article 24.
43. 1861 Census, Portessie, Banffshire
44. *The Statistical Account of Banffshire* (Edinburgh, 1842), p. 331.
45. R. Neish, *Old Peterhead* (Peterhead, 1950), p. 287.
46. Ibid., p. 277.
47. Ibid., p. 284.
48. R. Carwardine, 'The Welsh Evangelical Community and "Finney's" Revival', *Journal of Ecclesiastical History*, 29, (1978), p. 472.
49. M. Barclay-Harvey, *A History of the Great North of Scotland Railway* (London, nd), p. 225.
50. Robbie, *James Turner*, p. 92.
51. *P.S.*, (24 May 1861), p 2.
52. Ibid., (21 January 1859), p. 2.
53. Ibid., (4 March 1859), p. 3; (28 October 1859), p. 2.
54. Ibid., (1 July 1859), p. 2.
55. Ibid., (28 September 1860), p. 2.
56. Ibid., (21 October 1859), p. 4.
57. Ibid., (24 February 1860), p. 2.
58. Ibid., (3 March 1860), p. 2.
59. Ibid., (25 May 1861), p. 2.
60. Robbie, *James Turner*, p. 23.
61. E. McHardie, *James Turner; or, how to reach the masses* (Aberdeen, 1875), p. ix.
62. Robbie, *James Turner*, p. 92.
63. Ibid., p. 95.
64. McHardie, *James Turner*, p. ix.
65. *A.H.*, (16 June 1860), p. 6.
66. Ibid.
67. Robbie, *James Turner*, p. 129.
68. R. Carwardine, *Transatlantic Revivalism: Popular Evangelicalism in Britain and America, 1790-1865* (Westport, Connecticut, 1978), p. 151.

CHAPTER 10

Conclusion

The 1859 revival, as it appeared across the north east of Scotland, was a disparate movement. Revealed in a variety of different forms in Aberdeen, in its rural hinterland and along the Moray Firth, it was not a tidy, uniform affair. There were many differences between the manner and expression of the awakening as it occurred in the three separate contexts within Aberdeenshire. This final chapter seeks to compare and contrast the various manifestations of the revival and to locate these distinct appearances within the historical tradition of awakenings. Then an appraisal will be made of the principal schools of revival studies which have sought to understand these remarkable events. In addition, the influences of the particular local and the broader national situations of the late 1850s upon the north east's experience of the movement will be explored. The resulting analysis will reveal the rich diversity that lay within this awakening, and the fundamental power which indigenous circumstances exercised upon this 'season of grace'.

I

The 1858-62 revival in north east Scotland was precipitated by one common feature in each of the places where it was experienced. It was desired and expected in every community that felt its influence. James Douglas, author of a revival pamphlet in 1839, said that, 'where no revivals are expected, none are likely to take place, for men will only pray for blessings which they hope to obtain'.[1] Peter Drummond's *British Messenger*, which began publication in 1853, carried news of the American and Ulster revivals and so served to stir the thoughts of Christians. It gave them confidence to hope that a similar movement would begin amongst them. As local groups of men and women met in Aberdeen, in the neighbouring countryside and along the Moray Firth to read these reports, a climate of excited anticipation began to seize their minds, with the result that they prayed more earnestly for a revival to descend upon them. Wherever the revival appeared it was preceded by a spirit of longing and waiting. Indeed, this substructure of anticipation was not sufficiently created in Peterhead and this, above all, explains why the fishing town did not experience the 1859 revival.[2] Nonetheless, it remains that a desire for and an expectancy of revival were the only regular characteristics of the three separate situations within which this movement appeared.[3] These were the foundation stones upon which this awakening was built.

II

It is apparent from the factors examined that the 1859 revival was a diverse movement which appeared in a variety of different forms within a number of dissimilar contexts. The three manifestations of this movement in north east Scotland were not only located in separate social settings. Each also reflected a particular ethos of revival. In the first instance, the rural movement was set within long established settled communities. Notwithstanding the social and economic changes during the early nineteenth century, the fermfolk had lived and worked on their land for many generations and, as a result, strong bonds united them together. Led principally by Free Church ministers, this movement relied upon the accustomed means of grace, the preaching of the word of God and the celebration of the Lord's Supper. Indeed the Presbyterian communion season was the basis upon which the rural revival was erected. These five-day community religious festivals were infused with enormous spiritual power and became again celebrated 'seasons of grace'. In this way the revival flowed in a gentle manner through the countryside, and fitted comfortably into the slower, more gradual rhythm of life that governed the work and rest routines of the farming people.[4] The experience of conversion in the countryside was often protracted, the result of many weeks and months of anxious struggle that required both patience and perseverance, habits which the fermfolk learnt and exercised in their work upon the land each day. The greater proportion of those who were affected were the children of church members, and thus the movement appears to have spread through the families of those already within the guidance of the church. Also most of the converts were young, unmarried women. Accordingly, the revival of 1859, as it appeared in the rural hinterland of Aberdeenshire, displayed many of the characteristics of a seventeenth-century Scottish Presbyterian awakening.

The experience of revival in the fishing communities along the Moray Firth was very different. These settlements were comparatively recent creations, many of them having been founded by local lairds in the seventeenth and eighteenth centuries. Nevertheless, despite their relative youth they were close knit settlements. Cut off from the surrounding farming people and 'neglected' by the established churches, the fisherfolk were an isolated, marginalised group of men and women. The revival among them was precipitated by a poor herring season which appears to have inclined them towards religious concerns. More importantly, it was led by a local itinerant Methodist preacher who was well known by those to whom he preached, and it thrived during a brief season of long, protracted all-night meetings when the fisherfolk were less engaged with their work.[5] Abrupt in its appearance and undisciplined in its enthusiasm, the revival among the fishing people was dramatic, intense and noisy. Unchecked by the local Presbyterian ministers, many of whom were unable or unwilling to become involved, this religious epidemic raged uncontrolled along the Moray Firth until almost everyone had been affected. People understood their conversions to be an immediate event which they could locate to a particular place at a certain time, and frequently their 'new birth' was accompanied by long periods of physical prostration. Often, according to one eye witness, 'they were falling on the floor, and, in fact, appeared to be dead or dying'.[6] The fishing revival lasted barely two months. Quickly the unbridled enthusiasm upon which it thrived was burnt out. In its typology the fisherfolk's religious movement along the Moray Firth in 1859 manifested many of the features of a late eighteenth-century Methodist revival.

Thirdly, in Aberdeen, the birthplace of the movement in November 1858 and the centre from which it was diffused across the north east of Scotland, the revival appeared in a fluid, urban situation. Around the middle of the nineteenth century Aberdeen, like many places of its size, was developing rapidly into an important industrial centre. It was becoming a modern successful city. In many regards, the 1859 urban revival was the product of the influence of Charles Finney, the architect of modern revivalism. Organised by a band of highly motivated laymen, it was carefully planned in order to fit around the disciplined lifestyle of the city's working population and to target their leisure time. Moreover special services were arranged for certain times of the week to suit the convenience of selected portions of the population. In the city the revival was administered with the same care and attention to detail that its leaders would have devoted to their business affairs.[7] Furthermore, it was led by professional itinerant evangelists who conducted large meetings in public halls. Also it was dignified and respectable, and did not display any of the cruder elements of traditional, spontaneous revivals. At the heart of the city movement was the increasingly common gospel that presented conversion as an instantaneous work of God's Spirit. According to his biographer daughter, 'there was no more characteristic element in Mr Radcliffe's preaching than his insistence on the doctrine of instant salvation . . . he would use such expressions as this: "You may be saved by believing in Jesus even before you have time to kneel down"'.[8] Undoubtedly this alienated some ministers and churches who maintained a more strictly Calvinist opinion. The most important feature of the city revival was its remarkable popularity among young men. In the 1850s they had become the goal of modern revivalists who were anxious to reverse the gender imbalance within churches. They were disproportionately well represented among those who were converted in Aberdeen, and this suggests further that this was a well orchestrated evangelistic crusade. In many ways the city revival was a forerunner of the Moody and Sankey campaign and similar movements that have followed in the twentieth century. Accordingly the 1859 revival, as it was conceived in the urban context of Aberdeen, was a modern, nineteenth-century evangelistic campaign.

III

There are many features of the whole movement which contribute to the discussion of why and how revivals have appeared at certain times in particular places. There is no doubt this awakening had an internal spiritual dynamic which defies historical analysis.[9] It was conceived, born and nurtured in prayer meetings. Indeed these gatherings were consistently the chief characteristic of this revival. Hence a purely reductionist approach that seeks to explain awakenings in non-religious terms is considered inadequate. Yet notwithstanding the significance of the spiritual forces that operated during the movement, any purely theological interpretation remains deficient if it ignores a number of other important temporal conditions. Indeed there were a number of external factors that exercised a weighty influence upon its appearance.

Economic factors, it appears, exercised an effect upon the timing of this revival in at least some situations. The movement began in Aberdeen almost ten years after the end of the most severe economic recession which the city experienced in the nineteenth century, and thus there is no clear correlation between the urban revival and poor commercial conditions. Meanwhile, notwithstanding the prosperity that accompanied the rise of the cattle trade after the 1830s, it appears that the exceptionally poor harvests of 1860 and 1861 probably affected the progress of the revival among the fermfolk.[10] However, there can be no doubt that the poor herring season endured by the fisherfolk along the Moray Firth in 1859 had an explicit effect upon the timing of their religious movement. It is particularly significant that the failure of the herring season was the main reason for Turner's evangelistic tour of the fishing villages which acted as the catalyst of the awakening among the places he visited. Although adverse economic circumstances were not a consistent influence upon the timing of the revival in each situation, they made a vital contribution to the creation of the fishing context in which it arose.[11]

John Kent's wry assessment of mid-nineteenth-century revivals that denied their effectiveness for outreach has been further exposed to be wanting. The composition of those affected by the Aberdeen movement clearly reveals how its influence extended beyond the pale of the Christian sub-culture and affected the city's unchurched working classes. Furthermore, his judgment that the 1859 revival represented 'the old forms of pietist renewal [which] showed themselves capable of a last major outburst of popular feeling' is ill-founded.[12] Rather, this movement exhibited features of traditional and modern revivalism in different situations, and was, certainly in Aberdeen, a precursor of the Moody and Sankey campaign of 1873. Nevertheless, the definitive factor that explains the appearance of the movement in 1858 was the climate of expectancy and desire that descended upon groups of praying people in north east Scotland. The news of the American and Ulster revivals had a powerful effect upon local Evangelicals. It created the excited anticipation and gave rise to the growth in prayer meetings that preceded the movement. Accordingly, the evidence from this region lends strong support to Carwardine's theory of revivals being preceded by a climate of yearning and hope.[13]

It is also apparent that local circumstances affected the course of this revival. The importance of indigenous factors is perhaps most obviously demonstrated by the manner in which the work and leisure patterns of the townsfolk, the fermfolk and the fisherfolk affected the appearance of the revival. The Aberdeen movement was organised carefully to fit around the disciplined working routines of the townsfolk in order to target their free time.[14] Meanwhile, in the rural hinterland the traditional five-day communion season, that was knitted around the patterns of work and rest which governed the lives of the farming people, was the focal point of the awakening.[15] The fisherfolk's revival was also affected by their annual habits of labour and recreation. It arose and flourished during the winter when they were less active and ended abruptly as soon as the busy herring season began in May.[16] Accordingly a notable feature of this revival was the manner in which its appearance was fashioned by the different patterns of work and rest which governed the lives of those amongst whom it was felt. This confirms the important influence which local situations exercised upon the appearance of this movement.

The power of native conditions to affect the course of revivals is illustrated further by noting the common characteristics and distinguishing aspects of this awakening as it arose in Glasgow and Aberdeen in 1859. In the first instance there were a number of features that appeared in both centres. Clifford Marrs has shown that during the period immediately before the revival Glasgow had experienced sustained growth in industry and agriculture, and therefore there was no correlation between a poor economic climate and the awakening.[17] On the contrary, he considers that the atmosphere of expectancy and desire, created by news of the Ulster revival, was the most important influence upon the timing of the movement.[18] Likewise in Aberdeen, the revival was not precipitated by adverse economic conditions, but rather emerged from an environment that was anticipating an awakening. Marrs also found that the Free and the United Presbyterian Church, along with other small dissenting congregations, were keen supporters of the awakening, while the Established and Episcopal Church adopted a less than wholehearted approach towards the movement.[19] A similar ecclesiastical pattern of enthusiasm and antipathy existed in Aberdeen. Moreover, Marrs carefully plotted the rise and fall of the Glasgow revival through a cycle of advent, expansion, consolidation, initial decline, recovery, recession and terminal decline.[20] Again this resembled closely the ebb and flow of the Aberdeen awakening that enjoyed periods of intense activity and endured spells of suspension. Above all, Marrs noticed the organised nature of the awakening and how, unlike previous spontaneous revivals, it was meticulously planned and prepared for in the city.[21] This accords with the nature and manner of the Aberdeen movement. Accordingly there were a number of similarities between the manifestations of the revival in Glasgow and Aberdeen.

Notwithstanding the resemblance of the movement in these two Scottish cities, there were other notable local differences. During its first eighteen months the revival in Glasgow appears to have been led principally by local ministers. Alexander Somerville, Jacob Alexander, Dugald M'Coll and Andrew Bonar were the chief agents of the work. Indeed the earliest reference to the work of an itinerant evangelist is in February 1861 when E. P. Hammond was invited to lead a series of church-based meetings in the west end of the city in an attempt to arrest a decline in the revival. He was followed later that year by William Carter, Reginald Radcliffe, and Richard Weaver. However, there was concern about this new tactic and the reliance upon guest celebrities to generate support for the movement.[22] By contrast, itinerant lay preachers acted as the catalyst and were among the foremost protagonists of the Aberdeen movement. Also, it was observed that protracted late-night meetings and physical prostrations appeared in Glasgow at the beginning of the revival.[23] However, such gatherings and the behaviour that attended them did not arise in Aberdeen. Moreover, the revival was actively supported in Glasgow by only ten per cent of the city's churches and ministers, while in Aberdeen it attracted the loyalty of atleast a third of the clergy and their congregations.[24] Of greater significance, Marrs suggests that most of those affected by the movement in Glasgow had a prior church affiliation, that they were 'predominantly the skilled or regularly employed working classes and the middle classes', and perhaps most importantly, that men and women were converted in equal numbers.[25] By contrast, the revival in Aberdeen penetrated successfully beyond the boundaries of the Kirk's membership, it affected a large proportion of the unskilled working classes, and most significantly, it embraced a disproportionately large number of men. Lastly, it would appear that the revival produced a less noteworthy impression upon Glasgow than upon Aberdeen. Marrs is anxious to prove that the revival 'did not have the impact perceived and previously claimed'.[26] Therefore he remarks that the attendance of 20,000 people at a revival open-air meeting constituted less than five per cent of the city's 443,639 inhabitants in 1859.[27] Meanwhile in Aberdeen, crowds of more than ten thousand gathered regularly to listen to evangelists on the Broad Hill. They represented more than an eighth of the city's population of 75,805 people. Hence it appears that the revival occupied the attention of a larger proportion of the city's population, and consequently it is suggested that it exerted a greater influence in the Granite City. It remains true, despite the common characteristics, that there were marked differences between the appearance of the 1859 revival in Glasgow and Aberdeen. This serves to confirm further the considerable effect which local situations exert upon religious movements.

There is a reasonable explanation for the differences between the manifestations of the awakening in Glasgow and Aberdeen, which lies within their separate origins. The Aberdeen revival that began in December 1858 was 'imported' directly from America and as a result it bore all the characteristics of the modern evangelistic campaign that had become the religious movement in New York. The Glasgow revival, however, started in earnest in the city in September 1859 after ministers had returned from scenes of the awakening in Ulster during the previous summer. The Irish movement, hugely dissimilar to the American awakening, was decidedly traditional in manner and expression. Accordingly it served to condition the expectations and experiences of those who embraced the revival in the south west of Scotland. In this way, the 1859 religious movement appeared in contrasting forms in Glasgow and Aberdeen.

IV

Besides the importance of local factors, there were other broader, national circumstances that also exercised an influence upon the appearance and course of this awakening. There were, in particular, two pressing issues that were confronting the Free Church towards the end of the 1850s, and it is clear that the Church's response to these matters served to create the environment within which the revival flourished. Firstly, the Free Church was in a state of decline in some areas. The Church Extension Charges Report of 1862 recorded that there were ninety-six weak congregations, including sixty-eight Lowland and twenty-eight Gaelic-speaking churches, each with less than one hundred members. Some of them had once been in a flourishing condition, but they were 'now smitten with a decline that threatens their extinction'.[28] As a result the delicate and difficult question was raised concerning the viability of these churches and 'whether there are not some congregations which do not need the full services of a minister . . . and whether it is not necessary to take some steps for re-organising and reviving such congregations'.[29] It is clear that the fortunes of the Free Church were beginning to deteriorate in a large number of its congregations around the time of the revival. Secondly there are indications that the financial circumstances of the Free Church were not altogether favourable during this period. Even during the year 1861-2 the collection for the Home Mission Fund of the Church raised only £2237, which was appreciably less than the expected target of £3000. This 'disheartening feature' was noted, and the question raised, 'What would Dr (Thomas) Chalmers have said to such paltry contributions to an enterprise which engaged the noblest energies of his soul?'[30] Moreover, James Buchanan, who delivered the Sustenation Fund Report in 1862, commented that 'it was indeed discouraging that they had not yet reached the point at which they had been so long aiming'.[31] Meanwhile another minister, George Dalzeil, lamented that the Disruption ministers and laymen were fast disappearing, and he said that 'he was afraid that . . . there was reason to fear it would be difficult to supply their [minister's] places in a pecuniary point of view.'[32] Hence it is manifest that, in its congregational strength and national finances, the Free Church was not in a prosperous condition around the period of the revival.

Despite the decline of individual congregations and the economic problems that were confronting the Church, it appears from the Home Mission and Church Extension Report of 1862, that the Free Kirk was, in response to these difficulties, engaged in evangelism to an unprecedented level. Indeed in 1862, when the 'Home Mission was never in a more thriving condition . . . was never conducted on a larger scale . . . was never better consolidated . . . nor more full of "mercy and of good fruits"', there were forty-four probationers employed at mission stations, a further fourteen at missions in large towns, five catechists at other outreach centres, nine ordained ministers of sanctioned territorial charges, seventeen students under the Committee's supervision, twenty-four ministers of Church Extension Charges and forty-six ministers who had been engaged in evangelistic work during the summer.[33] There is no doubt that the Free Church, in response to its difficulties, was actively involved in the work of aggressive evangelism during the period of the revival. It was anxious to stem the tide of decline. Consequently, the religious movement of 1859 arose in the midst of a campaign of outreach organised by the Free Church. Anxious and hopeful of new growth in the face of its pressing problems, the Free Church was particularly eager to welcome revival. There can be little doubt that their renewed commitment to mission had a vital bearing upon the wholehearted manner in which the awakening was received in many parts of Scotland.

Beyond the immediate concerns of the Free Church, the awakening emerged in the midst of at least two noteworthy religious developments that were continuing to evolve around the middle of the century. In the first instance, the relationship between the Scottish Presbyterian Churches and the Westminster Confession was beginning to change. Despite the effect of the creation of the Free Church and its adoption of the Confession as its subordinate standard in 1843, which served to strengthen the cause of conservatism, by 1850 James Buchanan 'conceded that people were becoming increasingly uneasy with all dogmatic or confessional statements'.[34] Around this time several indications appeared that demonstrated how a different mood was beginning to occupy the minds of religious people towards the subordinate standard of their Presbyterian Churches. In general, people became less satisfied with emphatic statements of faith and started to question these more thoroughly. This new spirit was perhaps most noticeably demonstrated in the writings of the Edinburgh advocate and lay theologian, Alexander Taylor Innes. He reflected the prevailing attitude of tolerance and tentativeness when he discussed the limited usefulness of any confessional statement.[35] Accordingly, a modern, inquiring approach to religious matters began to show dissatisfaction with a confessional formula which many were beginning to find wanting.

Secondly, there were important changes taking place concerning the doctrine of atonement during this period. As early as 1831 John Mcleod Campbell was condemned for arguing that Jesus Christ had died, not for the elect only, but for all people. Campbell's *The Nature of Atonement* was finally published in 1856, and gradually his view of the efficacy of Christ's death exerted a broader appeal.[36] In addition, in 1841 James Morison was expelled from the United Secession Church on account of his Sandemanian view of the atonement. As a result the Evangelical Union Church was established which upheld an Arminian theology. According to John Cairns, the outstanding United Presbyterian divine, these episodes 'exerted a valuable influence in liberalising the tone of Scottish theology'.[37] Increasingly, as the nineteenth century progressed, the authority of the older Calvinist emphasis upon election declined, while the love of God to all men grew to occupy the central place in the preaching from many pulpits across the land.

It was into the midst of these developments that the religious movement descended in 1859. Although the awakening did not directly encourage an explicit repudiation of the Westminster Confession, it did reflect some of the broader changes that were overtaking the Church around the middle of the nineteenth century. In rural areas during the movement, conversion continued to be understood and experienced in a traditional Calvinist manner. Nonetheless, the new approach to evangelism that characterised the Aberdeen revival reflected a break from long-established ways and demonstrated the increasing popularity of more modern views of the atonement that laid stress on the love of God. The organised 'inquirer's meetings', where instantaneous conversion was taught and expected, exhibited a higher estimate of the human ability to choose to be 'born again'. Hence the 1859 revival embodied a modern method of evangelism, at least in its urban expression and views, that were congruent with contemporary views of the atonement. In this manner the religious movement reflected the broader, transforming mood of the Church around the middle of the nineteenth century.

This book has developed further the most recent work undertaken by revival historians. It has pursued the new interest that has been created in the detail of the actual events of religious movements as they unfold, and it has carried out an extensive study into those who were affected by the revival. Despite the valuable insights of previous scholars of revivals, they have tended to examine them on a national or a strictly local level. In so doing they have dealt with either the broader course of events or the detailed conditions of a particular situation. This study is distinctive because it has examined the 1859 revival from a regional perspective. This approach has revealed the multifaceted nature of a movement that superficially appears unitary. This feature has been hitherto overlooked by scholars. What has been established for the north east of Scotland is the heterogeneous nature of simultaneous revival movements in the same vicinity.

Undoubtedly the most fascinating feature of this revival, as it swept across the north east of Scotland, was this rich diversity of forms in which it appeared. Within this one, simultaneous movement there were a number of separate campaigns. Each manifestation, set in a particular context, displayed a different ethos and belonged to a separate tradition of revival. The farmers' movement emerged in a settled community and reflected the Presbyterian model of seventeenth- and early eighteenth-century revival. The awakening that took place among the fisherfolk was altogether very different. Located along a 'neglected' coastline, it bore the characteristics of a more excitable late eighteenth-century and early nineteenth-century Methodist revival. Finally, the movement as it appeared in Aberdeen, took the form of a modern evangelistic campaign. Set within a growing and fast-changing urban environment it belonged to a new common Evangelical school of revival that had emerged in the mid-nineteenth century and was set to continue through Moody and Sankey, Billy Sunday and Billy Graham into the later twentieth century. Most significantly, the constitution of those who were affected by the revival, in each of the three different situations, did not simply reflect the social composition of that particular context. Rather it displayed further the distinct nature of the revival as it arose in these places. The 1859 revival in the north east of Scotland was not a single, uniform religious movement. Simultaneous in its appearance and yet disparate in its manifestation, this 'season of grace' demonstrates the definitive influence which theological and local circumstances exercise when 'the Lord is walking through the land'.[38]

Notes

1. J. Douglas, *The Revival of Religion* (Edinburgh, 1859), p. 10.
2. *P.S.*, (24 May 1861), p. 2.
3. T. T. Matthews (ed.), *Reminiscences of the Revival of Fifty-Nine and the Sixties* (Aberdeen, 1910), p. 6.
4. *A Report of a Conference on the State of Religion and Public Meeting held in the*

Free Church, Huntly, January 5, 1860 (Huntly, 1860), p. 29.
5. F.E.N.G., (24 April 1860), p. 3.
6. W. Robbie, *The Life and Labours of the late James Turner of Peterhead* (Aberdeen, 1863), p. 53.
7. Anon, *Times of Refreshing: Being Notices of the Religious Awakening which have taken place in the United Kingdom, with Special Reference to the Revival in Aberdeen* (Aberdeen, 1859), pp. 9-12.
8. J. Radcliffe, *Recollections of Reginald Radcliffe* (London, nd), p. 40.
9. D. N. Hempton, M. Hill, *Evangelical Protestantism in Ulster Society, 1740-1890* (London, 1992), p. 160.
10. A.F.P., (5 October 1860), p. 5.
11. Robbie, *James Turner*, p. 48.
12. J. Kent, *Holding the Fort: Studies in Victorian Revivalism* (London, 1978), p. 71.
13. R. Carwardine, *Transatlantic Revivalism: Popular Evangelicalism in Britain and America, 1790-1865* (Westport, Connecticut, 1978), p. 56.
14. A.H., (10 August 1861), p. 4.
15. *Report of Conference on State of Religion*, Huntly, p. 7.
16. F.E.N.G., (24 April 1860), p. 3.
17. C. J. Marrs, 'The 1859 Religious Revival in Scotland: A Review and Critique of the Movement with Particular Reference to the City of Glasgow', unpublished PhD thesis, University of Glasgow, 1995, pp. 117-19.
18. Ibid., pp. 134-5.
19. Ibid., pp. 158-62.
20. Ibid., pp. 214-323.
21. Ibid., p. 341.
22. Ibid., p. 311.
23. Ibid., p. 250.
24. Ibid., pp. 329-30.
25. Ibid., pp. 165-8.
26. Ibid., p. 342.
27. Ibid., p. 333.
28. Free Church of Scotland: *Assembly Proceedings 1862* (Edinburgh, 1862), p. 167.
29. Ibid., [Supplementary Report of the Sustenation Fund] p. 2.
30. Ibid., pp. 109,111.
31. Ibid., p. 150.
32. Ibid., p. 156.
33. Ibid., p. 108.
34. A.C. Cheyne, *The Transforming of the Kirk: Victorian Scotland's Religious Revolution* (Edinburgh, 1983), p. 67.
35. Ibid., p. 69.
36. Ibid., p. 63.
37. Ibid., p. 66.
38. *Report of Conference on State of Religion*, Huntly, p. 6.

Bibliography

MANUSCRIPTS
Census
Church Records

PERIODICALS
Denominational Journals
Religious Journals
Newspapers

OTHER PRINTED SOURCES
Sermons and Addresses
Pamphlets, Letters and Essays
Reports
Biographies
Books

SECONDARY SOURCES
Books
Component parts of books
Articles
Unpublished theses
Unpublished articles

MANUSCRIPTS

Census
The Census listed below are held at the General Register for Scotland, New Register House, Edinburgh.
1861 Census, Aberdeen, Aberdeenshire
1861 Census, Banchory Ternan, Kincardineshire
1861 Census, Banff, Banffshire
1861 Census, Buckie, Banffshire
1861 Census, Daviot, Aberdeenshire
1861 Census, Findochty, Banffshire
1861 Census, New Deer, Aberdeenshire
1861 Census, Peterhead, Aberdeenshire
1861 Census, Portessie, Banffshire
1861 Census, Portknockie, Banffshire
1861 Census, Rhynie, Aberdeenshire
British Parliamentary Papers: 1851 Census Great Britain Reports and Tables on Education England and Wales and on Religious Worship and Education Scotland (Dublin 1970).

Census of Scotland, 1861, Population Tables and Report (Edinburgh, 1862).
Tenth Decennial Census of the Population of Scotland taken 5th April 1891, with report. Volume One (Edinburgh, 1892).

Church Records

All of the following Church Records are held at the National Archives of Scotland, Edinburgh, with the exception of the following:
i. Those that are marked with a * are held at the Aberdeen City Archives.
ii. Those marked ^ are kept at the Special Collections Department of Aberdeen University Library.
iii. Those that are marked with + are held in various private hands.

1. Church of Scotland
Aberdour Parish Church Communion Rolls 1861-69
Aberlour Parish Church Communion Rolls 1843-71
Banchory Ternan Parish Church Kirk Session Minutes 1857-60
Banff Parish Church Kirk Session Minutes 1849-69
Chapel of Garioch Parish Church Kirk Session Minutes 1843-67
Cluny Parish Church Communion Rolls 1851-71
Cruden Parish Church Kirk Session Minutes 1844-67
Culsamond Parish Church Kirk Session Minutes 1855-1900
Daviot Parish Church Communion Rolls 1829-1873
Daviot Parish Church Kirk Session Minutes 1855-1915
Drainy Parish Church Kirk Session Minutes 1860-64
Echt Parish Church Kirk Session Minutes 1851-1908
Ellon Parish Church Communion Rolls 1860-70
Fraserburgh Parish Church Kirk Session Minutes 1835-59
Fraserburgh Parish Church Kirk Session Minutes 1859-76
*Greyfriars Parish Church Communion Rolls 1848-1865
Greyfriars Parish Church Kirk Session Minutes 1851-1868
*Greyfriars Parish Church List of Members 1848-1859
Holburn Parish Church Communion Rolls 1859-1861
*John Knox Parish Church Communion Rolls 1846-1863
Inch Parish Church Communion Rolls 1836-61
Insch Parish Church Kirk Session Minutes 1856-77
Inverurie Parish Church Kirk Session Minutes 1845-70
Meldrum Parish Church Communion Rolls 1856-61
Millbrex Parish Church Communion Rolls 1862-66
Millbrex Parish Church Kirk Session Minutes 1858-1894
Newhills Parish Church Kirk Session Minutes 1854-1911
Oyne Parish Church Kirk Session Minutes 1841-88
Peterhead Parish Church Kirk Session Minutes 1844-82
Rathen Parish Church Kirk Session Minutes 1856-70
Rathven Parish Church Kirk Session Minutes 1858-95
Rhynie Parish Church Communion Rolls 1857-58, 1859-72
Rhynie Parish Church Kirk Session Minutes 1855-1908
*St Clement's Parish Church Kirk Session Minutes 1851-1871

Bibliography

St Fergus Parish Church Kirk Session Minutes 1828-72
Savoch Parish Church Communion Rolls 1858-64
Woodside Parish Church Communion Rolls 1859-1868

2. *Free Church of Scotland*
i. Congregational Records
Aberlour Free Church Kirk Session Minutes 1848-96
Alves Free Church Kirk Session Minutes 1843-71
Ardelach Free Church Kirk Session Minutes 1843-1933
Auchendoir Free Church Kirk Session Minutes 1843-88
Auldearn Free Church Kirk Session Minutes 1843-78
+Banchory Ternan Free Church Communion Rolls 1853-68
+Banchory Ternan Free Church Kirk Session Minutes 1856-59
+Banchory Ternan Free Church Kirk Session Minutes 1863-66
+Banchory Ternan Free Church Session Record 1843-63
Banff Free Church Communion Rolls 1845-60
Banff Free Church Kirk Session Minutes 1843-66
Bellie Free Church Kirk Session Minutes 1843-96
Blackburn Free Church Communion Rolls 1860-1866
Blackburn Free Church Kirk Session Minutes 1844-1900
Boharm Free Church Kirk Session Minutes 1844-1907
Bon Accord Free Church Communion Rolls 1849-1868
Bon Accord Free Church Kirk Session Minutes 1843-1870
Botriphinie Free Church Communion Rolls 1846-56
Botriphinie Free Church Communion Rolls 1857-1930
Botriphinie Free Church Foreign Missions Cashbook 1853-66
Botriphinie Free Church Kirk Session Minutes 1841-79
Braemar Free Church Kirk Session Minutes 1843-93
Buckie Free Church Kirk Session Minutes 1857-77
Chapel of Garioch Free Church Kirk Session Minutes 1843-1906
Clola Free Church Kirk Session Minutes 1852-97
Cluny Free Church Kirk Session Minutes 1844-1933
Cruden Free Church Kirk Session Minutes 1843-83
Cullen Free Church Kirk Session Minutes 1845-1917
Culsamond Free Church Kirk Session Minutes 1843-92
Dallas Free Church Kirk Session Minutes 1845-1908
East Free Church Kirk Session Minutes 1843-1863
Echt Free Church Kirk Session Minutes 1843-1926
Elgin High Free Church Communion Rolls 1853-63
Elgin High Free Church Kirk Session Minutes 1852-61
Elgin High Free Church Kirk Session Minutes 1861-78
Enzie Free Church Communion Rolls 1857-72
Enzie Free Church Kirk Session Minutes 1843-60
Fordyce Free Church Kirk Session Minutes 1843-1909
Forgue Free Church Kirk Session Minutes 1843-83
Fraserburgh Free Church Kirk Session Minutes 1844-85
Fyvie Free Church Kirk Session Minutes 1843-81
Gartly Free Church Kirk Session Minutes 1843-80

Holburn Free Church Kirk Session Minutes 1837-1882
Huntly Free Church Deacons' Court Minutes 1851-71
Huntly Free Church Kirk Session Minutes 1849-89
Insch Free Church Kirk Session Minutes 1843-1923
Inveravon Free Church Kirk Session Minutes 1845-1904
Inverurie Free Church Kirk Session Minutes 1843-1923
John Knox Free Church Kirk Session Minutes 1854-1883
Kintore Free Church Kirk Session Minutes 1843-1903
Kirkmichael Free Church Kirk Session Minutes 1843-1907
Knockando Free Church Kirk Session Minutes 1844-1915
Longside Free Church Communion Rolls 1852-1929
Longside Free Church Kirk Session Minutes 1845-1929
Lumphanan Free Church Kirk Session Minutes 1845-65
Macduff Free Church Kirk Session Minutes 1843-1930
Maryculter Free Church Kirk Session Minutes 1857-1872
Mortlach Free Church Deacons' Court Minutes 1846-96
Nairn Free Church Kirk Session Minutes 1843-75
Newhills Free Church Communion Rolls 1852-1860
Newhills Free Church Deacons' Court Minutes 1846-1874
Newhills Free Church Kirk Session Minutes 1844-1878
North Free Church Deacons' Court Minutes 1849-1875
North Free Church Kirk Session Minutes 1843-1875
Old Deer Free Church Kirk Session Minutes 1845-97
Ordiquhill and Ord Free Church Communion Rolls 1844-77
Ordiquhill and Ord Free Church Kirk Session Minutes 1845-81
Oyne Free Church Kirk Session Minutes 1843-1917
Peterculter Free Church Kirk Session Minutes 1844-89
Pluscarden Free Church Communion Rolls 1843-71
Pluscarden Free Church Kirk Session Minutes 1843-68
Portsoy Free Church Communion Rolls 1854-76
Portsoy Free Church Kirk Session Minutes 1843-59
Portsoy Free Church Kirk Session Minutes 1859-1911
Rafford Free Church Kirk Session Minutes 1855-1936
Rothes Free Church Kirk Session Minutes 1857-96
Rhynie Free Church Kirk Session Minutes 1844-94
*St Clement's Free Church Deacons' Court Minutes 1851-1865
*St Clement's Free Church Kirk Session Minutes 1843-1859
Skene Free Church Kirk Session Minutes 1843-1901
South Free Church Kirk Session Minutes 1855-1871
South Free Church Young Men's Mutual Improvement Association
Strachan Free Church Kirk Session Minutes 1843-1914
Stricken Free Church Kirk Session Minutes 1843-90
Trinity Free Church Communion Rolls 1855-1867
Trinity Free Church Kirk Session Minutes 1843-1867
West Free Church Kirk Session Minutes 1843-1859
West Free Church Kirk Session Minutes 1859-1878
Woodside Free Church Kirk Session Minutes 1843-1876

Bibliography

ii. Presbytery Records
Aberdeen Free Church Presbytery Minutes 1853-69
Aberlour Free Church Presbytery Minutes 1854-66
Alford Free Church Presbytery Minutes 1843-64
Deer Free Church Presbytery Minutes 1843-70
Ellon Free Church Presbytery Minutes 1856-85
Fordyce Free Church Presbytery Minutes 1857-84
Forres Free Church Presbytery Minutes 1843-73
Garioch Free Church Presbytery Minutes 1843-66
Kincardine O'Neil Free Church Presbytery Minutes 1851-76
Strathbogie Free Church Presbytery Minutes 1847-64
iii. Synod Records
Aberdeen Free Church Synod Minutes 1857-72

3. United Presbyterian Church
Banff United Presbyterian Church Communion Rolls 1850-1914
Banff United Presbyterian Church Kirk Session Minutes 1830-76
Belmont Street United Presbyterian Church Communion Rolls 1850-1875
Belmont Street United Presbyterian Church Kirk Session Minutes 1858-1883
Belmont Street United Presbyterian Church Managers' Minutes 1841-1878
Buckie United Presbyterian Church Kirk Session Minutes 1859-71
Craigdam United Presbyterian Church Kirk Session Minutes 1848-1863
Forres United Presbyterian Church Kirk Session Minutes 1852-68
Huntly United Presbyterian Church Kirk Session Minutes 1849-79
New Deer United Presbyterian Church Communion Rolls 1856-1907
New Deer United Presbyterian Church Kirk Session Minutes 1856-1908
St Nicholas Lane United Presbyterian Church Kirk Session Minutes 1842-1865
St Nicholas Lane United Presbyterian Church Managers' Minutes 1857-1888
Shiels United Presbyterian Church Congregational Roll Book 1857-1898

4. Congregational Church
*Belmont Street Congregational Church Roll Book 1817-1937 (Previously George Street Congregational Church 1797-1865)
*Blackfriars Street Congregational Church Minute Book of Church Meetings 1844-1861
*George Street Congregational Church Minute Book of Church Meetings 1797-1862
*George Street Congregational Church Minute Book of Deacons' Meetings 1801-1876
*Frederick Street Congregational Church Minute Book of Church Meetings 1851-1871

5. Episcopal Church
^ Register of Persons Confirmed by Bishop Thomas George Suther 1857-1881
*St James Episcopal Church Copy Letter Book of Manager's Secretary including letters from John Avery 1854-1858 and John Crombie 1858-1880
*St James Episcopal Church Extracts from Minutes Books 1854-1914
*St James Episcopal Church Minutes of Congregation and Management Committee, Aberdeen 1854-1881

+St James Episcopal Chapel, Cruden, List of Communicants, 1844-69
+St James Episcopal Chapel, Cruden, List of Confirmations, 1850-65
^ St Paul's Episcopal Church, Aberdeen, Minute Book 1860-1874
+St Ternan's Episcopal Chapel, Banchory Ternan, List of Communicants, 1856-68

6. *Evangelical Union Church*

*St Paul Street Evangelical Union Church Communicants Roll Book 1846-1872
*St Paul Street Evangelical Union Church Minutes of Church Meetings 1850-1878
*St Paul Street Evangelical Union Seat Letting Book 1855-1865

7. *Baptist Church*

+Union Terrace Baptist Church Membership List of 4 January 1862
+Union Terrace Baptist Church Minute Book 1821-68

PERIODICALS

Denominational Journals

The Baptist Magazine
The Free Church Monthly Record
The Free Church Weekly Record
The Home and Foreign Record of the Church of Scotland
The Home and Foreign Record of the Free Church of Scotland
Missionary Record of the United Presbyterian Church
The Scottish Congregational Magazine
The United Presbyterian Magazine
Wesleyan Times

Religious Journals

British Evangelist
British and Foreign Evangelical Review
The British Messenger
The Day Star
The News of the Churches and Journal of Missions
The Revival
The Wynd Journal

Newspapers

Aberdeen Citizen
Aberdeen Free Press
Aberdeen Herald
Aberdeen Journal
Aberdeen Saturday Post
Banffshire Journal
Banffshire Mercury
Elgin Courant
Elgin Courier
Forres, Elgin and Nairn Gazette

Bibliography

Fraserburgh Advertiser
Morayshire Advertiser
Nairnshire Telegraph
Northern Advertiser
Northern Telegraphic News
Peterhead Sentinel
Stonehaven Journal
The Scotsman
The Times

OTHER PRINTED SOURCES

Sermons and Addresses

J. Adam, *The Preaching of the Word in Relation to the Times* A Sermon Preached before the Free Synod of Aberdeen (Aberdeen, 1861).

Address by the Promoters of a Proposed National Bible Society of Scotland (Glasgow, 1860).

Addresses on the Revival of Religion, and on Prayer Meetings, delivered at a Special Meeting of the United Associate Presbytery of Cupar (Edinburgh, 1840).

R. Balmer, *Address to Elders on the Means to be used by them for Promoting a Revival of Religion* (Berwick, 1841).

D. Brown, *On United and Universal Prayer throughout the Church of God* A Paper read at the Annual Conference of the Evangelical Alliance in October 1860 at Nottingham (London, 1860).

J. M. Cramp, *An Address to British Christians on the Importance and Necessity of a Revival of Religion* (London, 1832).

R. Forbes, *The Pastoral Care of the Children of the flock* A Sermon Preached before the Free Synod of Aberdeen (Aberdeen, 1859).

W. Gibson, *Present Aspects of the Irish Revival* A Paper read at the Annual Conference of the Evangelical Alliance in October 1860 at Nottingham (London, 1860).

Hofmeyr, *A Brief Account of the Present Revival of Religion in some parts of this Colony* An Address delivered at the Annual Meeting of the South African Evangelical Alliance (Cape Town, 1860).

J. M'Cosh, *The Present Tendency of Religious Thought throughout the Three Kingdoms* A paper read before the British Organisation of the Evangelical Alliance (Edinburgh, 1864).

H. MacGill, *On the Present Revival of Religion in Scotland* A Paper read at the Annual Conference of the Evangelical Alliance in October 1860 at Nottingham (London, 1860).

Memorial of Mr Spurgeon's Visit to Aberdeen Two Sermons and an Address delivered by C. H. Spurgeon (Aberdeen, 1861).

Pastoral Address on the Subject of Religious Revival from the Reformed Presbyteries of Dumfries and Newtownstewart to the Congregations under their Care (Lockerbie, 1859).

Proposal for United Prayer An address by Ministers of the Gospel, and others of the Evangelical Churches in England, Scotland and Ireland (Edinburgh,

1855).

A. Reid, *Hindrances to Ministerial Success, or Some of the Causes of the Present Low State of Religion in the Church* A Sermon preached before the Free Synod of Aberdeen (Aberdeen, 1850).

D. Smith, *In Memoriam: An address on the National Affliction occasioned by the Death of the Prince Consort* (Edinburgh, 1861).

J. Smith, *Farewell Sermon* (Aberdeen, 1862).

J. Venn, *The Revival in Wales* A Paper read at the Annual Conference of the Evangelical Alliance in October 1860 at Nottingham (London, 1860).

Pamphlets, Letters and Essays

J. Alexander, *Prize Essay on the Present Condition of Farm Servants in Scotland with Means to be Adopted for its Amelioration* (Aberdeen, 1852).

J. W. Alexander, *Revival Lessons* (Edinburgh, 1859).

Aliquis, *The Revival: A Great Work of the Spirit of God, with Notice of some Objections* (Aberdeen, 1861).

Anon, *Aberdonia: Footdee in the Last Century* (Aberdeen, 1872).

Anon, 'The Agricultural Labourer of Scotland.' *Fraser's Magazine* 3, 1871.

Anon, *The Appearance of God's Work in the Chief Towns of Scotland: With Special Reference to Aberdeen and Dundee* (Aberdeen, 1859).

Anon, 'The Effect of Farm Overseers on the Morals of Farm Servants.' *Blackwoods Edinburgh Magazine* 3, (1818).

Anon, *Eleven Years at Farm Work, Being a True Tale of Farm Servant Life from 1863 Onwards* (Aberdeen, 1879).

Anon, *A Narrative of the Surprising Work of God in the Conversion of Souls in Kilsyth, Finnieston and Cumbernauld and the Revival of Religion in Anderston and Paisley with an Account of the Remarkable Occurrence which took place at the Dispensation of the Sacrament at Kilsyth on 22 September 1839* (Glasgow, 1839).

Anon, *Times of Refreshing. Being notices of some of the Religious Awakenings which have taken place in the United Kingdom, with Special Reference to the Revival in Aberdeen* (Aberdeen, 1859).

E. Bird, *Some Account of the Great Religious Awakening now going on in the United States* (London, 1858).

A. A. Bonar, *Thirty Years of Spiritual Life in the Island of Arran* (Glasgow, 1889).

F. W. B. Bouverie, *The Pastor to His Flock* (Annual Addresses from the Minister to his Congregation) (Aberdeen, 1858-1864).

G. Campbell, *The Revival Meeting and Other Poems* (Aberdeen, 1864).

Catalogue of a Collection of Books being portions of the Libraries of the late Rev Robert Reid, Banchory, and others, to be sold by auction, by the Aberdeen Auction Company Limited within their rooms, 120 Union Street, Aberdeen, on successive evenings, commencing 28 February 1894. Sale at 6.30 pm each evening. John F Smyth, Auctioneer (Aberdeen, 1894).

E. Davies, *Revivals in Wales* (London, 1859).

J. Douglas, *The Revival of Religion* (Edinburgh, 1839).

P. Drummond, *Showers of Blessing* (Stirling, 1858).

Evidence on the Subject of Revivals taken before a Committee of the Presbytery of Aberdeen (Aberdeen, 1841).

A. Fraser, *The Condition of the Agricultural Population and the Best Means of Ame-*

liorating their Condition, Morally and Socially (Edinburgh, 1859).
J. Gerrard, *Rural Labourers in the North of Scotland: Their Medical Relief and House Accommodation as they effect Pauperism and Illegitimacy* (Banff, nd).
W. H. Harding, *The Ulster Revival of 1859* (Belfast, 1859).
G. King, *Brief Historical Sketch of the Congregational Church formerly in George Street, Aberdeen, now in Belmont Street* (Aberdeen, 1870).
A Letter from Rev Alexander Stewart, Minister of the Parish of Moulin to Rev David Black, Minister of Lady Yester's Church Edinburgh (Glasgow, nd).
J. MacFarlane, *Scriptural Warrant for Women to Preach the Gospel* (Peterhead, nd).
H. M. MacGill, *Thoughts on Revival, with a Reference to the Present Religious Movement in the United States* (Glasgow, 1858).
A. MacGillvray, *The Revival of Religion: The Claims of the Times* (Elgin, 1860).
A. MacGillvray, *Sketches of Religion and Revivals of Religion in the North Highlands during Last Century* (Edinburgh, 1859).
G. Marr, *Essay on the Condition of the Agricultural Population, and the Best Means of Ameliorating their State, Morally and Socially* (Aberdeen, 1858).
J. Murker, *Revival Meetings: Some of their Good Works and Occasional Perversions* (Aberdeen, 1865).
W. Nixon, *An Account of the Late Work of God at Ferryden* (London, 1860).
Omicron, *Five letters on the Religious Movement in Aberdeen: With an Appendix on the Nature, Probability and Necessity of a Religious Revival* (Aberdeen, 1859).
R. Peddle (ed.), *A Consecutive Narrative of the Remarkable Awakening in Edinburgh under the Labours of Messrs Moody and Sankey, the City Ministers and Christian Laymen* (London, 1874).
E. Porter, *Letters on Revivals of Religion in America during the Present Century* (Edinburgh, 1840).
A. Reed, *The Revival of Religion: A Narrative of the State of Religion at Wycliffe Chapel, London, during the year 1839* (Glasgow, 1840).
W. Ruxton, *An Essay by a Farm Servant in Aberdeenshire* (Inverurie, 1865).
'A Short History of Aberdeen and Its People.' (A Series of 48 Articles from the *Free Press*, printed from 12 July 1890.)
W. T. Stead, The Revival in the West: A Narrative of Facts (London, 1904).
H. Taylor, *A Letter on Religious Revivals: Containing Words of Wisdom and Warning to Authors and Editors, Magistrates and Ministers from President Edwards* (Glasgow, 1860).
W. Watson, *Pauperism, Vagrancy, Crime and Industrial Education in Aberdeenshire, 1840-1875* (Aberdeen, 1877).
W. Watson, *Remarks on the Bothy System and Feeing Markets* (Aberdeen, 1849).
G. R. Watt, *On the Improvement of Farm Servants* (Inverurie, 1865).
A. Whyte, *Revival: A Letter Written by the Rev Principal Alexander White in Response to a Request from Two Friends* (Edinburgh, 1913).

Reports

Aberdeen Association for Reclaiming Fallen Females: Appeal for Support (Aberdeen, 1861).
Aberdeen City Mission: Annual Report, 1849 (Aberdeen, 1850).
Abstract Report of the Aberdeen Temperance Society (Aberdeen, 1863).
Fifteenth Annual Report of the Aberdeen Temperance Society (Aberdeen, 1860).

Fifth Report of the Aberdeen Evangelistic Association (Aberdeen, 1865).
Fifth Report of the Ladies Association for the Rescue of Fallen Females (Aberdeen, 1865).
First Annual Report of the Aberdeen Young Men's Christian Association (Aberdeen, 1859).
First Report of the Aberdeen Evangelistic Association (Aberdeen, 1861).
First Report of the General City Mission (Aberdeen, 1854).
Fourth Annual Report of the Aberdeen Young Men's Christian Association (Aberdeen, 1862).
Fourth Report of the Aberdeen Evangelistic Association (Aberdeen, 1864).
Free Church of Scotland: Assembly Proceedings 1859 (Edinburgh, 1859).
Free Church of Scotland: Assembly Proceedings 1860 (Edinburgh, 1860).
Free Church of Scotland: Assembly Proceedings 1862 (Edinburgh, 1862).
Nineteenth Annual Report of the Aberdeen Temperance Society (Aberdeen, 1864).
Northern Temperance Record (Aberdeen, 1841).
Report by the Committee of Elders appointed by the Free Presbytery of Aberdeen on the State of Religion (Aberdeen, 1850).
Report by a Committee of the Free Synod of Aberdeen upon the State of Religion within their Bounds, presented 12 April 1870 (Aberdeen, 1870).
A Report of a Conference on the State of Religion and Public Meeting, held in the Free Church, Huntly, January 5, 1860 (Huntly, 1860).
Report of the Aberdeen Free Church Divinity Students' Missionary Association (Aberdeen, 1865).
Report of the Aberdeenshire Association of Ladies for the Rescue of Fallen Women (Aberdeen, 1863).
A Report of the Free Church General Assembly on the State of Religion, 1846 (Edinburgh, 1846).
Second Annual Report of the Aberdeen Young Men's Christian Association (Aberdeen, 1860).
Second Annual Report of the Scottish Evangelistic Association (Edinburgh, 1864).
Second Report of the Aberdeen Evangelistic Association (Aberdeen, 1862)
Sixth Annual Report of the Aberdeen Young Men's Christian Association (Aberdeen, 1864).
Sixth Report of the Aberdeen Evangelistic Association (Aberdeen, 1866).
Third Report of the Aberdeen Evangelistic Association (Aberdeen, 1863).
Thirteenth Annual Report of the Aberdeen Temperance Society (Aberdeen, 1858).
Twentieth Annual Report of the Aberdeen Temperance Society (Aberdeen, 1865).
Twenty-first Annual Report of the Aberdeen Temperance Society (Aberdeen, 1866).
Twenty-ninth Annual Report of the Scottish 'Monthly Visitor' Tract Society (Edinburgh, 1862).

Biographies

JAMES BEGG
T. Smith, *Memoirs of James Begg* (Edinburgh, 1888).
ANDREW BONAR
M. Bonar (ed.), *Andrew A. Bonar DD: Diary and Letters* (London, 1893).
ROBERT BUCHANAN

N. L. Walker, *Robert Buchanan DD: An Ecclesiastical Biography* (London, 1877)

ROBERT CANDLISH
W. Wilson, *Memorials of R. S. Candlish* (Edinburgh, 1880).

WILLIAM CUNNINGHAM
R. Rainy, *Life of William Cunningham* (London, 1871).

PETER DRUMMOND
J. Birkbeck, *Peter Drummond: Man of Conviction and Action* (Stirling, 1984).
M. J. Cormack, *The Stirling Tract Enterprises and the Drummonds* (Stirling, 1984).

CHARLES FINNEY
G. M. Rosell, R. A. G. Dupois (ed.), *The Memoirs of Charles G. Finney* (Grand Rapids, Michigan, 1989).

DUCHESS OF GORDON
G. Gordon, *The Last Dukes of Gordon and their Consorts, 1743-1865* (Aberdeen, nd).

HAY MacDOWALL GRANT
M. M. Gordon, *Hay MacDowall Grant of Arndilly: His Life, Labours and Teaching* (London, 1876).

JESSIE McFARLANE
H. I. G., *Jessie McFarlane: A Tribute of Affection* (London, 1872).

DUNCAN MATHESON
J. MacPherson, *Life and Labours of Duncan Matheson: The Scottish Evangelist* (London, 1910).

JOHN MILNE
H. Bonar, *Life of the Rev John Milne, MA* (London, 1868).

DWIGHT L. MOODY, IRA SANKEY
J. MacPherson, *Revival and Revival Work: A Record of the Labours of Messrs Moody and Sankey* (London, 1876).

JOHN MURKER
J. Stark, *John Murker of Banff: A Picture of Religious Life and Character in the North* (London, 1887).

ROBERT MURRAY M'CHEYNE
A. Bonar, *Memoir and Remains of Robert Murray M'Cheyne [1844]* (Edinburgh, 1978).

ASAHEL NETTLETON
B. Tyler, *A. A. Bonar, Nettleton and His Labours [1854]* (Edinburgh, 1996).

BROWNLOW NORTH
K. Moody-Stuart, *Brownlow North: Records and Recollections* (London, 1878).

REGINALD RADCLIFFE
J. Radcliffe, *Recollections of Reginald Radcliffe* (London, nd).

ALEXANDER THOMSON
G. Smeaton, *Memoir of Alexander Thomson of Banchory* (Edinburgh, 1869).

JAMES TURNER
E. McHardie, *James Turner or How to Reach the Masses* (Aberdeen, 1875).

W. Robbie, *The Life and Labours of the late James Turner of Peterhead, with a brief notice of his brother, George Turner* (Aberdeen, 1863).

RICHARD WEAVER

R. C. Morgan, *The Life of Richard Weaver: The Converted Collier* (London, 1861).

J. Paterson, *Richard Weaver's Life Story* (London, nd).

GEORGE WHITEFIELD

H. S. Stout, *The Divine Dramatist: George Whitefield and the Rise of Modern Evangelicalism* (Grand Rapids, Michigan, 1991).

ALEXANDER WHYTE

G. F. Barbour, *The Life of Alexander Whyte* (London, 1923).

Books

Aberdeen Almanac (Aberdeen, 1859).

Aberdeen Almanac (Aberdeen, 1860).

W. Alexander, *Twenty-Five years: A Personal Retrospect* (Aberdeen, 1878).

J. Arbuthnot, *An Historical Account of Peterhead* (Aberdeen, 1815).

P. Buchan, *Annals of Peterhead* (Peterhead, 1819).

W. Carnie, *Reporting Reminiscences* (Aberdeen, 1902).

A. S. Cook, *The Evolution of the Temperance Movement 1837-1901* (Aberdeen, 1901).

W. L. Crammond, *The Making of a Banffshire Burgh: Being an Account of the Early History of Macduff* (Banff, 1893).

J. B. Craven, *Recollections and Collections in Connection with the Parish of Newhills, Aberdeenshire* (Kirkwall, 1922).

F. D. Davenport, *Primitive Traits in Religious Revivals* (New York, 1905).

C. Diack, *Sketches of Methodism in Aberdeen* (Aberdeen, 1901).

J. Edwards, *An Account of the Revival of Religion in Northampton* [1743] (Edinburgh, 1995).

J. Edwards, *The Distinguishing Marks of a Work of the Spirit of God* [1741] (Edinburgh, 1995).

J. Edwards, *A Narrative of Surprising Conversions* [1736] (Edinburgh, 1995).

J. Edwards, *The Religious Affections* [1746] (Edinburgh, 1997).

G. Eliot, *Adam Bede* [1859] (London, 1980).

Encyclopaedia Britannica (9th edition) (London, 1875).

W. Ferguson, *The Great North of Scotland Railway* (Edinburgh, 1881).

C. G. Finney, *Charles G. Finney: An Autobiography* (London, 1882).

C. G. Finney, *Revival Lectures* (np, nd).

J. Gillies, *Historical Collections Relating to Remarkable Periods of the Success of the Gospel* [H. Bonar ed.,Kelso, 1845] (Pennsylvania, 1981).

H. G. Graham, *The Social Life of Scotland in the Eighteenth Century* (London, 1906).

F. H. Groome (ed.), *Ordnance Gazetteer of Scotland: A Survey of Scottish Topography, Statistical, Biographical and Historical* (Edinburgh, 1882).

Handbook of the Ecclesiastical, Educational, Medical, Charitable and Provident Institutions of Aberdeen and Neighbourhood (Aberdeen, 1883).

J. Johnston, *The Ecclesiastical and Religious Statistics of Scotland* (Glasgow, 1874).

D. MacFarlan, *The Revivals of the Eighteenth Century Particularly at Cambuslang*

Bibliography

with Three Sermons by the Rev. George Whitefield (Edinburgh, nd).
J. McGibbon, *The Fisherfolk of Buchan* (Edinburgh, nd).
L. MacKinnon, *Recollections of an Old Lawyer* (Aberdeen, 1935).
A. MacRae, *Revivals in the Highlands and Islands in the Nineteenth Century* (Stirling, nd).
T. T. Matthews (ed.), *Reminiscences of the Revival of Fifty-Nine and the Sixties* (Aberdeen, 1910).
W. Paul, *Past and Present of Aberdeenshire or Reminiscences of Seventy Years* (Aberdeen, 1881).
Peterhead a Century Ago: Extracts from the Diary of the late Mr Alexander Murray of Blackhouse (Peterhead, 1910).
The Peterhead Almanac and Directory (Peterhead, 1853).
The Peterhead and Fraserburgh Railway (Aberdeen, 1856).
The Revival of Religion: Addresses by Scottish Evangelical Leaders Delivered in Glasgow in 1840 [1840] (Edinburgh, 1984).
Results of the Census of 1851 with Respect to the Religious and Educational Establishments of Scotland (Edinburgh, 1851).
W. Robbie, *Aberdeen: Its Traditions and History* (Aberdeen, 1893).
W. Robbie, *Bon Accord Free Church, Aberdeen: A Retrospect, 1828-1887* (Aberdeen, 1887).
A Short History of Aberdeen and its People (Aberdeen, 1890).
J. S. Simon, *The Revival of Religion in England in the Eighteenth Century* (London, nd).
J. Slater, *Revival Reminiscences* (np, nd).
A. Smith (ed.), *A New History of Aberdeenshire* (Aberdeen, 1875).
W. B. Sprague, *Lectures on Revivals of Religion* [1832] (London, 1959).
J. Stark, *The Light of the North* (Aberdeen, 1896).
J. Stark, *Priest Gordon of Aberdeen* (Aberdeen, 1909).
The New Statistical Account of Aberdeenshire (Edinburgh, 1843).
The New Statistical Account of Banffshire (Edinburgh, 1842).
The New Statistical Account of Scotland: Banff, Elgin, Nairn (Edinburgh, 1845).
W. L. Taylor, *Bibliography of Peterhead Periodical Literature* (np, 1889).
J. B. Thomson, *The Ministers of the North United Free Church, Aberdeen, 1843-1908* (Aberdeen, 1908).
J. Tracy, *The Great Awakening: A History of the Revival of Religion in the Time of Edwards and Whitefield* [1842] (Edinburgh, 1976).
J. Valentine, *Aberdeen as It Was and Is* (Aberdeen, 1871).
W. Whyte, *Revival in Rose Street: A History of Charlotte Baptist Church, Edinburgh* (Edinburgh, nd).
D. Wilson, *Methodism in Scotland* (Aberdeen, 1850).

SECONDARY SOURCES

Books

W. Alexander, *Rural Life in Victorian Aberdeenshire* [I. Carter ed.] (Edinburgh, 1992).
T. Allan (ed.), *Crusade in Scotland: Billy Graham* (London, 1955).

D. Amand (ed.), *The Moray Book* (Edinburgh, 1976).
R. D. Anderson, *Scottish Education since the Reformation* (Dundee, 1997).
P. F. Anson, *The Catholic Church in Modern Scotland 1560-1937* (London, 1937).
P. F. Anson, *Fisher Folklore* (London, 1965).
P. F. Anson, *Fishermen and Fishing Ways* (London, 1932).
P. F. Anson, *Fishing Boats and Fisherfolk on the East Coast* (London, 1930).
P. F. Anson, *Scots Fisherfolk* (Banff, 1950).
M. Barclay-Harvey, *A History of the Great North of Scotland Railway* (London, nd).
A. Baxter, *Bygone Days of Futtie* (np, 1953).
D. W. Bebbington (ed.), *The Baptists In Scotland: A History* (Glasgow, 1988).
D. W. Bebbington, *Evangelicalism in Modern Britain: A History from the 1730s to the 1980s* (London, 1989).
D. W. Bebbington, *Holiness in the Nineteenth-Century* (Carlisle, 2000).
C. Binfield, *George Williams and the YMCA: A Study in Victorian Social Attitudes* (London, 1973).
E. L. Blumhofer, R. Balmer (ed.), *Modern Christian Revivals* (Illinois, 1993).
D. Brailsford, *Sport, Time and Society: The British at Play* (London, 1991).
C. J. Brown, *The Social History of Religion in Scotland since 1730* (London, 1987).
K. D. Brown, *A Social History of the Nonconformist Ministry in England and Wales 1800-1930* (Oxford, 1988).
J. H. S. Burleigh, *A Church History of Scotland* (London, 1960).
D. Butcher, *Following the Fishing* (London, 1987).
D. K. Cameron, *The Ballad and the Plough* (London, 1978).
D. K. Cameron, *The Cornkister Days: Portrait of a Land and its Rituals* (London, 1984).
N. M. de S. Cameron (ed.), *Dictionary of Scottish Church History and Theology* (Edinburgh, 1993).
J. T. Carson, *God's River in Spate: The Story of the Religious Awakening of Ulster in 1859* (Belfast, 1958).
I. Carter, *Farm Life in North East Scotland, 1840-1914* (Edinburgh, 1979).
R. Carwardine, *Transatlantic Revivalism: Popular Evangelicalism in Britain and America, 1790-1865* (Westport, Connecticut, 1978).
A. C. Cheyne, *The Transforming of the Kirk: Victorian Scotland's Religious Revolution* (Edinburgh, 1983).
D. Clark, *Between Pulpit and Pew: Folk Religion in a North Yorkshire fishing village* (Cambridge, 1992).
N. Cohn, *The Pursuit of the Millennium* (London, 1957).
C. T. Cook, *London Hears Billy Graham* (London, 1954).
W. J. Couper, *Scottish Revivals* (Dundee, 1918).
J. Cranna, *Fraserburgh: Past and Present* (Aberdeen, 1914).
M. J. Crawford, *Seasons of Grace: Colonial New England's Revival Tradition in its British Context* (Oxford, 1991).
R. Currie, A. Gilbert, L. Horsley, *Churches and Churchgoers: Patterns of Church Growth in the British Isles since 1700* (Oxford, 1977).
M. J. Daunton, *Coal Metropolis: Cardiff 1870-1914* (Leicester, 1977).
A. Dickson, J. H. Treble (ed.), *People and Society in Scotland: Volume 3, 1914-1990* (Edinburgh, 1992).
N. Dorian, *The Tyranny of Tide* (Ann Arbor, 1985).

L. W. Dorsett, *Billy Sunday and the Redemption of Urban America* (Grand Rapids, Michigan, 1994).
A. L. Drummond, J. Bulloch, *The Church in Late Victorian Scotland 1874-1900* (Edinburgh, 1978).
A. L. Drummond, J. Bulloch, *The Church in Victorian Scotland 1843-1874* (Edinburgh, 1975).
R. Duncan, *Textiles and Toil: The Factory System and the Industrial Working Class in Early Nineteenth-Century Aberdeen* (Aberdeen, 1984).
F. M. Duthie, *Peterhead Methodist Church: Centenary Souvenir Programme* (Peterhead, 1966).
H. Escott, *A History of Scottish Congregationalism* (Glasgow, 1960).
E. Evans, *Fire in the Thatch: The True Nature of Religious Revival* (Bridgend, Mid Glamorgan, 1996).
E. Evans, *Howell Harris, Evangelist 1714-1773* (Cardiff, 1974).
E. Evans, *Revival comes to Wales: The Story of the 1859 Revival in Wales* (Bridgend, Mid Glamorgan, 1995).
E. J. Evans, *The Forging of the Modern State: Early Industrial Britain 1783-1870* (London, 1983).
A. Everitt, *The Patterns of Rural Dissent: The Nineteenth Century* (Leicester, 1972).
W. Ewing (ed.), *Annals of the Free Church of Scotland 1849-1900* (Edinburgh, 1914).
A. Fawcett, *The Cambuslang Revival: The Scottish Evangelical Revival of the Eighteenth Century* (London, 1971).
J. T. Findlay, *A History of Peterhead* (Aberdeen, 1933).
M. Ford, *Charisma Reports: The Brownsville Revival* (Florida, 1997).
J. Foster, *Class Struggle and the Industrial Revolution: Early Industrial Capitalism in Three English Towns* (London, 1974).
W. H. Fraser, *The Coming of the Mass Market, 1850-1914* (London, 1981).
W.H. Fraser, C.H. Lee (ed.), *Aberdeen 1800-2000 A New History* (East Linton, 2000).
A. Gammie, *Church Life in Fraserburgh Past and Present* (Aberdeen, 1908).
A. Gammie, *The Churches of Aberdeen: Historical and Descriptive* (Aberdeen, 1909).
P. Gibbon, *The Origins of Ulster Unionism: The Formation of Popular Protestant Politics and Ideology in Nineteenth-Century Ireland* (Manchester, 1975).
A. D. Gilbert, *Religion and Society in Industrial England: Church, Chapel and Social Change 1740-1914* (London, 1988).
I. R. Govan, *Spirit of Revival: The Story of J. G. Govan and the Faith Mission* (Edinburgh, 1938).
M. Gray, *The Fishing Industries of Scotland, 1790-1914: A Study in Regional Adaption* (Oxford, 1978).
H. Hamilton (ed.), *The Third Statistical Account of Scotland: The County of Banff* (Glasgow, 1961).
D. Hempton, M. Hill, *Evangelical Protestantism in Ulster Society, 1740-1890* (London, 1992).
D. Hempton, *Methodism and Politics in British Society 1750-1850* (California, 1984).
D. Hempton, *The Religion of the People: Methodism and Popular Religion c.1750-*

1900 (London, 1996).
K. Hylson-Smith, *Evangelicals in the Church of England 1734-1984* (Edinburgh, 1988).
K. S. Inglis, *Churches and the Working Classes in Victorian England* (London, 1963).
A. Keith, *The North of Scotland Bank Limited 1836-1936* (Aberdeen, 1936).
J. Kent, *Holding the Fort: Studies in Victorian Revivalism* (London, 1978).
J. Leatham, *Fisherfolk of the North East* (Turiff, 1930).
D. M. Lloyd-Jones, *The Puritans: Their Origins and Successors* (Edinburgh, 1987).
D. M. Lloyd-Jones, *Revival: Can We Make It Happen?* (London, 1986).
K. T. Long, *The Revival of 1857-58: Interpreting an American Religious Awakening* (New York, 1998).
J. MacInnes, *The Evangelical Movement in the Highlands of Scotland 1688-1800* (Aberdeen, 1951).
H. MacKenzie, *The Third Statistical Account of Scotland: The City of Aberdeen* (Edinburgh, 1953).
A. A. MacLaren, *Religion and Social Class: The Disruption Years in Aberdeen* (London, 1974).
H. McLeod (ed.), *European Religion in the Age of Great Cities, 1830-1930* (London, 1995).
W. G. McLoughlin, *Revivals, Awakenings, and Reform: An Essay on Religion and Social Change in America, 1607-1977* (Chicago, 1978).
J. D. MacMillan (ed.), *Restoration in the Church: Reports of Revivals 1625-1839* (Tain, Ross-shire, 1989).
W. D. McNaughton, *The Scottish Congregational Ministry 1794-1993* (Glasgow, 1993).
J. M. McPherson, *Primitive Beliefs in the North East of Scotland* (London, 1929).
D. Morgan, *The Villages of Aberdeen: Footdee* (Aberdeen, 1993).
I. H. Murray, *Pentecost-Today? The Biblical Basis for Understanding Revival* (Edinburgh, 1998).
I. H. Murray, *The Puritan Hope: Revival and the Interpretation of Prophecy* (Edinburgh, 1971).
R. Neish, *Old Peterhead* (Peterhead, 1950).
M. A. Noll, *A History of Christianity in the United States and Canada* (Grand Rapids, Michigan, 1992).
M. A. Noll, *The Scandal of the Evangelical Mind* (Grand Rapids, Michigan, 1994).
A. C. O' Dell, J. Macintosh (ed.), *The North East of Scotland* (Aberdeen, 1963)
J. Obelkevich, *Religion and Rural Society: South Lindsey 1825-1875* (Oxford, 1976).
J. Ogilvie Skea, *The Free West: A Record of the West Church of St Andrew, Aberdeen 1843-1961* (Aberdeen, 1963).
J. E. Orr, *Evangelical Awakenings in Africa* (Minnesota, 1975).
J. E. Orr, *Evangelical Awakenings in India* (New Delhi, 1970).
J. E. Orr, *The Light of the Nations* (Devon, 1965).
J. E. Orr, *The Second Evangelical Awakening in Britain* (London, 1949).
L. A. Orr MacDonald, *A Unique and Glorious Mission: Women and Presbyterianism in Scotland 1830-1930* (Edinburgh, 2000).
C. N. Peckham, *Heritage of Revival: A Century of Rural Evangelism* (Edinburgh, 1986).
G. A. Rawlyk, *Wrapped up in God: A Study of Several Canadian Revivals and*

Revivalists (Ontario, 1988).
L. E. Schmidt, *Holy Fairs: Scottish Communions and American Revivals in the Early Modern Period* (New Jersey, 1989).
H. Scott, *Fasti Ecclesiae Scoticanne: The Succession of Ministers in the Church of Scotland from the Reformation, Volume Six* (Edinburgh, 1926).
T. Shaw, *A History of Cornish Methodism* (Truro, 1967).
J. Sinclair (ed), *The Statistical Account of Scotland, 1791-1799: Kincardineshire and South and West Aberdeenshire* (Edinburgh, 1982).
A. Skevington Wood, *The Inextinguishable Blaze: Spiritual Renewal and Advance in the Eighteenth Century* (London, 1960).
J.S. Smith and D. Stevenson (ed.), *Aberdeen in the Nineteenth Century* (Aberdeen, 1988).
M. Smith, Religion in Industrial Society: *Oldham and Saddleworth 1740-1865* (Oxford, 1994).
R. Smith, *One Foot in the Sea* (Edinburgh, 1991).
T. L. Smith, *Revivalism and Social Reform in Mid Nineteenth Century America* (New York, 1957).
T. C. Smout, *A Century of the Scottish People* (London, 1986).
H. Sprange, *Kingdom Kids: Children in Revival* (Ross shire, 1994).
D. W. Summers, *Fishing off the Knuckle: The Fishing Villages of Buchan* (Aberdeen, 1988).
L. I. Sweet (ed.), *The Evangelical Tradition in America* (Georgia, 1984).
W. F. Swift, *Methodism in Scotland: The First Hundred Years* (London, 1947).
W. F. Swift, *The Romance of Banffshire Methodism* (Banff, 1927).
J. Taylor, *Rosehearty: Its History as a Fishing Town* (Rosehearty, 1982).
E. P. Thompson, *The Making of the English Working Class* (Middlesex, 1968).
D. M. Valenze, *Prophetic Sons and Daughters: Female Preaching and Popular Religion in Industrial England* (New Jersey, 1985).
H. A. Vallance, *The Great North of Scotland Railway* (London, 1965).
W. M. Walker, *Jutepolis: Dundee and its Textile Workers 1885-1923* (Edinburgh, 1979).
A. Walls, *The Missionary Movement in Christian History: Studies in the Transmission of Faith* (Edinburgh, 1996).
W. R. Ward, *Faith and Faction* (London, 1993).
W. R. Ward, *The Protestant Evangelical Awakening* (Cambridge, 1992).
W. R. Ward, *Religion and Society in England 1790-1850* (London, 1972).
M. R. Watts, *The Dissenters: Volume 2, The Expansion of Evangelical Nonconformity* (Oxford, 1995).
J. S. Werner, *The Primitive Methodist Connexion: Its Background and Early History* (Wisconsin, 1984).
E. Wilkinson, *The Story of Early Methodism in Aberdeen* (np, 1972).
G. Yuille (ed.), *History of the Baptists in Scotland* (Glasgow, 1926).

Component parts of books

J. Baxter, 'The Great Yorkshire Revival 1792-6: A Study of Mass Revival among the Methodists' in *A Sociological Yearbook of Religion in Britain, 7* (London, 1974).
D. W. Bebbington, 'Mission in Scotland, 1846-1946', in D. Searle (ed.), *Death or*

Glory: The Church's Mission in Scotland's Changing Society (Edinburgh, 2001).
T. Bilhartz, 'Sex and the Second Great Awakening: The Feminisation of American Religion Reconsidered' in P. Vandermeer and R. Swierenga (ed.), *Belief and Behaviour: Essays in the New Religious History* (New Brunswick, NJ, 1991).
L. Billington, 'Revivalism and Popular Religion' in E. M. Sigworth (ed.), *In Search of Victorian Values: Aspects of Nineteenth Century Thought and Society* (Manchester, 1988).
S. J. Brown, 'Presbyterian Communities, Transatlantic Visions and the Ulster Revival of 1859' in J. P. Mackey (ed.), *The Cultures of Europe: The Irish Contribution* (Belfast, 1994).
S. J. Brown, 'Thomas Chalmers and the Communal Ideal in Victorian Scotland' in T. C. Smout (ed.), *Victorian Values* (Oxford, 1992).
R.H. Campbell, 'The Landed Classes' in T. M. Devine, R. Mitchison (ed.), *People and Society in Scotland, Volume 1, 1760-1830* (Edinburgh, 1988).
R. H. Campbell, T. M. Devine, 'The Rural Experience' in W. H. Fraser, R. J. Morris (ed.), *People and Society in Scotland, Volume 2, 1830-1914* (Edinburgh, 1990).
I. Carter, 'Class and Culture among the Farm Servants in the North East, 1840-1914' in A. A. MacLaren (ed.), *Social Class in Scotland: Past and Present* (Edinburgh, 1976).
R. Carwardine, 'Religious Revival and Political Renewal in Antebellum America' in J. Garnett, C. Matthew (ed.), *Revival and Religion since 1700: Essays for John Walsh* (London, 1993).
J. Coffey, 'Democracy and Popular Religion: Moody and Sankey's Mission to Britain, 1873-1875' in E. F. Biagini (ed.), *Citizenship and Community: Liberals, Radicals and Collective Identities in the British Isles, 1865-1931* (Cambridge, 1996).
R. Colls, 'Primitive Methodists in the Northern Coalfields' in J. Obelkevich, L. Roper, R. Samuel (ed.), *Disciplines of Faith: Studies in Religion, Politics and Patriarchy* (London, 1987).
J. R. Coull, 'The Fisherfolk and Fishing Settlements of the Grampian region' in J. S. Smith, D. Stevenson (ed.), *Fermfolk and Fisherfolk: Rural Life in Northern Scotland in the Eighteenth and Nineteenth Centuries* (Aberdeen, 1989).
N. Dickson, 'Open and Closed: Brethren and their Origins in the North East' in J. Porter (ed.), *After Columba, after Calvin: Religious Community in North East Scotland* (Aberdeen, 1999).
M. Gray, 'Farm Workers in North East Scotland' in T. M. Devine (ed.), *Farm Servants and Labour in Lowland Scotland* (Edinburgh, 1984).
M. Gray, 'Fishing Villages, 1750-1880' in A. C. O' Dell, J. Macintosh (ed.), *The North East of Scotland* (Aberdeen, 1963).
M. Gray, 'North East Agriculture and the Labour Force, 1790-1875' in A. A. MacLaren (ed.), *Social Class in Scotland: Past and Present* (Edinburgh, 1976).
M. Gray, 'The Regions and their Issues: Scotland' in G.E. Mingay (ed.), *The Victorian Countryside* (London, 1981).
M. Gray, 'The Social Impact of Agrarian Change in the Rural Lowlands' in T. M. Devine, R. Mitchison (ed.), *People and Society in Scotland, Volume 1, 1760-1830* (Edinburgh, 1988).

D. E. Meek, 'Evangelicalism and Emigration: Aspects of the Role of Dissenting Evangelicalism in Highland Emigration to Canada' in G. MacLennan (ed.), *Proceedings of the First North American Congress of Celtic Studies* (Ottawa, 1988).

D. E. Meek, 'Gaelic Bible, Revival and Mission: The Spiritual Rebirth of the Nineteenth-Century Highlands' in J. Kirk (ed.), *The Church in the Highlands* (Edinburgh, 1999).

A. Noble, 'The Evangelical Tradition among the Fisherfolk of North East Scotland' in J. Porter (ed.), *After Columba, after Calvin: Religious Community in North East Scotland* (Aberdeen, 1999).

J. Rule, 'Methodism, Popular Beliefs and Village Culture in Cornwall, 1800-50' in R. D. Storch (ed.), *Popular Culture and Custom in Nineteenth-Century England* (London, 1982).

L. E. Schmidt, 'Time, Celebration and the Christian Year in Eighteenth-Century Evangelicalism' in M. A. Noll, G. A. Rawlyk, D. W. Bebbington (ed.), *Evangelicalism: Comparative Studies of Popular Protestantism in North America, the British Isles and Beyond 1700-1990* (New York, 1994).

T. C. Smout, 'The Landowner and the Planned Village in Scotland' in N. T. Phillipson, R. Mitchison (ed.), *Scotland in the Age of Improvement: Essays in Scottish History in the Eighteenth Century* (Edinburgh, 1970).

C. B. Turner, 'Revivalism and Welsh Society in the Nineteenth Century' in J. Obelkevich, L. Roper, R. Samuel (ed.), *Disciplines of Faith: Studies in Religion, Politics and Patriarchy* (London, 1987).

K. Walton, 'Regional Settlement' in A. C. O' Dell, J. Macintosh (ed.), *The North East of Scotland: British Association* (Aberdeen, 1963).

W. R. Ward, 'The Evangelical Revival in Eighteenth-Century Britain' in S. Gilley, W. J. Sheils (ed.), *A History of Religion in Britain* (Oxford, 1994).

D. J. Withrington, 'The Idea of Religious Community at the Disruption' in J. Porter (ed.), *After Columba, after Calvin: Religious Community in North East Scotland* (Aberdeen, 1999).

Articles

O. Anderson, 'Women Preachers in mid-Victorian Britain: Some Reflections on Feminism, Popular Religion and Social Change', *The Historical Journal*, 12, 1969.

S. R. Baillie, 'The Structure of Population in Traditional Communities of North East Scotland: Whitehills and Gardenstown', *Northern Scotland*, 6, 1984.

D. W. Bebbington, 'Evangelical Conversion, c. 1740 – 1850', *North Atlantic Missiology Project, Position Paper Number 21*, University of Cambridge, 1996.

C. G. Brown, 'The Sunday School Movement in Scotland, 1780-1914', *Records of the Scottish Church History Society*, 21, 1981.

S. Bruce, 'Born Again: Conversion, Crusades and Brainwashing', *The Scottish Journal of Religious Studies*, 3, 1982.

S. Bruce, 'Social Change and Collective Behaviour: The Revival in Eighteenth Century Ross shire', *British Journal of Sociology*, 34, 1983.

I. Carter, 'Social Differentiation in the Aberdeenshire Peasantry', *Journal of Peasant Studies*, 5, 1977.

R. Carwardine, 'The Welsh Evangelical Community and Finney's Revivals',

Journal of Ecclesiastical History, 29, 1978.
J. R. Coull, 'The Scottish Herring Fishery: Development and Intensification of a Pattern of Resource Use', *Scottish Geographical Magazine*, 102, 1986.
R. Currie, R. M. Hartwell, 'The Making of the English Working Class?', *Economic History Review*, 2, 1965.
N. Dickson, 'Brethren and Baptists in Scotland', The Baptist Quarterly, 33, 1990.
J.P. Dodd, 'The 1854 Agricultural Statistics for the North East of Scotland: An Analysis', *Northern Scot*, 5, 1983.
J. L. Duthie, 'The Fisherman's Religious Revival', *History Today*, December 1983.
J. L. Duthie, 'Philanthropy and Evangelism among Aberdeen Seamen, 1814-1924', *Scottish Historical Review*, 63, 1984.
C. D. Field, 'Adam and Eve: Gender in the English Free Church Constituency', *Journal of Ecclesiastical History*, 44, 1993.
B. Harrison, 'Religion and Recreation in Nineteenth-Century England', *Past and Present*, 38, 1967.
M. Hill, 'Ulster Awakened: The '59 Revival Reconsidered', *Journal of Ecclesiastical History*, 41, 1990.
P. L. M. Hillis, 'Presbyterianism and Social Class in Mid-nineteenth-Century Glasgow: A Study of Nine Churches', *Journal of Ecclesiastical History*, 32, 1981.
W. Jamieson, 'Methodist Churches in the North East of Scotland', *Wesleyan History Society Scottish Branch Journal*, 23, 1993.
K. S. Jeffrey, 'Physical Phenomena in the 1859 Ulster Revival', *The Rutherford Journal*, 5, 2, 1998.
N. Landsman, 'Evangelists and Their Hearers: Popular Interpretation of Revivalist Preaching in Eighteenth-Century Scotland', *Journal of British Studies*, 28, 1989.
D. G. Lockhart, 'Migration to Planned Villages in Scotland between 1725 and 1850', *Scottish Geographical Magazine*, 102, 1986.
D. G. Lockhart, 'The Planned Villages of Aberdeenshire: The Evidence from Newspaper Advertisements', *Scottish Geographical Magazine*, 94, 1978.
D. Luker, 'Revivalism in Theory and Practice: The Case of Cornish Methodism', *Journal of Ecclesiastical History*, 37, 1986.
D. E. Meek, 'Evangelical Missionaries in the Early Nineteenth Century Highlands', *Scottish Studies*, 28, 1987.
D. E. Meek, "Falling Down as if Dead': Attitudes to Unusual Phenomena in the Skye revival of 1841-42', *Scottish Bulletin of Evangelical Theology*, 13, 1995.
D. E. Meek, "Fishers of Men': The 1921 Religious Revival, its Cause, Context and Transmission', *Scottish Bulletin of Evangelical Theology*, 17, 1999.
D. W. Millar, 'Presbyterianism and "Modernization" in Ulster', *Past and Present*, 80, 1978.
I. A. Muirhead, 'The Revival as a Dimension of Scottish Church History', *Scottish Church History Society Records*, 20, 1980.
J. Sharp, 'Juvenile Holiness: Catholic Revivalism among Children in Victorian Britain', *Journal of Ecclesiastical History*, 35, 1984.
T. C. Smout, 'Born Again at Cambuslang: New Evidence on Popular Religion and Literacy in Scotland', *Past and Present*, 97, 1982.
E. P. Thompson, 'Time, Work-Discipline and Industrial Capitalism', *Past and*

Present, 38, 1967.
M. Van Die, 'The Marks of a Genuine Revival: Religion, Social Change, Gender and Community in Mid Victorian Brantford, Ontario', *The Canadian Historical Review*, 79, 1998.
R. B. Walker, 'The Growth of Wesleyan Methodism in Victorian England and Wales', *Journal of Ecclesiastical History*, 24, 1973.
C. R. Williams, 'The Welsh Religious Revival, 1904-5', *British Journal of Sociology*, 3, 1952.
D. J. Withrington, 'The 1851 Census of Religious Worship and Education: with a Note on Church Accommodation in Mid-Nineteenth-Century Scotland', *Records of the Scottish Church History Society*, 18, 1973.

Unpublished theses and dissertations

A. R. Acheson, 'The Evangelicals in the Church of Ireland, 1784-1859', unpublished PhD thesis, Queen's University, Belfast, 1967.
R. J. Carwardine, 'American Religious Revivalism in Great Britain c1826-c1863', unpublished D.Phil. thesis, University of Oxford, 1974.
R. E. Chadwick, 'Church and People in Bradford and District, 1880-1914: The Protestant Churches in an Urban Industrial Environment', unpublished D.Phil. thesis, University of Oxford, 1986.
N. Dickson, 'The History of the Open Brethren in Scotland, 1838-1999', unpublished PhD thesis, University of Stirling, 2000.
J. E. Holmes, 'Religious Revivalism and Popular Evangelicalism in Britain and Ireland, 1859-1905', unpublished D.Phil. thesis, Queen's University, Belfast, 1995.
K. S. Jeffrey, 'The Ulster Revival of 1859', unpublished undergraduate dissertation, University of Stirling, 1992.
L. Jeffrey, 'Women in the Churches of Nineteenth Century Stirling', unpublished M.Litt. thesis, University of Stirling, 1996.
C. J. Marrs, 'The 1859 Religious Revival in Scotland: A Review and Critique of the Movement with Particular Reference to the City of Glasgow', unpublished PhD thesis, University of Glasgow, 1995.
P. B. Morgan, 'A Study of the Work of American Revivalists in Britain from 1870-1914, and of the Effect upon Organised Christianity of their Work Here', unpublished B.Litt.thesis, Oxford University, 1961.
R. J. Rice, 'Religious Revivalism and British Methodism, 1855-65', unpublished PhD thesis, University of Illinois, 1979.
G. B. Robertson, 'Spiritual Awakening in the North East of Scotland and the Disruption of the Church in 1843', unpublished PhD thesis, University of Aberdeen, 1970.
H. J. Rowe, 'The Geographical Distribution of Non-Established Protestant Churches in Stirlingshire and Clackmannanshire in the Mid Nineteenth Century', unpublished undergraduate dissertation, University of Stirling, 1998.
A. R. Scott, 'The Ulster Revival of 1859', unpublished PhD thesis, Trinity College, Dublin, 1962.

Unpublished articles

W. Chalmers, 'Brief History of the Testimony on the Moray Coast'

I. Hutchison, 'Residential Distribution of the Elite of Aberdeen, 1860'

K. S. Jeffrey, 'Work, Rest and Play: The Integration of the 1859 Revival into the Social and Working Lives of the Townsfolk, Fermfolk and Fisherfolk of the North East of Scotland', a paper presented at the Ecclesiastical History Society Annual Summer Conference at Cambridge, July 1999.

Appendix 1

The method by which those who were affected by the revival were identified

An attempt was made to analyse the converts of the 1859 revival by identifying those who joined churches during the period of the movement. Church documents, including kirk session minutes, communion rolls and membership lists, were examined. They provided various details of men and women who constituted the new members. On occasions only the number of people who joined congregations was recorded, in other places names were provided, while in some instances names and addresses were chronicled. Subsequently an attempt was made to find these people in the relevant published census of 1861. When this was successful a more complete profile emerged of the new church members, including details of their age, marital status and employment. Then it became possible to examine the type of person who was most likely affected by this religious movement.

However, certain problems arose in this attempt to identify the converts of the revival. In the first instance it would appear that a number of those who were influenced by the movement were already nominal members of the congregations that were examined. Alexander M'Kenzie, the Free Church minister at Nairn in 1859, noticed how the revival 'quickened' religious people and that 'communicants were no longer satisfied with being members of the church' but felt the need to be 'born again'.[1] It seems likely then that a significant minority, perhaps as many as a third, of those who were affected by the revival were communicant members of congregations. They were not counted among the new members who joined the churches during the movement, and as a result it was not possible to include them in the examination of the 'converts'.

Also the membership rolls and kirk session minutes did not provide a detailed account of the circumstances that surrounded how each person became a young communicant of the church. Consequently it was not practicable to distinguish those who converted as a result of the revival from those who professed faith for the first time during the same period apart from the movement. It is fortunate, however, that those who joined a congregation by transfer from another church could be separated from those who were admitted to the fellowship upon their first profession of faith. Therefore the inference was made that a large proportion of those who joined the church upon a first profession of faith at this time can be considered as likely converts of the revival.

The identification of converts is an important feature of the thesis because the composition of those who were affected by the revival in each of the three separate situations reveals further the distinctive appearance of the movement as it became manifest across the north east of Scotland.

Note

1. *A Report of Conference on the State of Religion and Public Meeting, held in the Free Church, Huntly, January 5, 1860* (Huntly, 1860), p. 15.

Appendix 2

Social Classification System Used

High Status (Upper Middle Class)

A. *Professional Group (Usually University Graduates)*
   1. Advocates.
   2. Lecturers, physicians, surgeons.
   3. Ministers of religion.

B. *Commercial Group*
   1. Bank managers
   2. Accountants

C. *Large Merchant – Manufacturing Group*
   1. Suppliers of consumer goods and services catering for the middle classes, for example, suppliers of food and wines.

D. *Retired – Rentier Group*
   1. Ship Owners
   2. Those retired and living on private means. Annuitants and those living on interest from shares or capital. House and landed proprietors.
   3. Farmers

Middling Status (Lower middle class)

E. *Public Servants I*
   1. Local government officials.
   2. Ship masters, army sergeants, station masters.
   3. Post masters.

F. *Public Servants II*

1. Teachers
2. Bankers clerks, law clerks.

G. *Small Merchant – Tradesman Group*

1. Shopkeepers, hotel keepers.
2. Spirit dealers, chemists, antique dealers, tobacconists, china merchants.
3. Self-employed tradesman, commercial travellers.
4. Foremen, small timber merchants, managers
5. Dancing masters, lodging house keepers.

The Working Classes

H. *Artisans*

1. Bakers, joiners, tailors, coach makers, smiths, milliners, painters, carpenters, plumbers, dressmakers and others involved in skilled employment.
2. Domestic servants. (20%)

I. *Unskilled*

1. Labourers, carters, porters, farm servants, washer women, power loom turners, cleaners, lamp lighters, guides, factory hands, dairymen.
2. Domestic servants. (80%)

Sources

P. L. M. Hillis, 'Presbyterianism and Social Class in mid-nineteenth-century Glasgow, a study of nine churches', *Journal of Ecclesiastical History*, 32, 1981, pp. 48-9.

L. Jeffrey, 'Women in the Churches of Nineteenth-Century Stirling', unpublished M. Litt. dissertation, University of Stirling, 1996, p. 112.

Index

A

Aberdeen 1, 2, 9, 39, 40, 42, 43, 44, 49, 50, 51, 52, 53, 54, 55, 56, 57, 58, 59, 60, 61, 63, 64, 65, 69, 70, 75, 76, 77, 78, 79, 81, 83, 84, 85, 86, 87, 89, 90, 91, 93, 94, 95, 97, 98, 99, 100, 101, 103, 104, 105, 107, 108, 113, 114, 115, 122, 124, 128, 129, 130, 135, 159, 162, 165, 173, 174, 177, 185, 190, 192, 193, 196, 220, 227, 234, 235, 245, 246, 249, 253, 256, 257, 258, 259, 260, 261, 263, 264
Aberdeen Almanac 132
Aberdeen Bible Society 63
Aberdeen Citizen 43
Aberdeen City Mission 52
Aberdeen Evangelistic Association 53
Aberdeen Free Press 43, 58, 63, 133, 196, 235, 239
Aberdeen Harbour 50
Aberdeen Herald 42, 75, 81, 195, 210, 226, 249
Aberdeen Journal 43, 68, 185
Aberdeen Music Hall 58, 61, 108
Aberdeen Musical Association 60
Aberdeen Saturday Post 43
Aberdeen University 58, 67, 106
Aberdeen Young Men's Missionary Union 122
Aberdeenshire 113, 114, 115, 116, 117, 118, 125, 127, 152
Aberlour 142, 145
Aboyne 135
Adam, John 86
Africa 1
Agricultural Improvements 113
Ahoghill 49
Albion Street Congregational Church 56, 77, 85, 99
Albion Street, Aberdeen 57
Alexander, J. 116
Alexander, Jacob 259
Alford 162
Allan, Alexander 226
Allan, Jessie 226
Allan, John 197, 209
Allen, John 98
Alves 127
America 1, 2, 3, 9, 10, 15, 29, 32, 34, 38, 55, 75, 117, 118, 135, 189, 200, 260
American Awakenings 32
American revival of 1857-58 16, 36, 44, 52, 54, 55, 56, 62, 65, 69, 75, 98, 108, 118, 122, 135, 187, 189, 234, 236, 246, 253, 258, 261
Anglican Church 11, 155
Anson, Peter 183, 211, 228
anxious seat 18, 63
Arbuthnot, J. 239
Archibald, George 127
Ardclach 119, 132
Arminian 79, 263
Armley 98
Armstrong, Miss 108
Arran 2
Asia 1
Atonement 263
Auchendoir 145

B

Baillie, Susan 199
Bain, George 116, 118, 128, 130, 134, 174
Bala 98
Baldernock 2
Balfour, John 6
Ballater 124
Ballymena 189
Banchory 116, 124, 125, 128, 131, 134, 135, 151, 157, 165, 170, 174, 175

Banchory Parish Church 142
Banchory Ternan Free Church 146,
    168, 171, 172, 173, 175
Banff 124, 125, 133, 181, 182, 185,
    189, 193, 196, 207, 209, 211, 212,
    216, 217, 218, 219, 220, 221, 222,
    223, 224, 226, 227, 240, 245, 247
Banff Free Church 190, 215, 216, 218,
    220, 221, 223, 224, 226
Banff United Presbyterian Church
    217, 220, 221, 223, 226
Banffshire 195, 233
Banffshire Journal 43, 135, 192, 209,
    224
baptism 184
Baptist Church 9, 11, 12, 102, 103
Baptist Church in Aberdeen 43, 76,
    93
Baptist Church in Aberdeenshire 141
Baptist Church in Brantford, Ontario
    95
Baptist Church in Broadford 8
Baptist Church in Elgin 212, 217
Baptist Church in Fraserburgh 229
Baptist Church in Grantown on
    Spey 33
Baptist Church in Highlands and
    Islands 10
Baptist Church in Lossiemouth 212
Baptist Church in Peterhead 229, 239
Baptist Preacher 18
Barritt, Mary 12
Barrowclough, William 212
Barvas 21
Baxter, John 28
Baxter, Richard 129
Baxter, Thomas 124, 133, 182, 189,
    207, 212, 216, 219, 224, 249
Bebbington, D.W. 13, 19, 28, 35, 98
Bede, Adam 12
Belfast 128
Bellie Free Church 214, 226
Belmont Street Congregational
    Church 54
Belmont Street United Presbyterian
    Church 56, 60, 77
Bertram, James 198
Bible and tract distribution 63

Bilston 33
Birse 162
Bo'ness 189
Boddam 233
Bon Accord Free Church 54, 65, 67,
    85, 94
Bonar, Andrew 67, 129, 259
Botriphinie 145
Bourne, Hugh 13
Bouverie, Fred W.B. 78
Bowman, Robert 9
Boyndie 125
Bradford 103
Braemar 125
Braemar Free Church 145
Bramwell, William 12
Bramwell-Pipe revival 30
Brand, Alexander 234
Brantford, Ontario 17, 31, 36, 91, 95,
    97, 103, 107
Breadalbane 10, 11
Brethren Assemblies 226, 228, 229,
    230
Brethren Assemblies, Closed 227
Brethren Assemblies, Open 227
Brethren Assembly, Aberdeen 227
Britain 1, 3, 32, 38, 49, 51, 55, 102,
    250
British and Foreign Evangelical
    Review 54, 108
British Association 51
British Evangelist 42, 54, 56, 65, 77
British Messenger 42, 52, 53, 54, 55,
    62, 64, 94, 99, 106, 117, 183, 187,
    191, 195, 207, 253
Broad Hill, Aberdeen 260
Broad Street Hall, Peterhead 244
Broadsea 197, 233
Brown, Callum 30, 90, 155
Brown, David 55
Brown, J.C. 56
Brown, K.D. 19, 98
Brown, S.J. 35
Brownlow North 42, 53, 56
Bruce, Steve 29
Buchan, P. 239
Buchanan, James 261, 262
Buchanan, Robert 37, 52

Index 293

Buchanhaven 185, 235
Buckie 182, 183, 192, 198, 207, 211, 216, 217, 224, 229, 233, 247, 249
Bulloch, James 3, 68
Burghead 192, 193, 206, 211, 233
Burleigh, J.H.S. 3
Burnhaven 185, 235, 240
Burns, W.C. 64, 98
Burns, W.H. 34

C

Cairnbulg 233
Cairns, John 263
Caithness 193
Calder, George 185
Calvinist 130, 257, 263
Calvinists 18, 129
Cambuslang 2, 3, 5, 6, 7, 8, 9, 29, 30, 38, 90, 91, 95, 97, 98, 103, 176
Cameron, David Kerr 132
Camp Meeting 135
Campbell, Duncan 2, 21
Campbell, George 58, 61, 81, 85
Campbell, John Mcleod 263
Captain Shepherd of Kirkville, Skene 89
Carnie, William 59
Carter, I. 115, 153
Carter, William 259
Carwardine, R. 17, 29, 32, 33, 35, 258
Castleton 125
Catholicism 4
cattle trade 114, 165, 257
cattlemen 171
Cellardyke, Fife 35
Chadwick, R.E. 103
Chalmers, Thomas 52, 261
Chapel of Garioch 116, 118, 135, 142, 174
Chapels of Ease 85
Charlestown 233
Chicago 18
child converts 224
children 99, 173, 174, 224, 229, 235
cholera epidemic of 1832 33, 34
Church of England 11

Church of Scotland 2, 43, 77, 141, 142, 144, 162, 176, 181, 182, 183, 227, 237, 239
Church of Scotland, Aberdeen Presbytery 81
Clackmannanshire 155
Clatt 155
clearances 30
Clola Free Church 119
Clowes, William 13
Cluny Parish Church 143
Cockburn, Lord 114
Coffey, John 32
Coleraine 128
Colton, Calvin 15, 129, 244
communion seasons 4, 5, 6, 9, 134, 135, 136, 254, 258
Congregational Church 9, 12, 102, 103
Congregational Church in Aberdeen 76
Congregational Church in Aberdeenshire 141
Congregational Church in Banff 217
Congregational Church in Brantford, Ontario 17, 95
Congregational Church in Elgin 212
Congregational Church in Highlands and Islands 10
Congregational Church in Macduff 217
Congregational Church in Peterhead 235, 236, 238
Congregational Church in Portsoy 217
Congregational Church, Albion St., Aberdeen 57
Congregational Church, George St., Aberdeen 76, 97
Congregational Church, George Street, Aberdeen 105
Congregational Churches in Aberdeen 43, 92, 93
conversion 9, 13, 19, 53, 64, 68, 70, 76, 98, 125, 126, 129, 130, 131, 136, 184, 185, 191, 192, 200, 224, 236, 246, 248, 254, 256, 257, 263
Converts of Aberdeen Revival of

1859 – Class Composition 90
Converts of Aberdeen Revival of 1859 – Gender 102
Converts of Aberdeen Revival of 1859 – Geographical Distribution 87
Converts of Aberdeen Revival of 1859 – Marital Status 95
Converts of Aberdeen Revival of 1859 – Religious Background 86
Converts of Aberdeen Revival – Age 97
Converts of Aberdeenshire Revival of 1859 126, 136
Converts of Aberdeenshire Revival of 1859 – Age 172
Converts of Aberdeenshire Revival of 1859 – Class Composition 170
Converts of Aberdeenshire Revival of 1859 – Gender 174
Converts of Aberdeenshire Revival of 1859 – Marital Status 172
Converts of Aberdeenshire Revival of 1859 – Religious Background 168
Converts of Cambuslang Revival of 1742 8
Converts of Moray Firth Revival of 1839 125, 190
Converts of Moray Firth Revival of 1859 – Age 222
Converts of Moray Firth Revival of 1859 – Class Competition 220
Converts of Moray Firth Revival of 1859 – Gender 224
Converts of Moray Firth Revival of 1859 – Marital Status 221
Converts of Moray Firth Revival of 1859 – Religious Background 218
Cornwall 10, 11, 30, 207, 218
Couper, W.J. 5, 20, 27, 38
Couper, William 129
Covenanters 2
Cowan, Professor 58
Craigdam United Presbyterian Church 148, 149
Cranna, John 184, 227

Crathes 165
Craven, John 86
Crawford, M.J. 5
cricket 59, 60
Crimean War 115
Crimond 187
Crombie, John 78
Crovie 227
Crown Street, Aberdeen 89
Cullen 41, 182, 199, 217, 227, 244
Cullen Free Church 213
Culsamond 127, 130, 142
Culsamond Free Church 119, 130
Culter 165
Cults 165
Currie, R. 29
Cutler, Ann 12

D

Dalzeil, George 261
Daviot 162, 165, 168, 171, 172, 173, 175
Daviot Parish Church 143, 144, 171, 172, 173, 175
death 35, 185, 186, 200, 244
Deer 162
desire 9, 118, 120, 135, 187, 190, 245, 248, 254, 258, 259
Desire of Revival 250, 253
Deskford 117, 124, 126, 128, 130, 153, 157, 170, 174, 184
Dickson, David 5
Diffusion of the Revival 122, 125, 162, 192, 193
Disruption 79, 86, 89, 261
domestic servants 91, 94, 171, 220, 221
Donald, William 233, 238, 241
Dorian, Nancy 30
Douglas, James 108, 253
Dow, Lorenzo 135
Dower, William 125
Drainy Parish Church 212
Drum 165
Drummond, Andrew 3, 68
Drummond, Peter 42, 56, 66, 253

Index

Drumoak 162
Duncan, John 85
Duncan, Robert 51
Dundas, Alexander 185
Dundee 2, 16, 94, 236, 246
Dunnet Bay 185
Durham 6, 238
Durham, James 6
Durris 135, 162
Duthie, J.L. 30
Dyce 165

E

East Coast Mission 239, 240
East Lothian 37
Echt 142
economic circumstances and revival 30, 49, 114, 186, 200, 257, 258
Edinburgh 2, 16, 42, 43, 236
Edwards, Jonathan 1, 9, 35
Elgin 175, 196, 208, 212, 217
Elgin and Morayshire Courier 192, 208, 217
Elgin High Free Church 147, 168, 172, 175
Eliot, George 12
Ellon 142, 162
Emslie, William 145
enclosure 113, 114
England 9, 10, 14, 33, 34, 155
English Episcopal Chapels 76, 78
English Episcopal Church in Aberdeen 78
Enlightenment 14
Entwisle, Joseph 13
epidemic illnesses 33
Episcopal Church in Aberdeenshire 141, 150, 176
Episcopal Church in Glasgow 259
Episcopal church in Peterhead 237, 238, 239
Episcopal Churches in Aberdeen 43
Established Church 69, 76, 77, 79, 80, 85, 89, 141, 142, 144, 152, 159, 162, 176, 190, 212, 213, 237, 238
Established Church in Glasgow 259

Established Church in Peterhead 237, 238, 239
ethnic and cultural homogeneity 199, 200
Europe 1, 34
Evangelical Alliance 64
Evangelical Union Church 77, 263
Evangelical Union Church in Aberdeen 43, 76, 84, 93, 105
Evangelical Union Church in Peterhead 239
Evangelicalism 238
Evangelicals 250
evangelists 66, 67, 127
Everitt, Alan 152, 153
Expectancy of Revival 9, 118, 120, 122, 135, 187, 189, 190, 200, 250, 253, 254, 258, 259

F

Falkirk 155
farm servants 116
Fawcett, Arthur 2
feeing markets 133, 134
Field, C.D. 98, 102
Findlay, George 183, 197
Findochty 124, 181, 182, 183, 189, 192, 193, 195, 196, 197, 206, 207, 208, 217, 227, 229, 233, 240
Finney, C.G. 15, 17, 18, 19, 20, 32, 38, 63, 64, 70, 129, 256
Fintray 115
Fishing Villages 181, 186, 203, 233, 237, 242, 243, 244, 245, 258
Fleming, Robert 3
Footdee 185, 195, 198
Forbes, Sir J.S. 185
Fordyce 162, 193
Fordyce Free Church 213
Fordyce Free Presbytery 118
Forgue Free Church 119
Forlong, Gordon 53, 116, 234, 235, 238, 248, 249
Forres 216, 217
Forres, Nairn and Elgin Gazette 206
Forrester, John 209

Fraser, Alexander 40, 116
Fraser, Donald 120
Fraser, W.H. 59
Fraserburgh 41, 184, 187, 196, 197, 204, 213, 217, 227, 229, 233, 240
Fraserburgh Advertiser 186, 189
Free Church 37, 38, 43, 52, 54, 67, 69, 76, 77, 81, 83, 85, 115, 116, 117, 118, 119, 120, 127, 128, 129, 131, 136, 141, 142, 144, 145, 147, 152, 159, 162, 176, 183, 184, 190, 192, 207, 209, 212, 213, 216, 218, 219, 226, 227, 228, 229, 234, 237, 238, 239, 261, 262
Free Church General Assembly 52, 55
Free Church in Portsoy 215
Free Church – Aberdeen Synod 99, 116
Free Church, Aberdeen 90
Free Church, Bon Accord, Aberdeen 77
Free Church, East, Aberdeen 76, 77
Free Church, North, Aberdeen 77
Free Church, Presbytery of Aberlour 162
Free Church, Presbytery of Deer 162
Free Church, Presbytery of Fordyce 190
Free Church, Presbytery of Forres 162
Free Church, South, Aberdeen 54, 60, 76, 77, 92, 96, 100, 104
Free Church, West, Aberdeen 76, 77
Free East Church, Aberdeen 86
Free North Church, Aberdeen 58, 81, 85, 89
Free Presbytery of Ellon 127
Free South Church, Aberdeen 75, 81, 82, 86, 92, 93, 96, 97, 101, 105
Free Tron Church, Glasgow 52
Free Union Church, Aberdeen 76
Free West Church, Aberdeen 54, 81
French Revolution 34
French War 50
friendly societies 185
Friends 76
Fyvie 118, 135

G

Gallowgate 76, 89
Galway, Ireland 12
Gammie, Alexander 66, 79, 81
Gamrie Parish 241
Gardenstown 189, 193, 199, 206, 208, 211, 233, 241
Gardiner, James 181
Gardner, Archibald 120, 128, 130, 131, 170
Garioch 162
Garmouth 209
Gartly 165
Gauld, William 67
Gentle, Alexander 127
George Street Congregational Church, Aberdeen 77, 84, 92, 96, 100, 104
Gibbon, Peter 30
Gilbert, Alan 155
Gilcomston, Aberdeen 40, 89
Gilfillan, George 246
Gillies, John 1, 27
Glasgow 2, 6, 39, 42, 52, 58, 90, 91, 259, 260, 261
Glasgow Herald 17
Glassites 76
Glenbucket 157, 159
Glengairn 157, 159
Glenlivet 159
Glenmuick 157, 159
Golf Club, Aberdeen 60
Golspie 6, 9
Goodrich, Chauncey A. 250
Gordon of Parkhill, John 53, 56, 58, 65, 116
Gordon, Duchess of 125, 133
Gordon, Dukes of 153
Gordon, M.M. 42
Graham, Billy 2, 21, 103, 264
Graham, H.G. 183
Graham, Miss 108, 236
Grange 126
granite industries 51
Grant, Francis 181, 185, 187
Grant, Peter 239
Grantown on Spey 33

Index

Gray, Gordon 55, 56, 122, 165
Gray, Malcolm 196
Gray, Thomas 145
Great North of Scotland Railway 245
Greig, George 53
Greyfriars Free Church 89
Greyfriars Parish Church 57, 58, 67, 79, 80
Greyfriars Parish Church, Aberdeen 62, 77, 85, 89, 106
Greyfriars Parish, Aberdeen 89
Guinness, Grattan 56, 57, 63, 76

H

Haldanes 10
Halévy 28
Halley, William 6
Hammond, E.P. 18, 259
Hartwell, R.M. 29
Hawick 114
Hayslope 12
Hempton, David 10, 29, 34, 38
Henderson, George 181, 199, 244
Henry, David 1, 117, 120, 132
Henry, Matthew 129
herring fishing industry 186
Herring Fishing Season 187, 203, 204, 256, 257, 258
Heugh-head 157
Highlands 2, 4, 8, 10, 11, 12, 29, 30
Hill, Myrtle 36, 38
Hillis, P.L.M. 90, 91
historiography of revivals 27
Hobsbawm, E.J. 28, 29
Holburn Free Church 77
Holburn Parish Church 76, 77, 80, 85, 87, 92, 93, 96, 100, 101, 104, 105
Holburn, Aberdeen 40, 89
Holmes, Janice 36
Homogeneity of Fishing Villages 196
Hopeman 190, 192, 193, 206, 208
Hopper, Christopher 238
horsemen 132

Hull 33, 98
Huntly 1, 58, 116, 120, 124, 125, 128, 131, 133, 135, 153, 157, 165, 170, 175, 196
Huntly Conferences of Revival 125
Huntly United Presbyterian Church 118, 131, 148, 168, 171, 172, 175
hymn singing 3, 69
hymns 20, 68, 76, 190, 191, 210

I

Inch 142
Ingram, William 127, 131
Innes, Alexander Taylor 262
Inquiry meeting 64
Inquiry rooms 18
Insch 133, 142, 165
Insch Free Church 119, 145, 146, 168
Insch Parish Church 132
Inverallochy 185, 233
Inveraven 159
Inveravon 145, 157, 159
Inverness 120, 235
Inverurie 142, 157, 165, 171
Inverurie Free Church 145
Ireland 12, 64, 118, 128, 130, 189, 200
Irish ministers 189
Irish revival 128, 189
Irvine 2, 5, 9, 34
Isolation of Fishing Villages 196, 197, 200
itinerant evangelists 53, 66, 70, 116, 122, 127, 128, 136, 184, 192, 238, 259, 260

J

Jacobite Rising 29
Jedburgh 2
Jeffrey, Linda 90, 91
John Knox Parish Church, Aberdeen 77, 85

K

Keay, William 85

Keig and Tough 126
Keith 114, 209
Keith, Alexander 51
Keith, George 114
Kelso 2
Kemp, Joseph 2
Kendall, James 35
Kent, John 32, 38, 258
Kentucky 10
Ker, William 117, 120, 124, 126, 128, 130, 170, 174, 184
Kilsyth 2, 6, 33, 34
Kiltearn 4
Kincardine 162
Kincardine O'Neil 162
King Edward 125
Kinnethmont 129, 165
Kintore 165
Kintore, Lord 53, 116
Kirk of Shotts 4, 5, 6, 7
Kirkintilloch 2
Kirkmichael 145, 157, 159
Knockando 145, 157
Kyle, James 211

L

Lanarkshire 2
Lancashire 12
Landsman, Ned 7, 30
laymen 9, 62, 108, 127, 208
Leisure Patterns and Revival 204, 244, 256
Leslie and Premnay 117, 122
Leslie, William 127, 130, 214
Lewis 2, 21
Links, Aberdeen 61, 62, 75, 124
Liverpool 33, 57, 192
Livingston 5, 6
Livingston, John 5, 6
Logie Coldstone 157
London 10, 42, 50, 233
Long, Kathryn 36, 37, 44, 75, 107
Longside 145, 239
Lonmay 187
Lord's supper 5, 6, 132, 144, 254
Lossiemouth 192, 193, 207, 208, 212, 217
Lowestoft 2
Luker, David 30, 31
Lumphanan 145
Lybster 193

M

M'Coll, Dugald 259
M'Culloch, William 6, 8, 9, 90, 103
M'Hardie, Elizabeth 42
M'Kay, Murdoch 213
M'Kenzie, Alexander 120, 174
MacDonald, Alexander 50
MacDowall Grant of Arndilly, Hay 42, 53, 99, 116
Macduff 127, 130, 193, 217
Macduff Free Church 213, 214
MacFarlane, Miss 108
MacGill, Hamilton 64
Mackay, John 213
MacLaren, Allan 84, 90
MacLennan, J. 55
Macphail, James 86
Maiden Street, Peterhead 234, 239
Mailler, James 118
Manhattan 16
Manson, John 118
Marischal College 57, 106
Marischall, George Earl 233
Marrs, Clifford J. 39, 58, 259, 260
Martin, William 57
Martinmas 133
Maryculter Free Church 54
Marywell Street School, Aberdeen 54, 99
Matheson, Duncan 107, 116
Matthews, T.T. 1
McCheyne, R.M. 129
McCleod, Henry 132
McCombe, Robert 122
McCombie, Robert 117
McGibbon, John 35, 182, 185, 195, 198, 199, 204, 228
McHardie, Elizabeth 184, 185, 218, 219, 220, 221, 222, 223, 224
McKenzie, William 6

Index 299

McLean, William 227
McLeod, Henry 119
McLoughlin, William G. 32
McQueen, James 8
Meek, D.E. 1, 28, 29, 33
Mencken, H.L. 18
Methodism 9, 13, 28, 29, 34, 79, 152
Methodists 11, 13, 14, 21, 34, 38, 78, 95, 217, 229, 238
Methodism in America 9
Methodism in Banff 212
Methodism in Brantford, Ontario 91
Methodism in Buckie 182
Methodism in Cornwall 11
Methodism in Peterhead 239
Methodism in Ulster 10
Methodist Church 11
Methodist Church in Aberdeen 76, 78
Methodist Church in Peterhead 238
Methodist Church, Crown Terrace, Aberdeen 79
Methodist Circuits at Bilston 33
Methodist Cornish fishermen 210
Methodist Evangelists 13
Methodist Itinerant Lay Evangelist 131, 184, 229, 248, 256
Methodist revivalism 28, 29
Methodist revivals 31, 98, 207, 218, 230, 250, 256, 264
Methodist Revivals in Ulster 12
Methodist Revivals in Yorkshire 12
Methodist, Itinerant Lay Evangelist 42, 64
Methodist, Primitive Connexion 13
Methodist, Primitive, Preachers 13
Methodist, Primitive, Revivals 10
Methodists in Aberdeen 79
Mieklejohn, Robert 114
mill workers 94
Millbrex 168, 175
Millbrex Parish Church 142, 143, 168, 171, 172, 175
Millseat 125
Milltimber 165
Milne, John 85
Mitchell, David 98
Moderates 162

Monthly Visitor 63
Monymusk, Sir Archibald Grant of 113
Moody, D.L. 2, 16, 17, 18, 19, 20, 32, 64, 257, 258, 264
Moody-Stuart, K. 42
Moore, Samuel 189
Moorhouse, Henry 18
Moray Firth 2, 21, 30, 37, 40, 41, 42, 43, 44, 58, 64, 124, 125, 131, 181, 182, 183, 184, 186, 187, 189, 191, 192, 193, 195, 196, 197, 198, 199, 203, 206, 207, 211, 212, 213, 224, 227, 229, 230, 233, 235, 237, 240, 241, 243, 245, 246, 250, 253, 254, 256, 257
More, Ingram 9
Morison, James 263
Morris, Dinah 12
Mortlach 145, 159
Moulin 2, 4, 7
Muirhead, Ian 34, 39
Munro, John 189, 193, 208
Murker, John 212, 217, 219
Murray, I.H. 27
Murtle 165
Muthill 2, 6
Mutual Improvement Association 244

N

Nairn 120, 174, 213
Nairn Free Church 214, 215, 226
Napoleonic Wars 114
National Intelligencer 55
Nettleton, A. 129
New Deer 120, 128, 131, 170, 171, 172, 173, 175
New Deer United Presbyterian Church 148, 168, 171, 172, 173, 175
New England 9
New Marnoch 1, 117, 120, 132
New Measure Revivalism 32
New Pitsligo 135
New York 16, 30, 54, 55, 69, 99, 260

New York Evangelist 55
Newburgh 227
Newhills 76, 77
Newhills Free Church 82, 83, 86, 92, 93, 96, 104
News of the Churches and Journal of Mission 42, 193, 195
newspapers 42, 43, 117, 187, 189, 211, 245, 246, 247, 250
Nigg 6
North British Agriculturist 115
North East Coast Mission 185
North Shields 33
North, Brownlow 67, 116, 117
Northampton, Massachusetts 35
Northampton, New England 1
Northern Ireland 33, 49
Northern Telegraphic News 43
Northfield 76
Nottingham 30

O

Obelkevich, James 35, 152
Obsdale 4
Old Deer Free Church 119
Oldmeldrum 142
Omicron 69
Open Brethren assemblies 227
open-air revival meetings 60, 62, 134, 135, 136, 239, 260
Orr J.E. 3, 27, 35, 38, 39
Ouseley, Gideon 12
Outer Hebrides 37
Oyne 142, 165
Oyne Free Church 119

P

Paisley 106
paraphrases 69
Pascommuck 35
patterns of work and leisure 59, 131, 132, 198, 203, 204, 206, 254, 258
Perth 2, 16
Perthshire 2, 10
Peterculter Free Church 54

Peterhead 35, 42, 44, 185, 187, 195, 196, 204, 207, 217, 227, 229, 233, 234, 235, 236, 237, 238, 239, 240, 241, 242, 243, 244, 245, 248, 249, 250, 254
Peterhead Sentinel 186, 187, 189, 191, 245, 246, 247, 248
Philadelphia 246
physical manifestations 7, 13, 14, 36, 64, 65, 124, 128, 130, 131, 203, 207, 208, 209, 210, 229, 246, 247, 248, 250, 256, 260
Pitcaple 165
Pitlochry 2
planned villages 155, 176
ploughmen 171
Pluscarden 175
Pluscarden Free Church 146, 147, 168, 172, 175
poor harvests 257
population 155, 176, 197, 240
Port Henry 241
Porteous, Moir 189, 234
Portessie 124, 181, 182, 183, 185, 192, 193, 195, 196, 197, 207, 209, 217, 224, 233, 240, 242, 243
Portgordon 41, 182, 183, 191, 192, 196, 197, 210, 217, 226, 240
Portknockie 124, 181, 182, 183, 187, 190, 191, 192, 196, 197, 204, 207, 208, 224, 227, 228, 233
Portknockie Free Church 190
Portsoy 117, 127, 174, 189, 193, 211, 217, 227
Portsoy Free Church 215, 226
Potarch 133
prayer meetings 54, 119, 122, 127, 135, 189, 199, 236, 257, 258
Premnay 122
Presbyterian Church in Brantford, Ontario 95
Presbyterian revivals of 17th & 18th Centuries 141, 176, 254, 264
Presholm 211
Primitive Methodists 14, 29, 35
professional itinerant evangelists 17, 256
prostitutes 75

Index 301

Protracted Revival Meetings 11, 209, 210, 256, 260
provident institutions 185
Psalms 69

R

Radcliffe, Reginald 42, 57, 58, 61, 62, 63, 64, 67, 68, 70, 75, 83, 94, 99, 106, 117, 122, 127, 128, 130, 133, 192, 234, 235, 238, 246, 249, 257, 259
radicalism 28
Rae, James 55
Rafford 145
railway 50, 51, 52, 114, 165, 196
Railway Companies 124
Rait, David 65, 106
Rait, William 54
Ramsay, Colonel 135
Rathven 181, 196
Redruth 11
Reid, Alexander 117, 120, 127, 174, 215
Reid, James 103
Reid, Robert 116, 124, 125, 126, 128, 129, 131, 134, 146, 170, 174
Reid, Tammas 35
Reith, Gordon 19
Relief Church 12
religious newspapers 42, 117, 122, 132, 187
remote 196
Revival and Demographic Change 155
Revival and Economic Change 30
Revival and Political Change 28
Revival and Rural Planned Village 153
Revival and Rural Settlement Patterns 152
Revival and Rural Topography 157
Revival and Social Change 29
revival historiography 37
revival preaching 18
revival sermons 6, 7, 190, 191
Revival, The 42, 43, 52, 106, 107, 122, 182, 185, 189, 193, 206, 224, 229, 234, 236
Rhynie 144, 162, 168, 171, 172, 173
Rhynie Parish Church 144, 168, 171, 172, 173
Rifle Corp 60
Robb, Alexander 146
Robbie, William 42, 187
Robe, James 6, 33
Robertland, Lady 7
Robertson, George Booth 162
Roman Catholic Church 35, 76, 159, 176, 211, 237, 238
Rose Street Baptist Church 2
Rose, Donaldson 129, 133
Rosehearty 187
Ross, Charles 85
Ross, Donald 227, 239
Rothiemay 127, 131
Rothiemay Free Church 120
Rowe, Heather 155
Roy, William 114
rural domestic industries 114
Russell, Douglas 18

S

Sandemanian 263
Sankey, Ira 2, 16, 18, 20, 32, 257, 258, 264
Savoch 142
Scotland 1, 2, 3, 9, 10, 12, 16, 18, 21, 33, 38, 44, 50, 52, 53, 55, 59, 77, 79, 103, 118, 195
Scottish Congregational Magazine 219
Scottish Episcopal Church 211
Scottish Reformation Society 189, 234
Shiels United Presbyterian Church 149, 150, 168, 171, 172
ship building 51
Shiras, Alexander 246
Shotts 2, 3, 37
Simpson, William 103
Skea, J. Ogilvie 81
Skene 135

Skene Free Church 145
Skye 2, 8
Smellie, Alexander 212
Smith, James 57, 67, 106
Smith, R.H. 235
Smith, Robert 236
Smith, William 126
Smout, T.C. 8, 90, 95, 98, 153
Solway 37
Somerville, Alexander 259
South Lindsey 11, 35, 152
sport 59, 60
Sprague, W.B. 86
Spurgeon, C.H. 108
St Clement's Parish Church, Aberdeen 53
St Combs 187, 204, 233
St Fergus 187
St James E 78
St James Episcopal Chruch, Aberdeen 150
St Nicholas Lane United Presbyterian Church, Aberdeen 76, 77, 83, 92, 96, 100, 101, 104
St Paul Street Evangelical Union Church, Aberdeen 76, 77, 78, 84, 85, 92, 96, 100, 104
St Peter's Well, Peterhead 234
St Ternan's Episcopal Church, Banchory 151
Stark, James 57, 69
steam ship service to London 114
Stewart of Garth, Major-General 11
Stewart, R. 246
Stewarton 2, 3, 4, 5, 7, 34, 38
Stirling 9, 42, 90, 91, 240
Stirling, James 234
Stirlingshire 155
Stonehaven 114
storm of 1860 115
Strachan 145
Strathbogie 126, 162
Strathdon 114, 155, 157, 159
Street preaching 61
students 75
Sturrock, J.B. 106
Sunday, Billy 264
Sunderland 33
superstition 10, 183, 184, 200, 243
Sutherland, John 6
Swift, Wesley 182, 217
Swing riots 28

T

Tain 5
Tarbat 5
targeting 75, 76
Tell Scotland Campaign 21
Temperance Societies 60
Ten Years' Conflict 34
Tennyson, A. 60
textile industry 50, 51
theatre 60
Thompson, E.P. 28, 29, 31
Thomson, Alexander 134
Thomson, James 204
Thorne, George 239
timing of the revival 49, 52, 115, 117, 118, 122, 134, 181, 204
Tongue 4, 6
Topping's Hall, Peterhead 239
Towie 157
tract distribution 63
Tractarian 78
Troup, Jock 21
Truro 30
Tullich 157, 159
Tulloch, Charles 207
Turiff 152, 162
Turner, Christopher 35
Turner, James 42, 64, 131, 184, 187, 190, 192, 193, 200, 207, 209, 210, 212, 218, 219, 221, 222, 223, 229, 243, 245, 247, 248, 249, 250, 258

U

Udny 127
Ulster 1, 9, 10, 30, 34, 35, 38, 52, 117, 135, 189, 236, 239, 246, 258, 259, 260
Ulster Presbyterians 35
Ulster revival of 1859 36, 189, 234, 246, 253

Union Terrace Baptist Church, Aberdeen 76, 77, 84, 85, 92, 96, 100, 104, 105
Unitarians 76
United Christian Church 76
United Irishmen 34
United Presbyterian Church 43, 64, 76, 92, 93, 105, 124, 141, 142, 148, 150, 152, 182, 189, 208, 212, 216, 218, 224, 234, 235, 237, 238, 259, 263
United Presbyterian Magazine 99
United Presbyterians 77
United Secession Church 263

V

Van Die, Marguerite 31, 36, 91, 95, 103, 107
Varley, Henry 18
Vasey, Thomas 217
Volunteer Movement 60

W

Wales 2, 33, 35
Walker, R.B. 31, 33
Walker, W.M. 94
Ward, W.R. 34
Wardhouse 165
Washington 55
Watts, M.R. 97
Weaver, Richard 58, 259
weddings 204
Werner, Julia 29, 30, 33, 35
Wesley, John 34
Wesleyan Methodism 10, 14, 33, 98, 102, 103, 248
West Riding 10, 12, 30
Western Isles 2
Westminster Confession 262, 263
Whitefield, George 2, 6, 7, 9, 129
Whitehills 182, 193, 217
Whitney Cross 30
Whitsunday 133
Williams, George 20, 65
Williamson, Henry 1, 116, 120, 125, 126, 128, 133
Wilson, D. 78
Wilson, James 83, 85
Wilson, Thomas 241
Windmill Street Congregational Chapel, Peterhead 234
women 107, 208, 229
women evangelists 12
Wood, Julius 38
Woodside 40, 51, 85, 94, 105
Woodside Free Church 54
Woodside Parish Church, Aberdeen 76, 77, 80, 81, 85, 87, 92, 93, 96, 100, 104
Wynd Journal 42, 122, 133, 171, 206
Wynds District, Glasgow 52

Y

Yale 250
Yorkshire revivals 12, 13, 28, 34
Young Men's Christian Association 20, 56, 63, 65, 66, 70, 76, 107
Yuille, James 238

Studies in Evangelical History and Thought
(All titles uniform with this volume)
Dates in bold are of projected publication

Andrew Atherstone
Oxford's Protestant Spy
The Controversial Career of Charles Golightly
Charles Golightly (1807–85) was a notorious Protestant polemicist. His life was dedicated to resisting the spread of ritualism and liberalism within the Church of England and the University of Oxford. For half a century he led many memorable campaigns, such as building a martyr's memorial and attempting to close a theological college. John Henry Newman, Samuel Wilberforce and Benjamin Jowett were among his adversaries. This is the first study of Golightly's controversial career.
2006 / 1-84227-364-7 / approx. 324pp

Clyde Binfield
Victorian Nonconformity in Eastern England
Studies of Victorian religion and society often concentrate on cities, suburbs, and industrialisation. This study provides a contrast. Victorian Eastern England—Essex, Suffolk, Norfolk, Cambridgeshire, and Huntingdonshire—was rural, traditional, relatively unchanging. That is nonetheless a caricature which discounts the industry in Norwich and Ipswich (as well as in Haverhill, Stowmarket and Leiston) and ignores the impact of London on Essex, of railways throughout the region, and of an ancient but changing university (Cambridge) on the county town which housed it. It also entirely ignores the political implications of such changes in a region noted for the variety of its religious Dissent since the seventeenth century. This book explores Victorian Eastern England and its Nonconformity. It brings to a wider readership a pioneering thesis which has made a major contribution to a fresh evolution of English religion and society.
2006 / 1-84227-216-0 / approx. 274pp

John Brencher
Martyn Lloyd-Jones (1899–1981) and Twentieth-Century Evangelicalism
This study critically demonstrates the significance of the life and ministry of Martyn Lloyd-Jones for post-war British evangelicalism and demonstrates that his preaching was his greatest influence on twentieth-century Christianity. The factors which shaped his view of the church are examined, as is the way his reformed evangelicalism led to a separatist ecclesiology which divided evangelicals.
2002 / 1-84227-051-6 / xvi + 268pp

Jonathan D. Burnham
A Story of Conflict
The Controversial Relationship between Benjamin Wills Newton and John Nelson Darby

Burnham explores the controversial relationship between the two principal leaders of the early Brethren movement. In many ways Newton and Darby were products of their times, and this study of their relationship provides insight not only into the dynamics of early Brethrenism, but also into the progress of nineteenth-century English and Irish evangelicalism.

2004 / 1-84227-191-1 / xxiv + 268pp

Grayson Carter
Anglican Evangelicals
Protestant Secessions from the Via Media, c.1800–1850

This study examines, within a chronological framework, the major themes and personalities which influenced the outbreak of a number of Evangelical clerical and lay secessions from the Church of England and Ireland during the first half of the nineteenth century. Though the number of secessions was relatively small—between a hundred and two hundred of the 'Gospel' clergy abandoned the Church during this period—their influence was considerable, especially in highlighting in embarrassing fashion the tensions between the evangelical conversionist imperative and the principles of a national religious establishment. Moreover, through much of this period there remained, just beneath the surface, the potential threat of a large Evangelical disruption similar to that which occurred in Scotland in 1843. Consequently, these secessions provoked great consternation within the Church and within Evangelicalism itself, they contributed to the outbreak of millennial speculation following the 'constitutional revolution' of 1828–32, they led to the formation of several new denominations, and they sparked off a major Church–State crisis over the legal right of a clergyman to secede and begin a new ministry within Protestant Dissent.

2007 / 1-84227-401-5 / xvi + 470pp

J.N. Ian Dickson
Beyond Religious Discourse
Sermons, Preaching and Evangelical Protestants in Nineteenth-Century Irish Society
Drawing extensively on primary sources, this pioneer work in modern religious history explores the training of preachers, the construction of sermons and how Irish evangelicalism and the wider movement in Great Britain and the United States shaped the preaching event. Evangelical preaching and politics, sectarianism, denominations, education, class, social reform, gender, and revival are examined to advance the argument that evangelical sermons and preaching went significantly beyond religious discourse. The result is a book for those with interests in Irish history, culture and belief, popular religion and society, evangelicalism, preaching and communication.
2005 / 1-84227-217-9 / approx. 324pp

Neil T.R. Dickson
Brethren in Scotland 1838–2000
A Social Study of an Evangelical Movement
The Brethren were remarkably pervasive throughout Scottish society. This study of the Open Brethren in Scotland places them in their social context and examines their growth, development and relationship to society.
2003 / 1-84227-113-X / xxviii + 510pp

Crawford Gribben and Timothy C.F. Stunt (eds)
Prisoners of Hope?
Aspects of Evangelical Millennialism in Britain and Ireland, 1800–1880
This volume of essays offers a comprehensive account of the impact of evangelical millennialism in nineteenth-century Britain and Ireland.
2004 / 1-84227-224-1 / xiv + 208pp

Khim Harris
Evangelicals and Education
Evangelical Anglicans and Middle-Class Education in Nineteenth-Century England
This ground breaking study investigates the history of English public schools founded by nineteenth-century Evangelicals. It documents the rise of middle-class education and Evangelical societies such as the influential Church Association, and includes a useful biographical survey of prominent Evangelicals of the period.
2004 / 1-84227-250-0 / xviii + 422pp

Mark Hopkins
Nonconformity's Romantic Generation
Evangelical and Liberal Theologies in Victorian England
A study of the theological development of key leaders of the Baptist and Congregational denominations at their period of greatest influence, including C.H. Spurgeon and R.W. Dale, and of the controversies in which those among them who embraced and rejected the liberal transformation of their evangelical heritage opposed each other.

2004 / 1-84227-150-4 / xvi + 284pp

Don Horrocks
Laws of the Spiritual Order
Innovation and Reconstruction in the Soteriology of Thomas Erskine of Linlathen
Don Horrocks argues that Thomas Erskine's unique historical and theological significance as a soteriological innovator has been neglected. This timely reassessment reveals Erskine as a creative, radical theologian of central and enduring importance in Scottish nineteenth-century theology, perhaps equivalent in significance to that of S.T. Coleridge in England.

2004 / 1-84227-192-X / xx + 362pp

Kenneth S. Jeffrey
When the Lord Walked the Land
The 1858–62 Revival in the North East of Scotland
Previous studies of revivals have tended to approach religious movements from either a broad, national or a strictly local level. This study of the multifaceted nature of the 1859 revival as it appeared in three distinct social contexts within a single region reveals the heterogeneous nature of simultaneous religious movements in the same vicinity.

2002 / 1-84227-057-5 / xxiv + 304pp

John Kenneth Lander
Itinerant Temples
Tent Methodism, 1814–1832
Tent preaching began in 1814 and the Tent Methodist sect resulted from disputes with Bristol Wesleyan Methodists in 1820. The movement spread to parts of Gloucestershire, Wiltshire, London and Liverpool, among other places. Its demise started in 1826 after which one leader returned to the Wesleyans and others became ministers in the Congregational and Baptist denominations.

2003 / 1-84227-151-2 / xx + 268pp

Donald M. Lewis
Lighten Their Darkness
The Evangelical Mission to Working-Class London, 1828–1860
This is a comprehensive and compelling study of the Church and the complexities of nineteenth-century London. Challenging our understanding of the culture in working London at this time, Lewis presents a well-structured and illustrated work that contributes substantially to the study of evangelicalism and mission in nineteenth-century Britain.

2001 / 1-84227-074-5 / xviii + 372pp

Herbert McGonigle
'Sufficient Saving Grace'
John Wesley's Evangelical Arminianism
A thorough investigation of the theological roots of John Wesley's evangelical Arminianism and how these convictions were hammered out in controversies on predestination, limited atonement and the perseverance of the saints.

2001 / 1-84227-045-1 / xvi + 350pp

Lisa S. Nolland
A Victorian Feminist Christian
Josephine Butler, the Prostitutes and God
Josephine Butler was an unlikely candidate for taking up the cause of prostitutes, as she did, with a fierce and self-disregarding passion. This book explores the particular mix of perspectives and experiences that came together to envision and empower her remarkable achievements. It highlights the vital role of her spirituality and the tragic loss of her daughter.

2004 / 1-84227-225-X / xxiv + 328pp

Don J. Payne
The Theology of the Christian Life in J.I. Packer's Thought
Theological Anthropology, Theological Method, and the Doctrine of Sanctification
J.I. Packer has wielded widespread influence on evangelicalism for more than three decades. This study pursues a nuanced understanding of Packer's theology of sanctification by tracing the development of his thought, showing how he reflects a particular version of Reformed theology, and examining the unique influence of theological anthropology and theological method on this area of his theology.

2005 / 1-84227-397-3 / approx. 374pp

Ian M. Randall
Evangelical Experiences
A Study in the Spirituality of English Evangelicalism 1918–1939
This book makes a detailed historical examination of evangelical spirituality between the First and Second World Wars. It shows how patterns of devotion led to tensions and divisions. In a wide-ranging study, Anglican, Wesleyan, Reformed and Pentecostal-charismatic spiritualities are analysed.

1999 / 0-85364-919-7 / xii + 310pp

Ian M. Randall
Spirituality and Social Change
The Contribution of F.B. Meyer (1847–1929)
This is a fresh appraisal of F.B. Meyer (1847–1929), a leading Free Church minister. Having been deeply affected by holiness spirituality, Meyer became the Keswick Convention's foremost international speaker. He combined spirituality with effective evangelism and socio-political activity. This study shows Meyer's significant contribution to spiritual renewal and social change.

2003 / 1-84227-195-4 / xx + 184pp

James Robinson
Pentecostal Origins
Early Pentecostalism in Ireland in the Context of the British Isles
Harvey Cox describes Pentecostalism as 'the fascinating spiritual child of our time' that has the potential, at the global scale, to contribute to the 'reshaping of religion in the twenty-first century'. This study grounds such sentiments by examining at the local scale the origin, development and nature of Pentecostalism in Ireland in its first twenty years. Illustrative, in a paradigmatic way, of how Pentecostalism became established within one region of the British Isles, it sets the story within the wider context of formative influences emanating from America, Europe and, in particular, other parts of the British Isles. As a synoptic regional study in Pentecostal history it is the first survey of its kind.

2005 / 1-84227-329-1 / xxviii + 378pp

Geoffrey Robson
Dark Satanic Mills?
Religion and Irreligion in Birmingham and the Black Country
This book analyses and interprets the nature and extent of popular Christian belief and practice in Birmingham and the Black Country during the first half of the nineteenth century, with particular reference to the impact of cholera epidemics and evangelism on church extension programmes.

2002 / 1-84227-102-4 / xiv + 294pp

Roger Shuff
Searching for the True Church
Brethren and Evangelicals in Mid-Twentieth-Century England
Roger Shuff holds that the influence of the Brethren movement on wider evangelical life in England in the twentieth century is often underrated. This book records and accounts for the fact that Brethren reached the peak of their strength at the time when evangelicalism was at it lowest ebb, immediately before World War II. However, the movement then moved into persistent decline as evangelicalism regained ground in the post war period. Accompanying this downward trend has been a sharp accentuation of the contrast between Brethren congregations who engage constructively with the non-Brethren scene and, at the other end of the spectrum, the isolationist group commonly referred to as 'Exclusive Brethren'.

2005 / 1-84227-254-3 / xviii+ 296pp

James H.S. Steven
Worship in the Spirit
Charismatic Worship in the Church of England
This book explores the nature and function of worship in six Church of England churches influenced by the Charismatic Movement, focusing on congregational singing and public prayer ministry. The theological adequacy of such ritual is discussed in relation to pneumatological and christological understandings in Christian worship.

2002 / 1-84227-103-2 / xvi + 238pp

Peter K. Stevenson
God in Our Nature
The Incarnational Theology of John McLeod Campbell
This radical reassessment of Campbell's thought arises from a comprehensive study of his preaching and theology. Previous accounts have overlooked both his sermons and his Christology. This study examines the distinctive Christology evident in his sermons and shows that it sheds new light on Campbell's much debated views about atonement.

2004 / 1-84227-218-7 / xxiv + 458pp

Kenneth J. Stewart
Restoring the Reformation
British Evangelicalism and the Réveil at Geneva 1816–1849
Restoring the Reformation traces British missionary initiative in post-Revolutionary Francophone Europe from the genesis of the London Missionary Society, the visits of Robert Haldane and Henry Drummond, and the founding of the Continental Society. While British Evangelicals aimed at the reviving of a foreign Protestant cause of momentous legend, they received unforeseen reciprocating emphases from the Continent which forced self-reflection on Evangelicalism's own relationship to the Reformation.
2006 / 1-84227-392-2 / approx. 190pp

Martin Wellings
Evangelicals Embattled
Responses of Evangelicals in the Church of England to Ritualism, Darwinism and Theological Liberalism 1890–1930
In the closing years of the nineteenth century and the first decades of the twentieth century Anglican Evangelicals faced a series of challenges. In responding to Anglo-Catholicism, liberal theology, Darwinism and biblical criticism, the unity and identity of the Evangelical school were severely tested.
2003 / 1-84227-049-4 / xviii + 352pp

James Whisenant
A Fragile Unity
Anti-Ritualism and the Division of Anglican Evangelicalism in the Nineteenth Century
This book deals with the ritualist controversy (approximately 1850–1900) from the perspective of its evangelical participants and considers the divisive effects it had on the party.
2003 / 1-84227-105-9 / xvi + 530pp

Haddon Willmer
Evangelicalism 1785–1835: An Essay (1962) and Reflections (2004)
Awarded the Hulsean Prize in the University of Cambridge in 1962, this interpretation of a classic period of English Evangelicalism, by a young church historian, is now supplemented by reflections on Evangelicalism from the vantage point of a retired Professor of Theology.
2006 / 1-84227-219-5 / approx. 350pp

Linda Wilson
Constrained by Zeal
Female Spirituality amongst Nonconformists 1825–1875

Constrained by Zeal investigates the neglected area of Nonconformist female spirituality. Against the background of separate spheres, it analyses the experience of women from four denominations, and argues that the churches provided a 'third sphere' in which they could find opportunities for participation.

2000 / 0-85364-972-3 / xvi + 294pp

Paternoster
9 Holdom Avenue,
Bletchley,
Milton Keynes MK1 1QR,
United Kingdom
Web: www.authenticmedia.co.uk/paternoster

July 2005

www.ingramcontent.com/pod-product-compliance
Lightning Source LLC
Chambersburg PA
CBHW071230230426
43668CB00011B/1372